12/95

ACCOUNTING INFORMATION SYSTEMS

A Book of Readings with Cases

JAMES R. DAVIS
University of South Carolina

BARRY E. CUSHING
University of Utah

ADDISON-WESLEY PUBLISHING COMPANY

Reading, Massachusetts
Menlo Park, California • London • Amsterdam • Don Mills, Ontario • Sydney

ISBN 0-201-01099-2
ABCDEFGHIJ-HA-89876543210

PREFACE

The theme of this first edition is "accounting information systems in transition." With the myriad changes taking place in this area it is difficult to keep abreast of all the things that are having an impact on the accounting profession. In recent years many articles have been written and a multitude of speeches and papers presented on this topic. Because of this, the material selection process for this book was extensive; but we feel that the most appropriate literature available has been chosen.

A survey conducted by our publisher of approximately 50 educators indicated very positive support for most of the readings that we have selected. The response to the inclusion of the two cases was much stronger than we anticipated. With such positive preliminary responses to the content we believe that this book will contribute to the available literature in accounting information systems.

In many professional disciplines, acceptance of new concepts and methods evolves at a very slow pace. The purpose of this book of readings is to improve the flow of ideas from accounting writers to the classroom. New concepts and a few traditional ones are included and the user should find that the book is compatible with both traditional and contemporary accounting systems textbooks.

The rapidly increasing body of knowledge affecting accounting information systems poses a challenge to all accountants, but especially to accounting educators. With so much literature available for classroom use, many educators find it impossible to expose the students to all the relevant literature in the area. Hopefully, this book provides much of the screening that is required to present only the most relevant material to the students.

With many technical areas affecting accounting information systems, the selection of articles had to include a broad spectrum. Many good articles were reviewed and those selected were based on characteristics of topic, readability, and lack of widespread availability. This last characteristic was chosen because not every library has access to certain excellent, but poorly circulated, periodicals. Therefore, we have attempted to effectively expand the available literature for many students and professors.

The Introduction and Chapter One provide the reader with an overall view of accounting information systems and the justifications for including this topic in the accounting curriculum. While most schools offer a course in accounting information systems, only a slim majority require such a course for graduation. Chapter Two covers the broad area of technology and most of the important current topics have been included.

Chapters Three and Four concentrate on the systems aspect of accounting information systems. Articles related to design, implementation, and management were considered necessary for the accounting student because the relationships of accounting and information systems cannot be separated. Chapter Five contains articles on control and computer fraud. While computer, accounting, and administrative controls are extensively discussed in textbooks, little space is devoted to actual computer fraud cases. The readings in auditing selected for Chapter Six closely relate to the topics in Chapter Five. When evaluating computer systems the predominant concern of auditors is control. These readings stress the importance of the relationship between the accountant, the auditor, and the systems designer in dealing with computer controls and the need for audit trails. Chapter Seven brings together many of the facets of accounting information systems and illustrates some of the various possible applications and related uses of a sound information system.

To enhance the learning process the last two chapters are cases which can be integrated into the normal accounting systems course. Before assigning material for a course it is advisable for educators to read the introductions to each case to evaluate their uses for a particular term. The first case requires the student to evaluate and reconstruct an accounting information system, either in whole or in part. The second relates to the control of a system, and several improvements are needed before the system can operate with the confidence of management. Some users may find the two cases to be the most useful learning aspects of the book.

These readings and cases are intended for use with introductory accounting systems courses at either the undergraduate or graduate levels. The book may be coordinated with both systems and auditing courses because of the overlapping of relevant material. Also, management information systems classes will find the material relevant to most of the situations discussed from a general business viewpoint.

The editors would like to express appreciation to the authors, publishers, and accounting firms whose kind permissions to reprint their material made this book possible. Also, the suggestions and work of Al Hartgraves related to content and format were generously received. We would like to thank Kent McMath and Jean Swinton for their work in proofing, assembling, and typing the manuscript.

We and the publishers welcome comments.

Columbia, South Carolina   J. R. D.
Salt Lake City, Utah   B. E. C.
October 1979

CONTENTS

INTRODUCTION

Virtually every organization has an accounting information system. Such systems consist of people, machines, procedures, controls, documents, files, and reports. Their basic purpose is to provide operating and management personnel with information which can be used to effectively and efficiently execute the mission of the organization. Evidence indicates that accounting information systems have played a central role in organizations of all types for many years.

Until recently the accounting information system was virtually the exclusive domain of the accountant. He or she designed and implemented systems of documents, files, and reports; devised methods, procedures, and controls; operated business equipment; and advised management on matters relating to financial planning and control. The accounting information system was by far the largest and most pervasive information system within the organization, and the accountant was responsible for virtually every feature of the accounting information system.

Then, in the 1950s, there arrived a revolution in information technology. The computer-based information system was introduced as a tool for commercial data processing, and most of its early applications—payroll, inventory, billing—involved accounting data. This presented a challenge to the accountant's domain.

Of course, business data processing equipment was not new in the 1950s. Over the previous 100 years a variety of machines had been developed for business and accounting purposes, including the adding machine, the typewriter, the bookkeeping machine, and a variety of mechanical punched-card devices. But the technology of those machines was relatively simple. The accountant could easily understand how they worked, and then incorporate them into the accounting information system.

However, the computer was different. In terms of technical complexity, it was several orders of magnitude beyond other forms of business machines. And the technology didn't stand still, but kept mushrooming. The most modern system available at a particular time might be obsolete the next year. This cycle didn't slow down, it escalated. The revolution created whole new professions—programming, systems engineering, and systems analysis. New developments such as real-time systems, minicomputers, data base software, distributed data processing, and microcomputers flooded the marketplace.

Where did these developments leave the accountant? The accountant's first reaction was to absorb the new technology into the accounting information system, as he or she had done with previously developed business machines. Many organizations bought a computer and assigned responsibility for it to the accountant. Payrolls, billings, inventories, and other accounting applications were implemented.

It soon became clear, however, that this arrangement was not totally satisfactory. Two problems emerged. First, the accountant had difficulty understanding the new technology in sufficient depth to effectively manage and control it. And second, other voices in the organization demanded a share in the harvest of this new technology. Production executives, marketing managers, engineers, personnel administrators, and others requested that their information systems be implemented on the computer.

And so there emerged in medium-sized and large organizations a new functional department—the information systems department. The computer was not destined to be just another business machine operated by the accounting department, but a data processing tool for the entire organization. Different organizational arrangements were tested. In some organizations, the head of the systems department was responsible to an accounting executive, while in other organizations this relationship was severed. But in all cases the end result was clear—the computer-based information system was not just another cog in the accounting wheel, but a separate entity with its own identity in the organization.

How did the accountant react to this development? His or her formerly safe and secure domain had been invaded, and part of it carried away. Accounting data were now processed, stored, and reported by the information systems department. Some rash souls even predicted the demise of the accountant, as the computer gradually took over more and more accounting functions.

Out of this rather uncertain state of affairs, there gradually developed an understanding of the respective roles of the accountant and the computer specialist. It became clear that they must act as partners in the development and operation of an effective and efficient management information system (MIS). The accounting information system is but a subset—although a very important one—of the larger MIS. The role of the computer specialist is to adapt the information technology to the needs of the organization in an optimal fashion.

And what is the role of the accountant? The computer-based information system has taken over some of the accountant's functions. Therefore, we might expect that the accountant's role has declined in comparison to the precomputer era.

Such an expectation is incorrect. In his or her partnership with the computer specialist, the accountant must play an active role, not a passive one. The computer specialist has an intimate knowledge of the new systems technology, and this knowledge is indispensable. However, because of the technical depth required for such specialization, computer personnel often have only limited understanding of management information requirements, principles of management planning and control as they relate to the new information technology, and methods of internal control and audit of information systems. These are areas in which the accountant has long been recognized as an expert.

The present situation, then, is that the effective and efficient operation of accounting and management information systems requires a combination of knowledge and skills which no single individual is likely to possess. What is required is two types of individuals—the accountant, and the computer specialist—working in a close partnership. However, this does not imply that their separate knowledge and skills are mutually exclusive. Indeed, there is a rather large body of knowledge with which both the accountant and the computer specialist must be familiar, for otherwise they would have no common ground enabling them to communicate and work productively with each other.

It is this shared body of knowledge which is the subject matter of this book. Our goal in selecting articles for inclusion in the book has been to provide the student of accounting with sufficient insights to the new systems technology so that he or she can effectively begin to operate as a partner with the computer specialist in the design, implementation, and management of both accounting and management information systems. While we have primarily adopted an accounting perspective, we believe that the student of computer technology can benefit in an analogous manner from studying this book.

Let us review briefly the nature of the accountant's role in his or her partnership with the computer specialist. First and perhaps most obvious, the accountant must be able to communicate with the computer specialist. This means that the accountant must have some understanding of the existing state of systems technology, and of its current trends. Of course, the accountant's knowledge in this area will generally be limited as compared to that of the computer specialist. However, the accountant should be able to communicate intelligently with the computer specialist about those current developments which are likely to affect the accounting function. With this in mind, we have devoted an early chapter of the book to nine articles dealing with a variety of recent developments in information technology.

A second important role of the accountant involves management of the new information technology. For many years this was a neglected area, and lots of organizations paid the price of this neglect. Now it is understood that the same principles of management control which accountants have long advocated for other functional areas within an organization can also be beneficially applied to the information systems department. By applying these principles, the accountant can assist the information systems department in planning and organizing its activities, and in measuring and controlling its costs. The accountant's experience in financial planning and budgeting, understanding cost behavior, identifying relevant costs for decision making, measuring the financial performance of responsibility centers, developing transfer pricing systems, and so forth, is extremely useful in establishing a systematic and professional approach to the management of computer technology. Accordingly, we have devoted a chapter of this book to the topic of managing the computer.

Another important role of the accountant involves the design of computer-based information systems. Accountants have always been intimately involved in the analysis and design of information systems. Many years before the computer arrived on the scene, accountants were concerned about the information requirements of managers, the optimal structure of management reports, the appropriate content and format of files and documents, and the human factor in the information system. Many of the same concepts and principles apply in the computer environment. Therefore, the accountant's understanding of these concepts and principles is still needed. In most organizations, systems analysis, design, and implementation are now a team effort, and the accountant plays an important role on the team. In recognition of the significance of this role, we have included in this book a chapter dealing with some of the major issues of systems analysis and design. In addition, one of two cases provided in the book introduces the students to many of the practical aspects of systems analysis and design.

Internal control has for many years been one of the primary responsibilities of the accountant. Using such techniques as separation of functions, procedural documentation, and internal check to assure accurate accounting records, accountants have established important safeguards over cash, inventories, and other assets. However, to a large extent the computer has taken over the maintenance of accounting records, and therefore new techniques of internal control had to be devised. At first accountants were slow to respond to this challenge, and some organizations incurred losses caused by poor internal control in the computer-based information system. Now, accountants have begun to realize that they must bear a primary responsibility for the entire internal control system, including controls over computer processing of not only accounting data, but all types of data. The performance of this role is another reason why the accountant's participation on the systems analysis and design team is crucial to the success of the design effort. Therefore, another chapter of this book is concerned with some of the more important considerations in the design of internal control systems for computer data processing. Furthermore, a second case is provided which exposes the student to many of the computer control and management problems which are frequently encountered in the real world.

The auditing function, as performed by both internal and external auditors, has long been closely associated with the accounting function. And once again we find that the computer has had a substantial impact. Auditing techniques that were appropriate for records maintained by manual or semi-automated systems became obsolete in the computer environment. Accountants were forced to develop new concepts and techniques for both financial and operational audits. Among the new techniques were the use of computer audit software and a number of variations of the test data concept. In light of these developments, we have devoted a separate chapter of this book to the topic of auditing computer-based information systems.

Accounting information has always been useful for a variety of purposes. For example, in a manufacturing company accounting information relating to sales and profitability is useful to marketing executives; accounting information dealing with inventories is useful to production personnel; and accounting information concerning financial performance is useful to financial executives and top management. Accordingly, the accountant has long been a partner with managers and other information users throughout the organization. The advent of the computer has affected the manner in which accounting data are processed to provide such information, and has enhanced the quantity and quality of the information. In order to fulfill his or her traditional role as a supplier of accounting information to a variety of management users, the accountant must understand the impact of the new technology on the processing of accounting data. The final chapter of this book reviews some of the most significant applications of computer data processing to accounting data. The perspective provided by the articles in this section should enable the accountant to be a more effective participant in the design of computer-based accounting information systems.

In conclusion, it should be clear that the new information technology has had a substantial impact on the role of the accountant in modern organizations. While it was once thought that the accountant's traditional skills and concerns might be rendered less significant by the computer revolution, it is now evident that such traditional skills and concerns are even more important in the computer environment. If an effective and efficient information system is to be obtained, the accountant and the computer specialist must work in close harmony. For this to be possible, each must have a clear perspective on the factors of greatest concern to the other. Our goal in this book is to provide students with a first step toward achieving this perspective.

CHAPTER 1

INFORMATION SYSTEMS
AND THE ACCOUNTANT

Upon starting a career as an accountant most graduates will likely be involved with some sort of computer or computerized system. With the increasing popularity of minicomputers even the smallest of organizations will expect their new employees to be familiar with the basic aspects of the computer. Whether the student enters the public, private, or not-for-profit field of accounting, the computer will be encountered—and the time to prepare for this encounter is before graduation. Accounting graduates should have a knowledge of the benefits and drawbacks of computerized systems and a general understanding of accounting information systems. Tomorrow's accountant must be aware of the impact of computers on the organization as well as on all areas of accounting, especially auditing.

To put the academic emphasis of information systems into context and to give the accounting student the proper perspective, the first article by Gordon B. Davis, "Computer Curriculum for Accountants and Auditors—Present and Prospective," presents several possible alternatives for placing information systems in the accounting curriculum. This article discusses four courses which the writer believes are fundamental to the needs of accounting students. He includes both the pros and cons for the inclusion of each course. Suggested outlines for the courses are presented along with currently available texts and relevant readings.

While discussions of systems-related courses included in the accounting curriculum are important, it is probably more important to promote the need for inclusion of such courses in accounting curriculums. Davis estimates that only 60 percent of the accounting programs offer a systems course. Hopefully, as the importance of the computer relationship to accounting is realized, more schools will begin implementing accounting systems courses.

Firmin, in "The Potential of Accounting as a Management Information System," discusses the importance of having accounting become a formal information system. He elaborates on the conditions and requirements of a management information system with regard to accounting. After defining the criteria for an effective information system he addresses the question of whether or not accounting systems qualify as management information systems. While the accounting system has been the only information system in many organizations for years, the value of the information provided has been questioned in recent years. Firmin discusses what the profession must do to overcome this problem and how the full potential of accounting as a formal information system can be realized. To accomplish recognition as an information system, he argues, accounting must broaden its scope, especially in the area of nonmonetary reporting. He feels one can express an organization's activities simultaneously, in both monetary and nonmonetary terms, through the concept of multiple values.

While not everyone will agree with Firmin's assessment of accounting, the article does provide inquiry into what direction the accounting information system should pursue. It is an excellent reading to stimulate the accounting student and to broaden his or her perspective as to what accounting does or should encompass.

To properly evaluate the role of the accounting information system it is necessary to examine the relationship of the accounting information system to the total information system. The authors of "The Changing Management Information Systems Environment" elaborate on the changes which have taken place in management's information needs during the last 20 years. Public reporting requirements and data processing capabilities have increased concurrently during this period and these trends have resulted in the need for a more sophisticated information system. As advances have been made in computer technology, the problems of control and coordination have become more complex. This reading does not describe how to cope with the myriad changes, but it does provide an excellent survey of many of the changes that have taken place and of some of the impacts they have had on information systems. The outlook is for a continuation of rapid growth in all computer-related areas, and if organizations are to survive, systems development must continue to advance with the technology.

This reading, in fact, briefly mentions many of the concepts which are covered by specific readings in succeeding chapters and can be considered as a capsule of what is to follow, especially in Chapter Two. The perspective that this reading provides should enable the student to better understand the relationships of the different aspects of information systems technology included in Chapter Two.

Having been exposed to readings which justify, define, and describe the accounting information system in this chapter, the reader will better appreciate the material presented in the succeeding chapters. From our experience, many students have difficulty relating systems to accounting, and the first two readings in this chapter provide insights into the importance of accounting and information systems to each other. For the modern organization to be successful, the accounting system and the total information system must be properly integrated so that they are compatible with the overall goals and objectives of the organization.

The last article in this chapter, which was commissioned by the Institute of Internal Auditors, emphasizes that accountants should know and understand not only accounting systems, but also management information systems in general. Particularly in large organizations, the accountant cannot remain in a debit-and-credit shell, even if he or she is satisfied to do so; there are simply too many demands placed upon the accounting system for it to stand alone.

Computer Curriculum for Accountants and Auditors— Present and Prospective

GORDON B. DAVIS

Most of my remarks concern a curriculum which would provide a suitable academic background for the accounting student who will be primarily an accountant and auditor rather than a management services consultant.

Since the typical accounting curriculum can absorb only a certain amount of additional material, it is perhaps most useful to consider the fundamental courses which should be available for students in accounting. These are:

1. a computer data-processing course,

2. some exposure to computer programming, using either an algebraic language or a data-processing language,

3. an information system analysis and design course, plus

4. an auditing and EDP course.

I will discuss each of these briefly, mentioning what I consider a suitable content and the support material that is generally available.

THE COMPUTER DATA-PROCESSING COURSE

Probably more than three-fourths of all accounting programs have an introduction to computer data processing, either required or as an elective course. The content of the computer data-processing course is fairly well understood. (A typical outline for a computer data-processing course is described in Figure 1.) The data-processing course for accountants should tend to emphasize control over the quality of computer processing as a major topic and also include flowcharting exercises. There are a large number of textbooks for such a course; perhaps twenty textbooks could be located which would meet most of the needs of the accounting student. A professor seeking to upgrade, change, or introduce a basic computer data-processing course should have no difficulty in obtaining suitable material, outlines, and appropriate exercise material.

General Content

I. Introduction to Computer Data Processing
   1. Historical perspective
   2. Overview of computers for data processing
   3. Computer-based information systems

II. Short Survey of Computer Hardware Technology
   4. Internal operation
   5. Storage and retrieval of data in a computer

III. Development of Computer Data-Processing Applications
   6. The system master plan and life cycle of development of applications
   7. Tools for analyzing and planning computer applications
   8. Computer program structure and design
   9. Programming in low-level languages
   10. Programming in high-level algebraic languages
   11. Programming in high-level data-processing languages

IV. Processing Methodology and System Technology
   12. Input/output and file storage devices
   13. Data-processing methods
   14. Organizing and processing computer-stored data
   15. Data communications in data-processing systems
   16. Control over quality of computer processing

V. The Computer System in Use
   17. Sharing the use of a computer
   18. Evaluating and installing computer hardware and software
   19. Operation and management of the computer installation
   20. Impact of computer on society, organization, and individuals

Exercises

   Flowcharting of processing application
   Flowcharting of program logic
   Other documentation
   Short cases

Textbooks

   Several available

Fig. 1 *Outline of typical computer data-processing course for accountants and auditors*

PROGRAMMING FOR STUDENTS IN ACCOUNTING

A major problem in curriculum design is the question of experience in coding and debugging computer programs. (In considering the design of such a curriculum, there are several curriculum reports which a faculty should consider listed in

Figure 2.) Those who advocate this instruction feel that programming is an activity that is best understood by experience and that comprehension of computer data processing is enhanced by exposure to computer programming. Those who oppose the inclusion of actual coding say that learning a language which the student may not use takes time that might be better spent elsewhere. I believe a student needs to have participated in the actual designing, coding, and debugging of a computer program in order to understand the process by which a computer program is prepared. The cost of learning the rudiments of a computer language is small compared to the experience and understanding that comes from genuine practice.

- ACM graduate in information systems. R. L. Ashenhurst (ed). "A Report of the ACM Curriculum Committee on Computer Education for Management," *Communications of the ACM*, May 1972.

- ACM undergraduate program in information systems. J. Daniel Couger (ed). "Curriculum Recommendations for Undergraduate Programs in Information Systems," *Communications of the ACM*, December 1974.

- Canadian Institute of Chartered Accountants Curriculum Report, 1976 (Updated, 1973) *CA Magazine*, September 1974.

- AAA 1968-69 Committee on the Role of the Computer in Accounting Education, *Accounting Review*, XLV, 1970.

- *Horizons for a Profession*, Roy and MacNeill. AICPA. 1967.

- "Technical Proficiency for Auditing Computer Processed Accounting Records," *Journal of Accountancy*, October 1971 (Updated October 1975).

- AICPA AAA. Report of a Task Force on Inclusion of EDP in an Undergraduate Curriculum, *Journal of Accountancy*, December 1974 and *Accounting Review*, October 1974.

Fig. 2 *Some curriculum recommendations to consider in designing an EDP curriculum for accountants and auditors*

Even after deciding that students should be exposed to computer programming, we still have several issues to be resolved. (These are summarized in Figure 3.) The depth of instruction is related directly to how much a student should know. Should students do only a few simple coding programs or should there be reasonable proficiency in the language chosen? A modest proficiency is certainly most satisfactory because the learning of a language is not as crucial as understanding the process of designing, coding, and debugging programs. This process requires learning the rules of a specific language but does not require high proficiency.

The next issue is whether to locate the instruction as a separate programming course or as part of the data-processing course. At Minnesota, we found that when programming is included with a regular data-processing course the exercises tend to drive the course since programming problems and the instruction overshadow the conceptual material being presented. Separating the programming makes descriptive conceptual material easier to present and more meaningful. We have developed an approach based on one-credit programming modules that a student can use at his own pace without attending formal lectures. The first day of the course the student obtains the description of a set of problems, course materials describing how to gain access to the computer, and so forth. In order to complete the course the student must design, code, and debug a set of five problems and take a set of four or five examinations. Theoretically, the student could appear the second meeting of class and turn in all problems and take all of the examinations. There is no required attendance at lectures. (These are informal and consist primarily of consulting with students.) There are three modules currently operating—FORTRAN, Elementary COBOL, and Intermediate COBOL. Various proposals were made for an RPG module and a simulation language module, but none have been implemented.

There are other advantages to the modular approach. If a course needs a knowledge of COBOL as part of the prerequisites, the students can be required to take the one-credit COBOL module before taking the course needing it. A transfer student may have had COBOL but not FORTRAN; the modular approach allows the student to take only that language in which he or she is deficient.

Alternative Views

Depth of Instruction	A few simple programs written and debugged	Good proficiency
Location of Instruction	Separate programming course	Programming as part of data-processing course
Type of Language	Algebraic • BASIC • FORTRAN • PL/I • PASCAL • etc.	Data Processing • COBOL • PL/I • RPG • etc.
Language Philosophy	Language elements for coding	Program structure and programming discipline

Fig. 3 *Alternative views for teaching computer program-ming to accounting students*

The type of language to require of accounting students is a difficult question to answer. In course work, the student will find that an algebraic language is most useful. For example, a knowledge of BASIC, PL/I, FORTRAN, and so forth, allows the student to use the computer effectively in simulation or statistical processing. The algebraic language is therefore preferred for the academic environment. In the data-processing world, however, COBOL dominates, with RPG a close second. This suggests that students who wish to learn something about the environment of commercial data processing should have an exposure to COBOL. At Minnesota, the students are required to learn BASIC as part of a prerequisite mathematics course. Either FORTRAN or COBOL is required as a prerequisite for the computer data-processing course which they are required to take. The accounting students, therefore, tend to choose COBOL over FORTRAN as the language to take. If students can learn only one language, my preference would be for them to learn an algebraic language because of its usefulness in academic processing.

Remaining is the question of how to teach the programming language. One can merely teach the language elements necessary for coding as a rote system: learn these instructions, code them this way, put them in this order, and they will work. An alternative approach is to teach programming discipline. This is often termed *structured* programming. In some respects, it is quite effective to teach the students merely the language elements, have the students write a few simple programs in such a way that they work, and ignore efficiency or discipline. However, we are making a major transitional effort at Minnesota. COBOL will be taught completely in the framework of programming discipline and all exercises will be done in a structured format. In other words, the student will be taught from the beginning to use rules-of-programming discipline and to format programs using the concepts of structured programming, all as a natural part of the programming exercises. FORTRAN does not lend itself quite as well to this approach, but even there an emphasis upon a disciplined style will be given so that the resulting programs are readable and maintainable.

THE INFORMATION SYSTEMS ANALYSIS AND DESIGN COURSE FOR ACCOUNTING STUDENTS

Wherever the computer data-processing course is generally required, the information systems analysis and design course is either elective or not offered. Perhaps only 60 percent of the schools offer a systems course and this figure may be high (see Figure 4). The traditional accounting systems course has had serious problems; the replacement has probably more intellectual content and more utility to the typical accountant/auditor, but there is less agreement as to an outline for such a course. (A useful outline is shown in Figure 5.) The course idea is to present the way by which an information system is developed in both the overall system plan and individual application. Such a process is difficult to teach in the abstract, because there needs to be student involvement in the process through case experience. A teaching of tools and techniques and material relative to the design of applications is required. The student should be apprised of principles and guidelines for data preparation, input procedures, document design, and output procedures. The student may be exposed usefully to common applications, perhaps one or two in some detail to see the entire flow. The student also needs to be aware of alternatives in application theory.

	Number of Schools	Percent
Requires both systems and EDP course	5	5%
Requires EDP; systems is elective	23	22
Requires systems; EDP is elective	5	5
Both systems and EDP are elective	13	12
Requires systems; EDP not offered	5	5
Requires EDP; systems not offered	22	21
Systems is elective; EDP not offered	10	10
EDP is elective; systems not offered	9	9
Neither course is offered	11	11
*Total	103	100%

*Survey of 103 schools by Joan Schroeder, "Systems and Electronic Data-Processing Courses in the Accounting Curriculum," *The Accounting Review*, April 1972, pp. 387-89.

Fig. 4 *Comparison of requirements for courses in systems and electronic data processing*

The text material is not as well developed for such a course, although a number of recent texts have been brought out in the field which certainly should be considered. Generally, however, the textbook support material for the course is not yet adequate. They tend to be conceptually weak, offering descriptions of the process and what analysts do but insufficiently describing why things are done the way they are. Consequently, it is desirable for the students to have good case experience so that they can learn by following a process.

Because of the absence of a large body of case support material, an information systems analysis and design course is difficult to teach. A school must be prepared, therefore, to devote considerably more resources than for the basic computer data-processing course or for the teaching of programming. As textbook support becomes better, this course should become a regular offering for accounting students.

General Contents
  The development of an information system master plan
  The process by which an information system application is developed and implemented
  Tools and techniques for use in information analysis and system design
  Application design -- data presentation, input procedures, processing, document design, output procedures
  Common applications
  Alternatives in application design

Exercises
  A comprehensive case problem which carries the student through the application development process

Fig. 5 *An outline for the information systems analysis and design course for accountants*

THE CONTROL AND AUDIT OF AN
EDP COURSE FOR ACCOUNTING AND AUDITING STUDENTS

One can introduce computer audit concepts and techniques in the regular auditing course. However, it would appear desirable for an optional course to be available which handles the specific problems of auditing and control in an EDP environment. The combination of the two topics is sufficiently rich in concepts and techniques to justify a separate course. (An outline of such a course is included as Figure 6.) Some good material exists in this area, although the textbook support is fairly weak. Material which should be considered when teaching such a course is listed.

IIA *et al.*	EDPACS
	Auditing Computer Centers
	Auditing Fast Response Systems
AICPA	SAS No. 3
	Auditing & EDP (in revision)
	Service Center Audit Guide
	The Auditor's Study and Evaluation of Internal Control in EDP Systems (*in process*)
	Report of Special Committee on Equity Funding
Canadian Institute of Chartered Accountants	Computer Control Guidelines*
	Computer Audit Guidelines*
Firms	Touche Ross
	Computer Controls and Audit (1975 edition)
	Arthur Young
	Computer Auditing in the Seventies (1970)
National Computer Centers (Great Britain)	Data Control Guidelines
AFIPS	Security-System Review Manual (1974)
Recent Textbooks	Jancura, Elise G., *Audit & Control of Computer Systems,* Petrocelli/Charter, New York. 1974. 355 pages.
	Porter, W. Thomas, *EDP Controls and Auditing,* Wadsworth Publishing Company, Inc., Belmont, California. 1974. 240 pages.

---

* Available from the AICPA.

Major Topics
  Concepts of control in EDP
  EDP organizational and management controls
  EDP control functions
  EDP physical security
  EDP application controls
  The EDP Audits
    Management audit
    Application post audit
    Financial control audit
  Tools and techniques for auditing EDP

Exercise Material
  An audit software system plus data files and problems
    (generally available for classroom use)
  A test data problem (e.g., the Minnesota COMBI problem)
  Case studies—not completely satisfactory

Fig. 6 *Outline of a control and audit of an EDP course for accounting and auditing students*

The instructor teaching an auditing controls course should have access to *EDPACS*, a publication rich in useful material. Although somewhat expensive, it is a must. Case and exercise materials, however, are still a problem. There needs to be, for example, exercise material that would allow a student to use computer audit software and to perform test data. At Minnesota we developed a test data problem based on a software package called COMBI, thus allowing the students to prepare test data and get computer-generated feedback indicating how well the test data tested all the documented code. It also illustrates how undocumented code cannot be detected by test data. We have used CARS, a computer-audit software system, although we have access to STRATA and AUDITAPE, because it is completely COBOL-based and therefore easily adapted to the control data equipment at the university.

An introductory course on the concepts and structure of a management information system possibly would be valuable for accounting students. Such a course has been taught successfully at Minnesota using a new text designed especially for it. (An outline of the course is given in Figure 7.) A readings book containing a number of classic or well-stated supportive readings is also available. We use the readings plus the text as an introduction to management information systems.

The last problem to be considered is the training of faculty. It is difficult to teach that which you have not had a chance to study. A faculty member should have, of course, a depth of knowledge greater than that which is required for the students. This involves, therefore, a continuous commitment to the updating of knowledge. A few references which are useful for keeping abreast of developments in the computer data-processing field are the following.

- *Computing Newsletter for Schools of Business* ($20/yr.)
- *Datamation* (Free to qualified individuals)
- *Computerworld* ($15/yr.)
- *Computing Reviews*
- *Datapro* ($325/yr.)
- *EDP Analyzer* ($35/yr.)
- *EDPACS* ($35/yr.)

In the College of Business at the University of Minnesota we have been involved in the implementation of a comprehensive management-information-systems curriculum for the past seven years. It is probably one of the more strongly developed MIS options currently available. Our experience has been that curriculum development, development of teaching materials, and updating of these materials has been a major, on-going undertaking. I believe that bringing the computer-oriented accounting curriculum up to the standard described here is a difficult task. We had extra resources for the Minnesota MIS development. In the absence of

Section One -- Conceptual Foundations

1. An Overview of Management Information Systems
2. Concepts of Information
3. Human Information Processing
4. System Concepts and Information Systems
5. Concepts of Organization and Management Relevant to Information Systems
6. Decision-Making Concepts for Information Systems
7. Value of Information for Decision Making

Section Two -- Structure of a Management Information System

8. Structure of a Management Information System
9. The Hardware, Software, and Control Environment for Information Processing Systems
10. The Transaction Processing System
11. The Data Base Subsystem
12. Information System Support for Decision Making
13. Information System Support for Planning and Control

Section Three -- MIS Development and Management

14. Organization and Management of Information Systems
15. The Development of a Management Information System
16. Evaluation of Information Systems
17. Current Issues, Societal Implications, and Future Developments

*Based on Gordon B. Davis, *Management Information Systems, Conceptual Foundations, Structures and Development* (New York: McGraw-Hill, 1974).

Fig. 7 *Outline for an introduction to a management information course**

such additional resources, the instructor needs to rely even more heavily upon existing course materials, textbooks, and so forth. The number of textbooks in process or recently issued suggests, however, that textbook support is improving. Continuing motivation for curriculum development comes both from the instructors who recognize the need and from the firms who insist that it is important. It would help if it also came from the CPA exam, which should require that the candidates taking the examination have a reasonable knowledge of computer data processing.

The Potential of Accounting as a Management Information System

PETER A. FIRMIN

CRITERIA FOR A MANAGEMENT INFORMATION SYSTEM

Much of contemporary literature in management, accounting, data processing, and allied disciplines is concerned with the need for timely and relevant information to facilitate the decision-making process at all levels of management.[1] Discussions about structuring and operating an effective management information system usually center around the following criteria.[2]

1. Management's objectives must be defined clearly. In each organization, management must engage in the introspective process necessary to resolve the question, "What are our (firm's) objectives?"

2. A good management information system must yield information which will enable management to evaluate entity position vis-a-vis entity goals.

3. This evaluation must be sufficiently timely to permit (sometimes, to cause) necessary adaptations to be made in the operation of the entity, or in its objectives.

4. Evaluation of alternative choices of action must be facilitated by the management information system.

---

[1] See, for example: Adrian M. McDonough, *Information Economics and Management Systems* (New York: McGraw-Hill Book Company, Inc., 1963); F. T. Tyson, "Providing Management with Control Information," *Cost and Management,* Vol. XXXIX, No. 1 (January, 1965), 9–23; James W. Vair, "Management Information Systems," *Cost and Management,* Vol. XXXVI, No. 10 (November, 1962), 450–53; and D. Ronald Daniel, "Management Information Crisis," *Harvard Business Review,* Vol. 39, No. 5 (September-October, 1961), 111–21.

[2] See, for example, H. B. McGuire and T. L. Stoddard, "Information Presentation Systems," *Electrical Engineering,* Vol. 80, No. 2 (February, 1961), 111–17; George Kozmetsky and Paul Kircher, *Electronic Computers and Management Control* (New York: McGraw-Hill Book Company, Inc., 1956), Chapter 9; and S. A. Spencer, "The Dark at the Top of the Stairs: What Higher Management Needs from Information Systems," *Management Review,* Vol. 51, No. 7 (July, 1962), 4–12.

5. A procedure for measuring cost and value of information generated by the management information system should exist.

6. The management information system must recognize functional and personal relationships within the entity.

7. The management information system must be flexible. It must be capable of generating a great variety of information for a multiplicity of users, both within and without the firm, whose objectives are diverse and who will use the information in different ways.

DO ACCOUNTING SYSTEMS QUALIFY?

Accounting systems long have functioned as major sub-systems in the total information system of many firms. In most cases, the accounting system has been the major information system. In recent years, however, the value of accounting information—especially for decision-making purposes—has been questioned. "Most management information systems," some assert, "are really only accounting systems . . . designed more for governmental requirements than for management of the business."[3] Complaints about long delays in generating accounting reports, often attributed to un-warranted preoccupation with needless accuracy, are legion.[4]

The business organization has been compared to a cybernetic system whose survival requires the maintenance of effective information and communication networks.[5] Inevitably, then, if "conventional" accounting information systems possess such serious inadequacies as those alleged above, and if they do not qualify as satisfactory management information systems, there will arise in the business organization a variety of supplemental and independent information systems, often on *ad hoc* and informal bases.[6] Whenever this phenomenon occurs, it is to be regretted—for the following reasons:

1. A variety of independent systems cannot be expected to deal effectively with the multiplicity of inter-relationships in the business organization.

2. Unnecessary—and costly—duplication of effort will occur.

---

[3] S. A. Spencer, *op cit.*, p. 7.

[4] Spencer A. Tucker, for example, argues in "A System of Managerial Control Using 'Live' Ratios and Control Charts," *NAA Bulletin,* Vol. XLIII, No. 12 (August, 1962), at p. 5, "If upper management controls its business on the basis of periodic operating statements, then it is managing 'after the fact,'. . .".

[5] See, for example, Stafford Beer, *Cybernetics and Management* (New York: John Wiley and Sons, Inc., 1959).

[6] See, for example, Neil Milroy, "The Disintegration of an Information System," *The Canadian Chartered Accountant,* Vol. 82, No. 5 (May, 1963), 338-44.

3. As this paper will demonstrate, the accounting information system, with its highly developed structure, could constitute the fundamental framework for the entire information system. Where it does not, the full potential of the accounting system is not being realized.[7]

TOWARDS A REALIZATION OF THE POTENTIAL OF ACCOUNTING: IMPROVING THE EXISTING SYSTEM

Defining Business Entity Objectives

It has been argued in many places that business objectives are more complex than profit maximization and that they include such goals as achievement of superior positions in product innovation, market share, and employee morale; discharge of community and social responsibility; and a host of others.[8] Some assert that each of these specific objectives can be viewed as a sub-goal to, or even (at some minimum level) a *sine qua non* for achieving, the total system goal of entity survival. The fulfillment of each sub-goal, of course, is constrained by other sub-goals and by the total system goal. Thus, for example, even where feasible, market shares are not increased to the limit of pure monopoly if such activity might provoke retaliatory action which would threaten survival. Firms do not attempt to promote such an exalted image of social responsibility that long-run survival is threatened. The objective of maintaining high employee morale does not override that of maintaining high productivity, if the two conflict.

If "assets" are defined broadly as resources at an organization's or entity's disposal, the goal of survival can be translated into one of asset preservation. In a dynamic economic environment, "preservation" may translate literally into "maximization," or, at least, "satisficing," for an organization which does not preserve its relative position with respect to its environment does not survive. In some contexts and for some purposes, the "net asset" position, defined as owner's equity in organizational resources, may be the appropriate transformation.

---

[7] Some appreciation of the power accounting system may be obtained from Hector R. Anton, "Some Aspects of Measurement and Accounting," *The Journal of Accounting Research*, Vol. 2, No. 1 (Spring, 1964), 1–9, where an isomorphism is established between the properties of an accounting system and the basic system properties of a military command-control system.

[8] See, for example, Peter Drucker, *The Practice of Management* (New York: Harper & Brothers, 1954), p. 63. Also see William J. Baumol, *Business Behavior, Value, and Growth* (New York: The Macmillan Co., 1959), pp. 45–53, in which it is argued that business' objective is to maximize *sales*, subject to the constraint of maintaining an acceptable minimum profit level.

A defensible argument is that entity position relative to the goal of survival and to each of its sub-goals is accounted for in the measurement of changes in the organization's assets. Thus, high employee morale, for example, will be reflected in the "above normal" productivity (measured qualitatively or quantitatively), which will in turn be reflected in the "above normal" increments in net assets. Assessing entity position relative to its goals, then, is primarily a matter of measuring increments or decrements in assets.

The Accounting System Model: Theoretical Construction

The theoretical objective of the conventional "double entry" accounting system model is to measure changes in assets. Traditionally, the primary focus of the measurement process has been on those facets of the asset character which could be expressed in financial terms, but this limitation is not fundamental to the accounting system model. The mathematics of the accounting system model are simple. Nothing in its construction impairs its usefulness as a vehicle for measuring the magnitudes of changes in net asset or equity amounts. Furthermore, the model provides for any number of account classification schemes, so that the input values can be partitioned in a large variety of ways. Sales data, for example, may be accumulated by country, by salesman, by product, or by price class. Costs may be arrayed in similar fashion, as well as by activity, project, or internal cost center. Judicious combination of sales and cost data may permit the establishment of profitability as well as responsibility centers.

If the asset maximization (or "satisficing") criterion is a valid construct for evaluating entity achievement relative to any one of its subobjectives, the accounting system model is a useful framework for designing a management information system. Furthermore, the input and output values assigned to changes in asset and equity accounts are not constrained by the model to a single mode of expression. Rather, value coefficients for any asset and equity account given in the model can be viewed as an "n" component vector, each component expressing the value coefficient in a different unit of measurement.

The Accounting System Model: Operational Problems

If measurement of changes in net assets is a valid way of evaluating the position of the business relative to its goal of survival, then failure of the accounting model to realize its full potential must stem not from imperfections in the model itself, but from operational difficulties.

The problem of convention and tradition At the root of many operational problems is the heritage of conventions which constrain many accounting systems. Many accounting systems apply "generally accepted financial accounting principles" without discrimination to the problem of generating internal accounting reports for management and other uses. Some firms use the same account classification for internal purposes as they employ on published statements. The concept that the output of the accounting information system should be tailored to serve the needs of a variety of internal users is not always implemented.

The remedy for this problem is simple. Management has the authority to specify the accounting practices which it wishes to be accepted as standard *within a company*. No public interest need be safeguarded when only internal considerations are important. Information relevant for management needs should be provided, even though the underlying principles conflict with those which are "generally accepted" for the purpose of preparing statements for wider circulation. The accounting system must, of course, continue to generate "generally accepted" accounting information as well as that needed for management's purposes, when interests of parties outside the firm are involved, or when effective communication requires it.

The problem of transaction definition The necessity for safeguarding interests of parties other than management has caused accountants to demand "objective, verifiable evidence" (usually of a documentary nature) of a change in net value. This demand is often tempered by a desire to be "conservative" in assessing net assets. Thus, the accounting system does not process all changes in asset value. In other cases, however, changes are anticipated. Typically, for example, appreciation in asset values caused by price level movements and by general economic progress will not be admitted as inputs to the system until validated by an exchange. Yet anticipated decrements may be recognized by establishment of account "reserves" or direct asset write-downs.

Again, it is not necessary to subscribe to these conventions for internal purposes, for in many cases their employment may impair the effectiveness of the management function.[9] Rather, for internal purposes, accounts should reflect "current" values of assets and equities whenever such values are the relevant ones. Further, for example, if the "sale" test for entry into the accounting system does not permit vital information about order backlogs to be part of the information system output, then the sales order itself also should be viewed as a transaction.

The problem of the measurement unit Much has been written about the accounting assumption that the monetary unit of measurement is stable. In a sense many of

---

[9] Examples include the understatements of asset values which may occur through failure to recognize increments in market or current values of assets, application of the "cost or market, whichever is lower" convention, employment of "accelerated" depreciation methods, and arbitrary "write-down" of fixed and intangible asset values. Such "conservative" asset valuations often will be reflected in calculations involving invested capital, and may, irrationally, influence the decision in capital budgeting and other problems.

the problems in communication are created because the monetary unit of measurement is *not* stable. Reporting changes in current values of assets and equities might resolve this problem and enhance the effectiveness of the accounting information system.

The problems of timeliness and control One of the imperatives in a management information system is that the information output be timely, *i.e.*, that it facilitate control of the process.

Achieving necessary timeliness in an accounting information system requires that the accounting system model be used for budgetary purposes, and that predictive reports be generated to permit current evaluation of progress towards goals at appropriate points in time. For some variables, "appropriate points in time" may mean daily, or even hourly. For other variables, less frequent comparisons may be needed. In some cases, required timeliness may be attained only through the use of sampled data input and standard costs.[10]

Significant research in the use of the accounting system model for purposes of control has been accomplished by Ijiri, who has used it as a basis for a linear programming model for optimizing the survival (profit maximization, in his work) function subject to other system constraints. The linear programming model is used to generate predictive accounting reports, and the dual is used to evaluate the opportunity cost implicit in the constraints.[11]

Evaluation

So far, it has been suggested in this paper that the accounting information system can be made more useful if certain unnecessary constraints of convention and tradition are disregarded. A *sine qua non* of an effective accounting information system is the incorporation of the budget as an explicit part of the accounting system. No attempt yet has been made, however, to remove the constraint of the double entry concept,[12] to impair the constraint that the domain of accounting is limited to those economic phenomena which can be measured in terms of the

---

[10] The exigencies of dealing with parties external to the enterprise (customers, creditors, *e.g.*) will usually demand "scorekeeping" accounting and the generation of accounting information by census rather than by sample. But where such demands cause a significant time delay in the information processing system, other methods may have to be used to generate input information for control purposes.

[11] Yuji Ijiri, "Goal Oriented Models for Accounting and Control" (Ph. D. dissertation, Carnegie Institute of Technology, 1963).

[12] The double entry concept envisioned here relates to the accounting convention of contemplating two facets of every transaction, *i.e.*, its effect on assets, and on equities. "Double entry" as used here does not refer to the "debit-credit" or "input-output" network flow concept.

monetary unit, or to otherwise broaden the scope of accounting. The concern of this paper, thus far, has been to demonstrate that with only minor modifications within a conventional structure, the accounting system model may be made more effective. We now turn our attention to expanding the boundaries of accounting concepts.

TOWARDS A REALIZATION OF THE POTENTIAL OF ACCOUNTING: BROADENING THE SCOPE OF THE ACCOUNTING SYSTEM

Non-monetary Information Is Needed

Even if the uniqueness of the profit maximization objective were acknowledged universally, management information systems still would have to be concerned with non-monetary data. Lower echelons of management would be concerned with rate of absenteeism and its effect on scheduling and production. Other levels of management might be concerned with ratio of seat occupancy to capacity on airlines; with the effectiveness of maintenance quality control; or with depth of management potential at various submanagerial levels. Required in many instances by regulatory authorities, demanded by other consumers of information, such data also may constitute necessary—*and often superior*—measurement constructs for evaluating entity or sub-entity performance.[13] In many cases, interpretation of monetary information is facilitated by concomitant analysis of supplementary non-monetary data.

The obvious advantages of integrating business information systems, coupled with the indisputable need for an accounting information system, leads logically to an inquiry into the possibility of utilizing the structure of the accounting information system as a framework for the integrated information system.

The Nature of Non-Monetary Information Requirements

The dominant characteristic of management information requirements is variety. Management concern with survival can be translated into care about production, finance, foreign markets, the role of government relative to business, long-range forecasts, and a myriad of other matters.[14]

---

[13] Spencer A. Tucker for example, in both *Successful Managerial Control by Ratio-Analysis* (New York: McGraw-Hill Book Company, Inc., 1961), and *The Break-Even System* (Englewood Cliffs, N.J.: Prentice-Hall, Inc, 1963), emphasizes the crucial importance of analyzing certain non-monetary indices.

[14] See, for example, H. F. R. Catherwood, "Information Needs of the Chief Executive," *The Canadian Chartered Accountant*, Vol. 83, No. 6 (December, 1963), 402–5.

Because the accounting model translates entity activity within its domain, however measured, into monetary equivalence, *it also is possible, conceptually, to express simultaneously any given entity activity in non-monetary and monetary terms.* Both physical and dollar costs per unit of machine down time can be calculated. Customers' orders, first stated in terms of physical quantities, are then translated into dollars of sales. They may be classified by type of customer. "Lost" orders are expressed in physical and dollar terms. Fruitless customer contacts by salesmen can be measured in terms of their cost—in time as well as in dollars. (Measures of salesmen's frustrations are more difficult to make.)

Processing Methodology

Conventional accounting systems view a transaction as single valued. But multiple values for a given transaction can be expressed by an "n" dimensional vector, "n" large, where each vector component represents a different basis for or scale of measuring the change in an object or in some aspect of an object. As an example, the sale of 300 units of finished product Z, costing $5,000, to a new customer number 0143 for $8,000, with a probability of collection of .96, could be represented by a vector T with the following components:

$8,000	$5,000	Z	0143	.96	300	1
Sales Price	Cost	Product Category	Customer Number	Probability of Collection	Quantity	Customer Class (new, old)

Additional vector components may be used to express other facets of the transaction and other classification schemes. For example, geographical sector, salesman initiating the transaction, rate of salesman's commission, sales taxes due each of several governments, excise taxes, method of delivery, and a wide variety of other information, may be catalogued. The detailed "m × n" sales transactions matrix would then appear as follows, with the rows representing individual transactions T_1, the columns expressing various facets F_1 of each transaction.

	F_1	F_2	F_k	F_n
T_1	a_{11}	a_{12} $\cdots$	a_{1k} $\cdots$	a_{1n}
T_2	a_{21}	a_{22} $\cdots$	a_{2k} $\cdots$	a_{2n}
.	.	. . . .	. . . .	.
.	.	. . . .	. . . .	.
.	.	. . . .	. . . .	.
T_k	a_{k1}	a_{k2} $\cdots$	a_{kk} $\cdots$	a_{kn}
.	.	. . . .	. . . .	.
.	.	. . . .	. . . .	.
.	.	. . . .	. . . .	.
T_m	a_{m1}	a_{m2} $\cdots$	. . . .	a_{mn}

Appropriate partitioning, column operations, and matrix multiplication may be performed to facilitate accumulation and reporting of sales and sales-related data in any desired form. For example, the "Probability of Collection" column (transpose) may be multiplied by the "Sales Price" column to generate the estimated net sales revenue; sales accumulations may be accomplished by matrix multiplication. Partitioning operations will facilitate multifaceted analysis of sales data. Finally, for purposes of summarization, the sales transactions matrix may be reduced to a single multicomponent vector representing the accumulation of all components for a specific time period.[15] Similar treatment may be afforded other standard transaction forms.

If "transactions" matrices facilitate a multi-dimensional recording of changes in assets and equities, then "inventory" matrices may also be maintained which depict asset and equity status at any given time. In such matrices, each element may describe a unique aspect of a particular resource (or equity).

For example, descriptive data on each employee may be catalogued in vector form, each component representing a "measurement" of the employee. In such a manner might his skills, physical qualities, rate of pay, chronology, and other vital data be stored. Appropriate matrix operations would generate many varieties of reports from such a base manpower matrix, and would be compatible manipulatively with appropriate transactions matrices.

It is important to note that the "double entry" principle may be preserved in both of its conceptions. Each aspect of a transaction may be considered with respect to its effect on both assets and equities; and the debit-credit network flow mechanism is preserved as asset-equity changes are recorded. But unlike an accounting system which measures only the monetary equivalence of asset-equity levels and flows (and occasionally physical inventory levels and flows), the matrix accounting system envisaged here measures—as an integral part of the account process—many non-monetary as well as intangible aspects of asset-equity "transactions" and "inventories."

One of the very important and exciting possibilities suggested by the transactions vector approach is that additional vector components might be used to express the effect of a transaction on entities other than the business organization. For example, one problem area in national income accounting is the reconciliation between private industry and national government concepts of income which is inevitably necessary. Appropriate definition of vector components in data processing systems could capture at the point of generation the transactions data for subsequent accumulation in national income accounts.[16]

---

[15] Not all components of the resultant "summary" vector would have significance. For example, the accumulation of components expressing skills possessed by employees would have no significance unless a separate column in the transactions matrix had been used to designate each skill.

[16] Indebtedness to Dr. Louis Perridon for this suggestion is gratefully acknowledged.

Facilitating the ready consideration of many aspects of assets, equities, and transactions involving them also invites an expansion of the concept of the asset. Some who have questioned the utility of accounting data have suggested broader conceptions of assets. Churchman, for example, defines an asset as ". . . any aspect of an individual's environment which produces a potentiality of choice for a set of actions."[17] Viewing this definition in an operational context we can argue that skills possessed by employees constitute a potentiality of choice for the employer, and that a wider range of skills creates a greater potentiality of choice than does a smaller range. Thus the "inventory" of usable skills "possessed" by an employer is an asset which should be reckoned and perhaps measured in some meaningfully quantitative way. Does not the business organization suffer an impairment of its potential for choice, a reduction in its "worth," upon the loss of a skilled employee or the deterioration of his skill?

In the same vein, such intangibles as "management effectiveness" might be considered an asset. Levels of such an asset might be measured by qualities like aggressiveness, propensity to use sophisticated techniques, and creativity—all subjective measurements, but indirectly quantifiable through the use of substitute constructs.

While the two examples cited may be difficult to implement on a systematic basis, they are nonetheless within the realm of the feasible. And they are consistent with the flexible accounting process described.

Even more importantly, the multi-dimensional approach to transactions analysis described herein can include predictive elements and discounting for uncertainty. "Sales lost," alternative rates of return, and hence, opportunity costs can be comprehended within the system on a fairly systematic basis.

The Concept of the Transaction Revisited

One of the most powerful operational constraints in any accounting information system is the concept of the transaction which is adopted. Its significance is obvious: entry into the accounting information system is afforded an event only if it meets the test of the transaction. Earlier in this paper, it was noted that the interests of more effective communication and control would be served if the traditional concept of the transaction were modified to permit entry of the sales order into the system, for example, and if changes in market values of assets were to be recognized. Later, further departures from the traditional concept of the transaction were urged.

Important as these modifications are, however, they do not cope effectively with another critical problem. Accounting information systems are oriented towards internal entity activities, even when the public interest is an issue. They do

---

[17]C. West Churchman, *Prediction and Optimal Decision* (Englewood Cliffs, N.J.: Prentice-Hall, Inc., 1961), p. 324.

not regard all interactions between the entity and its environment as being within the domain of accounting. Thus, for example, a good conventional accounting information system will identify the costs of manufacturing and selling a product, facilitate control of the process, and encourage a variety of analyses. It will not so readily *explain* a variance between actual and projected sales volume, or measure consumer reaction to a product. In short, it does not recognize some relationships between the entity and the external environment, particularly those relationships in which the environment acts upon the business entity. For this reason, management scientists often find it wanting.

Deficiencies in formal information systems frequently spawn independent information systems to remedy the illness. Because model builders frequently need data for predictive models which differ in chronology and orientation from much accounting-type historical data, finding a transactions concept which serves this purpose becomes an imperative.

Returning to Churchman's conception of an asset, the size of an entity's net assets seems to symbolize and measure its power, its total potentiality of choice. A transaction, then, can be viewed as *any* event which changes the probability distribution of the size of the entity assets at some later time.[18] Were this concept of the transaction implemented, the accounting system routinely would admit entry into the system of such "transactions" as changes in the probability distribution of consumer demand (perhaps classified by cause of change), changes in the cost of capital, risk of obsolescence, expected delays in incoming materials, and other active external environmental factors.

An information system which provided for the routine collection, storage, and processing of this variety of data would have much potential power to provide meaningful information for all users. Realization of this potential would be more likely if it reflected an effective integration of all of the organization's information sub-systems.

IMPLEMENTING THE SYSTEM

Summary of Central Issues

The recommendations in this paper focus on the following points:

1. Transactions, as business events which affect the magnitude and nature of the net assets of the business entity, have many dimensions.

---

[18] Churchman's definition of a transaction seems to restrict it to actions *of the entity* which change the shape of the probability distribution. The necessary conditions for a good information system would seem, however, to include explicit recognition of changes in the probability distribution which were caused by the action of the environment on the entity. The fact of a change in the size of entity net assets is independent of its cause, although, for purposes of control and analysis, the accounting information systems should afford the distinction.

2. Accounting for the many dimensions of a transaction facilitates planning, reporting, analysis and control in the business organization. Conventional accounting rules, while important for some purposes, must not constrain the data processed. Non-monetary as well as monetary, predictive as well as historical, data must be generated, reported, and evaluated.

3. The double entry network flow mechanism which is characteristic of the accounting model is an excellent mechanism for tracing the flows of resources, viewed in their many facets, through the various organizational activities and levels. Vector and matrix concepts provide a particularly useful structure for the accounting model.[19]

The "data bank" concept An essential recommendation of this paper is that an adequate management information system provide for the generation and processing of a wide variety of data. Some of the data will be used immediately and in well-structured situations. The usefulness of other data may be less certain and well defined, but probable future usefulness may militate in favor of its generation.[20] The transactions concept espoused in this paper comprehends both classes of data, and the matrix procedures described contemplate data storage in a kind of "data bank," wherein ordered classification will permit easy entry, manipulation, and withdrawal of data. As Henderson has said ". . . relative to management, we need to provide access in depth to basic data. Quick, cheap access—with ability to respond to variable demands."[21]

Perhaps obviously, the data generation and processing procedures suggested in this paper are contemplated within the framework of an automatic (electronic) data processing system. Only with such a system could *full* implementation of the concepts discussed here be achieved. And even where large electronic data processing systems exist, rigidity in existing systems, inertia, and a multitude of other factors may impede their implementation. Nonetheless, the rewards of even partial implementation seem important enough to justify small scale (even non-EDP) attempts to incorporate selected modifications of existing accounting systems.

---

[19] For an illustration of matrix applications within the bounds of conventional accounting rules, see A. Wayne Corcoran, "Matrix Bookkeeping," *The Journal of Accountancy*, Vol. 117, No. 3 (March, 1964), 60–66.

[20] In fact, a very small probability of subsequent usefulness may justify generation of data, unless the cost of generating and processing is very high. As Paul Henderson, Jr. has pointed out, "We do not know what data management 'ought' to have and have little indication that managers know what constitutes complete and perfect data services. It is apparent that the needs are not static. . . " Paul B. Henderson, Jr., "On the Design of Data Systems for File Analysis and Information Retrieval" (Unpublished paper presented at the Eleventh Annual Meeting of The Institute of Management Sciences, Pittsburgh, March 12, 1964), p. 2.

[21] *Ibid.*, p. 4.

Better accruals can be made. Current asset values can be reflected in the accounts. Multiple classifications of data can be made, and separate reports and analyses can be prepared for different purposes. Budget periods can be shortened, and comparisons can be made more frequently. Emphasis can be shifted from "How did the company do last period?" to "How is the company going to do this period?" Non-monetary and monetary data can be reported, and non-financial aspects of recourse utilization can be disclosed.[22]

In some cases implementation of the concepts expressed here may be accomplished by such simple techniques as applying a scalar (index) to selected or total asset and equity measurements, existing or projected. A normal level of customer dissatisfaction might be established, for example, and deviations from that norm expressed as an index and transformed into an operator on asset and equity measurement.

The value of generating such data is related to the level of any given company's operations, and to the ability of its management to utilize information effectively. This value is measured in terms of the relative advantage of decisions made on the basis of more sophisticated data (or the cost of decisions made on the basis of cruder information), and is apt to vary with the size of the enterprise. The cost of generating these kinds of data, which also may vary generally with the size of the enterprise, is a function of the data processing system's characteristics.[23]

---

[22] For a particularly eloquent plea for better information systems, see Gerald G. Fisch, "The Integrated Management Organization," *Financial Executive*, Vol. XXXII, No. 5 (May, 1964), 13–16.

[23] For interesting discussions on the cost vs. value of information, see McDonough, *op. cit.*, Ch. 9, and Robert H. Gregory and Richard L. Van Horn, *Automatic Data Processing Systems* (Belmont, Calif.: Wadsworth Publishing Company, 1963), Ch. 15.

The Changing Management Information Systems Environment

THE INSTITUTE OF INTERNAL AUDITORS

Management's information needs have changed dramatically during the last 20 years as a result of the growth and diversification of business activities. Government regulation and regulatory reporting requirements have increased concurrently. These trends have resulted in the need for more comprehensive and sophisticated computer-based information systems. During this same period and particularly since the early 1960s, new data processing technology and concepts have been applied to satisfy management's information needs. As new technology is successively introduced and applied, computer application systems and control have become more complex. For example, data communication capabilities bring data processing users closer to the computer, and thus allow faster access to needed data. The implementation of such technology has, however, resulted in fundamental changes in the structure of computer application systems and controls. As a result, audit and control techniques appropriate to earlier business operations have, to some extent, become outmoded. In addition, with increasing reliance upon data processing, management is increasingly concerned about insufficient controls and the complexity of data processing. These concerns are translated to data processing management's increasing concerns about losses arising from errors and improper controls that may occur and remain undetected. In this environment, the audit and control of computer application systems and supporting data processing activities are becoming more important to management.

CHANGES IN MANAGEMENT'S INFORMATION NEEDS

The information needs of both business and government have increased dramatically in recent years. The private sector of the economies in Canada, Western Europe, Japan, and the United States grew rapidly during the 1960s and early

1970s, until the slowdown was experienced. With economic recovery now under way in most areas, there is no reason to believe management's information needs will not continue to grow in the years ahead.

Economic growth has occurred as a result of an expansion of existing markets and products. Business activity has also expanded geographically within countries and across national borders. The latter is exemplified by the multinational corporation phenomenon, which became prominent during the mid and late 1960s. The geographic spread of business increases the need for communication facilities to allow the exchange of information between business locations. In response to this need, communication and digital computer technologies have been joined to provide the high-speed data communication capabilities now used by many businesses. Multinational business operations share the need for data communications capabilities, but also have other requirements that increase the complexity of management information needs. For example, multinational corporations must accommodate currency conversion, additional regulatory reporting, and variations in practices in developing computer-based information systems.

Expanding markets and product lines have involved acquisitions for many businesses. This has led to consolidation of operations in some situations and diversification in others. Consolidation is often accompanied by increased transaction volumes and an expansion of existing information systems. Diversification through acquisition has, in contrast, often required an information exchange between previously unrelated management information systems. In some situations, diversification has resulted in a significant expansion of data processing capabilities in order to provide necessary management information on a consolidated basis.

The rapid growth of the private sector of the economy has been paralleled by increasing government activities. Legislation and governmental regulation to control business increased significantly during the 1960s and early 1970s. Such regulation and associated regulatory reporting have caused an increase in the amount and complexity of information that must be captured and processed. Top management, data processing management, and internal audit management in SRI's Primary U. S. Mail Survey sample were asked, "What governmental, professional, or other trends do you see emerging that will have a definite impact on your data processing and internal auditing operations?" Government regulation and reporting were the most frequently reported trends. Privacy legislation was one form of regulation frequently mentioned. A second frequently cited governmental trend was the Security and Exchange Commission's requirement for quarterly reviews. National health insurance, affirmative action programs, new rules for pension plan reporting, and consumer protection laws require modifications and extensions to the computer application systems maintained by many firms. Such reporting is quite often different from the usual reports prepared for management and necessitates modification and expansion of existing systems in many instances. Government regulation and regulatory reporting present substantial new requirements for computer application systems.

INCREASING DATA PROCESSING CAPABILITIES

The business trends described above (i.e., growth in transaction volumes, geographic distribution of operations, and increasingly complex product line reporting needs) have occurred during a period when important advances were being made in data processing technology and its application. These advances include:

- Increased computer system usage
- Increased use of data communication facilities
- New data processing application areas
- Distributed data processing
- Integrated computer application systems
- Centralized shared data files.

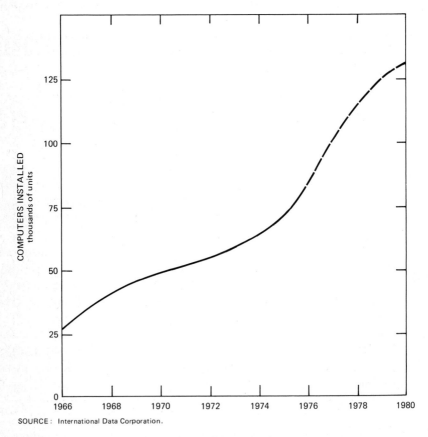

SOURCE: International Data Corporation.

Fig. 1 *General purpose computer systems installed, 1966–1980 (U.S.)*

Figure 1 shows the increasing number of business-oriented computer systems installed during the past 10 years. In 1966, more than 25,000 general-purpose computer systems were installed in the United States. In 1975, over 70,000 were installed. This reflects the increasing use of data processing to provide the information that management needs to evaluate, control, and plan business operations.

Figure 2 shows the increasing number of installed data communications terminals. This characterizes the growing use of data communications in bringing computer capabilities closer to users and improving the flow of information between remote facilities. For example, a large automobile manufacturer has data communication links to its widespread suppliers, thus providing overall production control from the suppliers' facilities to the manufacturer's assembly plant. In another situation, a manufacturer has data communication links between its facilities and its distributors to provide nightly order entry for replenishment of the distributors' inventories. In the financial services industry, bank clearing systems are being linked using data communication facilities to speed interbank fund transfers and settlements.

The use of data communications has become substantial during the last five years. The use of data communications is expected to continue to grow in the years ahead, as shown by the projections in Figure 2.

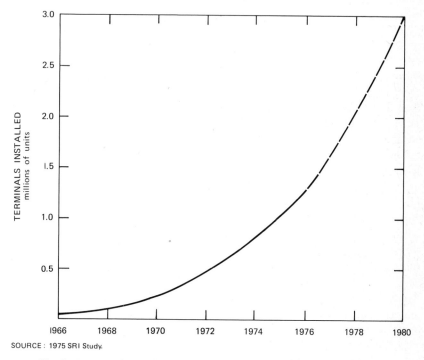

SOURCE: 1975 SRI Study.

Fig. 2 *Data communication terminals installed, 1966–1980 (U.S.)*

Electronic funds transfer is an example of a new data processing application area that will require extensive use of data communications. Developments in electronic funds transfer affect financial institutions, retailers, and the consumer. This will be, perhaps, the area of greatest data processing growth during the next 10 years. Electronic funds transfer is in its early stages of development. The concept usually encompasses:

- Electronic interbank clearing.
- Automated teller machines and unattended remote terminals to dispense currency.
- Retail point of sale terminals that combine retail and banking transactions at supermarket checkout counters, for example.

Many regulatory and business problems remain to be resolved before electronic funds transfer application systems are available and widely used. Consumer acceptance is an important factor that will pace and perhaps constrain their wide use in the near future. Electronic funds transfer is an example of how data processing technology can affect both business and the consumer public.

The use of minicomputers in business began in 1969. By 1975, minicomputers installed for use in business applications reached nearly 40,000 units. The number of minicomputers used for business applications is expected to grow to 86,000 units in 1980.

The concept of distributed data processing based on the use of minicomputers is gaining importance with the increasing geographic distribution of business operations and the acceptance of minicomputers for business data processing. During the 1960s there was a trend toward consolidating data processing on large centralized computer systems. Such computer systems were several times faster than their smaller counterparts. They could perform the work of four or five smaller computers concurrently and in less elapsed time. Accordingly, there were economies of scale that resulted in consolidation and centralization of computing resources. Distributed processing is a currently growing countertrend resulting from the adaptation of low-cost, high-speed minicomputers to business needs.

For example, a midwestern manufacturer has 15 geographically distributed plants. Product transportation costs are a potentially large component of product cost, so plants are located in the areas they serve. The firm maintains a central accounting department and data processing facility with communication links to terminals at each plant location. It has recently installed minicomputers in each plant location to handle order entry, customer billing, and accounts receivable. This equipment replaced manual bookkeeping machines and is connected to the firm's central computer system. Order entry, production backlog reporting, billing, and accounts receivable are performed locally at each plant. Sales, production, and accounts receivable information is transmitted to the central data processing facility each night and used to prepare consolidated operating reports. In selecting this approach, the firm considered a larger central computer system with remote terminals at each location. They concluded it was more economical for them to process detailed information locally and transmit only summary statistics to the central facility. In specific situations, distributed processing may have advantages over totally centralized data processing facilities.

As a result of changing management information needs and the availability of new data processing technology, computer application systems are changing from traditional forms. In the past, for example, order processing, customer billing, and accounts receivable were developed as separate computer application systems. They were processed separately with files of related transactions passed between computer application systems. Order processing might occur one night, with billing the next, and accounts receivable processing only twice a month. Manual control logs and procedures were used to ensure the accuracy and completeness of successive processing cycles and the flow of transactions between computer application systems.

Computer application systems being designed and developed today involve the use of remote terminal entry, transaction processing, and central data base concepts. Remote terminal operations were described earlier. Transaction processing is a complementary concept. It involves integrating processing procedures so that a single transaction is entered and processed by all appropriate computer application systems in a single sequence. For instance, order entry, inventory control, billing, and accounts receivable application systems can be integrated into a single transaction that automatically flows through the entire sequence. Orders are entered and customer acknowledgments prepared, inventory records posted, warehouse packing documents prepared, and customer records posted. Terminal operators entering orders are automatically notified if discrepancies, such as items out of stock, are encountered during the processing sequence.

The concept of centralized shared data files (i.e., a "data base") has been a factor in the integration of computer application systems as described above. The data base concept is to capture and maintain data in a single central file, which can be accessed by those programs that have a need for specific data elements. In the past, each computer application system was designed around its own files. The same data elements would occur in different files, and would even have different values because of inconsistent processing procedures and/or schedules. Centralized files eliminate redundancy. When this concept is first explained, one might assume that all an organization's data reside in a single file. In fact, most data bases represent a federation of files serving logically related computer application systems. The elimination of redundant files and the logical association of data files with computer application systems are fundamental to the data base concept.

Several important changes in the data processing environment are summarized in Table 1.

In summary, management's needs and data processing capabilities have both become more complex and have merged. As more business functions have been computerized, business operations and management have become dependent upon data processing and the internal controls that ensure accuracy and completeness.

Traditional control and audit methods, tools, and techniques have become outmoded as a result of changes in the structure and form of computer application systems. With greater reliance on data processing have come new potentials for loss. Loss exposures are described in the following section.

TABLE 1
CHANGES IN THE DATA PROCESSING ENVIRONMENT

Areas of Change	1956–1965	1966–1975
Processing equipment	Separate, stand-alone installations	Computers and terminals linked with data communication facilities
Computer application system development	Limited coordination and discipline	Formalized coordination of development and use of standards within individual organizations
Computer application system design	Single-function batch processing applications	Interdependence among application systems
File usage	Overlapping and partial data files	Common masterfiles shared by several application systems
User relationship with data processing	Limited direct links to processing equipment	User has direct access to processing equipment and data files

LOSS EXPOSURE

The potential for loss associated with the use of data processing is increasing and taking new forms, as procedures once performed manually are automated. Traditional systems and procedures relied on manual checks and verifications to ensure the accuracy and completeness of data and records. In such an environment, exceptions could be handled as they were encountered. Decisions could be made without much delay in processing. Manual control was maintained over most, if not all, phases of transaction processing and record keeping.

Computer Application Systems Error Potential

As business data processing expands, manual controls are replaced by computer application program control functions. Computer application program routines are needed that anticipate exceptions previously handled manually on an ad hoc basis. Without such control routines, incomplete or incorrect transactions can be processed unnoticed. When computer application systems are linked and integrated, an undetected error that is accepted by one application can result in errors in several others. Once accepted, an erroneous transaction can be processed against several files without any manual checking until the processing cycle is complete. The potential effects of a single error are much greater in this environment. When such errors are detected, their correction can require extensive manual analysis in order to determine what files and records have been affected, and to prepare proper correcting entries.

Internal audit and data processing management interviewed report that the primary area of emphasis for a further reduction in loss exposure will be computer application systems.

Computer Service Center Loss Potential

Increasing dependence upon data processing facilities and a continuing trend toward centralization and concentration of data processing resources are major concerns of a majority of top executives interviewed by SRI. Interruptions in the availability of either data or processing capability can have catastrophic consequences for organizations highly dependent upon data processing. Top management as well as data processing and internal audit management are concerned that effective programs be developed to protect data processing facilities and minimize this loss exposure. Controls in use generally include:

- Computer service center security (i.e., limited access, special fire protection, standby or uninterrupted power sources).
- Backup processing and data files, including alternative processing facilities and off-site storage of important data files.
- Disaster planning, including documented recovery plans for various disaster situations such as fire, vandalism, flood, accidental or intentional destruction of vital data files.

Most of the firms interviewed have implemented improved computer service center security programs. Steps to enhance the security of computer facilities and to develop disaster plans require relatively short lead times and expenditures compared with the lead time to review computer application systems and eliminate vulnerabilities.

Loss Identification and Reporting

Despite a growing awareness of the potential for loss, top management interviewed by SRI seems confident that losses are minimal. Several of the managers said that they had no knowledge of loss relating to data processing within their organizations but at the same time indicated that they had no formal procedures to identify and report incidences of data processing loss. In confirmation of this, in only 17% of the organizations in the Primary U.S. Mail Survey does top management receive periodic reports of time or dollars lost due to data processing errors and omissions.

A few of the organizations visited by SRI indicated that they had formalized procedures for reporting data processing losses and believe such reporting and subsequent investigation discourage loss due to fraud, embezzlement, or inadequate computer application system controls. These procedures are used to report individual instances of loss. No one interviewed had been able to establish a method of measuring or estimating the overall extent of loss, either detected or undetected loss, or loss potential associated with data processing. As part of the Primary U.S. Mail Survey, data processing and internal audit management were asked to identify the areas of potential loss exposure within data processing. Their responses, which are given in Table 2, show that, whereas internal auditors most often indicate a major concern is loss from improper controls, data processing management most often indicate a major concern is loss from errors and omissions. In response to the same question, about 85% of Japanese and 50% of European data processing management indicate their highest ranking concern is with potential loss resulting from inadequate system design. Of the Japanese internal auditors who responded, 60% indicate their highest ranking concern is with errors and omissions, while 50%

TABLE 2
DATA PROCESSING LOSS POTENTIAL

Which *two* of the following areas of potential loss exposure in the data processing department are you most concerned about? (Check two)

	Percentage of organizations selecting each category*	
	Data processing	Internal audit
Potential loss from errors and omissions	61.8%	46.8%
Potential loss from improper controls	47.4	67.1
Potential loss from inadequate system design	43.3	41.2
Potential loss from fraud and defalcation	17.1	15.6
Potential loss from failure to comply with standards or procedures	14.9	20.9
Potential loss from inadequate conversion methods	7.5	6.7
Other	8.0	1.7

Note: Number of respondents = 222 from data processing and 221 from internal audit.

* Percentages equal 200% because each respondent checked two categories. Percentages are based on actual responses weighted to reflect the probable response distribution of all organizations in the sampling frame.

of the European internal auditors indicate their highest ranking concern is with improper controls. Internal auditors interviewed reported that proper manual controls governing the origination, transmittal, and balancing of transactions in user areas can significantly reduce errors and omissions relating to source transactions. Improved computer application system controls can ensure the detection of errors and omissions and prevent their subsequent processing.

As part of the Primary U.S. Mail Survey, data processing managers were asked in which two areas improvements are needed most to reduce the potential loss exposure about which they were most concerned. The responses of those who checked the top three categories listed in Table 2 are shown in Table 3. The latter table indicates that among data processing management who are most concerned about losses from either errors and omissions or improper controls, controls on processing procedures are most often reported as being in need of improvement. Among those who are most concerned about losses from inadequate system design,

TABLE 3
CONTROLS NEEDED BY DATA
PROCESSING TO REDUCE LOSS POTENTIAL

In which *two* of the following areas are improvements needed the most to reduce the potential loss exposure you checked above? (Check two)

	Percentage of organizations that are concerned about potential loss from*		
	Errors and omissions	Improper controls	Inadequate system design
Controls on			
1. Processing procedures	55.2%	67.8%	46.0%
2. Analysts/programmers	33.6	27.5	58.2
3. Operations personnel	31.0	31.2	22.3
4. Data access	24.0	32.7	14.0
5. Applications programmers	15.7	6.4	11.2
6. Data conversion (source data entry)	15.3	14.2	10.5
7. Systems programmers	11.3	3.8	18.0
8. Contingency planning	4.6	2.8	7.1
9. Physical access	4.0	10.2	2.8
10. Other	5.3	3.4	9.9

Note: Number of respondents = 214

* Percentages equal 200% because each respondent checked two categories. Percentages are based on actual responses weighted to reflect the probable response distribution of all organizations in the sampling frame.

however, controls on analysts and programmers are most often reported as being in need of improvement. Data processing managers interviewed by SRI also stressed the importance of procedures governing the handling and processing of data within the data processing organization. Many also reported that improvements are needed in the controls governing system analysts and programmers involved in computer application systems development and maintenance. Controls governing computer application systems development are required to ensure that adequate control procedures are built into computer application systems and programs being developed and maintained, and that adequate acceptance testing is performed.

In a related Primary U.S. Mail Survey question, top management was asked to develop its two major concerns about data processing. Table 4 summarizes the results of this question. The top management concerns most frequently reported are insufficient controls, the complexity of data processing, and insufficient user involvement. Despite the attention computer abuse and fraud have received in the media, potential loss due to fraud was only the fifth most frequently reported concern.

TABLE 4
TOP MANAGEMENT'S DATA PROCESSING CONCERNS

What are your *two* major concerns about data processing in your organization? (Check two)

	Percent of total*	Percentage of organizations with major concerns selecting each category*†
Organizations indicating no major concerns	5.3%	
Organizations indicating two of the following concerns	94.7	
Insufficient controls		39.4%
Complexity of data processing		29.5
Insufficient user involvement		25.1
Lack of data processing standards		23.9
Exposure to fraud		21.3
Lack of adequate independent review		19.8
Inadequate return on investment		17.1
Other		13.3

Note: Number of respondents = 221

* Percentages are based on actual responses weighted to reflect the probable response distribution of all organizations in the sampling frame.

† Percentages sum to 189.4% = 2 × 94.7% because respondents with major concerns checked two categories.

The top-ranking concern about data processing, as expressed by about 40% of the Japanese and 30% of the European top management, was with an inadequate return on investments. While insufficient controls were the second-ranking concern of European top management (about 25%), insufficient control was only the fourth-ranking concern of Japanese top management (about 20%). The top four concerns of Canadian top management are the same as those in the Primary U.S. Mail Survey. It is interesting to note that 65% of state government organizations responding to this question indicate insufficient controls as a major concern.

SUMMARY

Economic growth in the private sectors and growth in the scope of government activities have resulted in increasingly complex management information requirements. As data processing technology has been successfully applied to these management information needs, management at all levels has become increasingly reliant upon data processing for the information needed to effectively plan, evaluate, and control its organization's activities. The degree of reliance upon data processing is often not fully realized. However, a prolonged interruption of data processing can result in business disruption of catastrophic proportions.

Changes in data processing technology have occurred concurrent with the expansion of management information needs. Data processing has become more complex as more business functions are automated and as advanced data processing technology is applied. As a result, traditional control techniques and procedures as well as audit techniques used in the past must be reevaluated in light of these developments. New audit and control techniques are needed to ensure the integrity of data processing. Changes in the role of the internal auditor are occurring and are presented in a subsequent chapter.

With the broader application of, and greater reliance upon, data processing, the potential for losses resulting from undetected errors and omissions has increased. Error potential exists in the areas of computer applications systems, computer service center operations and application systems development. Many organizations have taken steps to improve computer service center control procedures. The security of computer facilities has received much emphasis. Steps to improve controls in these areas are relatively easy to implement; relatively short lead times and only modest expenditures are usually involved. In contrast, action programs to improve computer application system controls involve more cost and are longer term. Because of the progress that has been made with computer service center control procedures, the primary emphasis in the future will be on application system controls.

Few of the organizations interviewed by SRI, or which responded to the SRI mail survey, have established formal programs to identify, report, and investigate losses associated with data processing. Those interviewed who have such programs, however, report them to be effective in preventing losses. No organization contacted during the study reported having a satisfactory method of measuring over-all loss or loss potential. In general, existing programs handle loss reporting and investigation on an individual basis. The potential losses most frequently reported by data processing and internal audit are errors and omissions, inadequate systems design, and improper controls. In addition, internal auditors report that a better integration of manual and automated controls can reduce undetected errors and omissions originating during source documents preparation. Improved automated controls are important to ensure the detection of input errors and omissions and subsequent processing errors. Data processing management report controls governing processing procedures and systems development activities are the areas that need the most improvement.

EVALUATION AND OUTLOOK

The outlook is for a continuation of the trends that have characterized the growth of data processing in recent years: the automation of more business functions, an increasingly complex data processing environment, and greater management reliance upon computer-based information systems. However, because internal audit and control capabilities have not kept pace with the expansion of data processing and the introduction of new technology, new data processing control techniques and internal audit approaches are needed to ensure the accuracy, completeness, timeliness, and security of computer application systems. Greater emphasis is needed on systems auditability and control if they are to catch up and keep pace with rapidly advancing data processing technology.

Management programs are needed to improve the effectiveness of internal audit and control. These programs should focus attention on three areas: first, closer cooperation and coordination between data processing and internal audit to ensure that effective control procedures and audit facilities are established; second, more emphasis on the importance of controls, particularly computer application system controls in situations that involve the use of new technology or new system design concepts; third, formalized programs to develop needed data processing skills, knowledge, and capabilities within the internal audit organization.

Management attention and follow-up are needed to ensure that plans for greater cooperation and the upgrading of internal audit capabilities are prepared and executed. It is also important that the expanding role of internal audit is understood throughout the organization.

CHAPTER 2

INFORMATION TECHNOLOGY

Information technology as it relates to accounting information systems is such a broad topic that it is impractical to select articles to cover every aspect. Therefore, we have selected only articles that deal with the topics of most interest to today's readers. Of particular importance in the selection process was the relative newness of the topic to accounting and the timeliness of the material presented.

With the greatest demand for computers currently being for minicomputers, our first article by Dowell, "So, You Want to Buy a Minicomputer?," discusses the pros and cons of these small mechanical wizards. The author of this article has been associated with minicomputers for many years. He has witnessed their growth and acceptance, and from this experience he derived the material for this article. Because not all aspects of minicomputers are positive the author discusses various points that must be considered before investing in such a system. The background information from actual minicomputer operations should prove useful as a checklist for evaluating the potential of such a system in a given organizational situation.

Related to the development of the minicomputer has been another fast growing semiconductor machine, the microcomputer. The background, opportunities, and challenges of this machine are explained in the second article of this chapter. Howson, in "The Microcomputer Challenge," explains the characteristics of these computers in relation to other computers. A technical appendix is included to provide explanations of the more common terms, and a schematic illustrates a typical microcomputer system application. Throughout the article the author relates the challenge of the microcomputer to professional accountants and stresses that the professional must extend his computer expertise to this new and fast developing area.

Structured programming is a technique that has developed along with computer technology. "A Brief Look at Structured-Programming and Top-Down Program Design," by Yourdon, describes structured programming as a type of modular programming. The characteristic "top-down" implies an orderly approach to the designing of such programs. The author begins by defining the concepts and contrasting modular and structured programming. After defining the objectives and explaining the theory behind such programming, the author discusses its techniques and applications. The pros and cons are also discussed, but only briefly.

An area which is quickly gaining prominence in accounting systems literature is data base systems. "Computer 'data base management systems' (DBMS) have been surrounded by excitement, controversy, and misunderstanding since their first appearance several years ago," according to Singel in "Computer Data Base Systems: Who Needs Them?" Singel goes on to give a brief history of DBMS and to define it in current terms. He provides reasons for using such a system and offers several "real world" applications. Key issues that should be considered when adopting a DBMS are presented, and the components of such a program are listed.

The advantages and characteristics of a DBMS suggest a new and expanding role for accounting, and Nusbaum et al. in their article, "Data Base Management, Accounting, and Accountants," suggest several ways that DBMS has influenced the work and role of accountants. The authors describe the benefits to be derived by accountants from DBMS and provide some insights into its potential for accounting. The data base structure flowcharts are very informative and assist in understanding the relationship of the DBMS to the traditional accounting information system. Although somewhat bold, the authors suggest that accountants be placed in charge of the data base system to supervise its implementation and management because they are the ones who will benefit most from it. The prototype system suggested in the article could be used as a foundation for developing a complete DBMS at the corporate level and adapted to meet the needs of almost any type of organization. Again, this is an area where accountants should perhaps expand their expertise to maintain their prominent role in information systems.

Because of the ever-increasing use of small computers, the data processing function of many organizations is being redeployed. This major change in computer systems philosophy is going to have a major impact on both computer personnel and information users. Statland and Winski present an analysis of what can be expected in this area in "Distributed Information Systems: Their Effect on Your Company." According to the authors many small and medium size computers are being distributed for use by functional areas of businesses, and a movement towards decentralization is taking place—trends that are rapidly accelerating. To put the impact of distributed processing into perspective the authors review two major phases in the evolution of computer usage. Next, they discuss the conditions that are conducive to distributed processing and the impact that this change has on the management information system. Lastly, they specifically list the impacts of the change on information users. While they admit that advocates of centralization may disagree with their arguments, the authors believe that there are enough benefits to start opponents thinking about shifting away from extreme centralization.

"Cost-Performance Trade Off in Real-Time Systems Design," by Cushing and Dial, attempts to develop a method of communication by which managers can become more familiar with the concepts and technology of real-time systems. The article's primary objective is to develop an understanding of the trade-offs that must be made in the design process between conflicting objectives of cost minimization and performance maximization. After defining the five basic elements of real-time systems they discuss the concept of performance as related to information systems. Next, the factors in a cost-performance system are examined. Because real-time systems are continuing to gain in popularity it is more desirable than ever to be able to distinguish justifiable uses from unnecessary ones in decisions relating to system elements.

A chapter on information technology would be incomplete without the inclusion of an article on electronic funds transfer systems (EFTS). The title of the article by Schaller, "The Revolution of EFTS," aptly describes what is occurring in this area. This article discusses a dramatic change that is taking place in our society—a change that will very soon affect all businessmen, and eventually everyone. A brief history of EFTS is given and its current status is discussed. Next, the impact of EFTS on businessmen, auditors, and society is analyzed. While comprehensive predictions about impact may still be premature, a number of observations are made. The author describes the types of EFTS and provides evidence to show that in the near future EFTS are going to have a permanent impact on the business environment. While many banks and a few retail businesses are currently using EFTS, the trend is just beginning. The author predicts that there will be many growing pains and that the rate of growth will depend upon the resolution of many issues such as customer acceptance, legal problems, and audit-trail developments.

"Beyond 1984: A Technology Forecast," by Withington, sheds light on other developments that can be expected to occur in information systems. He begins by predicting the hardware changes that will take place in computer capabilities, specifically mentioning microcoding, multiprocessing, and component processors. A separate prediction is made with respect to storage, with emphasis on auxiliary storage. Other hardware items included in his predictions are input-output equipment and terminals.

The most drastic changes in information systems will probably be made in software. Operating systems, software management, and data management are all scheduled to undergo major changes in the next few years. The last major prediction in the article deals with the broad area of communications. Stand-alone controllers will receive much attention in the next few years because of their close association with EFTS. While not all of Withington's predictions will come true, he has made a realistic attempt to examine those areas where change appears either necessary or highly probable.

Not everyone will be interested in all of the topics included in this chapter, but a knowledge of them is important for tomorrow's accountants. Our profession has been criticized often because of its failure to make changes. If it is unwilling to keep up with and adapt to the changing world of information systems it will not be criticized but simply left behind and eliminated. In the business world "status quo" means "self-destruction."

So, You Want to Buy a Minicomputer?

J. RICHARD DOWELL

Executives of smaller businesses are being inundated with information about the use of minicomputers. Most such businesses have previously been unable to afford their own electronic data processing systems. Therefore, smaller-business executives have not had the experience needed to recognize the complexities of developing and implementing application systems for computers—especially minicomputers, which require some special considerations.

The author of this article has been associated with the application and installation of minicomputers for the last ten years, initially on the staff of a minicomputer vendor and subsequently as a consultant. He has observed that the smaller-business executive in most cases has no readily available source of information that evaluates the promises of benefits and the possible pitfalls that may occur during an otherwise successful installation. The smaller-business executive often cannot expect the salesman for the company from which he is purchasing a system to emphasize anything but the positive aspect. Executives of other companies who have installed minicomputers will have a tendency to stress the benefits of the installation rather than dwelling on the problems.

Consultants who may be able to provide some objective, independent judgments about the smaller-business executive's minicomputer acquisition decision and the subsequent planning process are all too often not called until after the decisions have been made. At that point the potential user asks the consultant, "Have I made the correct decision?" instead of "How do I go about making a sound decision?" and "What are the pitfalls that I must avoid?"

THE EXECUTIVE'S DILEMMA

Most smaller-business executives—especially those involved with repetitive cycles of manufacturing, distributing, or retailing—would like to use automated record keeping to contend with the volume of business records they need to effectively manage their businesses. Few, however, have been able to afford traditional electronic data processing solutions to their record processing problems. The heavy cost of equipment, coupled with the expense of an internal staff of programmers, key punch operators, and computer operators, has set a high operating cost threshold for computer operations.

Many smaller-business executives in this dilemma have used a data processing service bureau to supplement their manual data processing activities and inhouse billing and posting machines. These data processing service bureaus pick up transactions data on a periodic basis, process them, and return the reports and other output later—sometimes after several days. Service bureaus have been quite effective for cycle-type applications such as payroll, accounts payable, accounts receivable, inventory accounting, and general ledger accounting. These areas have a common trait: they deal with completed transactions.

Service bureaus, however, haven't dealt effectively with the more time-critical processing and information requirements that accompany order processing, shipping, billing, and inventory/warehouse management. Indeed, these latter applications are not only the most time-critical; they also trigger management actions. As such, they tend to be important to profitability.

The smaller-business data processing dilemma is being solved increasingly in the 1970's through the use of minicomputers. The overall success of these small, versatile computers is illustrated by their phenomenal growth over the last few years. The estimated number of U.S.-manufactured minicomputers installed worldwide increased from approximately 32,000 in 1972 to some 190,000 in 1976. By 1980, the latter figure is expected to more than double to 400,000.

The growth of minicomputers has resulted in, or perhaps has been the result of, numerous stories about their benefits—chiefly involving low-cost minicomputer solutions to business data processing problems. These stories are told by minicomputer vendors when they call on executives of smaller businesses, by fellow executives at trade and business association gatherings, and in business trade journal advertisements.

There are tales about a successful competitor whose telephone salesmen have a video display terminal in front of them which, with the pressing of a few keys, displays on a cathode ray tube (television screen) information about stock availability and delivery dates. This same competitor may also tell all who will listen of his improved inventory management and cash flow position as well as of his reduced bad debt. One can also hear about the chief executive who has a video display terminal on his desk which helps him make the tough business decisions, such as what products to offer, whether to make or buy products, and when to order or manufacture them. All of these stories contain a common ingredient: they state that the data processing system doesn't require expensive, specialized personnel for programming, key punching, and operations; rather it is run by the people currently involved in the day-to-day operations of the business.

These stories perhaps sound somewhat contrived but they are, in fact, typical of the benefits being realized by many smaller businesses.

This article provides background information to assist the smaller-business executive in examining three common promises of minicomputer benefits:

- Low initial cost
- Low operating cost
- Business management improvements

The following discussion will serve as a checklist for the smaller-business executive in appraising minicomputer alternatives and implementing plans.

PROMISE NO. 1: LOW INITIAL COST

First, let's look behind the promise of low initial cost, which actually has two components: the equipment (hardware) and the application systems (software).

Minicomputer hardware is usually manufactured by cost conscious companies in a very competitive environment. There are currently some three dozen U.S.-based companies offering minicomputers. Moreover, most minicomputer manufacturers don't sell directly to smaller businesses. So, they haven't spent large sums of money, as the large computer manufacturers have, on application system software for specific processing functions or industries. The application systems that are needed by most smaller businesses, which don't have or don't want to hire programmers, are usually supplied by third parties.

That's because most smaller businesses want to buy the solution which the application system offers—they often tend to view the particular type of minicomputer they acquire as a secondary consideration. The third party that offers the application system solution may purchase the minicomputer from the manufacturer and resell it, complete with application systems, to the smaller business. These third parties are often referred to as original equipment manufacturers, or OEMs. Those application systems suppliers that don't buy and sell hardware are usually referred to as software or systems houses. OEMs and systems houses are usually characterized by a small number of employees and limited capital. And, they sell solutions which they have developed and sold several times, thus lowering the cost of each usage by spreading the development expense over several installations.

The obvious benefit of low equipment cost and shared applications development expense is the lower cost threshold for entry into electronic data processing. Smaller businesses with significant processing volumes can in this way now afford EDP.

The risks may not be so obvious. First, the manufacturer of the equipment may not survive. The total number of minicomputer manufacturers in the U.S. dropped from over 50 to 36 between 1972 and 1976. As was the fate of quite a few large computer manufacturers, many other minicomputer manufacturers may well not survive the shakeout period that characterizes the development of sophisticated technology as its products impact a more mature market.

The most serious impact of the business failure of your minicomputer's manufacturer would be the lack of replacement parts and maintenance services. Unlike many of the large computers made by companies no longer in the business, there may not be enough of a particular minicomputer in existence to support a viable business of replacement parts and maintenance, should the manufacturer go under. Indeed, unlike many large computers which can be rented, most minicomputers are purchased. So, you could find yourself buying a machine that may be totally useless without maintenance support.

Less serious, but probably more likely, the minicomputer manufacturer may not be able to provide adequate maintenance service. This may result from poor spares logistics, inadequate training, or too little business in a particular location to support a service person. Poor service may bring your machine down for days at a time, stranding you without alternatives for processing your normal work load. What's more, whether the maintenance is adequate or not, it's likely to cost more than you anticipated. You can expect that a maintenance contract covering service calls during normal business hours will, on an annual basis, cost approximately 10% of the equipment's purchase price.

In addition, the systems house or OEM may be unable to provide an effective application system. If the systems house should go bankrupt during systems implementation, it would seriously set back the realization of any benefits. This would be especially true if the hardware has been purchased by your firm and is already in place. If the systems house should fail after your installation is complete, it may affect your ability to deal with software errors and/or system changes that most certainly will occur. Failure after the installation will also mean more expense if another firm needs to alter the application system in response to your changing business needs.

One of the most serious failures known to us concerned a manufacturer who purchased a minicomputer for $70,000, based on the recommendation of a hardware vendor and a systems house. The systems house then spent five months trying to convert an application system from a larger computer to the minicomputer. After the company had put five months of payments into a machine and $12,000 into software that, as it turned out, couldn't be used, the systems house withdrew from the job. It said the hardware was inadequate for the business volumes required. The manufacturer was left with a hardware system too small to be used in his application, $82,000 worth of liabilities, and no offsetting benefits. The whole ordeal had practically put this manufacturer out of business because of the resources it had absorbed, primarily the time of his most valuable operating people.

PROMISE NO. 2: LOW OPERATING COST

The second promise, low operating cost, is possible primarily because of what may be referred to as on-line, transaction driven systems. These systems promise the ability to accomplish processing requirements with line personnel who are normally involved in processing a particular transaction, anyway, rather than with such specialized personnel as key punchers and computer operators.

For example, an order processing system in a traditional EDP environment may require that the salesperson fill out an order form that will be transcribed into computer form by a data transcriber (key punch operator). The orders are stacked into batches and the computer operator initiates a process to edit and validate all of the orders. (Are the customers, credit limits, and products valid? Are the products in stock?) A listing of errors then goes back to the sales department for correction before processing can continue. Once all information is corrected, possibly several days later, the orders are processed to create picking tickets and bills, update inventories, and debit accounts receivable.

On the other hand, in a well designed, on-line, transaction driven system, the salesperson accepting the order keys it into the machine as quickly as the order form can be completed. Entry of the order information initiates the process to edit and validate the information, which is immediately corrected, if required, by the person keying in the order. The order transaction then "drives" the process to create a bill, update the inventory file, and debit the customer's accounts receivable file. In other words, the separate process of data transcription is eliminated and there is no operator needed to initiate the processes and load the proper files.

Several features of minicomputers can be combined to facilitate on-line, transaction driven systems. One of the primary features is the video display terminal that allows keying in of information and quickly displays messages, instructions, or other pertinent information on the video screen. Another important element is the disk file that allows for direct and timely location of a particular data record, thus eliminating the need to examine all the records in order to find one. Finally, today's minicomputers have system control programs which facilitate on-line, transaction driven systems and, in some cases, concurrent transaction processing for various applications from different video display terminals.

The chief benefit of on-line, transaction driven systems is that the data processing can be accomplished without additional steps and personnel. This, of course, saves time and, therefore, money (primarily, salary expenses).

The risk is that the system may not perform as expected. In that event, either more people will have to be hired to enter data as a normal function of their job or special input personnel will have to be hired. This can happen when the input keying and machine interaction requirements are too lengthy or too complicated for the line personnel to deal with in the normal course of their work.

PROMISE NO. 3: BUSINESS MANAGEMENT IMPROVEMENTS

The third minicomputer promise is improved business operations. These improvements are, in part, possible due to timely processing. Because the minicomputer is located inhouse and the complete processing of each transaction takes only a matter of minutes, management is able to see the complete effect of each transaction on a timely basis.

Data concerning product availability (inventory level) can be updated immediately so that the availability will be known at the time of the next order. On-line systems also allow a manager to interact with the machine on "what if" questions, such as how long it will take to get a purchased part delivered. Similarly, more timely inventory updates may allow a lower inventory level with the same or a higher level of customer service. Timely data also may allow on-line credit checking and more timely billing, which may improve cash flow and reduce bad debts. Indeed, there are many such decisions that timely information can improve.

The risks inherent in this third promise are that no business benefit may be achieved, or worse, that business may suffer. All business decisions don't require timely processing and information. For example, if you're obtaining a minicomputer primarily to perform general ledger and payroll processing, you may be just as well off at a data processing service bureau.

Inaccurate information is another problem. Sometimes this occurs because the application system doesn't perform in the expected manner. Inaccurate information can also occur because the conversion to the new system brings over inaccurate data, or worse, because of poor internal processing controls within the system.

Many applications designed by inexperienced EDP professionals won't include the necessary data security and internal processing controls to ensure that the usage of on-line, transaction driven systems is properly controlled. The application system design should provide for levels of authorized access, where certain critical transactions can be initiated only by supervisory or management personnel. The system should also provide audit trail features that can be used to ensure control over transactions entered from each terminal. File balancing program routines and processing totals should be provided to verify the integrity of all files.

AVOIDING THE RISKS

The dangers to the smaller company of failing to achieve the benefits of any of these minicomputer promises aren't actually very different than those faced by larger businesses. The smaller businessman does, however, face some special risks which aren't as likely to confront the larger businessman. The primary reason is a general lack of understanding of electronic data processing's intricacies and the smaller-business executive's almost total dependence on persons outside of his business. This is compounded by the previously mentioned risks of dealing with vendors with limited business resources.

Besides recognizing the risks involved, one of the more important aspects of avoiding or minimizing danger in acquiring your minicomputer is defining the processing requirements of your business. Not many manufacturers would purchase a new automated manufacturing machine without understanding the machine's specifications and exactly how it would integrate with other processes. But this often happens in purchases of minicomputers and application systems—there is a lack of understanding about the requirements and/or the specifications of the new system.

Keep in mind that the applications sytems that are the least costly may turn out to be the most expensive to install. The low priced application system (under $10,000) may appear to do what a more expensive system does but, in fact, it may not do it as well, it may do it wrongly, it may do it in an uncontrollable manner, or it may not perform the expected functions at all. Part of the additional cost of the higher priced application system may be in tailoring it to fit the specifics of your business. For example, the low priced application system may work fine if you are willing to change the way you do business to conform with the processing requirements for which the system was designed. The more expensive system may allow greater benefits and cause fewer training and conversion problems by adapting more easily to your specific business.

SUMMARY

This article has attempted to provide executives of smaller businesses with points they should consider when debating whether to try a minicomputer as a solution to their data processing problems. It points out potential risks that may not have been obvious so that minicomputer users may apply good business judgment in evaluating the acquisition, just as they apply such judgment to other decisions affecting important capital assets.

Many managers of smaller businesses have solved the dilemma of affordable electronic data processing with the implementation of minicomputer application systems and the installation of one or more minicomputers. The majority of them have realized the promised benefits discussed in this article. They also have often been able to minimize potential risks through their own careful approaches and the timely use of consultants' expertise.

Minicomputer solutions to smaller business data processing problems can indeed allow executives to realize low initial cost, low operating cost, and business management improvements. Executives of larger businesses found similar benefits with the introduction of electronic data processing some 25 years ago and have learned through experience how to maximize them. Executives of smaller businesses should be able to profit from that earlier experience.

The Microcomputer Challenge

HUGH R. HOWSON

This past spring, major computer manufacturers announced unprecedented price reductions in their computer equipment. New systems—ranging from very large systems to minicomputers—were announced, emphasizing cost-performance improvements in the order of 30%. Although market strategies were partly responsible for the timing and nature of all this activity, a recent issue of *Business Week* noted that the reductions generally reflect continuing advances in electronic technology:

"The forcing factor behind the emergence of new computer systems is the continuing price plunge of semi-conducter circuits. Such circuits—thousands of transistors on a single chip of silicon—make up the logic and memory circuits of all computers. As semi-conductor makers squeeze more and more circuits on a chip, the cost per circuit falls, making it economically feasible to use more of them and thereby increase computer power."[1]

In contrast to the approach of the established computer manufacturers—more computing for the same dollar—the microcomputer[2] is forcing its way into the marketplace by providing a smaller package of computer power for many fewer dollars. For example, a microcomputer with a small memory and limited input/ output can be purchased, ready to run, for about $300. This includes an operating system in read-only memory! It is really more of a toy (other than for specialized uses)—that is, until you add on up to 64K bytes of memory, a couple of floppy disks for secondary storage, one or two typewriter terminals or CRTs and, possibly, a line printer. Then, at a total cost of $3,000-$10,000, you have a very practical data processing system. Microcomputers can, therefore, provide a low cost means of starting into data processing and an alternative to some minicomputer time-sharing and service bureau applications.

This article will review the background of the microcomputer and consider some of the opportunities and challenges it offers for the professional accountant.

Reprinted with permission from *CA magazine*, published by the Canadian Institute of Chartered Accountants, Toronto, Canada (August 1977), pp. 50-53.

As many readers will wish to remain abreast of microcomputer terminology, a technical appendix is included, defining the more common terms and providing a schematic illustration of a microcomputer.

DEVELOPMENT OF THE MICROCOMPUTER

The first commercial microprocessor, the Intel 4004, was introduced in 1971 by Intel Corporation,[3] a manufacturer of semi-conductors. It was developed primarily as a product for special purpose calculators. Other manufacturers and other designs quickly followed, and a recent survey[4] listed 55 different microprocessors on the market.[5] Supporting the microprocessor was the concurrent development of memory and input/output chips that could be combined, with relative ease, to satisfy the requirements of the specific design or user.

The main marketing thrust of the semi-conductor firms has been toward industrial markets, such as process-control applications, with automobile and home appliances seen as large potential mass markets. The microprocessor is also used as a component of larger computer systems (in channels and device controllers) and peripheral devices (terminals, cash registers, etc.). The microprocessor can replace many of the individual components in almost any electronic device, utilizing instead the control capability of a stored program. In addition to saving costs, the microprocessor also achieves design flexibility because designs can now be changed by modifying the stored program without having to modify the circuitry.

The development of the microcomputer as a stand-alone computing system has come about independently and almost in spite of the industrial orientation of the semi-conductor manufacturers. Intermediate firms, purchasing the components, designed systems and software that attracted the interest of the home hobbyist. The extremely rapid growth of the home hobbyist market[6] led, in turn, to the entry of additional small specialized firms to satisfy the demands for inexpensive peripheral devices and software. And the hobbyist market is now expanding even further and changing. Whereas the early market focused on "build-your-own" computer kits, reduced costs have allowed more and more users to purchase fully assembled systems. The latest development in the U.S.—also just starting in Canada—is the retail store where customers can buy their system components off the shelf in ready-to-run condition.[7] The personal computer is coming into the home and is ready to move into the office.

WHAT CAN IT DO?

Basic stored-program computer power is virtually free;[8] the relevant costs are for memory, peripheral devices and software. Opportunities for effective use depend primarily on the imagination of the potential users, and extend far beyond the scope of this paper. Three areas that may be particularly relevant for the professional accountant are:

- Traditional data processing applications.

- Dedicated applications.
- Applications in an existing data processing environment.

Traditional Data Processing Applications

A business microcomputer system can be programmed to perform all the activities of mini and standard computers. Applications such as order entry, receivables, inventory control, accounting and payables are all practical for the smaller firm or division. There may be advantages, however, in having a separate microcomputer for a specific higher volume application. The March 1977 issue of *CAmagazine* contained a case study of a construction firm's successful use of a minicomputer for accounting and reporting purposes.[9] The same types of applications could be processed on a microcomputer for a smaller organization. As a rule of thumb, Mal Lockwood of ASI, an American firm developing accounting packages for microprocessors, suggests that firms with up to 200 employees or sales of up to $5 million might consider using the microcomputer.[10] Although packaged application programs are still limited, MITS, the firm that produced the most popular microcomputer, the Altair 8800, has recently set up a new company—the Altair Software Distribution Company—to distribute quality applications software. Its first products are directed to the small business market and, in addition to accounting and inventory control products, it provides a word processing package.[11] These are the forerunners of many more specialized application packages that will soon be available.

The Dedicated Application

A microcomputer can be designed to handle one specific application economically because of the flexibility in selecting only the minimum set of components required for the task. Also, it is relatively easy to incorporate data-collection components to collect analogue signals from sensing devices, such as weigh scales or counters. A biologist recently assembled a system to record and analyze test data with hardware costing under $1,000. This replaced a $12,000 measuring device and eliminated intermediate manual steps of examining graph plots and entering digital values into a computer for statistical analysis. The microcomputer performed the complete operation and analysis immediately while the experiment was in progress.

In the commercial environment, a store servicing retail and commercial customers has a microcomputer in its salesroom; customers use it to enter their job requirements and receive an immediate quotation. A university book store has a microcomputer linked to the cash register to maintain control over inventory and cash, in addition to interpreting the signals from a hand-held wand that reads bar codes on each item to provide the product code and price. A small medical practice is developing a microcomputer system to handle patient appointments and billing. A large New York bank is experimenting with linked microcomputer systems to reduce the volume of paper in interdepartmental correspondence. From the local pharmacy's prescription and drug control to the local parking lot, the microcomputer provides opportunities for simple but effective dedicated applications. As experience and markets develop, package systems incorporating both hardware and software for specific applications will be available, much like the word processing stations now on the market.

Within an Existing EDP Environment

It will be beneficial to rethink some aspects of existing computer-based systems. Newer "intelligent" terminals incorporate a microprocessor that provides computing capability at the terminal. This capability can be used to improve the efficiency and accuracy of data capture and entry, and reduce the load placed on the central processor. According to R. Wicham: "The whole object of the game in the future is to shield the host processor from this huge number of interrupts that will occur. . . . It's getting to be a locally online world with a batch or highly structured transmission to the host computer. And microprocessors in all their forms are what's making this possible."[12]

The possibility of maintaining local data files close to the user, in a distributed data base system, is also an important consideration. Considering the technical aspects, L. Thomas of Bell Labs commented: "The microprocessor is a memory revolution. Properly viewed, the CPU is a servant of memory and nothing else. If there is one generalization I can make from the many applications we've had over the last two years, it is that every time we've done something clever, it has not been from some clever choice of the CPU. It has been from clever use of memory."[13]

From the managerial viewpoint, however, it is important to consider the relationship of ever increasing salary costs to the rapidly decreasing costs of the computer system. This indicates that making the computer system the servant of the user is still the major task. The objective must be to increase productivity and job satisfaction. Paul Strassman, of Xerox Corporation, recently suggested that this emphasis on people is a major factor in managing information systems costs: "One of the problems I see in most existing information systems that rely mainly on computer terminals is their relatively narrow task orientation. People do not fit readily into such an environment."[14]

A review of information systems must focus on the tasks to be performed and how these tasks can be combined into meaningful productive jobs for employees.

THE CHALLENGE

The microcomputer poses exactly the same challenge to professional accountants as the minis, maxis, third generation, second generation, etc. did. Logically, the microcomputer is no different than its forebears. The need is as important now for careful assessment, planning and control, if not more so, than it was in the past. The problems of control can, in fact, be more pressing, as both hardware and software will be provided by more firms with varying abilities and skills—ranging from very competent to total incompetence. Hardware controls, which we have come to expect from most established manufacturers, may not be present. Many of the errors and problems of the 1960s will be repeated in poor systems and program designs. (For example, the customer quotation system mentioned earlier works very well—until there is a price change. Then price constants are part of the program and cannot be changed without changing the program!)

The CA profession has established an enviable reputation for its knowledge of the computer field—the challenge is to extend this knowledge to the new technology and avoid at least some of the pitfalls of the past. Microcomputers, because of their small size and modular construction, are easier to understand; all that is necessary is to get involved. Here are two suggestions as to how you can go about it: (1) Subscribe for a year to one or more of the microcomputer journals—*Byte*[15] and *Interface Age*[16] are particularly recommended. (2) Consider getting a microcomputer in the office. As mentioned at the start of this article, a basic system can be purchased for about $300-$500. There are also well packaged instructional systems that include the microcomputer, programs and instructional material. This will give you and your staff the opportunity to become familiar with the technology. As a second step—or as an alternative—find a simple application in your own or a client's office that could support the investment of $1,000-$5,000 for a more advanced system. Consider the costs of development as a worthwhile educational investment; you will find many future opportunities for earning a return.

NOTES

[1] "More tumult for the computer industry," *Business Week* (May 30, 1977), p. 59.

[2] Terminology is based on current usage rather than technical criteria, so it is difficult to provide absolute definitions. A "microprocessor" is a central processing unit contained on one or two silicon chips; a "microcomputer" is the collection of a microprocessor, memory and peripheral devices. Microprocessors typically operate at a machine cycle frequency of 1 microsecond, have an 8-bit word-length and have the capability to address 64K of memory. (There are, of course, 16- and 24-bit word microprocessors and some operate at cycle times of 250 nanoseconds.)

Using cost as a criterion to distinguish between microcomputers, minicomputers and conventional computers, one arbitrary classification defines a microcomputer as a system with a CPU costing less than $1,000 and a minicomputer as a system with a CPU costing less than $20,000. A CPU costing between $20,000 and $50,000 may be classed as a midicomputer, and anything above $50,000 would be just a computer!

[3] J. L. Hilburn and P. N. Julich, *Microcomputers/Microprocessors: Hardware, Software and Applications* (Englewood Cliffs, N. J.: Prentice-Hall Inc., 1976).

[4] "Microprocessor Specifications," *Databook 70, Volume I.* (Toronto: Maclean-Hunter Limited, June 1976). These 55 microprocessors were manufactured by 27 different firms.

[5] Microprocessors have their own geneology: current 8-bit machines are considered as 2nd generation processors; 3rd generation processors include 16- and 24-bit machines.

[6] Computer clubs are springing up in almost every city and several local and national magazines are published regularly. The most popular national magazine, *Byte,* has grown to a circulation of 90,000 in 20 months of publication. Some of

the more colourful US journals are the *Homebrew Computer Club Newsletter,* published monthly in Mountain View, California and the *Silicon Gulch Gazette.* Silicon Gulch, where much of the semi-conductor development work has taken place, can be located on the map under the name Santa Clara Valley, California.

[7] A chain of Computer Shack stores is in the planning stages; also, denoting respectability, Heathkit is expected to announce its entry into the market in the fall.

[8] The microprocessor chip, alone, can be purchased for $20–$30. To emphasize its low cost, some industry speakers have thrown out handfuls of the chips to attentive audiences.

[9] D. M. Fleming, "On time, in balance and under control—a computer success story." *CAmagazine* (March 1977).

[10] M. Lockwood, "Micro-Business," *Interface Age* (September 1976).

[11] "Computers for Small Businesses," *ETI Canada* (March 1977).

[12] R. Wicham, Vantage Research Inc., cited in *Datamation* (February 1976), p. 73.

[13] L. Thomas, cited in *Datamation* (February 1976), p. 72.

[14] P. A. Strassman, "Managing the costs of information," *Harvard Business Review* (September–October 1976).

[15] Byte Subscriptions, P. O. Box 361, Arlington, MA 02174 USA.

[16] Interface Age, P. O. Box 1234, Cerritos, CA 90701 USA.

TECHNICAL APPENDIX

A microcomputer system is illustrated schematically in Figure 1. The individual components are drawn in full size. The microprocessor has all the control, arithmetic and logic circuitry and a set of 70 to 150 machine instructions. It has an instruction register, program counter, one or more arithmetic registers, general purpose registers, one or more index registers and, possibly, a stack pointer. Second generation systems process one byte of data at a time. The clock provides machine cycle pulses at frequencies from 250 nanoseconds to one microsecond.

Main memory is provided by RAM (random access memory) chips that include the necessary circuitry to decode address and control pulses and either read or write data at the memory location specified by the signals coming from the address lines. Access time is in the order of 200 to 500 nanoseconds. Also ROM chips (read only memory) may be used for unchanging programs loaded in the manufacturing process. There is also PROM (programmable read only memory) that the user can load, and EPROM (eraseable programmable read only memory) which enables the user to erase contents and reload new data. The typical system can address up to 64K bytes, limited by the 16 address lines. However, this limitation should be relaxed in the near future. For example, an Ontario firm, EMA Industries Ltd., has designed a PLRAM (program locatable random access memory). This is a 4K memory board in which the starting address can be changed by program logic. Using this approach, a much larger main memory can be utilized by having several boards that can, in turn, be assigned the same memory addresses under control of the program during execution.

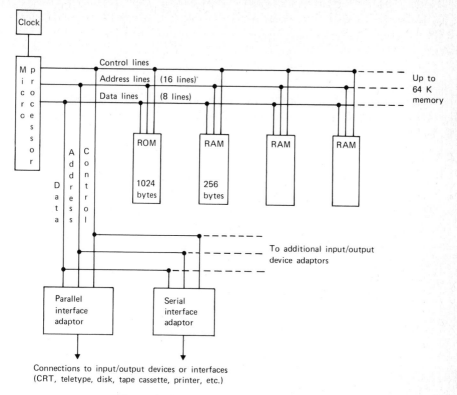

Connections to input/output devices or interfaces
(CRT, teletype, disk, tape cassette, printer, etc.)

Figure 1 *A typical microcomputer system*

Input/output devices are accessed through special purpose chips for either parallel or serial transmission. Each chip will service one input/output device, and is treated as a one-byte memory location by the microprocessor. Input/output operations are initiated when the microprocessor moves data to or from the chip.

The components are linked together by a common set of connections (a bus) that include eight data lines, 16 address lines and several control lines to provide common timing pulses, read-write, control and interrupt signals. On a small system all components may be on one PC (printed circuit) board. As more memory is added, the memory and input/output functions may be placed on separate boards. A common base into which the separate board connections can be inserted is referred to as a mother-board.

Programming. The CPU processes exactly the same types of machine instructions as regular computers. It is important to clarify the distinction between microprogram and microprocessor. They are completely unrelated concepts. A microprogram is the set of instructions controlling each switching operation that must be performed to achieve one machine instruction. For example, the one machine instruction "add memory contents to accumulator" would be represented by several microprogram instructions. Some microprocessors and standard computers may be microprogrammed; most do not have this capability.

Assembler language is normally provided by the manufacturer. Also, a cross-assembler may be available for development of programs on a larger computer, which will produce the machine language program for the microprocessor.

High level language compilers are also available with BASIC being the most popular. FORTRAN and a modified version of PL/I is also available.

A Brief Look at Structured Programming and Top-Down Program Design

EDWARD YOURDON

Structured programming is a "buzz-word" that has been used for the past few years to describe a rigorous form of modular programming. Much of the credit for "inventing" structured programming is given to Professor E. W. Dijkstra, who first began publishing papers on the subject in 1965 [1,2]. A variety of other papers have been published in the literature since then, but the concept was largely ignored by the EDP community until IBM published the results of its now-classic *New York Times* project in January 1972 [3]. Structured programming is now used by a variety of computer manufacturers, user organizations and universities; indeed, it is considered the best way of teaching beginners how to write computer programs.

Top-down *program design* is another idea attributed largely to Dijkstra, though a number of others have also helped develop the concept. Top-down *design* is an orderly approach to the design of a program or a system—beginning with the identification of major functions (or modules) and their interfaces, and breaking those functions into successively smaller functions. Top-down *coding* refers to the idea of writing the code in parallel with the design, i.e., so that the higher levels of design are coded before the lower levels are even designed. Finally, top-down *testing* refers to the concept of testing the higher levels of logic within a program, with the lower levels implemented as "dummy" modules—in contrast to the classical approach of performing module testing, then program testing, then system testing.

DIFFERENCES BETWEEN MODULAR PROGRAMMING AND STRUCTURED PROGRAMMING

A number of programmers feel that "structured programming" is simply another buzz-word for something they have been doing for years, namely modular programming. It is important to recognize that while there are obvious similarities between the two concepts, *they are not the same*.

Reprinted by permission from *Mini-Micro Systems* (June 1974), pp. 30–32, 34–35.

Attempts at modular programming often begin well: the programmer decides to break a large program into modules. However, he often makes no further attempt to break each of the modules into even smaller modules; thus, the result is often a program with a large main section and a few large (e.g., several hundred statements) modules that cannot be easily subdivided. Note the importance of this: if the modules cannot be subdivided, they must be treated as a single unit—which means that any testing, debugging, maintenance or attempt at understanding the module will be complicated by the need to comprehend a large block of indivisible coding. The situation is further complicated by the fact that the "modules" that are developed in the traditional attempt at modular programming are often not *independent* of one another—they alter each other's logic, share each other's working storage, etc.

The basic problem with modular programming, then, is that it is usually attempted in a somewhat *ad hoc* manner; good programmers presumably do a good job at it, but the large number of average programmers make quite a mess of it.

Structured programming, on the other hand, provides some very rigorous mechanisms which help ensure that a program can be broken into smaller modules, each of which can be broken into even smaller modules by a process that continues until we are left with "atomic" modules consisting of a few individual statements. This is done by forcing the programmer to use carefully defined program structures that help ensure that the programmer will *not* inadvertently end up with an unmodular program.

THE OBJECTIVES OF STRUCTURED PROGRAMMING

There are three major objectives of structured programming: vastly reduced testing time; increased programmer productivity; and greater clarity and comprehension of programs (which obviously improves the maintainability of programs). The testing aspect is usually considered the most important; in a recent article in *Datamation* [4], IBM claims to have developed a major project with an average of only one bug per 10,000 lines of coding; other structured programming projects have been completed and have been run in a production mode for two years with only a handful of minor bugs.

Greater programmer productivity is obviously somewhat related to the area of testing; nevertheless, it is interesting to note that several projects have experienced a five-fold improvement in the number of lines of debugged code produced by their programmers each day. This can lead to smaller programming teams working on a project—which in turn can lead to reduced management problems, reduced communication problems, and improved programmer morale.

Clarity of programming has recently become more important in many organizations. A recent survey [5] has found that the average EDP organization spends approximately 50% of its budget maintaining existing programs; clearly this could be reduced (though not eliminated) if programs were easier to read and easier to understand. Structured programming improves the clarity of programs considerably by (a) proposing a standardized *style* of programming, (b) organizing programs into modules that are generally no longer than one page of coding, and (c) arranging the program logic so that it can be read in a top-to-bottom fashion instead of the helter-skelter organization found in most programs.

THE THEORY BEHIND STRUCTURED PROGRAMMING

Much of the theoretical basis for structured programming comes from a classic paper by Bohm and Jacopini [6] in which a "structure theorem" is presented; any proper program can be constructed from three basic building blocks known as

    a. Process boxes

    b. IF-THEN-ELSE mechanisms

    c. DO-WHILE mechanisms

These structures are illustrated in Figure 1.

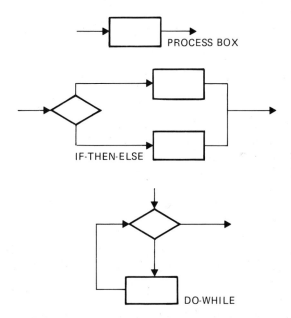

Fig. 1 *The basic Bohm & Jacopini mechanisms*

    The proof that any program *can* be constructed from these three mechanisms is rather complex, and is not generally required by the ordinary programmer. However, it is obviously important to see how the mechanisms can be implemented in the common programming languages, e.g., in COBOL, PL/I, FORTRAN, and assembly language. With each of these languages it is possible (though sometimes not trivial) to develop a set of basic statements that will implement the Bohm and Jacopini mechanisms: the programmer is then told to use *only* those statements when writing a program.

One of the aspects of structured programming that has caused a great deal of controversy is the fact that, in a reasonable programming language, the Bohm and Jacopini building blocks are easily implemented without the use of the GO-TO statement. After a great deal of arguing, most programmers can be convinced that while the GO-TO statement is not inherently evil, it can certainly be misused. And if the structured programming conventions make it unnecessary, why use it?

TECHNIQUES OF STRUCTURED PROGRAMMING

Depending on the programming language, the programmer must be taught which "tools" will facilitate the development of structured programs. In COBOL, for example, the programmer requires the PERFORM statement, the PERFORM-UNTIL structure, and judicious use of IF-THEN-ELSE statements—as well as the "primitive" MOVE statements, ADD statements, etc. Similarly, the PL/I programmer makes use of IF-THEN-ELSE structures, DO-WHILE structures and a variety of other forms. Since the FORTRAN language lacks these powerful constructs, the programmer must be told how to simulate them, or he must be encouraged to use some of the available preprocessors that provide IF-THEN-ELSE and DO-WHILE statements as a "superset" of the basic FORTRAN. Similarly, assembly language programmers must be shown the appropriate macros that will provide the IF-THEN-ELSE and DO-WHILE mechanisms.

Unfortunately, it is often not sufficient to show the structured programming mechanisms to a programmer and then assume that he will use them. There are a variety of programming situations where the use of the basic Bohm and Jacopini mechanisms—or, more simplistically, the elimination of the GO-TO statement— is not obvious. One of the more common situations which seems to cause difficulties is shown in Figure 2, which represents a phenomenon often referred to as "branching into common sections of code." Another example of a difficult programming situation is shown in Figure 3. In this case, the program has various *loops* that would seem to require something other than the basic Bohm and Jacopini mechanisms.

A number of techniques have been developed to cope with these situations; what is most interesting about them is that they require a method of programming somewhat alien to the programmer's usual techniques (techniques that are the result of several years of programming in an unstructured fashion). Thus it is necessary not only to explain the techniques, but also to encourage programmers to practice them until they become natural.

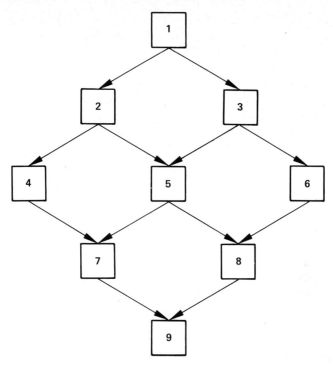

Fig. 2 *"Branching into common sections of code"*

One of the techniques for dealing with situations such as the one shown in Figure 2 is known as *duplication of coding*. It involves duplicating those modules that are entered from more than one place so that the "converted" program can be represented as a nested IF-THEN-ELSE structure. Another technique is based on a paper by Ashcroft and Manna [7]. It requires a "state variable" to be introduced into the program, and is useful for dealing with programs of the nature shown in Figure 3. The resulting structure is often implemented with a CASE structure or a GO-TO-DEPENDING-ON statement. Still another technique requires the introduction of a Boolean flag into the program. The flag is initialized at some point outside a loop (a loop that had originally been programmed in an unstructured fashion), is used to control the loop with a DO-WHILE or PERFORM-UNTIL structure, and is reset at some point within the body of the loop.

A number of other approaches are currently being developed to deal with other "difficult" programming situations, e.g., how to deal with end-of-file conditions without resorting to unstructured techniques. Similarly, new structured programming mechanisms have been proposed to supplement the basic Bohm and Jacopini mechanisms. As long as the new mechanisms conform to the one-entry-one-exit "black box" programming, they should also lead to well-structured programs.

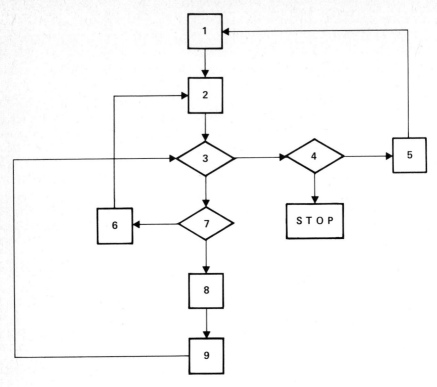

Fig. 3 *A typical programming situation involving looping*

OTHER CONSIDERATIONS

There are a number of additional programming conventions that are helpful—and often quite necessary—for the success of a structured programming project. Formatting conventions, for example, make the program listing more readable by showing, in a very graphic sense, the level of nested structures. It is also important to establish conventions for avoiding the use of "common" intermediate working storage; for avoiding ALTER statements and other means of changing the logic in another module; for keeping the length of a module to a reasonable number of statements (e.g., 50 or 60) and so forth.

TOP–DOWN PROGRAM DESIGN

As was mentioned above, top-down programming consists of a design phase, a coding phase, and a testing phase. Most programmers and system designers find the top-down design concept attractive, and often state that they have been designing in this manner for several years. Indeed, they have been doing something akin to top-down design, just as modular programming is somewhat akin to structured programming. The current approach to top-down design is an attempt to formalize what has previously been an *ad hoc* design process. A number of computer scientists are still refining this process of formalization, and there is some hope that a rigorous approach of the same nature as the Bohm and Jacopini paper will be developed shortly.

One of the arguments in favor of top-down design is that it can facilitate the eventual *proof* of program correctness. We do this by (a) first viewing the program as a collection of major functions, e.g., as a main program that simply calls a number of major modules, (b) assuming that those modules are working correctly, and (c) attempting to demonstrate that the overall logic of the program—e.g., the logic represented within the main program itself—is correct, and that the interfaces are correct. Once this is done, we then turn our attention to each of the major modules, breaking them into smaller modules, and going through the same three-step process. Eventually, we hope to reach the lowest level of modules, whose correctness can be demonstrated or proved in a straightforward fashion.

The approach suggested above is an *analytical* one: we are hoping to prove the correctness of a program in much the same way we prove geometry theorems, beginning with a set of axioms. In practice, of course, it is usually very difficult to prove the correctness of a computer program in this fashion; instead, we resort to top-down testing: that is, providing test data that will help demonstrate, in a top-down manner, that the higher levels of logic (and the major interfaces between modules) are working before worrying about local bugs within a module.

The top-down testing approach is often considered somewhat radical because of its contrast with the traditional "bottom-up" testing philosophy. However, a number of strong arguments can be made for the top-down approach: it helps expose major logic flaws early in the project, rather than at the end; it allows a partially-completed program or system to be demonstrated to users, thus giving them an early chance to see if it gives them what they want; it makes debugging *considerably* simpler (for reasons that are not immediately obvious); it provides a natural "test-harness" for testing of lower-level modules; it improves the morale of the programming team, who are able to see tangible results of testing progress; and so forth.

CONCLUSIONS

Top-down program design and structured programming have been heralded as a "revolution in programming" in recent articles [8]. The data processing community has come to realize that a solidly tested, bug-free, maintainable system is worth its weight in gold, especially when it can be produced five times more quickly than by conventional methods! There has been some question about the overhead (in terms of CPU time and memory) of the structured approach, but these have proved groundless in most cases; even when there is a measurable increase in overhead, it can almost always be justified by the savings in maintenance, testing, and development time—not to mention the cost of program bugs and "crashes" during production runs.

Structured programming and top-down design are often discussed in connection with some other recent developments—most notably the concept of the "chief programmer team" and the "program librarian." These concepts, developed primarily by IBM [3], deal largely with the organization and management of programming teams. While they are enormously helpful and quite interesting, they do not—in a strict sense—have anything to do with structured programming. Because of IBM's interest in a "package" approach involving the "chief programmer team" concept and "program librarian" concept *together with* structured programming and top-down design, it is desirable that programmers be made aware of them; on the other hand, it is clear that programmers can be taught how to write structured programs within the conventional programming organizations found in most companies.

It has been found in several recent training courses and structured programming projects that the *concepts* of structured programming are rather easy to describe. The *techniques* of structured programming (e.g., "Yes, but how can I write my master file update program without using any GO-TO statements?") are considerably more difficult and do not seem to be taught very widely. The ease with which the programmer accepts these techniques is also a function of the language in which he programs. Finally, a *belief* in structured programming seems possible, for some programmers, only after they have been forced to try it with some nontrivial programs; otherwise, they are likely to remark (as one programmer remarked to the author in a recent training course), "I've been programming for five years in COBOL without ever using the PERFORM statement, and I don't see why I should start now."

REFERENCES

[1] E. W. Dijkstra, "Programming Considered as a Human Activity," *Proceedings of IFIP Congress 65,* Spartan Books, Washington, D.C., 1965.

[2] E. W. Dijkstra, "GO-TO Statement Considered Harmful," Letter to the Editor, *Communications of the ACM,* March 1968.

[3] F. T. Baker, "Chief Programmer Team Management of Production Programming," *IBM Systems Journal,* January 1972, pages 56–73.

[4] F. T. Baker and H. D. Mills, "Chief Programming Teams," *Datamation,* December 1973, pages 58–61.

[5] "That Maintenance Iceberg," *EDP Analyzer,* October 1972.

[6] Bohm and Jacopini, "Flow Diagrams, Turing Machines and Languages with only Two Formation Rules," *Communications of the ACM,* May 1966, pages 366–371.

[7] E. Ashcroft and Z. Manna, "The Translation of 'GO-TO' Programs into 'WHILE' Programs," *Proceedings of the 1971 IFIP Congress.*

[8] D. McCracken, "Revolution in Programming: An Overview," *Datamation,* December 1973, pages 50–51.

Computer Data Base Systems: Who Needs Them?

JOHN B. SINGEL, JR.

Computer "data base management systems" (DBMS) have been surrounded by excitement, controversy, and misunderstanding since their first appearance several years ago.

Some authors have portrayed DBMS's as the latter day incarnation of that widely discussed but never implemented concept of the 1960's—the total Management Information System. Others have warned of enormous expense and disappointing results attached to the use of DBMS technology. As usual, the truth is somewhere in between. But where?

Management still must decide: "Does my company need a DBMS?" This article will explore the tradeoffs involved in this decision—specifically the potential benefits and costs associated with a DBMS. It will become clear that the "DBMS decision" is an investment decision in that many of the costs must be paid at the front end, while the benefits accrue over time. Parenthetically, there is a second important and equally complicated question: "If we need one, which one?" This question will be touched upon only briefly.

First, a real understanding of the issues involved in the DBMS decision requires some familiarity with the historical and technical background of DBMS.

TRENDS IN DATA PROCESSING AND DBMS

Over the brief and volatile history of data processing, certain trends have emerged:

- Hardware "costs per computation" have dropped regularly. This has taken the form of vast increases in hardware capability, coupled with only moderate increases in price.

- The unit cost of storing data has plunged sharply—again in the form of much larger devices for slightly higher prices.

- Personnel costs for designing and implementing computer-based systems have risen steadily, initially due to a shortage of skilled people and more recently as a result of inflation.

- The number of complex, multi-user applications has increased, resulting in a corresponding increase in the average number of man-months expended per application developed.

- As the base and complexity of installed applications has grown, the cost and amount of systems and programming effort devoted to application mainten- ance work has also increased steadily.

One reaction to these trends has been a continual effort to mechanize the recurring parts of the system development task that are common to different appli- cations. This has been done by separating application problem-solving activities from computer implementation activities that are commonly required regardless of application. Some of the results of this effort were the development of higher level languages (for example, COBOL), operating systems, communication control systems, and other types of software. Viewed in this context, DBMS is clearly not an unprecedented development. However, DBMS is perhaps the one outgrowth of this process with the most far-reaching implications.

WHAT IS A DBMS?

Fundamentally, DBMS's were created to correct a mismatch between the way computers store and retrieve data and the way users would like to use the data. We can demonstrate the nature of this mismatch with a simple example.

Imagine a credit manager who maintains a set of folders—one for each of the company's customers. These are filed in customer number sequence in a set of file drawers. However, this manager is burdened with an unusually dull file clerk. The only kind of instruction this clerk can understand is: "Get me the 7th folder from drawer number 13." If the clerk were a computer this would be called giving the computer the *address* of the data and it is, in fact, the way computers are instructed to retrieve stored data. Furthermore, the clerk can only remember one such instruction at a time.

Unfortunately, the instruction our credit manager *wants* to give is: "Get me the folder for the J. T. Jones Company." The technical term for this is *content addressing*. Obviously, there is a problem in using our limited file clerk to obtain the desired data since there is probably no direct relationship between the name of the customer and the filing location of his folder.

However, it is possible to construct a *sequence* of instructions to the file clerk which is equivalent to the "Jones" instruction. There are a variety of strategies available to do this. For example, we could instruct the file clerk to obtain every folder one at a time until we get the one desired. There are other, more sophisti- cated, strategies available, such as keeping a set of alphabetically arranged file cards which contain the folder's location for each company. The choice of strategy is not the major point; rather, the crucial fact is that obtaining the correct file folder is a multi-step process.

If we don't want to burden our credit manager with the problem of giving the file clerk the appropriate sequence of instructions one at a time, we could introduce an *intermediary* between the executive and the file clerk. (Assume that the file clerk is a long-term employee who can't be dismissed.) The intermediary's job is to take the executive's request for information, interpret it, issue the appropriate sequence of commands to the file clerk, identify when the correct folder has been obtained and, lastly, deliver the folder back to the credit manager.

A DBMS is a computer program written to play just such an intermediary role—but between user-written programs (the manager) and the computer operating system (the file clerk). User programmers working in non-DBMS environments must deal directly with the operating system—that is, construct their own search strategies.

Let's examine what is at first a startling possibility presented by having such an intermediary. Suppose that, when the credit manager requests the Jones file, the intermediary goes down the hall to the accounts receivable department and gets a copy of Jones' current payment status. He then visits the customer service department and gets copies of Jones' credit reports, etc. Finally, the intermediary puts these copies into a folder, marks it with Jones' name, and gives it to the credit manager.

Conceivably, the credit manager could operate *thinking* he had an actual physical set of files. In fact, every folder he uses is created by the intermediary on an ad hoc basis using parts of other files.

A DBMS can assemble just such "pretend" files—called logical files—for a program to use. This permits the program to be written exactly as it would be if the logical file had an actual physical representation.

One consequence of this is the ability to gather together, from several physical files, all of the data related to a particular transaction. All of the data retrieval and processing required to complete the transaction process can then be performed at one time. This contrasts with the traditional approach of passing batches of transactions through a series of programs, each of which performs one aspect of the total processing.

WHY A DBMS?

It is the separation of the physical handling of data from the logical use of that data—termed data independence—which provides the features that are potentially advantageous in a DBMS environment.

Program independence implies an ability to change the content and physical arrangement of the data base (that is, the files) in significant ways without the need to make corresponding changes to existing application programs as has always been necessary before.

In principle, we need only change the way in which the DBMS performs its physical data handling tasks to correspond to the changes in the files. If we can do this, the application program need not even be aware that a change in files has occurred.

Nonredundant storage of data can be achieved because a DBMS can draw on separate physical files to create "custom-made" logical files for use by individual programs. A given data item need be stored only once to meet the combined needs of all users. This will both conserve storage space and avoid the inconsistencies that inevitably arise among multiple files containing the same data.

Machine independence results from the user programs dealing with the data entirely in terms of its content rather than in terms of its physical location. This is, in fact, a particular kind of data independence and can facilitate the process of moving applications from one machine to another.

Multiple paths of access to data are possible if the DBMS program contains a variety of sophisticated data retrieval strategies. This can greatly speed up the user's access to desired information. It is, therefore, of particular importance to certain on-line applications requiring rapid data retrieval and display.

Improved data security is possible if the DBMS provides mechanisms to restrict the way in which individual users can utilize individual data records or items.

More timely data is available since every time a data item is changed, the up-to-date data is immediately available to all users.

THE REAL WORLD TODAY

An important consideration management must weigh in deciding whether to acquire DBMS software is the current state of DBMS technology. DBMS software vendors differ in their ability to provide each of the features discussed above. This difference exists in terms of both method and extent.

For example, data independence in a DBMS is provided by means of two special "languages." The first language is used to prepare a data base description—a set of statements which specify the content and characteristics of the files making up the data base. This description is maintained in a file separate from both programs and data. Programs wanting to use the data make requests for data handling services to the DBMS software using the second language—called a data manipulation language. Referring to the data base description, the DBMS translates these requests into a sequence of physical input/output operations to be performed by the operating system. Various DBMS's provide markedly different capabilities with their data description and data manipulation languages in terms of ease of use, the variety of ways the data can be accessed, etc.

Each vendor has had to make numerous tradeoffs—balancing the implementation of each feature against the other features as well as performance considerations. In most cases, the features are provided in a mix which is weighted to allow a reasonable level of operational efficiency for applications with particular processing characteristics for which the vendor's DBMS is intended. The performance of a DBMS-based application is largely determined by two factors:

- The actual data storage access method used for physical files determines the type and extent of intermediate processing needed to interpret the requests for application data.

- The degree of correspondence between the application's logical files and the actual physical files determines the amount of processing the DBMS must do in reassembling the physical data to fill requests for logical records.

An application built around logical files which closely approximate the physical storage techniques used by the DBMS will perform well. Conversely, a particular DBMS will typically yield poor performance if used for other than these "preferred" application types.

The DBMS user can generally influence the degree to which his application's logical and physical files will correspond. This is frequently done by designing the application to "fit" the DBMS. However, the extent of this influence is usually quite limited. For example, no amount of user fitting will make a DBMS designed for information retrieval work well in an environment involving the processing of large data volumes.

Furthermore, there can be substantial differences in various special features provided by vendors such as inquiry languages, utilities to simplify installation, restart and recovery facilities, and many others.

Because of the still immature state of DBMS technology, a number of significant problems remain to be solved. The most obvious requirement is for improvements in the basic DBMS features discussed above. This is particularly true with respect to language facilities and the kinds of access data which are provided. Other pressing needs are for standards, improved reliability, and methods of measuring and predicting performance.

So far, vendors have been on their own in deciding not only how their DBMS's will work, but even what they will do. There are no generally accepted standards for data base description languages, data manipulation languages, and security features—to name just a few. CODASYL, the group which prepared the standard definition of the COBOL language, has prepared a set of recommended specifications for a standard DBMS. These, as yet, have not won general acceptance. If history is a guide, it took standard COBOL several years to win such acceptance— even with a strong push from the federal government.

Early DBMS installations have suffered frequent software failures, akin to the problems experienced with the first complex operating systems in the mid-1960's. Because of the complexity of DBMS software, it has been difficult to devise ways of identifying rapidly the cause of failures. Compounding the problem has been the lack of efficient mechanisms for recovering from such failures. An additional need is for more effective methods of "debugging" user programs. There has been considerable recent progress in this area, but much remains to be done.

A further problem is the unpredictability of DBMS performance. Many users who converted existing applications to the DBMS environment found these applications running several times slower than before conversion. The complexity of the DBMS software makes it difficult to identify the factors which have a significant effect on performance.

Possibly the most significant problem for the new DBMS user is the scarcity of technical personnel experienced in DBMS installation and operation. At a recent DBMS users seminar, the one piece of advice offered most often to the prospective user was: "Don't think you know what you're doing." Given the current state of the art, high quality technical support is essential to a successful experience with DBMS. With such help, DBMS's can and do work, problems notwithstanding.

WHAT ARE THE POTENTIAL BENEFITS OF USING A DBMS?

The features provided by a DBMS have the potential to yield some very impressive benefits:

Reduced program development costs, because DBMS's (1) eliminate the need for programmers to spend time devising and coding strategies to store and retrieve data, (2) eliminate the need to compensate for possible inconsistencies between files with overlapping contents, and (3) reduce the amount of program maintenance which must be performed. In fact, certain types of maintenance are eliminated entirely.

More flexible applications, because of the ability to use data from multiple, interrelated files in multiple ways.

Reduced storage costs and consolidation of EDP facilities through the elimination of separate files and separate applications processing.

WHAT ARE THE COSTS?

As might be expected, the benefits of DBMS have their associated costs:

Increased hardware to support the DBMS software. More flexible access to data means more complicated processing which requires more central processor and main storage resources. In particular, the overuse of flexibility (specifically, in trying to achieve a complete elimination of redundant data) nearly always leads to a significant degradation of performance.

Learning costs because of inexperience with a new tool, the need to retrain programmers, and the difficulty of effectively structuring the first few data base files and applications.

An increased requirement for planning of long range system development because of the greater interdependence among applications.

An increased requirement for additional processing controls because a data item might be updated by any one of a number of different applications.

The lack of standardization of existing data base languages and program interfaces may require extensive changes when (and if) a standard approach finally emerges.

COMPUTER DATA BASE SYSTEMS—WHO NEEDS THEM?

It is clear that computer data base technology has the potential to provide some very significant benefits at the price of some equally significant costs. How then, does management decide whether or not to acquire this technology?

First, it is essential to realize that the benefits obtainable from a DBMS accrue gradually as a result of qualitative changes in the application development and operating environment. Unfortunately, there is little in the way of experience-based results which can be used to prove the existence, much less the size, of any quantitative benefits. On the other hand, many of the costs are experienced immediately, including most of the learning cost and some of the increased equipment cost. Recognition of the cost outlay is particularly important because of the need to adopt a "go slow" approach to implementation.

Consequently, the acquisition of a DBMS can rarely be justified based on a purely quantitative cost-benefit analysis, if for no other reason than the inability to prepare such an analysis. A DBMS can almost certainly never be justified in terms of a single application. In fact, a cost-benefit analysis of the decision to go under the data base "umbrella" would almost surely show it to be a loss proposition until a substantial base of applications is developed or converted to use the DBMS.

Therefore, the decision to adopt a DBMS as the base of applications systems development must be based on management's judgment regarding the direction and amount of system change and development needed by the organization over the long term. The decision should turn on several key issues:

- A data base facilitates the development of flexible multi-user applications which share some of their data.

- A data base can improve the ability of systems to respond to change because of the greater separation of programs and data, if change is part of the strategic plan of business development.

- A data base offers the potential of reduced applications maintenance expenditures if management is willing to invest in converting existing applications to use the data base.

- The ability to develop flexible inquiry applications is facilitated by the complex search and data retrieval facilities available with some DBMS's.

- Finally, management must be willing to accept the risk of initial failures and the possibility that the particular DBMS selected may become obsolete when (if) standards finally emerge.

It seems reasonable to expect that evolving technology will in the next few years make data base systems an accepted way to operate. Given the amount of effort being expended by both vendors and users, we can expect the capabilities of DBMS's to improve. Similarly, most of the problems and risks described above will eventually be reduced to more manageable proportions. If management cannot identify an immediate need for flexible, multi-user applications, a reasonable strategy might be to decide: "We may adopt data base technology, but later."

While waiting for the technology to mature, management can undertake a comprehensive program of planning and preparation for the future use of computer data bases. Some of the components of such a program would be to:

- Improve existing data processing organization and management practices.
- Develop a long term plan for applications development tied to the business planning process.
- Begin to catalog and organize the company's data by determining who is maintaining what files, for what purpose, etc.
- Investigate recently developed improvements in the conventional methods of program development and program maintenance as an alternative to DBMS technology.

In this way, management may obtain significant short-term benefits and at the same time avoid the pioneer's penalty—an arrow in the back.

Data-Base Management, Accounting, and Accountants

EDWARD E. NUSBAUM, ANDREW D. BAILEY, JR.,
AND ANDREW B. WHINSTON

Every organization requires pertinent, reliable, and timely information for its decision-making; and a central part of the information system that provides this service to management is normally associated with the accounting function. Such information is traditionally organized into general and subsidiary ledgers and journals, but with the introduction of computer technology, these manual systems are being "computerized" along a computer file management line. Despite this computerization, however, the basic general and subsidiary ledger and journals format is maintained. In fact, these same ledgers and journals were initially the primary output of the computer information system. Later developments reduced the traditional "hard copy" output, but still retained the basic recognizable file structure.

BENEFITS OF DATA-BASE MANAGEMENT SYSTEMS

Traditional computerized accounting systems usually consist of separate general and subsidiary ledger files. These are processed separately. In a data-base system, on the other hand, all of the ledgers can be integrated into one file and stored on direct access storage devices. The data-base file must, therefore, consist of all the information necessary to generate the required reports and be able to process transactions, both through the use of application programs. In addition, the data base, with a very special query language, is able to retrieve data upon request. The system is also able to integrate traditionally non-accounting information needs— such as marketing and production data—into the common data base.

The characteristics of data-base systems might suggest an expanding role for accounting in the management of an organization's total information needs. Furthermore, as data-base systems eliminate traditional general and subsidiary ledger restrictions by integrating all of the corporate information, the data system becomes more flexible, reliable, and accessible. In general, the information system can be more useful in providing support for decision-making. Within the corporation, accounting provides the best background for analyzing the various information needs. Thus the accountant should be able to determine the optimal use of the data-base system for the entire corporation. In other words, the data-base corporate information system eliminates the conventional boundaries of accounting and the traditional accounting structure becomes the nucleus of an all-encompassing, improved information system.

Two major advantages of using a common data base instead of the traditional system are increased consistency and efficiency. With a data base, different users of the same information need not maintain their own separate (and therefore redundant) files. For example, in a traditional system, the marketing department might maintain a file of sales by territory while the accounts receivable department records sales by customer. The data-base approach would record each sale only once with a pointer indicating the territory and another pointer indicating the customer. By eliminating redundant data, less storage space is required and transactions and other changes in the files are processed only once, thus increasing the efficiency of the system. In a traditional system, different users of the same information maintain separate files and quite often update their files at different times with different methods. This practice increases the possibility for inconsistencies between the files. With a data-base system, these inconsistencies are almost impossible. Using the above illustration, within a data-base system, total sales by territory must always equal total sales by customer. Within the traditional accounting framework, a total of the balances in a subsidiary ledger should always equal the account balance in the general ledger.

Several problems can, however, arise with the use of a data-base system. Because data is stored only in one place, an error entered into the system by one user, if left undetected, can affect the data needs of other users. Thus with a data-base system, the integrity of the input is even more critical than with current segmented approaches and so, must constantly be reviewed. Data-base systems are more accessible to the users of the information than traditional systems. Although this may be advantageous, a company may not want all its information accessible to all system users. Research is currently being done to develop data base systems which limit accessibility.

DATA–BASE MANAGEMENT SYSTEM STRUCTURE

To comprehend a data-base system, one must first understand how the data-base is structured. Every phrase, word, name, or number to be stored is called an "item." A file of information usually consists of many occurrences of the same item type. For example, "account name" is an item type and "accounts receivable" is a particular occurrence of this item type. Related item types are combined to form a record type. The data structure normally maintained for a typical general ledger account could form a record type, and all the information for a specific account, such as accounts receivable, would be an occurrence of this record type.

In structuring the data-base network, record types (e.g. accounts receivable control) are linked to other record types (e.g. accounts receivable detail) in a set relationship. For each occurrence of the owner record (accounts receivable control) there is a set of occurrences of the member record type (specific customer accounts). Exhibit 1 expands on this point, where for each record type containing an account name and balance (R4), a set of occurrences of the record type containing the transaction amount (R2) exists. For the "accounts receivable" occurrence of the record type containing the account name (R4), a set of record occurrences (of the record type, R7) for specific customer accounts is maintained.

Many software systems are currently being marketed which permit the user to develop a data-base oriented information system. The great majority of these systems are developed in a manner consistent with the CODASYL committee recommendation. The approach presented here is consistent with CODASYL.[1]

Exhibit 1 is a diagram of a partial corporate data-base structure with the information necessary for a general ledger and subsidiary ledgers: payroll, fixed assets, and accounts receivable. This structure integrates the four ledgers and the transactions into one consistent, logical, and efficient data-base file. The general ledger accounts (R4), such as accounts receivable and cash, are organized into sets for each account type (R3), such as current assets, by using a group of pointers for each record occurrence in the file. For each transaction (R1) at least two dollar amounts (R2) must exist: one or more debit amounts and at least one credit amount. Every transaction amount is associated with some general ledger account. The transaction amounts that affect accounts receivable are linked to the invoice involved which, in turn, indicates the customer.

For the fixed assets occurrence of account type (R3), the general ledger accounts (R4), such as machinery and equipment or buildings, each maintains a set of record occurrences with specific data on the fixed assets owned (R6). With this data, one could easily compute depreciation. Similarly, with the set of employee information maintained under the payroll expense general ledger account, the standard payroll calculations could be made and checks printed.

DATA–BASE MANAGEMENT SYSTEMS POTENTIAL

The system described above has been implemented using a standard CODASYL structured data-base package (GPLAN) developed at Purdue University.[2] With this package, the data in Exhibit 1 has been set up, the data entered, and the following reports generated: income statement, balance sheet, aged accounts receivable, fixed asset depreciation schedule, and a payroll schedule. When transactions are processed, the account balances are updated and the appropriate subsidiary ledgers are corrected. As one would expect, the subsidiary ledgers were always consistent with the general ledger. To produce an aged accounts receivable report, each customer's open invoices were located, the amount due for each invoice computed, and the date of the initial sale used to age the balance was entered.

Exhibit 1 CORPORATE DATA-BASE STRUCTURE

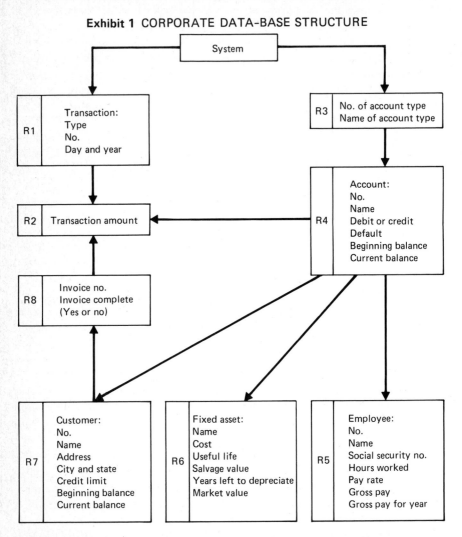

The data base presented in Exhibit 1 can easily be expanded to include the entire accounting system. Accounts payable, for example, can be handled with a structure similar to accounts receivable. A perpetual inventory system can be established, linking the sales and purchases to the customers and suppliers through invoices and purchase orders. This prototype data-base structure, with accounts payable and perpetual inventory added, is diagrammed in Exhibit 2.

Exhibit 2 COMMON DATA-BASE STRUCTURE

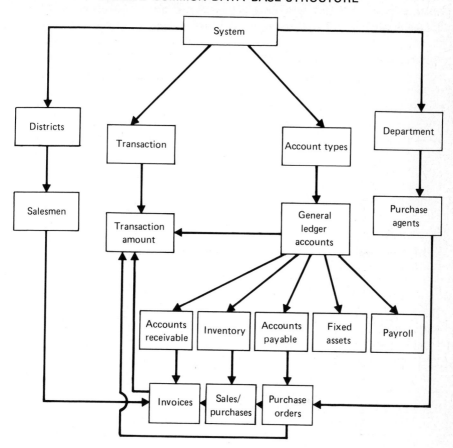

One major advantage of using this system is that one is able to integrate a company's traditionally non-accounting information needs into the accounting system. Marketing information concerning salesmen—possibly organized by district—can be linked to the sales invoices the salesmen are responsible for, thus indicating the actual sales transactions and the customers involved. Similarly, the purchasing agents, listed by department, can be added to the data-base structure. Production and operations management information needs, such as economic order quantities, can be included in the inventory portion of the data base. With this new system, the accounting, marketing, and production information needs become subsets of an efficient and consistent common corporate data-base information system.

The data-base system can also be developed to generate reports triggered by an event or by a change in a specific data item. When inventory stocks drop below a desired minimum level, a recommended purchase order can be printed indicating the item needed, the economic order quantity, the quantity on hand, the suppliers normally used, and past price information. Instead of being bogged down with volumes of data on inventory amounts, the manager receives, almost instantaneously, only the information he needs to maintain desired inventory levels.

By adding budgets and standards to the data base, accountants and managers can use the system to locate variances. Exception reporting can be effectively accomplished using the spontaneous reports mentioned above. Cost accountants are able to integrate their information needs for variance analysis into the same system maintaining financial accounting records.

For large companies it may be feasible to record all of the corporate information on one file in one computing center. But in these cases, the corporate data-base management system can be subdivided by division, subsidiary, or geographic region. Each division or region maintains its own common data-base system, which, in turn, can be linked to the corporate information system.

IMPLICATIONS FOR MANAGEMENT ACCOUNTING

The use of a data-base information system should have a major impact on the role of accountants within the organization, because the accounting system becomes a subset of a larger corporate information system. All of the information in this Thus, the accountant must be extremely concerned with the implementation of data-base systems. If he is to maintain his supervision over the accounting system, the accountant must be involved with the data base. Finally, because the accounting department, more than any other, benefits most from the use of a data-base system, the accountant should supervise its implementation and functioning rather than avoiding responsibility for it.

NOTES

[1] CODASYL: Conference on data systems languages, also known as CODASYL Data Base Task Group. See William D. Haseman and Andrew B. Whinston, *Introduction to Data Management*, Richard D. Irwin Inc., Homewood, Ill., 1977.

[2] GPLAN: Generalized Planning System, also referred to as GPLAN Data Management System.

Distributed Information Systems: Their Effect on Your Company

NORMAN STATLAND
AND DONALD T. WINSKI

The trend is here and accelerating. Computers are being distributed for use by functional business units and departments. Concurrently, we are seeing a significant deceleration of many data processing functions which, until recently, were within the domain of the centralized management information systems department.

The ever-increasing availability and usage of low-cost, powerful, small computers—whether they be "mini" or "midi"—is providing the economic impetus for this redeployment of data processing functions. This broader distribution, in turn, will have a major impact on the responsibilities of both information users and data processing personnel. Many corporations will move away from the environment of totally centralized processing of data toward decentralized end-user data entry, local processing, and subsequent integration, where required, by central computers using communication channels to collect the data from the remote processing site.

THE RAPID EVOLUTION

To put the impact of distributed information systems into perspective, let's review the two major phases of the evolution in computer usage that have already taken place. When computers came into major use during the early 1960s, it was common to find medium-sized computer installations established at divisional and plant sites throughout larger diversified companies. With this proliferation of computer equipment came a corresponding duplication of data processing personnel and, in many ways, a Tower of Babel mix of computer applications. Data processing costs increased at a rapid pace and central management was not able to effectively control the growth of related computer applications. As a result, separate and redundant processing was common.

The eventual outcome was the start of a movement toward consolidation of computer applications in the late 1960s and early 1970s as many diversified companies sought to control their rising computer costs. At the same time, larger and faster computers became available and were priced to provide economies of scale. Furthermore, data communications became a practical reality so that remote plants and divisional operations could be serviced from a central data processing facility, using larger, fast computers.

These technological advances and economies led to a pronounced swing to the establishment of centralized Management Information System (MIS) departments in many corporations. However, as the centralized MIS era progressed, serious management concerns developed that affected both MIS and the user.

MANAGEMENT CONCERNS

Typically, profit-oriented user management has come to view MIS as an overhead cost which should be minimized, instead of an investment on which return should be maximized. This viewpoint has been brought on by the following concerns:

- Frequently, MIS is organizationally too isolated from the user community to understand its real needs. Often, the data processing specialists (systems analysts and programmers) do not understand the user requirements for data processing.

- Much time is spent on maintaining and enhancing centrally developed common systems that frequently can't readily meet the divergent needs of various users. Indeed, local users frequently feel that new systems development projects for their own requirements are subverted in order to meet the data processing needs perceived at headquarters.

- Evaluation procedures for selecting high-profit projects for central development have many stages, as illustrated in Figure 1-A. This can cause time lags or, worse, encourage users to develop their own "bootleg" systems—often after the acquisition of a remote minicomputer was approved for some administrative function, such as word processing.

These concerns have resulted in a desire by some users to revert to the "good old days" of decentralized data processing, as depicted in Figure 1-B, that fostered many of the forgotten problems related to duplicate applications development and poor quality software. MIS management, on the other hand, has been equally concerned that there has never been an appropriate level of user responsibility in the development and use of new systems. The exercise of user responsibility and the involvement of user management in the systems development process is essential to maximizing the cost/benefit ratio for each new computer application.

As shown in Figure 1-C, distributed information systems can provide a practical means for resolving such concerns by placing operations and systems development responsibilities with the user when it is appropriate. But distributed

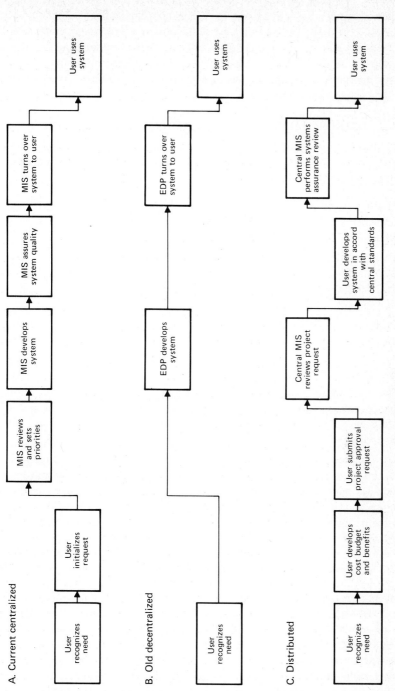

Fig. 1 *The system development process*

A. Current centralized

User recognizes need → User initializes request → MIS reviews and sets priorities → MIS develops system → MIS assures system quality → MIS turns over system to user → User uses system

B. Old decentralized

User recognizes need → EDP develops system → EDP turns over system to user → User uses system

C. Distributed

User recognizes need → User develops cost budget and benefits → User submits project approval request → Central MIS reviews project request → User develops system in accord with central standards → Central MIS performs systems assurance review → User uses system information systems can still provide for overall coordination and control through a central MIS function that promulgates standard procedures for systems development, testing, and operating practices—and one that exercises annual budgetary approval over all development projects. The exercise of the project approval procedure by centralized MIS is the key to providing management control over data processing activities and costs in a distributed data processing environment.

DISTRIBUTED INFORMATION SYSTEMS—THE SOLUTION?

Minicomputer-based distributed processing systems can cost less to develop and operate than large, centralized systems—if the controlled approach for use of minicomputer systems is enforced. Here's why:

- Distributed systems can be developed more quickly since they primarily address the immediate needs of a specific user group rather than the complex mix of needs of a diverse user population.

- Minicomputer equipment costs are usually less, assuming that the transaction and file volumes are low (say, several hundred transactions per day and less than 30,000 records) and the number of terminals concurrently used is limited (for instance, less than 12).

- Data communication costs are usually lower, since a major portion of the processing can be done through direct connection of terminals to an on-site minicomputer. This reduces the need for expensive, leased-line communication linkages to a remote central computer.

- The minicomputer approach, when limited to a few applications per computer, avoids the bottlenecks resulting from the traffic jams and work-overloads often encountered as new systems are added to already fully-utilized central computers.

- The corporate requirement for summary operating reports and tactical analyses of the same data against projected plans can be fulfilled by transmitting the data via administrative communication lines once or twice a day (or weekly) at no additional communication cost. Where the administrative lines are not present, low-cost, dial-up communications can be used to transfer data from the remote computer files to the central processing facility.

WHEN IS THE DISTRIBUTED APPROACH APPROPRIATE?

The answer to the above question lies in the analysis of the organization's hierarchical reporting structure. The more the daily information needs of the individual users are unique, the greater the likelihood that the data processing tasks can be deployed profitably onto distributed minicomputers. That is, providing corporate management can build a common account number structure for all divisions that can serve as the means to collect centrally information for corporate reporting by accessing the remotely shared files as required. Conversely, where there is a high degree of interrelated need among users, a central system should continue to prove advantageous.

These diverse situations can be best illustrated by an example. Consider an order processing system for two different multi-plant manufacturing companies. In the first case, each plant produces a full mix of products that are sold directly to a local customer base. This is common, for instance, in the building materials business. In the second case, each plant produces its own unique product mix that is sold nationwide. This is often found, for example, in the chemical industry.

A distributed systems approach would be more appropriate in the first situation and a centralized processing approach would be preferable in the second. If we were to consider a production planning and inventory control system for each of these situations, the processing requirements would be determined largely by the manufacturing organization's structure. Again, the decision would be influenced by the degree of unique information each plant requires.

THE DISTRIBUTED APPROACH'S ORGANIZATIONAL IMPACT ON MIS

To see the total impact of distributed systems on the user and MIS organizations, let us first analyze the functions MIS performs. A significant number of the functional responsibilities traditionally performed by MIS will be—in fact, already are—shifting to the user. The current MIS responsibilities are shown in a typical centralized MIS organizational chart in Figure 2-A.

The chart shows that the MIS manager normally has two major line functions reporting to him, systems development and operations, as well as two staff functions, quality assurance and technical support. Systems development is usually responsible for the design, programming, and maintenance of application systems. These activities may be performed in separate groups dedicated to each application area or they may be organized into project teams along application system subdivisions.

The operations organization is also usually divided into three functional activities: data entry, scheduling and input/output control, and computer operations, which runs the actual production work.

Two staff groups comprise the rest of the MIS organization. One, technical support, usually consists of the highly-skilled technicians required to maintain the operating system software. These technicians also provide technical advisory services to MIS in such areas as data base and data communications control software and new computer equipment acquisition.

The second, the quality assurance staff function, establishes and monitors system standards. These include: systems justification procedures, project management techniques, and system and acceptance testing mechanisms.

Although the actual structure of a particular MIS organization may differ somewhat from the one described here, the functions—though not always distinct—will still be present.

A. Classical

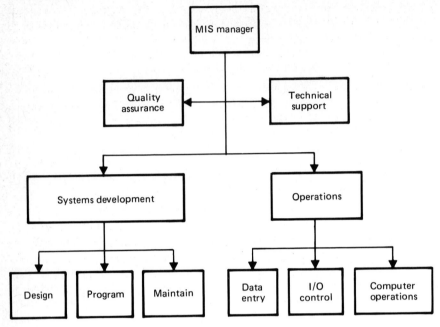

B. Distributed

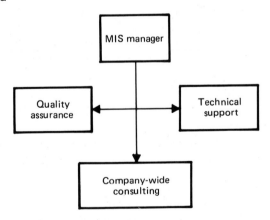

Fig. 2 *Central MIS organization*

How will the trend to distributed information systems affect this structure? Significant changes are likely within the next three to five years and these changes, in each of the functions described below, will be proportional to the growth in the use of distributed processing systems.

MIS Manager

- His department will become smaller in number of systems development and operations personnel and will require higher skill levels for systems evaluation and quality assurance. Many of the development personnel will migrate into user areas.

- His function will become more oriented toward controlling and coordinating overall system activities while providing a strong quality assurance function with emphasis on the total system planning responsibility.

- His job qualifications will change. He will become (1) more oriented toward managing a matrix organization of staff-oriented experts, rather than a line organization, (2) more innovative, less of a caretaker, (3) more planning oriented, (4) more likely to be a member of the company's general management, and (5) more oriented to translating the corporations' strategic business plan into reports designed to inform management of the success or failure of each tactical objective related to the plan.

Operations

- The data entry function, as part of the data processing function, will disappear along with the keypunch operator. Almost all data will be entered by the user through intelligent terminals.

- The input/output control balancing function will be incorporated in the computer programs. This brings up an interesting internal control question: Who will assure management that the users are properly using the processing control features? This will become an increased responsibility of the internal auditors.

- Operation of the remote computer will be a user responsibility in accordance with corporate-wide procedures, so that data may be periodically accessed by the central computer.

- The centralized operations manager's position will be transformed so that he will be responsible for data communications coordination and data base administration.

Systems Development

- Systems analysts, currently responsible for designing systems, will move into the user organizations, generally assuming line management responsibilities as well as participating in the development of computer applications. Or, they will become staff consultants in the new MIS organization.

- The centralized programmer analyst positions will decrease in number but increase in skill requirements. Current programmers will either become more technically proficient and join the technical support function or they will be attached to other organizational units.
- The systems development manager's position will be transformed as his functional organization is reshaped into a matrix-based planning, monitoring, and coordinating structure. The systems manager will become an architect who operates as an adjunct to the corporate planning group. It will be his function to determine which sets of information operating management will have to access in order to implement and monitor the strategic plans of the management group.

Technical Support

- The personnel here will become more oriented toward minicomputer software support in addition to enlarging their knowledge of data base and data communications control software.
- Ideally, someone will be appointed who has the responsibility for controlling all data definitions and who checks new definition entries or changes against those maintained within the software dictionary. The person acting as the data controller or data administrator should be the central focus through which all definitions of data elements are added or changed. His tool for keeping track of all data stored would be a set of software (computer programs), known as a data dictionary, that all systems analysts, programmers, and users should utilize as a central reference point for all data definitions.
- Technical advisory services will be provided primarily to remote users rather than to MIS staff.

Quality Assurance (QA)

- This will be the most rapidly increasing area of importance within the MIS department. In the past, there has been a tendency at times to use it as a resting ground for personnel whose career paths were cut off in other MIS functional areas. It should now become a high profile position for the most qualified individuals who will review systems development projects at designated checkpoints.
- QA personnel will become more directly responsible for administration and coordination in many areas including:

1. Providing and monitoring data security and processing controls.
2. Making the decision whether to have one remote location develop an application for use by several locations, rather than duplicating development costs.

3. Interfacing synchronization between linked application systems (such as order-invoicing, sales accounting, and accounts receivable).

4. Analyzing contractual agreements with outside software and equipment vendors.

5. Training systems personnel users.

6. Providing and monitoring documentation and testing standards.

So, the MIS function will become more of an in-house consulting group and less of a service bureau/software house as distributed information systems take hold. MIS will tend toward the organizational structure shown in Figure 2-B.

THE ORGANIZATIONAL IMPACT ON THE USER

A significant number of data processing functions will be transferred to the user as distributed information systems come to fruition. The user will become responsible for the daily operation of the system, including data entry, input/output control, and scheduling of the equipment. However, this should not be overly burdensome, since it will be necessary to limit the number of concurrent application systems on the local minicomputer in order to reduce the scheduling task and lessen the need for complex operating system software.

Here's what the net effect will be on user managers who take over system operations:

• They will have to be more knowledgeable about computerized data processing and its economics. New functions within the user organization will be required, particularly in the area of processing controls and physical security. For example, the user, in conjunction with his internal or external auditors and central MIS quality assurance personnel, must provide adequate controls to ensure data accuracy and integrity and adequate security to protect data files and programs.

• Users will initially have more work to handle but this should be a transient situation. In almost all cases, direct on-line data entry and information accessibility should eliminate redundant paper handling and manual procedures to the point where a more productive, smaller workforce results.

• The users will have to become more oriented toward using the new tools available so as not to suffer "future shock." It is likely that some of the current managers and line personnel will not adjust easily to the challenges of having greater control over, and immediate access to, their local information system. Such personnel will require considerable retraining or, in some cases, replacement.

• The user's top management will have new risk/reward balancing to do. Initially, they may decide to acquire outside technical assistance. In the longer term,

A. Centralized MIS control

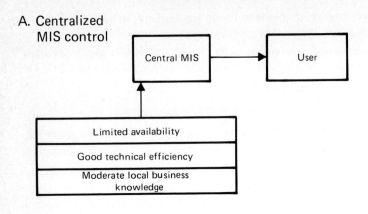

B. Decentralized user control

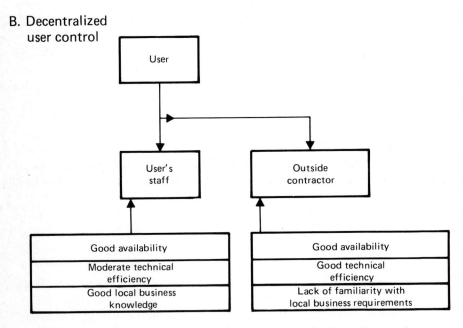

Fig. 3 *User options with technical personnel under distributed processing*

however, they should be able to use the consulting services that will be built up within the restructured central MIS function.

• The need for centralized user support functions should diminish. For example, the workload of corporate accounting staffs in correcting, reconciling, and consolidating local financial information should be reduced as a result of the more timely, accurate, and synchronized data entered and processed at local levels with distributed systems. This should provide for eventual staff reductions in such corporate support groups.

Yet another area of organizational impact on the user involves systems development responsibilities. In those cases where the needs are sufficiently unique to warrant local systems development activities, user management should be able to determine which technical resources are best utilized: central MIS, outside vendors, or an internal systems staff.

As shown in Figure 3, each resource alternative has its advantages and shortcomings. In many cases, there may not be a continuing need for a group of full-time systems personnel. The user then must decide to utilize either central MIS or outside resources. Certainly the user will have to familiarize himself with project management techniques in order to maintain control over his new systems development environment.

It would appear that a new breed of user may be needed to handle distributed information systems. This reorientation should be readily justified by the increased return on the system investment that will result from users being held responsible for the system's success.

SUMMARY

The trend toward distributed data processing is with us. The projected changes discussed here may run counter to the imbedded thinking of some people who are conditioned to the centralized MIS environment. If so, this article should provide a catalyst for rethinking. Members of the MIS fraternity may differ as to the timing of these changes but should not resist the need for organizational change.

Cost-Performance Trade-Offs in Real-Time Systems Design

BARRY E. CUSHING
AND DAVID H. DIAL

The increasing use of real-time computer systems in business and other administrative functions presents a new set of opportunities and problems to those managers concerned with getting the most out of expenditures on data processing. Real-time systems are being applied to manufacturing data collection, production scheduling, credit checking, airline and other travel reservations, sales order data entry, bank teller operations, and management simulation. The trend toward more efficient and reliable computer hardware and software, which is often less expensive than that which it replaces, is likely to increase the number and variety of real-time applications. These developments underscore the need for managers to become more familiar with the concepts and technology of real-time systems.

The purpose of this article is to discuss some important aspects of the design of real-time computer systems. The primary objective is to develop an understanding of the trade offs which must be made in the design process between the conflicting objectives of cost minimization and performance maximization. A definition of real-time systems is offered and the essential elements of real-time systems are reviewed. Cost-performance factors in systems design with respect to each of the basic elements are examined in turn. Our goal is to provide managers, system designers, and accountants with a framework for understanding problems of real-time systems design.

REAL-TIME SYSTEMS

A real-time system may be defined as a data processing system in which the time interval required to process and respond to input data is so small that the response itself is immediately useful in controlling a physical activity or process. The most important concept in the definition is that of response time. Real-time systems are sometimes associated with immediate response. However, the length of response time which will qualify a given system as real time is actually dependent upon the nature of the physical activity being controlled by the system. If the activity is the launching of a space satellite, a response time measured in fractions of a second is necessary in order for the system to effectively control the activity. If the activity involves a business function, a response time of several seconds or even a few minutes may be adequate for control purposes. Thus, the nature of the activity being controlled determines the response time which is necessary in order for control to be accomplished by a real-time system.

FIVE ELEMENTS IN SYSTEM

There are five basic elements of a real-time computer system. These are: (1) on-line direct-access files for storage of system data; (2) one or more central processors; (3) data terminals which provide the interface between the system and its users; (4) a data communications network which links the processor with the terminals; and (5) a software system, consisting of programs, documentation, and other user aids which enable users to operate the system effectively. A diagram of the elements of a real-time system and their relationship to each other is shown in Exhibit 1. Though not specifically illustrated in the exhibit, the element of software is inherent in each of the other four elements of the system. Each of these elements is discussed in turn in this article.

In discussing cost-performance trade offs with respect to real-time systems, it is necessary to clarify the concept of performance. There are two basic performance parameters in a real-time system: response time and reliability. Response time is basically the average elapsed time between data entry and system response. Reliability encompasses both avoidance of system breakdowns and accuracy of data processing. Other performance parameters may be significant in particular applications of real-time systems. Examples include system availability, convenience of

Exhibit 1 ELEMENTS OF A REAL-TIME COMPUTER SYSTEM

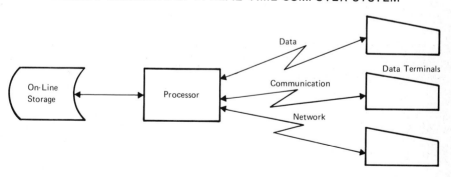

working with the system for human operators, and auditability of the system. The systems design process should seek an optimal trade off between cost minimization on the one hand and performance maximization with respect to these objectives on the other.

APPLICATION GOVERNS TIME

For a real-time business system, the required response time must be determined for each particular application. Unlike the process-control system which directs mechanical devices with response times measured in fractions of a second, the real-time business system controls the actions of human beings. Response times for interactive accounting and management information systems are measured in seconds or even minutes. When people are operating terminals to interact with a real-time system, the response times must be geared to human reaction times. A response time of less than one second is unnecessarily fast. Response times in excess of 15 seconds, however, may be so long that human operators become impatient. When the operator is engaged in a complex conversation with the computer, the response time needs to be relatively short. Some airline reservation systems, for example, are designed to react to 90 per cent of the transactions in less than three seconds.

Reducing response time will normally cause an increase in the cost of the system since more complex and expensive hardware is required. Increasing the response time may destroy some of the benefits expected from implementation of a real-time system. The importance of the response time becomes evident when the cost-performance trade offs in various components of the system are examined. A number of factors affect the response time of a real-time system, including the number of operating terminals in the system, the number of messages awaiting processing, the amount of computation required for each message, the speed of the central processing unit, the type of telecommunication network, and the response time of the file storage device.

The degree of reliability required within a real-time system is also dependent upon the particular application. In some applications it is essential that the system be "up" at all times, whereas in others an occasional breakdown may not be critical. In the latter case, however, it may be important to minimize the frequency and/or duration of system breakdowns. With respect to system accuracy, the nature of most real-time applications justifies design of a system which is as reliable as possible. Currently available hardware is highly accurate, and so most of the design problems relating to data accuracy concern the software system.

To achieve a highly reliable system requires duplication of some hardware and procedures and more elaborate hardware and software. These elements may add significantly to the costs of developing and operating a real-time system. However, if the system is less reliable than it should be, expected benefits will not be achieved and actual harm may be done to the organization. Careful analysis of the trade offs affecting system reliability is, therefore, essential in the design of real-time systems.

Real-time systems generally require a considerable amount of random access storage capacity. Since most transactions in a real-time system require the computer to access data in the storage files, the response time of the system depends largely on the response time of the storage devices. Certain techniques are available to reduce the response time of a random access file; however, most of these techniques also increase the storage capacity requirements. Such increases in storage capacity add significantly to the cost of the real-time system.

Since most real-time information systems are closely linked to the daily operations of the business, reliability of the storage files is an important factor in system performance. Increased reliability, however, usually means increased system costs for hardware and software. By properly analyzing the cost-performance trade offs in random-access storage files, the system designer can minimize the cost of the data storage and insure adequate system response time and system reliability.

The response time of the file storage device in a real-time system is based upon the number of records which must be accessed by the system before a message can be transmitted to the terminal operator, and upon the time required by the storage device to access a record in the file. Both the number of file references and the average file reference time involve cost-performance trade offs.

Number of file references—The number of file references required to assemble the information to be transmitted as a single message to the terminal operator depends upon two factors. First, the required data may be stored in more than one file or in several records within a single file. In such cases, more than one file reference must be made to obtain the data. Since numerous file references can substantially increase the system response time, frequently requested data should be stored whenever possible in a single record to minimize the number of file references. For example, if the total of certain amounts stored in numerous individual records is frequently requested, this total can be maintained in a separate record and updated each time the individual amounts are changed. The cost-performance trade off in this example involves comparing the sum of the cost of storing and additional total figures and the cost of increasing the processing time to update the file containing the total records to the benefit of faster response time.

The second factor affecting the number of file references is the file addressing technique used to locate a specific record in a file containing thousands or even hundreds of thousands of records. File addressing techniques often present distinct examples of cost-performance trade offs in file storage systems, since these techniques influence both the file response times and the file capacity requirements.

CODE IDENTIFIES RECORDS

In a real-time information system, each data record is identified by some unique code. For example, the data record for an inventory item might be identified by the inventory part number. Each data record is stored in a separate location in the random-access file. The file locations are also identified by unique numbers, often called file addresses. To access a specific record, the computer needs the file address of the record. The user, however, might provide the computer an inventory part number or a bank account number rather than the file address of the record. The purpose of a file-addressing technique is to provide the computer a method of locating a specific record using only the identifying information supplied by the terminal operator.

The two methods of file-addressing techniques most frequently employed, table look-up and randomizing, are used to illustrate the cost-performance trade offs inherent in selecting any file addressing technique.

The table look-up technique, also called the indexed-sequential method, has attracted considerable interest in recent years. Many computer systems are designed to provide this file-addressing method as a standard feature of the software. A primary characteristic of this technique is the use of one or more tables to provide an index to the random access file. At least two file references are required to locate the desired record: one file reference to read the appropriate indexing table and a second file reference to read the actual data record. With very large data files, the table look-up technique may require a hierarchy of indexing tables. In this case, several file references will be required to read the appropriate table at each level and finally to read the desired data record. Another factor influencing the file response time with the table look-up technique is the time required by the central processing unit to search the indexing tables for the desired entry after the tables have been read into memory from the random access storage file.

Another method of file addressing that is frequently used is a technique called randomizing. The randomizing method transforms a reference number into a random number within the range of file addresses where the desired record is located. This random number is the first address accessed to find the selected record. If the record is not located at the randomized address, another attempt must be made to locate the record at an overflow location. In some instances, several file locations must be accessed to locate the desired record. An important characteristic of the randomizing technique is that as the file packing density increases, the average number of file references required to locate a specific data record increases. In most instances, to achieve an acceptable file response time with the randomizing technique, at least 20 per cent of the file storage locations must remain unused.

The table look-up technique permits the user of smaller, and therefore less expensive, storage files to accommodate a specific number of data records than does the randomizing technique. The randomizing method, however, generally requires fewer file accesses to locate a selected data record than the table look-up method and thus permits a faster response time. When the randomizing technique is used, the average number of file references required to locate a data record can be reduced at the cost of providing a greater percentage of unused storage locations in the file.

COMPROMISE ALWAYS NECESSARY

The interrelation among file-addressing techniques, file sizes, and file reference times is an important aspect of random access file design. Every file design requires a compromise between response times and data storage costs. Careful analysis by the system designer of these cost-performance trade offs is required to achieve an optimal balancing of conflicting objectives.

Average file reference time—Regardless of the number of file references required to assemble the requested data, the system's performance can be improved by reducing the average file reference time. Reducing the average file reference time, however, requires a trade off in the cost of the random access files and perhaps in the storage capacity of the file device.

Three types of random access storage devices are magnetic drum, magnetic disk, and magnetic strip. A comparison of the access times, storage capacities, and monthly rental costs of these devices illustrates certain cost-performance trade offs inherent in file storage. An average-sized magnetic drum device provides a four-million-character storage capacity and rents for about $2,000 per month for a cost per character of $.0005 per month. The average access time provided by such a device is ten milliseconds, or .01 seconds. On the other hand, a typical storage capacity for a small disk unit is seven million characters. Such a unit might rent for around $500 per month, or $.00007 per character per month. The average time required to access a record stored in such a unit ranges from 30 to 75 milliseconds, depending on the unit. Large disk storage devices, with a capacity of 100 million characters, provide similar cost and access time characteristics.

The cost-performance trade offs in selecting file storage devices are further illustrated by the magnetic strip device, frequently called a data cell. The data cell is even slower, but is also less expensive, than the magnetic disk. A typical data cell unit has a capacity of 300 million characters and rents for about $2,500 per month, for a cost per character of $.000008 per month, which is about one-ninth the cost per character of disk storage. However, the average access time for a record in a data cell is 500 milliseconds, or seven to sixteen times slower than disk. An access time of 500 milliseconds may be too slow to provide an acceptable response time for a system which has a high volume of file inquiries and updates.

As these examples illustrate, trade offs exist among the three important characteristics of a file storage device: storage cost, access time, and storage capacity. A satisfactory compromise can be achieved in balancing these cost-performance trade offs only by carefully analyzing the requirements of the system and selecting the file storage device which can provide the required performance at the lowest cost.

FILE RECOVERY

A final example of cost-performance trade offs in file storage is provided by a comparison of the cost and desirability of various methods of recovering from loss of an on-line data file. Occasionally, through equipment malfunction, program errors or operator mistakes, complete files or portions of a file might be destroyed.

The most desirable approach to file recovery from a performance viewpoint is to duplicate the critical on-line files. The duplicate file is updated on-line at the same time that the primary file is updated. In the event data in the primary file should become unavailable, the computer system would automatically channel further file references to the duplicate file and notify the operator of the malfunction. Since this system requires a duplication of a substantial amount of the hardware and the use of specially developed software, the cost of providing file recovery in this manner is quite significant.

A less expensive technique for file recovery is to prepare a copy of the critical on-line files one or more times each day and to maintain a file of all changes that occur to the on-line files throughout the day. If an on-line file is damaged, the on-line system can be temporarily interrupted while one of the backup files prepared earlier in the day is updated for the transactions that have occurred since the backup file was copied. Since the on-line system is unavailable for a short period, procedures must be available for the system users to follow until the on-line system is again operative. In addition, some method must be available to permit updating the computer files for transactions that occur while the system is inoperative.

The cost-performance trade offs for file recovery require balancing the desired level of on-line service with the cost of providing this service. On one extreme, on-line service might not be interrupted more than a few seconds when a storage file is damaged or when a file device becomes inoperative. On the other extreme, the on-line system might be inoperative for several days or even weeks when a storage file is lost. The cost of a system that provides uninterrupted service is necessarily higher than the cost of a system that provides degrading service following a file breakdown. Thus, another decision involving cost-performance trade offs in file storage must be made during systems development.

CENTRAL PROCESSOR

Selection of the central processor configuration in a real-time system involves a number of complex cost-performance trade offs.

Size of primary storage—One of the most critical factors in real-time systems design is the size of the primary storage, or storage area within the central processor. Primary storage, consisting of either cores or semiconductors, is very expensive, ranging around five- to seven-tenths of a cent per character per month. This is ten to 14 times the cost of drum storage, and 70 to 100 times that of disk. However, if primary storage is too small, system response time may be adversely affected.

Most real-time systems use multiprogramming, which means that the system can process more than one program simultaneously, though at any one instant system control is devoted to only one program. Multiprogramming increases system throughput, and therefore the greater the degree of multiprogramming in a real-time system, the smaller will be the average system response time. However, the degree of multiprogramming in a system is often limited by the availability of primary storage. The greater the available primary storage area, the greater is the degree of multiprogramming possible.

A second illustration of this relationship involves the concept of "virtual storage." In a multiprogrammed system, as one program is being executed the system must provide storage area for all other programs and data which are in process and waiting their turn for the computer's attention. The use of primary storage for this purpose may be very expensive. A way of economizing on storage for this "work-in-process" is to store a portion of it on a high speed disk, drum, or other external storage unit. Programs or program sections may thus be relocated, or "swapped," back and forth between primary and external storage several times during their execution. Systems having this capability may appear to have virtually unlimited storage capacity, and are therefore referred to as "virtual storage" systems.

Though virtual storage systems provide a useful means of economizing on storage costs, these devices have an adverse effect upon response time in a real-time system. This is because the extra time required to swap programs back and forth between external and primary storage increases the average time required to process each user's transaction.

Careful analysis of cost-performance tradeoffs involving primary memory size is required in order to obtain a system having an adequate response time and yet avoid excessive expenditures for primary memory.

Processor configuration—A critical factor in real-time system reliability is the processor configuration. A configuration which consists simply of one central processor will at times cause the system to be shut down due to a failure of the processor. Very occasionally, an error in processing may be made as a result of an error by the central processor. The reliability of a real-time system may be considerably improved by configurations which include more than one central processor.

One example of a configuration which increases reliability in a real-time system is the duplex configuration. This system includes two central processors, with one serving as backup for the other. If a failure occurs in the on-line processor, all work is switched over to the backup processor. In such systems the backup processor is generally used for non-real-time functions at those times when both systems are operational. In addition, in the event of a file breakdown, the backup processor may be used to speed file recovery while the on-line processor continues to handle file inquiries and updates as best it can. The duplex configuration is quite common in real-time systems. It greatly increases system reliability in that the probability of failure of both processors concurrently is much smaller than the probability of failure of one processor.

While this example by no means exhausts the number of processor configurations which may be devised to improve reliability in a real-time system, it does illustrate the trade offs involved. Increases in reliability are achieved by duplication of processors, which may significantly increase the cost of the system. The cost of the additional software required is also a relevant factor. However, these additional costs are partially offset by the additional work that may be performed by backup processors while the real-time processor is functioning properly.

DATA TERMINALS

The data terminals in a real-time system are the interface between the system and its users. Therefore, decisions involving the terminal subsystem are often a critical factor in the success of a real-time system. Convenience may be a more essential performance factor than either reliability or response time.

A wide variety of terminal devices is currently available for use in real-time systems. The two major categories are (1) teleprinters or teletypewriters, and (2) cathode ray tube (CRT) or display devices. A comparison of some of the major features of these types of devices illustrates some of the cost-performance trade offs involved in the selection of data terminals.

Teleprinters are generally less expensive than display terminals. A purchase price of from $600 to $3,000 is typical for a teleprinter, whereas display terminal prices range from $1,000 to $10,000. Another advantage of the teleprinter is that it automatically produces a paper copy of all terminal activity, which in some cases significantly improves the convenience and auditability of the system.

The more expensive display terminal, however, has several performance advantages over the teleprinter. One important advantage is output speed. Typical printing speeds of teleprinters range from 10 to 30 characters per second. In contrast, display terminal output speeds depend upon the transmission speed of the data communication facility, and therefore speeds ranging from 60 to 240 characters per second or more are common. This factor is particularly important if output volumes are large.

Other advantages of display terminals over teleprinters include: (1) easier correction of errors in previously entered data by modifying only erroneous characters rather than retyping entire lines, (2) superior capability in displaying graphic output, and (3) noise-free operation. In addition, some display devices can store in memory more lines of data than can fit on the screen at any one time, in order that the operator can refer back to such data after it leaves the screen. Many display terminals can be equipped with a device which will produce a paper copy of whatever is on the screen when desired. However, all of these additional factors add to the expense of the terminal device.

Another critical decision relating to data terminals in a real-time system is the appropriate number of terminals in the system. User convenience is maximized if there is one terminal available for each user. However, this also requires a maximum expenditure on terminals. If several users can share each terminal, the expenditure on terminals may be reduced. However, such a reduction in cost is accompanied by a reduction in user convenience. This trade off involves evaluating the needs of the users relative to the cost of the terminals.

Still another factor relating to the selection of data terminals involves the possibility of using terminals which have a "stand-alone" capability. Such terminals can continue to perform such functions on their own even if the central computer system goes down. For example, some terminals can record and store transaction data on a machine-readable medium for transmission after the failure has been corrected and the system is available. Such terminals may also be capable of preparing a printed record of such transactions if one is desired. To obtain a stand-alone capability may require a more expensive terminal.

Several of these elements in selection of data terminals in a real-time system are illustrated by the case of a hospital which developed such a system for processing patient charges, laboratory test results, and related patient data. Terminals in each laboratory, in the pharmacy, and in other locations from which patient charges originated were used to enter transaction data into the system. Terminals were also located at nurses' stations throughout the hospital so that laboratory test results could be sent to them for inclusion in patient records, and so that doctors could use the terminals for fast retrieval of patient medical data. Still another terminal was located at the accounts receivable office for use in recording patient checkouts and preparing receipts for collections from patients.

The choice of terminals for the nurses' stations presented an interesting situation. Cost minimization was an important objective, and documentation of laboratory test results was essential. These criteria pointed to the selection of an inexpensive teleprinter, such as the Teletype Model 33 at a purchase cost of $600. However, due to the proximity of the nurses' stations to the hospital rooms, another essential objective was noise-free operation. Furthermore, due to the intended use of these terminals by doctors to retrieve patient data, output speed was very important. For these reasons, a small CRT display terminal with an attached hard copy unit was chosen at a purchase price of approximately $3,500. Though costing almost $3,000 more per unit, this device met all the performance criteria, including minimization of machine noise.

The selection of terminals for the pharmacy and for the accounts receivable department also required a compromise of the cost minimization objective. Because these departments dealt directly with patients and the general public, it was considered essential to utilize a stand-alone terminal which could record transaction data and provide receipts even while the central computer system was down.

DATA COMMUNICATIONS

The terminals used to communicate with the computer in a real-time system are often located at some distance from the computer. A telecommunication network is required to link the various terminals with the central computer. Basically, this telecommunication network consists of a transmission link and a set of electronic devices used to increase the efficiency of the network. A well planned network utilizes the combination of transmisssion links and peripheral devices that provides the required transmission rate and system response times at the lowest cost.

The cost of a telecommunication network is determined by several factors including the line transmission speed and the choice of leased or switched lines. Certain alternatives to the use of private lines are available such as Private Exchange (PBX) or multidrop lines. Each of these factors affects not only the cost of the network but also the performance of the system.

Line transmission speeds—Communication lines can be classified into three primary categories based upon the number of data bits per second that can be sent over the line. To measure transmission speeds in characters per second, the number of bits required to represent a character must be known. In the following discussion, a ratio of ten bits per character is assumed since this figure is representative of the transmission codes commonly used.

The lowest speed lines, called subvoice-grade lines, are designed for telegraph and similar machines transmitting at speeds generally not exceeding 300 bits per second. A subvoice-grade line can provide a low-cost communication link for a real-time system that uses only typewriter-speed terminals operating at transmission rates up to 30 characters per second.

Voice-grade lines, originally designed for telephone communications, provide transmission speeds as high as 9,600 bits per second. When the regular dial-up telephone lines are used however, the maximum attainable transmission rate is limited to 4,800 bits per second. The high speeds are possible on private lines that are specially conditioned for data transmission. Real-time systems using display terminals will usually require voice-grade channels to take advantage of the extremely high transmission speed possible between a computer and a display terminal.

Wideband lines provide the capability of transmitting data at speeds up to 500,000 bits per second. One application for wideband lines is high-speed communications between two computers. Subvoice-grade and voice-grade lines are currently the most important communication links for real-time business systems. The speed at which input data can be entered, or output data interpreted, by human operators using keyboard terminals is so severely limited that very high-speed transmission facilities are not usually required.

An obvious cost-performance trade off exists between subvoice-grade and voice-grade lines. Although the voice-grade line costs more to lease than the subvoice-grade line, the voice-grade line permits a substantially greater transmission speed. These performance factors and the cost differentials among various line transmission speeds must be carefully examined to determine the proper balance between line cost and transmission speed.

Leased versus switched lines—Two basic options are available with respect to usage of data communication facilities. These are (1) leased or private lines, and (2) switched lines or dial-up service. Leased lines are devoted exclusively to the use of a single customer. Dial-up involves simply using the long distance telephone service available to the general public. The cost of a leased line between two points is fixed and is determined by the length of the line. The cost of dial-up service is variable with distance and usage time. Therefore, dial-up service is less costly than a leased line—up to a breakeven volume, beyond which the leased line is more economical.

To illustrate the relative cost differential between leased and switched lines, consider the case of a company having a main office and computer center in Chicago and a branch sales office in Detroit. The company wishes to connect a data terminal in its Detroit office to the computer center in Chicago using data communication services, so that sales orders from its Detroit customers may be processed on a real-time basis. If a leased line is used, the differential cost per month will include approximately $30 for communications hardware at the Detroit and Chicago locations, plus the cost of the line itself. A rate structure embodying a decreased cost per mile as line mileage increases is used to compute the line cost. This computation, using actual Bell system rates in effect June 1, 1973 for a voice-grade line, and assuming a distance of 238 miles between the two locations, is illustrated in Table 1.

TABLE 1
COMPUTATION OF LINE COST FOR A LEASED LINE

Rate structure		Detroit–Chicago hookup	
Miles	Rate mile	Computation	Result
1–25	$3.00	25 X $3.00 =	$ 75.00
26–100	2.10	75 X $2.10 =	157.50
101–250	1.50	138 X $1.50 =	207.00
251–500	1.05	. . . .	. . . . . .
501–up	0.75	. . . .	. . . . . .
		Totals 238 miles	$439.50

The resulting line cost of $439.50, plus the additional hardware cost of $30, yield a total cost per month for the leased line of $469.50.

In contrast, the cost of switched lines (dial-up service) depends upon long distance rates, number of calls, and length of each call. For example, assume that the long distance rate from Detroit to Chicago is $0.90 for the first three minutes and $0.27 for each additional minute. If an average of 900 sales orders per month are received from Detroit, and if each requires a separate call of less than three minutes in duration, the cost will be $0.90 X 900 = $810 per month. However, if some calls are entered in groups of two or more, the average cost per order will be less due to the lower number of calls required and the smaller rate per minute once a call exceeds three minutes. To compute the actual cost would require knowledge of the pattern of receipt orders at the sales office and the average length of time required to enter order data over the terminal. For example,

TABLE 2
COMPUTATION OF SWITCHED LINE COST

No. of calls	Orders/call	No. of orders	Length of call	Cost/call	Total cost
600	1	600	2 minutes	$0.90	$540.00
100	2	200	4 minutes	1.17	117.00
20	3	60	6 minutes	1.71	34.20
10	4	40	8 minutes	2.25	22.50
	Totals	900			$713.70

assuming an average of two minutes connect time per order. Table 2 illustrates this computation under an assumed pattern of receipt of orders.

Exhibit 2 illustrates the relationship of usage volume and distance between hookup points to the breakeven point between leased lines and switched lines. Each point on the breakeven line represents a point where the monthly cost of a leased line for the number of miles given on the horizontal axis is exactly equal to the monthly cost of a switched line for that number of miles which is used for the amount of time per day shown on the vertical axis. The computations underlying the chart incorporate line costs only, and assume a month of 22 working days. Furthermore, the computations are based on the dial-up rate for each additional minute beyond the initial three minutes, which means that the chart reflects a situation in which transactions are entered in large batches (remote batch processing) such that the extra rate for the first three minutes increases total cost by an insignificant amount. If, alternatively, transactions are entered as they are received, the pattern of receipt must be known or assumed before a chart of this type may be prepared. Note that the breakeven line itself for any such chart would be almost identical in appearance to the line in Exhibit 2.

To further explain the breakeven line, note that each discrete drop in the line represents a mileage level at which a rate break occurs in the station-to-station dial-up rate. For example, at 676 miles the rate per minute increases from $0.32 to $0.35, causing a discrete drop in the economic desirability of switched lines. Furthermore, the change in the slope of the line at 500 miles reflects the decrease in the cost per mile of a leased line from $1.05 to $0.75 (see Table 1). In conclusion, the exhibit demonstrates that for short distances leased lines are more economical unless the volume of usage is quite small, whereas for long distances switched lines are more economical unless the volume of usage is quite high. In any given situation the cost differential between these two alternatives may be quite significant.

In addition to relative costs, the choice between leased and switched lines is affected by such performance factors as transmission speed, error rate, and flexibility. Transmission speed favors leased lines, since 4,800 bits per second is the maximum attainable transmission speed with dial-up lines. Error rates also favor

Exhibit 2 EFFECT OF USAGE VOLUME AND DISTANCE ON RELATIVE COST OF LEASED AND SWITCHED LINES.

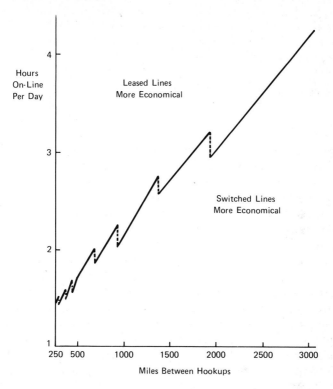

leased lines, which can be conditioned to reduce error rates significantly below those experienced on dial-up lines. However, flexibility favors the use of dial-up service in the sense that more than one system may be accessed from a single terminal.

In summary, the decision to use either a leased or a switched line involves analyzing transaction volume to determine the relative cost of these alternatives, and then balancing the cost differential against the performance features considered most desirable.

Private lines versus a Private Branch Exchange—To reduce network costs when long distances are involved, techniques must be used that reduce the total line mileage. When a separate leased line is provided between the computer and each terminal, the network will likely be highly inefficient as well as costly. This inefficiency arises from the fact that most of the terminals will not be operating at the same time.

When several terminals are installed in a small area located a long distance from the computer center, a Private Branch Exchange (PBX) can sometimes be used to reduce the total line mileage. One or more lines connect the PBX, which is actually a line switch, to the computer. Each terminal is connected by a separate line to the Exchange. A terminal is connected to the computer only while the terminal is being used. The economic feasibility of using the PBX depends upon whether or not the reduction in line mileage provides sufficient cost savings to offset the cost of the PBX.

One disadvantage of the PBX approach is that terminal operators may at times be unable to obtain a line to the computer because all lines are busy. The number of terminals that can be used simultaneously cannot exceed the number of lines from the Exchange to the computer. Thus, a cost-performance trade off arises as the reduction in network cost must be balanced against the possible reduction in system availability as an operator awaits a line to the computer.

Multidrop versus private lines—Another technique for reducing the total line mileage is to use a multidrop line, a single line connected to several terminals. If the terminals are installed at different locations, the line would be directed along the shortest path that connects all terminals to the computer.

QUEUEING NECESSARY

Two terminals on a multidrop line cannot transmit or receive at the same time. A system must be developed whereby each device waits in a queue for its opportunity to transmit. Usually the computer sends a signal to each terminal requesting the terminal to transmit any data it may have. This process of transmitting line control signals from the computer to the terminals is called "polling." The terminal cost will be somewhat higher because additional line control units must be included in the system to recognize the polling signals from the computer. Messages from the computer must always carry the address of the terminal to receive if the signal is to be received there. Likewise, messages from the terminals must include an identification of the terminal that transmitted the data.

Multidrop lines can be economically justified only if the reduction in line mileage provides a cost savings sufficient to offset the cost of the additional hardware required in the system. However, any cost saving achieved may be offset by a performance reduction in the form of increased system response time and decreased system reliability. While a message is being transmitted to or from one terminal, all other terminals on the line must wait, which means that system response time is increased in some cases. On the other hand, if one section of a multidrop line fails, the system is unavailable to all users located down the line from that point. A line failure in a system using point-to-point lines or a PBX will generally only affect one user. Thus the cost-performance trade off to be considered with multidrop lines is the reduction in total network costs achieved by increasing average system response time and sacrificing some degree of system reliability.

Many software decisions are inherent in decisions relating to the four areas of hardware already discussed. Examples include the selection of file reference method, the design of file structures, and the selection of processor configurations. These are not discussed further here.

Perhaps the most important cost-performance trade offs involving software in a real-time system relate to the reliability of the system. Software costs are the "personnel costs" of system analysis and programing. Software reliability is dependent upon such factors as the extent of system testing, the adequacy of system documentation, and the thoroughness of input data validation. These factors have been discussed extensively elsewhere in the literature* and are not belabored here.

SUMMARY AND CONCLUSIONS

Cost-performance trade offs are inherent in decisions relating to file storage, central processor, data terminals, data communications, and software in a real-time system. Though for convenience these five topics have been discussed separately in this article, they are closely interrelated in the design process. The decisions made have important implications for such performance factors as system response time, reliability and user convenience.

Real-time systems are the wave of the future in computerized data processing. Therefore it is important that the managers, accountants, and other non-specialists involved in the planning and evaluation of real-time systems develop a general understanding of the performance economics of such systems. Though a comprehensive treatment is beyond the scope of an article of this length, we have attempted to discuss some of the more important cost-performance trade offs in real-time system design.

---

* For a comprehensive treatment, see James T. Martin, *Programming Real-Time Computer Systems*, Englewood Cliffs, N.J., Prentice-Hall, Inc., 1965.

The Revolution of EFTS

CAROL A. SCHALLER

Whether you've paid by cash or check for a purchase, it's obvious that how consumers make payments for retail shopping has hardly changed in the past four decades. But a revolution in this payment system has begun to emerge. Soon Americans may be able to receive wages, pay their utility, insurance and department store bills, buy groceries and invest in mutual funds without using cash or checks. The checkless society will be brought about by electronic funds transfer systems (EFTS), which will affect almost everyone's life-style. Major changes will occur in financial transactions, and, as a result, the impact on the accounting profession will be great, and will extend to both large and small firms.

Although EFT systems are in an early stage of growth, they are increasing in number and importance. A large New York bank recently installed approximately 500 remote-banking terminals throughout its branches and an additional 3,500 terminals in retail stores. Other financial institutions have installed an estimated 20,000 terminals throughout the country. Supermarket checkout systems with optical scanners to recognize the merchandise and electronically ring up the price are beginning to appear; although only an estimated 600 stores will use scanners by the end of 1978, the rate at which they are being installed has increased substantially.

At least one brokerage house has a system that allows a customer to access his investment account from any store that accepts a VISA card. The store clerk simply calls the VISA authorization center. If the value of the customer's credit line (for example, the recent dividends and the value of his money market mutual fund account) exceeds the amount of the purchase, the transaction will be cleared.

EFTS can be defined as payment systems that use computerized electronic impulses rather than paper (money, checks, etc.) to effect an economic exchange. This difference in payment mode will have varied effects on participants in the payment system. The *banker* may find it reduces check processing, bad debt expense and the amount of float provided to checking account customers. Currently 81 percent of U.S. adults have checking accounts, and they write over 2.4 billion checks each month.[1] The potential savings are substantial.

For the *business community*, EFTS can mean guaranteed payments and an immediate use of funds because payments are usually initiated only when funds are available, and the funds are obtained on the day designated without the chore of depositing checks or waiting for a check to arrive in the mail. On the other hand, EFT systems present a new opportunity for white-collar crime. Embezzlement and manipulation of financial records could be more difficult to detect, unless new controls are developed for the new systems.

The effects on the *consumer* will be considerable. The reduction in the need to carry large amounts of cash will reduce robberies. The elderly and infirm could pay all their bills from home, and the average consumer could enjoy the convenience of paying bills by phone and writing fewer checks. (Fewer checks mean less postage, smaller checking account charges and less bother.)

For *auditors*, EFTS will mean that their clients may be using systems without a visible audit trail. Auditing financial transactions through a network of hundreds of computers, switches, telephone lines and terminals will require the application of new knowledge and techniques in the audit.

Auditors of smaller clients should be aware that some of their clients will be affected by EFTS. Besides EFTS services involving extensive retail chain stores and multinational corporations, EFTS "utilities" charging per-transaction fees are developing throughout the country, signing up many smaller financial institutions and merchants. Small banks will either use these services, set up cooperatives or employ the services of correspondents, as will savings and loan associations and credit unions.

EFTS will expand to small retail businesses as mechanical cash registers are replaced by electronic cash registers, many of which are easily and inexpensively upgradable to point-of-sale terminals. At least one large suburban shopping mall already has many of its shops participating in its system. The accounting firms for these shops are facing "future" systems now.

In short, clients will not have to develop multimillion dollar systems to be involved in EFTS. They will be able to use others' EFT systems in their financial transactions and the auditors will have to consider how much of the extensive EFTS network is part of their clients' accounting systems.

---

[1] *Payment Systems Perspectives '78*, a nationwide survey of consumer views on payment services, by Payment Systems, Inc. and Darden Research Corp.

TYPES OF EFTS

Most EFTS can be grouped into three general categories:

- Remote-banking services.
- Retail point-of-sale (POS) services.
- Direct deposit and preauthorized payment services.

Each is discussed in more detail below.

Remote-banking Services

These systems allow deposits, withdrawals, transfers between accounts, bill-paying and account status inquiries through the use of remote-banking terminals[2] or telephones. In a terminal system, the customer can accomplish these transactions by

- Inserting a plastic card into the terminal.
- Entering a personal identification number (PIN) or "password."
- Pressing the function key (e.g., "deposit") for the transaction he wishes to perform and, if appropriate, the amount of the transaction.
- Accepting from the terminal the receipt, cash (if applicable) and his plastic card.

The remote-banking systems that use telephones rather than terminals are normally limited to bill-paying, transfers between accounts and account status inquiries. Some telephone payment systems require discussion with a teller at the financial institution, but others are accomplished using only a touch-tone telephone to enter the transaction information. For example, a customer could pay a bill by

- Dialing the phone number of the system.
- Entering the account number and password.
- Entering the merchant's identification number and the amount of the payment.
- After listening to the computer's voice response (using prerecorded phrases) that repeats the information entered, pressing a button to confirm that the transaction is correct.

Remote-banking systems come in two varieties, depending on the number of financial institutions that use the system. If the terminals communicate with only one financial institution, the system is called *proprietary* (see Exhibit 1). If the

---

[2] Remote-banking terminals can be called automated teller machines (ATMs), customer/bank communications terminals (CBCTs) and remote service units (RSUs).

terminals communicate with a computer that services several financial institutions, the computer is called a switch and the system is called a switch system (see Exhibit 2). The auditor of smaller financial institutions will probably encounter switch systems, because the economies of scale favor sharing of costs.

Retail POS Services

The auditor of supermarkets and other retail outlets (see Exhibit 3) will find EFTS terminals performing three types of functions:

- Check verification/guarantee—Often this function can be performed more quickly and effectively by a POS system than by the store personnel (e.g., the clerk checking the customer's driver's license).
- Funds transfer—These functions are similar to remote banking services. Instead of obtaining credit by use of a plastic card, the customer uses the card to authorize a transfer of funds from his depository account to that of the merchant.
- Data capture—Some electronic cash registers or POS terminals record data to monitor inventory quantities and aid management in pricing and other decisions.

Some POS systems also perform remote-banking functions. Also like remote banking systems, POS systems can be proprietary or switch systems.

Direct Deposit and Preauthorized Payment Services

These EFTS allow recurring payments to be made electronically rather than manually. "Direct deposits" are direct payments into the recipient's account (see Exhibit 4). The most common of these are direct payroll and social security deposits. An example of the steps in a direct payroll deposit system follows:

1. The employees who want their payroll checks deposited directly sign an authorization form.

2. Before each payday, the employer's computer produces a magnetic tape with the machine-sensible "payroll checks" for the appropriate employees. The employees that do not participate in the direct deposit system get ordinary paper checks.

3. The magnetic tape is sent to the employer's bank, which debits its account for the entire direct deposit payroll and credits the accounts of each employee with an account at that bank. The remaining credits on the magnetic tape are transmitted to a clearinghouse for distribution to the other employees' financial institutions.

4. Each employee participating in the system receives a statement showing the deposit.

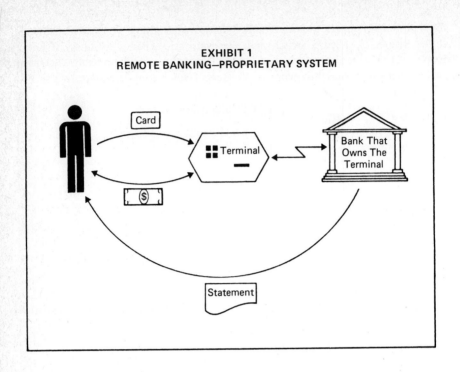

EXHIBIT 1
REMOTE BANKING—PROPRIETARY SYSTEM

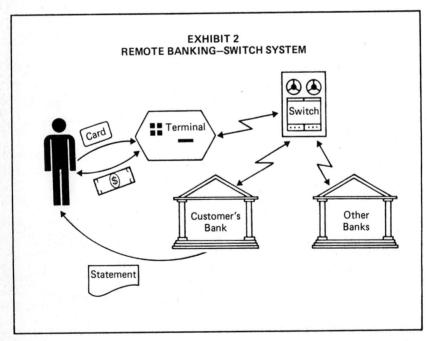

EXHIBIT 2
REMOTE BANKING—SWITCH SYSTEM

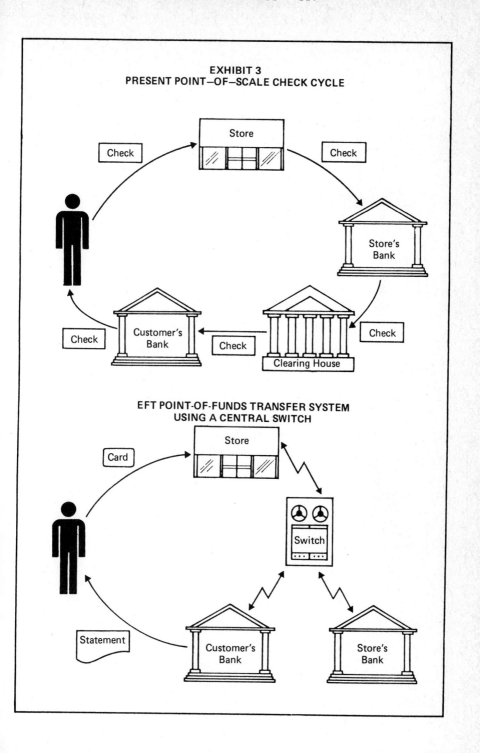

EXHIBIT 3
PRESENT POINT—OF—SCALE CHECK CYCLE

EFT POINT-OF-FUNDS TRANSFER SYSTEM
USING A CENTRAL SWITCH

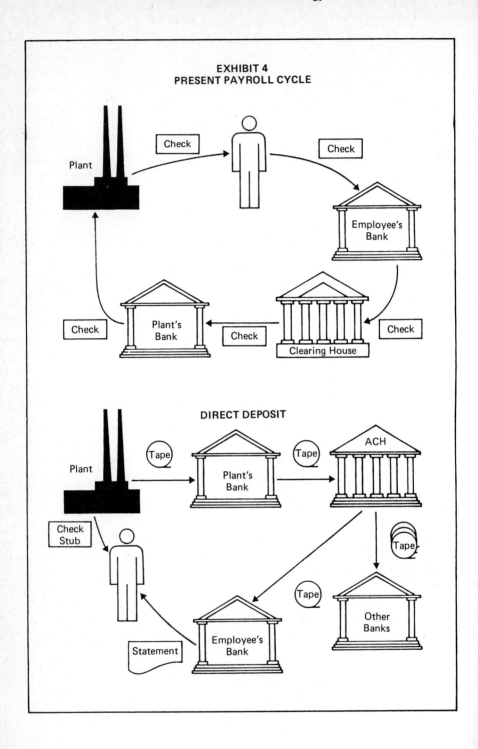

**EXHIBIT 4
PRESENT PAYROLL CYCLE**

DIRECT DEPOSIT

The use of direct deposits is already widespread. For example, both a successful local CPA firm in Perth Amboy, New Jersey, and the American Institute of CPAs use the direct deposit system to pay their employees.

"Preauthorized payments" are regular electronic payments of periodic bills such as mortgages, utility bills, car payments, etc. Example steps in this process are as follows:

1. The bill-payer signs an authorization form for a specific recurring bill, such as payments for life insurance. The authorization information is stored on a magnetic file that contains all the preauthorizations that are in effect for the bank's customers.

2. When the bank receives the insurance company's bill, it checks the authorization master file. If the bill is proper, the bill-payer's account is charged for the amount and a machine-sensible credit is forwarded to the clearinghouse for settlement with the insurance company's bank.

3. A memorandum bill is usually sent to the bill-payer. If sent in advance, it allows him to make sure enough funds are in the account, to check the amount of the payment and to prevent payment if a question arises. The bill-payer's bank statement serves as a receipt of payment.

"Mom and Pop" businesses as well as consumers find this a convenient way to pay bills.

LEGAL AND REGULATORY ENVIRONMENT

How soon will most auditors encounter these systems? And which ones will they be? The regulations and laws governing EFTS will influence the form of the systems developed, the speed of their adoption and the consumer's acceptance of the new payment systems. One of the major issues is whether a remote-banking terminal is a branch office of the financial institution. If it is, EFTS may be severely limited in states that limit branch banking (i.e., in number or location of branches or by requiring a high level of capital for each branch).

Various state legislatures, the U.S. comptroller of the currency, the Federal Home Loan Bank Board and many courts including the U.S. Supreme Court have considered this question and have taken very different views. Thirty-two states that do not consider the terminals as branches have enacted EFTS legislation. Of the remaining 18 states, 17 consider them branches and 1 has not addressed the issue.[3] Both the comptroller of the currency and the FHLBB did not consider the terminals to be branches, but their positions are now being challenged in court.

---

[3] *Analysis of Enacted State Legislation: Deployment* (Washington, D.C.: American Bankers Association, May 1978 revision).

Because of one case, the comptroller has had to rescind his ruling.[4] When the Supreme Court refused to hear an appeal of three cases involving the issue of the comptroller of the currency's ruling, the lower courts' decision to consider the terminals owned by national banks as branches remained in place.

On the other hand, the Nebraska Federal District Court upheld the FHLBB's view, finding by the court's interpretation of the regulations, that savings and loan association terminals are *not* branches. The standards are inconsistent, and the results will be that EFTS will tend to expand in different ways in different states.

Another issue, privacy of the individual, is increasingly important in an EFTS environment. Huge amounts of important personal data will be stored in the systems. They will be able to record most of an individual's financial transactions when and where they occur. A black market of confidential information could be developed. Problems could arise because of unauthorized access to the data, provision of incorrect or out-of-date information or the unauthorized sale of name lists.

In a 1974 case, the U.S. Supreme Court upheld the Bank Secrecy Act, which requires the maintenance of records and the reporting of individual financial data by financial institutions.[5] The act was intended to allow law enforcement agencies to review an individual's financial information without notifying the individual.

The National Commission on Electronic Funds Transfer Systems (NCEFTS) has recommended legislation to allow individuals to contest government access to their financial information and to provide them with notification of any inquiries. The legislation should consider law enforcement and other requirements, however. The NCEFTS has also recommended legislation similar in intent to the Fair Credit Reporting Act to protect the individual from the private sector's improper use of an individual's financial information.

An issue of interest to the auditor as well as to the participants in the payment system is liability for EFTS errors or irregularities. Computer crime will undoubtedly increase as more systems provide cash and payment for goods and services as their direct output. The Uniform Commercial Code's application to EFTS is unclear. The 1970 amendments to the Truth in Lending Act (that limit the consumer's liability on credit cards to $50) do not apply to "debit" cards used in remote-banking and POS services. Pending EFT systems legislation would limit the consumer's liability to $50.

That the future will see some form of EFTS seems certain, but the rate the EFT systems are installed, and certain aspects of how they will operate, will depend on the resolution of many issues, including those discussed above.

---

[4] *Independent Bankers Association of America v. James E. Smith, Comptroller of the Currency*, no. 75-0089, D.D.C. (October 10, 1975).

[5] *California Bankers Association v. Shultz*, 416 U.S. 21, 39 (1974).

CONCLUSION

This article was intended to provide a brief overview of the types of EFTS and some of the issues that will have to be resolved as these systems become commonplace. The effects of EFTS on the audit are considered in an article by Dana R. Richardson [see chapter six], and Norman Lyons expands on one one aspect of control in EFT systems in his article.[6]

---

[6] Norman Lyons, "Segregation of Functions in EFTS," *Journal of Accountancy,* (October 1978), pp. 89–92.

Beyond 1984:
A Technology Forecast

FREDERICK G. WITHINGTON

HARDWARE

Computers

Within the next five years, circuits for computer logic and storage will probably exist that have switching speeds on the order of 10^{-8} second, 10 to 50 times faster than today's devices. Beyond that level further improvements will become harder to achieve, though another order of magnitude could be obtained beyond 1985. However, appearance of improvements in the laboratory precedes their appearance in commercially usable, reliable computers by about five years. This suggests that the improvement in circuit performance per dollar cost will be no more than tenfold (relative to today's circuits) for computers being delivered in 1985. A rather simplistic inference is that circuits of today's performance level will cost about one-tenth the present price, while computers in today's medium-high price range will have speeds approaching 100 MIPS (million instructions per second).

However, an important factor in determining the architecture of tomorrow's processors derives from the desirability of manufacturing circuits in the most standardized form possible. It is and will remain expensive to design an individual integrated circuit, the more so as the scale of integration rises. On the other hand, the manufacturing cost of the individual circuit is extremely low, so it is more economical to effectively waste circuit functions than to design a new circuit. This influence, already visible in the design and functioning of electronic calculators, will be very important in determining the future architecture of computers. To the degree possible, modules at the microprocessor and even higher levels will be used in preference to the design of new specialized circuits.

Architecturally, increasing parallelism in commercial computers is likely to be used to reduce the wait times now encountered in interlinked data transfer and

---

manipulation operations. This parallelism is likely to be realized in the form of specialized processors dedicated to I/O and file management, memory management, interrupt processing, and similar functions. Paralleling of many identical, multifunction processors as in ILLIAC is unlikely in general purpose computers, because the jobs to be done (many of them involving emulation of today's programs) do not conveniently subdivide into array form.

Microcoding These specialized processors are likely to have their functions determined primarily by microcoded stored logic, with wired logic used only where high speed is essential. The use of microcode facilitates standardized manufacturing and maintenance, while permitting the functions of the processors to vary in support of system objectives.

The set of microcodes in the groups of processors forming a "computer" will, in addition to facilitating the basic scheduling and resource allocation functions, support the following system objectives now normally addressed by the operating system:

- Support of several run-time environments, both for the emulation of past programs (and related operating systems) and for the convenience of multiple users simultaneously desiring several modes of operation. Some version of virtual machine concepts will be involved.

- Separation of I/O, communications, and file processing from computational functions.

- Dynamic allocation of processor functions, both to meet varying workloads and to support fail-soft operations (which will, in some form, be all manufacturers' approach to increasing system availability).

- Automatic management of the memory and file device hierarchy at a symbolic level, to facilitate the ease of programming, convenience of use, and (through access tables associated with individual run-time environments) security and privacy of data.

- Self measurement, including error logging. This function will support routine maintenance, fail-soft operation, job accounting, and system tuning.

Other functions now associated with operating systems are likely to continue to be performed primarily by software, and are discussed below.

This set of system objectives applies to computers to be available in both 1977 and 1985, and across most of the computer price range. Success and generality in meeting the objectives (and cost/effectiveness in doing so) will be evolutionary, obviously greatest in the larger computers and the later ones.

Processors become components Computers of both 1977 and 1985 will, then, consist of complexes of component processors automatically sharing microcoded functions under control of the operating system in a manner largely invisible to the user.

The throughput of computers will be determined by that of their component processors. Three levels of component processors are defined here, designated level 1, level 2 and level 3, in order of increasing power. Then, four levels of end-user computers are defined in which they will be used. The four levels of end-user computers are enough to cover the normal price range for commercial data processing, and three levels of component processors appear to provide enough building blocks.

The price/performance forecasts for the component processors are summarized in Table 1. The level 1 processor is similar to today's microprocessor, manufactured on one or a few semiconductor chips. Initially simple with a small programmable read-only memory (PROM) and minimal complexity, it will evolve in the direction of higher complexity and speed. Its speed in 1985 is forecast to be the same as that of the level 2 processor, reflecting the expectation that by then there will be no cost benefit in manufacturing circuits with cycle times any slower than 250 nanoseconds. The level 2 processor will evolve similarly, but will in both 1977 and 1985 be considerably more complex: it will be required to perform the functions currently associated with an I/O channel controller, or with the cpu of a small computer system.

The level 3 processors will correspond to the central computers in today's medium to high priced computer systems, but will have raw speed equivalent to that of today's largest computers. They will be used singly in batch-oriented monoprocessor computers as they are today, and in multiples under multiprocessor operating systems in large-scale systems with high power and automatic fail-softness. The cost (to the vendor) of level 3 processors is not expected to drop as much between 1977 and 1985 as the costs of smaller processors, because the complexity increase required to support the evolving microcode software is expected to be greater (as shown by the quadrupling of PROM size). Pipelined instruction interpretation and execution, probably used to achieve speeds approaching the microcode equivalent to 100 MIPS, will also serve to keep complexity high.

Larger, more powerful component processors than level 3 will be possible in both 1977 and 1985 and will probably be built for large scientific systems, but they will not be needed for even the largest commercial systems (partly because at least two cpu's will be needed in such systems to permit fail-soft operations).

These component processors will be combined to form the "computers," or "processor systems," offered by the manufacturers. They will also be used in I/O subsystems (e.g., intelligent terminals and remote batch terminals) and in file storage subsystems; these are discussed below.

The expected characteristics of the four levels of computers are summarized in Table 2. Conventional terminology is used to identify them, mostly because terms such as "minicomputer" are traditionally associated with a price range that will still exist (though the power provided in each price class will change). Each computer is described as a module incorporating an average amount of main memory and of backing storage for program residence and working space. All file storage is additional; file modules are described below.

TABLE 1
FUTURE COMPONENT PROCESSORS

	Level 1 1977	Level 1 1985	Level 2 1977	Level 2 1985	Level 3 1977	Level 3 1985
Cycle time	2 usec	250 nsec	500 nsec	250 nsec	500 nsec	100 nsec
Bandwidth	4 bits	8-16 bits	16 bits	16-32 bits	32 bits	64 bits
Interrupt levels	0	1 level	1 level	2 level	2 level	4 level
PROM size	500 bytes	1,000 bytes	4,000 bytes	8,000 bytes	8,000 bytes	64,000 bytes
Cost to system vendor	$100	$50	$4,000	$2,000	$50,000	$30,000

TABLE 2
FUTURE COMPUTER CLASSES

	Microcomputer 1977	Microcomputer 1985	Minicomputer 1977	Minicomputer 1985	Mono-computer 1977	Mono-computer 1985**	Multi-computer 1977	Multi-computer 1985
Typical use								
On-line (users)	1	5-10	6-10	10-20	10-20	20-40	complete inter-mixing, job determines limit	
	or	or	and	and	and	and		
Batch (streams)	1	1	1	1	4-6	6-8		
Main memory(bytes)	4-8KB	32-64KB	32-64KB	0.2-0.5MB	0.5-2MB	2-4MB	2-16MB	8-64MB
Backing store*(bytes)	300KB	500KB	500KB	4MB	10MB	30MB	50-200MB	100-500MB
Operating system	minimal	minimal	real, fixed partitions	virtual	partitioned virtual	virtual	multiple virtual memory or machine	
User cost	$1-2K	$0.3-0.7K	$10-20K	$7-10K	$150-250K	$75-100K	$1.5-2.5M	$1-2M

* Auxiliary storage for system programs, current application programs, and data.

** This system will probably have multiple main processors by 1985.

Multiprocessing The microcomputer, including one level 1 component processor, will typically be used in intelligent terminals or satellites. By 1985, however, the power of the processor and the low cost of relatively large memory will enable the microcomputer to support small stand-alone systems of considerable versatility. The costs of such systems will be dominated by their peripheral equipment costs (see below).

The minicomputer will in both 1977 and 1985 be able to support a fully capable data processing system. The cpu will be a single level 2 processor, and from three to (in 1985) as many as 20 level 1 processors will be associated with peripheral equipment. Ease of use in interactive applications will be the primary design objective of these machines. This accounts for the very large average storage size of the 1985 machine and resulting slow decline in price. One batch stream is assumed in the background, though the 1985 machine could easily run more batch streams at the expense of some interactive capability (particularly since virtual memory management will be generally used).

The mono-computer is designed primarily for users whose intent is to perform fairly large amounts of batch processing, though some interactive capability will be present. In the 1977 system a single level 3 cpu will be employed and two or three level 2 processors for high-volume peripheral device control; level 1 processors will be used as needed for individual or low-volume peripherals. Because no multiprocessing will be present, and because (for efficiency) fixed partitioning of memory into batch and interactive virtual environments will be used, the functional system objectives listed above will be only partly met. In the 1985 system, however, the low costs of component processors will permit a second level 3 processor to be included and several more level 2 processors. These, together with larger memories, will permit the mono-computer to meet almost all the system objectives (except, perhaps, multiple run-time environments) even though its price will decline.

The multi-computer will incorporate at least two level 3 processors in 1977 and three, four or more in 1985. Four to six level 2 processors will be in the 1977 system and perhaps twice as many in the 1985 system, together with multitudes of level 1 processors.

The multi-computer's price difference from the mono-computer is due not so much to having more processors as to the much larger storage of the multi-computer, particularly the large backing store (which may use magnetic bubble or charge-coupled device technology as early as 1977. See discussion of auxiliary storage). This very large storage is needed to provide numerous run-time environments (one or more emulating past generations, several running batch streams, several varieties of interactive environments, etc.). Also, the multi-computer will be designed to completely intermix a wide variety of file-based interactive, batch, and system development applications. The multi-computer will in fact be a network of computers providing a number of processing environments simultaneously. The common elements will be two: the central data base around which the processing is distributed, and a central system executive that controls the functions of each component computer and provides overall monitoring. It is these two common elements which prevent the multi-computer from being broken up into a "federated network" of physically dispersed minicomputers. Perhaps in the farther future ways will be found to provide these common system elements in a dispersed network, but this seems unlikely in products being delivered by 1982.

Comparing the estimated purchase costs of the different classes shown in Table 2, it appears that wide gaps will develop in the price spectrum. This is partly an illusion caused by this article's objective of providing standard cost forecasts for typical modules; as now, variations in configuration will cause wider variations in price than those shown here. Nevertheless, between the mono-computer and multi-computer, a genuine price gap seems likely; the implication is that there will be no high-priced batch processing computers (except perhaps specialized scientific ones), and that there will be a minimum cost of entry to the high volume, interactive, data base oriented environment.

Auxiliary Storage

A great deal of research is being performed into novel auxiliary storage technologies including magnetic bubbles, charge-coupled devices, laser-holographic devices, cyrogenic devices, and others. This will gradually result in the introduction of new types of auxiliary storage subsystems. However, much improvement potential still exists in conventional magnetic technology. Most of the improvement will be in the form of increased area density of recording: more tracks per inch laterally across a magnetic disc face, and more bits per inch longitudinally. An area density improvement factor of at least 40 appears theoretically possible. This will result in a much lower cost per bit for magnetic discs, lower through at least 1983 than newer technologies can match. However, access time to magnetic discs will remain a problem even if head-per-track arrangements become general. For this reason it seems likely that hierarchies of auxiliary storage devices will continue to be used through 1985, with the newer technologies appearing first at the high speed, low capacity end of the spectrum, and then gradually superseding slower technologies as their costs per bit drop. Either magnetic bubble or charge coupled device technology (or both) will be in widespread use by 1983, and are likely to appear in some product lines by 1977.

Table 3 summarizes the situation: four levels of auxiliary storage (in addition to the computer's main memory) are likely to remain in use in 1977 and beyond; only in the 1980s does the improvement potential of the new high speed technologies indicate that the number of levels of storage may be reduced. The multilevel hierarchy will be of less concern to the user than it is now, however, because virtual memory management techniques will be used to move data sets up and down the hierarchy depending on usage. The recent announcement of IBM's 3850 system exemplifies the trend in this direction.

Auxiliary storage module performance and cost forecasts have been developed for 1977 and 1983, and compared with 1974 levels. These forecasts are summarized

TABLE 3

AUXILIARY STORAGE TECHNOLOGY PERFORMANCE CHARACTERISTICS

	Storage capacity (bits/unit)	Access time (sec)	Cost/bit (cents)
A. 1974 Technologies			
High speed/Low capacity (large core, hpt disc, drums)	$10^7 - 10^8$	$10^{-5} - 10^{-2}$	0.1 - 2.0
Moderate speed/Moderate capacity (moving-head discs)	$10^8 - 10^9$	$10^{-1} - 10^{-2}$	$10^{-3} - 10^{-2}$
Low speed/High capacity (ultra-large storage devices)	$10^{11} - 10^{12}$	1.0 - 10	$10^{-5} - 10^{-4}$
Archival storage (magnetic tapes)	Unlimited (10^8/tape)	10 - 100	$10^{-6} - 10^{-5}$
B. 1977 Technologies			
High speed/Low capacity (hpt discs, early bubbles or CCD)	$10^8 - 10^9$	$10^{-4} - 10^{-3}$	0.1 - 1.0
Moderate speed/Moderate capacity (moving-head discs)	$10^9 - 10^{10}$	$10^{-3} - 10^{-2}$	$10^{-4} - 10^{-3}$
Low speed/High capacity (ultra-large storage devices)	$10^{11} - 10^{13}$	1.0 - 10	$10^{-6} - 10^{-4}$
Archival storage (magnetic tapes)	Unlimited (10^9/tape)	10 - 100	$10^{-7} - 10^{-6}$
C. 1983 Technologies			
High speed/Moderate capacity (CCD, magnetic bubbles)	$10^8 - 10^9$	$10^{-7} - 10^{-5}$	0.01 - 0.1
Moderate speed/Very high capacity (discs, holographic, cryogenic)	$10^9 - 10^{14}$	$10^{-5} - 10^{-1}$	10^{-6}

in Table 4. The modules were configured on the basis of the typical size and access time requirements assumed for the four classes of computers (multiple modules could, of course, be used to obtain higher capacity). Controllers are included in the cost of each module, ranging from a controller requiring a single level 1 component processor at the low end to a controller with dual level 2 processors at the high end.

In addition to the auxiliary storage modules for conventional random file access, forecasts are also summarized in Table 4 for very large, slow access archival storage systems that could be added to multi-computer configurations. These require advanced technology to obtain the very high capacities required; early models are available now and they are expected to see general use in the late 1970s. These modules are shown as if they are independent, for clarity and ease of reference. Their actual use in systems of both 1977 and 1985 will be in hierarchical arrangements, with data movements at least partially transparent to the user.

TABLE 4
AUXILIARY STORAGE MODULE COST/PERFORMANCE FORECASTS

	1974	1977	1983
Microprocessor **auxiliary storage**			
Capacity	1 million bytes	5 million bytes	5 million bytes
Medium	small fixed disc	small fixed disc	semiconductor, CCD
Access time	10 msec	10 msec	10 usec
Cost	$5,000	$2,500-3,500	$1,500-2,500
Minicomputer **auxiliary storage**			
Capacity	20 million bytes	50 million bytes	50 million bytes
Medium	small removable disc	small removable disc	bubble memory
Access time	100 msec	30 msec	100 usec
Cost	$35,000	$15-20,000	$15-25,000
Product example	IBM S3/10 disc (5445)		
Monoprocessor **auxiliary storage**			
Capacity	200 million bytes	200 million bytes	500 million bytes
Medium	head/disc cartridge	head/disc cartridge	head/disc cartridge
Access time	25 msec	25 msec	20 msec
Cost	$60,000	$35-45,000	$25-35,000
Product example	IBM 3340	IBM 3340	
Multiprocessor **auxiliary storage**			
Capacity	1 billion bytes	2 billion bytes	2 billion bytes
Medium	multiple disc unit	multiple disc unit	multiple discs
Access time	30 msec	25 msec	20 msec
Cost	$260,000	$180-220,000	$90-130,000
Product example	IBM 3330		
Archival **storage option**			
Capacity	200 billion bytes	1 trillion bytes	10 trillion bytes
Medium	tape cartridge	laser, video recording	holographic systems
Access time	10 sec	10 sec	1 sec
Cost	$1,000,000	$400-600,000	$700-1,200,000
Product example	IBM 3850		

Forecasts for magnetic tape auxiliary storage modules are summarized in Table 5. (The controller in each module is assumed capable of handling simultaneous data transfer to all drives.) An eventual doubling of packing density (and therefore of data rate) and some reductions in cost are forecast, but the relatively mature electromechanical technology involved seems to preclude major improvement.

TABLE 5
MAGNETIC TAPE COST/PERFORMANCE FORECASTS

	1974	1977	1983
Low performance (single drive with controller)			
Data rate	40,000 bytes/sec	40,000 bytes/sec	40,000 bytes/sec
Cost	$10,000	$7,500-8,500	$6,500-7,500
Example	IBM 3411-2		
Medium performance (three drives with controller)			
Data rate	600,000 bytes/sec	1.2 million bytes/sec	1.2 million bytes/sec
Cost	$75,000	$45-60,000	$25-40,000
Example	IBM 3420-5		
High performance (six drives with controller)			
Data rate	7.5 million bytes/sec	7.5 million bytes/sec	15 million bytes/sec
Cost	$220,000	$140-180,000	$80-120,000
Example	IBM 3420-8		

Batch I/O Equipment

The spectrum of I/O device types, speeds, and functions is so broad that for purposes of the Air Force report individual devices were combined into clusters or "stations," each station forming a cost/performance module that could be used in configuring over-all networks with approximate accuracy even though the exact number of readers, printers, etc., would probably be somewhat inaccurate. The same procedure is followed in this article. Forecasts were developed for two types of basic batch I/O stations in which a line printer is combined respectively with punched card and magnetic I/O equipment; then two optional, additional batch options were forecast: optical readers and computer output microfilm stations.

Punch card/line printer The first of the batch I/O stations includes one card reader, one punch, and one line printer. Forecasts were developed for low, medium, and high speed versions of this station, and for 1977 and 1985. These are summarized in Table 6.

TABLE 6
COST/PERFORMANCE FORECASTS FOR
BATCH STATION (PUNCH CARD/LINE PRINTER)

	1974	1977	1985
Low speed			
Performance	300 cpm read, 60 cpm punch, 100 lpm print	400 cpm read, 100 cpm punch 200 lpm print	400 cpm read, 100 cpm punch, 300 lpm print
Station Cost	($15,000-20,000)	($12,000-16,000)	($12,000-15,000)
Medium speed			
Performance	900 cpm read, 200 cpm punch, 600 lpm print	1,000 cpm read, 200 cpm punch, 800 lpm print	1,000 cpm read, 200 cpm punch, 900 lpm print
Station Cost	($32,000-37,000)	($32,000-37,000)	($32,000-37,000)
High speed			
Performance	1,200 cpm read, 300 cpm punch, 1,100 lpm print	1,200 cpm read, 300 cpm punch, 1,300 lpm print	1,200 cpm read, 300 cpm punch, 1,300 lpm print
Station Cost	$65,000-75,000	$65,000-75,000	$65,000-75,000

During the last 10 years there has been little change in the price/performance of the card readers and punches offered for use with the larger computer systems. The only major innovation has been the 96-column card introduced by IBM: this did not cause a great deal of change in demand, and the price/performance of units designed to handle the 96-column card is comparable to that of conventional units.

A check of devices offered by 15 vendors showed that maximum speed of punched card readers now available is 1,200 cpm, and the maximum punch speed is 300 cpm. These speeds were first achieved more than 10 years ago. Further speed increases obviously pose mechanical problems, but if there had been substantial market demand for units of higher speeds, it would have been technically possible to develop them. We infer that these speeds are regarded by the market as adequate for high-performance units. Prices of high-performance units have also changed little.

The growth of the minicomputer has brought with it a set of slower card readers and punches at lower prices designed to match the throughput capabilities and prices of the minicomputers. Readers capable of handling 400 cards per minute typically have a purchase price of about $1,200, and punches capable of handling 100 cards per minute typically cost about $9,000.

Price/performance evolution of these devices will be constrained by the fact that they are predominantly electromechanical and reflect a mature technology. We may expect manufacturers to substitute electronics for mechanical components wherever they can, and there is some possibility of using different technologies (such as fluidics) for the direct control of mechanical modules. It is also likely that the manufacturers, faced with the inherent high failure rates of these devices, will continue to work to improve their reliability. However, their willingness to invest in either new technology or more reliable designs will be moderated by the fact that the total demand for card readers and punches will probably decrease; the popularity of data collection with other media should diminish the overall use of card readers and punches. We therefore forecast relatively little change in price/performance over the entire period 1977–1985.

Printers are similarly constrained by the limits of electromechanical technology, but nonimpact techniques (thermal, electrostatic, electrographic, inkjet and Xerographic) have led to a greater rate of change. In the time period of this article, the development of nonimpact devices may lead to improvements of 15%–30% in overall printer price/performance with greater improvements at speeds of 3,000 lpm and up. This improvement factor appears in Table 6 as an increase in speed for the medium and high speed printers without any decrease in cost; for the low speed printer, both speed and cost are forecast to improve.

The forecast for the second type of batch I/O station simply substitutes magnetic tape drives for the card reader and punch, arriving at only slightly different cost forecasts.

OCR station System designers are rapidly developing more sophisticated circuit designs that, combined with LSI technology, are producing character recognition logic components of much lower cost and smaller size. Electro-optics developments are also contributing very small, light, inexpensive scanning arrays for low-cost units, and also very fast, more accurate scanning elements (using such technologies as laser beam control) for the larger, more complex systems. The most difficult design barrier to dealing with the less constrained patterns of handprinting and script is still the development of a true "gestalt" pattern recognition methodology (probably of a software nature) with powerful heuristic capabilities. Little progress in this area is foreseen.

A combination of continued rapid development of newer electro-optic materials and improvements in the power, speed, and cost of integrated circuits will lead to an increase in the price/performance of all types of OCR's by an overall factor of at least 2 and, in some cases, as much as 4 by 1985. These assumptions are expressed in tabular form in Table 7. The most significant product development will be that of a family of multiple-font, medium-speed document readers in the $50,000–75,000 price range with flexible software by 1985. In high-speed modules there should also be substantial improvement by 1985 in the reliability of recognition of more unconstrained, hand printed numeric information and some alphabetic forms.

The emergence of effective low-speed (and low-cost) OCR stations in the 1977–85 period should also enhance the development of sophisticated, modular, multi-media data entry systems combining low-speed, batch processing, character recognition stations with keyboard data entry and editing terminals, a local processor, and auxiliary memory.

TABLE 7
COST/PERFORMANCE FORECASTS FOR OCR STATION

	1974	1977	1985
Low speed			
Performance	50-100 lpm*	50-100 lpm	50-100 lpm
Station Cost	$35-75,000	$25,000-50,000	$20,000-30,000
Medium speed			
Performance	100-500 lpm	100-500 lpm	100-500 lpm
Station Cost	$75,000-100,000	$60,000-80,000	$50,000-75,000
High speed			
Performance	500-1,200 lpm	500-1,200 lpm	500-1,200 lpm
Station Cost	$100,000-500,000	$100,000-250,000	$75,000-125,000

* Average line length of 50 characters

A computer output microfilm station was assumed to include an off-line COM printer, a developer, a duplicator, and binding equipment. Significant price declines are believed likely because of reduction in LSI and electro-optical costs, and because of economies of scale as manufacturing volumes rise. These are expected to be moderated by the highly electromechanical nature of the system, with the results summarized in Table 8. No low-speed units are shown, because

TABLE 8
COST/PERFORMANCE FORECASTS FOR COM STATION

	1974	1977	1985
Medium speed			
Performance:*	5,000-10,000 lpm	5,000-10,000 lpm	7,000-10,000 lpm
Station Cost	$50,000-75,000	$40,000-60,000	$25,000-50,000
High speed			
Performance:*	10,000-25,000 lpm	12,000-25,000 lpm	20,000-30,000 lpm
Station Cost	$75,000-125,000	$60,000-70,000	$50,000-65,000

* COM printer speed only, not system throughput

developments in display devices are believed likely to satisfy any demand that may exist.

Terminals

Remote batch terminals require no separate forecast; a combination of the appropriate speed level of batch I/O station and a component processor (probably level 2) results in a price/performance forecast which should be grossly accurate. Interactive or "transaction" terminals were separately forecast, however.

Again, to simplify configuration details the forecast was developed on the basis of "stations" in which each basic terminal would have sufficient electronics to interface directly with a line connected to the host computer, whether the host be remote or a local satellite. The purpose of this assumption was to eliminate the need to allow for shared controllers and modems; this trend to integral electronics is visible in recent products. "Intelligent" terminals were assumed to contain a level 1 component processor and auxiliary memory in addition.

As Table 9 shows, three kinds of transaction terminal stations are considered. The two "standard" stations are the familiar combinations of keyboard with low speed, serial printer and of keyboard with "soft" display. Forecasts of the costs of these are shown for 1977 and for 1985, and for two versions: "basic," with only minimal interface electronics, and "intelligent," incorporating a degree of independent processing capability. Two "optional" stations are also shown; these are in the form of optional additions to standard stations. (An intelligent hard-copy printer is considered nonexistent within these definitions since it would be associated with an intelligent standard station. Basic OCR units are also considered nonexistent since all OCR devices require at least the intelligence associated with a level 1 processor.) Finally, three kinds of "special stations" are shown: a small badge reader for credit checking, identification, and similar applications (no intelligent version needed), and voice input and response subsystems (both of which require intelligence).

Keyboard and low-speed serial printer mechanisms are not expected to change much in price. While thermal printers will largely replace mechanical ones and bring

TABLE 9
COST FORECASTS FOR TRANSACTION TERMINAL STATIONS

	Basic	Intelligent*
Standard stations		
No. 1 keyboard/teleprinter	1977: $ 700–2,500	$ 4,000–9,000
	1985: $ 600–2,000	$ 2,000–2,500
No. 2 keyboard/display	1977: $ 900–3,000	$ 4,000–8,000
	1985: $ 700–1,500	$ 2,000–2,500
Optional stations		
No. 3 hardcopy printer	1977: $2,000–5,000	nonexistent
	1985: $1,000–4,000	
No. 4 low-cost OCR unit	nonexistent	1977: $ 500–1,000
		1985: $ 500–750
Special stations		
No. 5 minimal badge reader	1977: $ 500–600	nonexistent
	1985: $ 300–600	
No. 6 voice input	nonexistent	1977: $ 8,000–12,000
		1985: $ 7,000–10,000
No. 7 voice response**	nonexistent	1977: $50,000–150,000
		1985: $25,000–100,000

* Including small processor and auxiliary memory

** A special case combining telephone receivers as remote I/O stations plus a specialized unit associated with the central system.

a substantial speed improvement, they will not cost much less. A somewhat greater cost reduction is forecast for "soft" displays, primarily because of the larger amounts of circuitry associated with the displays which will drop in cost very sharply. For large displays (over 1,000 characters), the crt will remain the dominant technology in 1977 and perhaps in 1985. Planar gaseous displays and/or light-emitting diodes will become steadily more competitive, however, dominating the smaller displays (under 500 characters) and eventually challenging the crt.

The intelligent versions of the standard stations incorporate a level 1 component processor of very low cost. They also require a substantial memory, however, as well as interface electronics, power supply, etc., which add considerably more costs. Between 1977 and 1985 decreasing electronics cost and increased manufacturing volumes should bring these costs down sharply.

Nonimpact printing technology will have a major effect on the hard-copy printer option (number 3), not so much in price as in speed. A typical speed range of 120–200 cps is forecast for such printers in 1977, rising to 200–1,000 cps in 1985.

The low-speed OCR device (number 4) is assumed to be hand fed, often using a hand-held "wand" rather than an automatic scanner. The cost of a paper feed mechanism is thereby avoided, so the cost of the device is largely determined by its case, power supply, and the very low cost of its electronics. Similar logic applies to the badge reader (number 5); marketing, packaging, and similar costs become dominant as electronics cost becomes insignificant.

The voice input device (number 6) is novel; only a few exist today in limited applications. Limitations on the recognition capability of the devices are expected to remain severe, but gradual improvement should permit the devices to see more use in controlled applications. Costs are not expected to decline much between 1977 and 1985, because complexity is expected to increase as recognition limitations are reduced. The voice response device (number 7) which might complement a voice input device is a central subsystem rather than a terminal; the need to handle multiple lines at high speed will keep its costs relatively high. In this area, too, there will be a tendency to trade off lower electronics cost for greater flexibility.

The purpose of this article is to forecast the capability of future software as perceived by the user, and as it affects his system development and operating resource needs. Coverage of such matters as scheduling algorithms of operating systems, evolution of specific language features, and data base structure is therefore relatively light.

SOFTWARE

Operating Systems

As was indicated in the discussion of computers, many of the functions now performed by operating system software are likely by 1985 to be performed by computer microcode. The major functions that remain, such as job scheduling, non-shareable device allocation, error monitoring, and recovery, will be performed by relatively simple monitors dedicated to specific modes of operation (e.g., batch, time-sharing) operating in some form of virtual machine environment. Evolution to this functional pattern will be slow and will still be in its early stages in 1977, but the trend is already visible.

Operating systems today also perform a set of functions designed to help the user manage the flow of work fed to the computer, its effective overall utilization, and the events surrounding it. These system management software functions are expected to increase steadily in importance and sophistication, but are also expected to become more clearly separated from the operating system proper. They are therefore considered separately in the article.

System Management Software

By 1985, computer systems should automatically log and report the data needed to control related external activities including tape and disc library control, external job scheduling, and user accounting and billing. Logging will also be automatic for references to protected files: the file management system will control access codes symbolically, and the logging system (inaccessible to any user) will record all

references. This capability, a subset of the automatic recove[...]
should provide adequate file access control for many users.

System performance measurement facilities will be needed [...]
logging facilities, so that users can observe the performance of pr[...]
ing of system resources, and the like. These measurement fac[...]
interface with the diagnostic and error-detection software. Sys[...] [...]
and specialized software firms have already developed very competent performance
measurement software; little further evolution is needed for adequacy of measurement at an overall level. System simulation software, to help users predict the behavior of changed systems and configurations, will be based on the results of the
measurement software and is similarly well advanced.

Data Management

The structure of data base management systems will evolve toward that shown in
Figure 1. The major elements of such systems will be a unified data management

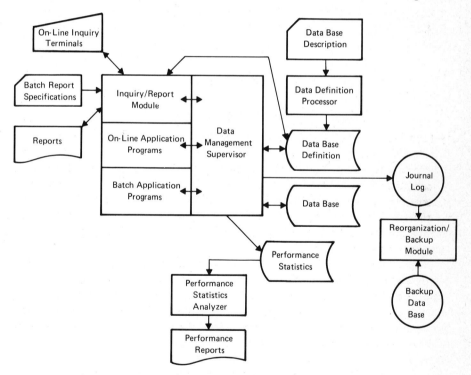

Fig. 1. *Data base management systems will evolve toward the structure shown here,
with the unified data management supervisor as the heart of the system. The inquiry/
report module acts as a front-end to the supervisor, while the reorganization/backup
module and the statistics analyzer help to constantly improve efficiency. A greater
degree of independence between the data definitions and the applications programs
can be expected, as well as more flexible data structures.*

rvisor (roughly corresponding to current host language processors), an inquiry/ report module which will become a front end to the DMS, a data definition processor, a reorganization/backup module, and a performance statistics analyzer. The evolution and function of each of these modules is described below.

The data management supervisor (DMS) is the heart of the data management system. Its main function is to manage inputs to and outputs from the data base that originate from on-line or batch application programs or from the inquiry report module. To do this, it makes use of the separately stored data base definition, which is output from the data definition processor. The DMS may call upon standard I/O service programs or special ones built to support itself. One of the reasons for this will be the trend toward modularity in system level software; this will enable users to select certain options which the DMS provides and to omit other options, thereby reducing overhead for features which are not desired.

Specific functions which will be provided by the data management supervisor are as follows:

• *Access control.* One function of the DMS will be to control access from programs to the data base. Users accessing the system via the inquiry/report module or interfacing directly from application programs will have to supply passwords or equivalent identification means. The DMS will ascertain whether a particular user or class of users is entitled to access the data base in a variety of ways. This includes read-only and read-and-write capabilities.

• *Record performance statistics.* Another function of the DMS will be to record access and usage statistics in a variety of ways. These statistics will be utilized for several purposes: (1) they will enable the data base administrator to determine who is accessing the data base and how; (2) they will enable him to tune or reconfigure the data base structure for optimal performance by the application programs; and (3) they will help him to reorganize the data base at appropriate points for performance or backup purposes.

• *Handle concurrent updates.* Partially through improved software, but possibly including additional hardware facilities such as test and set instructions, the ability to handle and resolve conflicts in multiple concurrent update situations will be greatly enhanced. Lockout mechanisms at the individual record level will be provided. Deadlock resolution capabilities will be provided which will enable the system to hold one particular requestor in a suspended state and allow another transaction to be processed to completion before the first transaction gains control of any record. Improved performance in handling multiple requests of all types will be provided through reentrant coding of the DMS.

• *Backup/recovery.* The DMS will record on an independent device all activities which have affected the data base. This will entail the writing on a data base journal log file of before-and-after images of data base records, which are time stamped and linked to the source that caused the change. Using this file, the DMS will be able to restore the data base to its condition prior to a failure, either by applying after-images to a backup copy, or by applying before-images to the present copy if the failure was not physical in nature.

• *Integrity checking.* Future data management supervisors will pay increased attention to insuring the integrity of the data base. This will include the ability to code into the data base definition certain relationships and consistency checks which must exist between individual records or fields. Each time a record or field is altered, these consistency checks will be invoked and the transaction rejected if the prescribed conditions are not met.

The functions of the inquiry/report module will evolve into a front-end general purpose routine for the unified data management supervisor. From the user's point of view, it will provide many of the same features that current inquiry/report systems provide, such as the ability to specify a variety of searching criteria, to locate records which satisfy these criteria, to perform elementary calculations on appropriate data, and to format specialized or one time output reports from the data base. In addition, provided authorized access permission has been obtained, the user will be able to write simple programs that, in effect, update the data base. These can be used for data entry operations or can be utilized to process simple transactions.

As greater numbers of systems are built with a data base system in mind, normal output report requirements will be met through the inquiry report module. This will permit easy modification of report formats and contents as desired by user departments. The reporting function will be carried out by application programs only in the case where reports are a direct byproduct of application program update functions or where complex computations or high volumes are involved that require high efficiency.

The data definition processor is utilized to define the structure of the data base and other characteristics such as access limitations. Two evolutions can be seen in data definitions for future data management systems. These are:

• A greater degree of data independence. Data independence refers to the separation of the data definition and processing from the application program. This is provided by the independently stored data base definition, which is output from the data definition and processing application program. The individual programmer will need to know less about the structure of the data base, and additional degrees of freedom in reorganizing or altering the data base structure will be possible without affecting the operation of individual programs. Specifically, it will provide for independence from physical media, the ability to add new record types to the data base, the ability to add new fields to existing records, and the ability to alter relationships among elements and records.

• Additional flexibility in data structuring and access methods. Currently, most data management systems impose a primary data structuring scheme, usually a variant of an inverted index or chained organization. Future systems will allow the user more flexibility in selecting data structures and access methods, and will make it easier to accommodate different and more complex data structures. This will be done in such a way as to optimize the data structure for the given application and thereby improve the performance of the system.

The functions of the reorganization and backup module include selectively copying the data base and reorganizing it for improved efficiency. These functions are included in the same module because they can be done concurrently. Backup copies of the data base need to be kept on a volume basis so that recovery from an individual volume failure is possible.

The performance statistics analyzer module is responsible for analyzing the statistics which are output by the DMS and reporting them to the data base administrator. This is one way that the administrator will monitor the activity against the data base. He may either choose to reorganize the data base or restructure it on the basis of the analyzer output.

Languages

Job control or command languages will become simpler, partly because the greater degree of automation within computer systems will mean that the user is required to provide less detailed instructions, and partly because of specific efforts to make them so. Simplifications will include higher level symbols closer to natural language and interactive command language facilities to help users specify their wants. In the inquiry/report module of the data management system, command language and programming language will have combined, in a sense; the user will not be conscious of providing one or the other but addresses the machines in a combination of both. Command languages with these features have already appeared in some systems: they can be expected to become general early in the forecast period.

The functional capabilities of APL, PL/1, COBOL, and FORTRAN will not have changed dramatically by the early 1980s. Dialects for these languages will have been developed to accommodate structured programming techniques and to help with testing and event synchronization problems. They will also have better capabilities for dealing with data bases.

For the smaller machines, cross-compilers will be available and subset dialects of the full-scale languages will be used for these machines. For the medium- and large-scale monoprocessor or multiprocessor machines, compiling will be done on the target machine, and complete sets of the languages will be available. Special versions of these common languages will be utilized on machines which have special architectures, such as array processors.

The development of very high level languages (problem-oriented languages) will continue, perhaps to the point where users can more easily develop standard applications such as payroll, accounts receivable, billing, materials control, accounts payable, and similar systems. These will be implemented most widely on minicomputer-class systems so that the user can be his own programmer; several software offerings approaching this ideal have already appeared. Problem-oriented languages will not, however, become the standard way of developing an application system. Most systems that require heavy production use will probably be developed using procedure-oriented languages. An "end-user language" may become available for the nonprogrammer, evolved from COBOL, BASIC and inquiry languages.

Program Development Aids

While programming languages are not expected to change much, facilities for supporting programmers will evolve considerably. Concepts of structured programming will have evolved enough by the early 1980s to be incorporated in interactive syntax and logic checking software that automatically accumulates code into modules for subsequent batch linking and initiation; a combination of interactive and batch debugging processes will be used. Listings prepared as a result will probably be useful as part of the documentation for programs. System testing, where numerous programs are involved, will be facilitated by automatic generation of test data (a by-product of the data base management system), and by automatic linking and generation of tables including data names, and symbolic identifications of system resources used, and the like. These, too, will be available to form part of program documentation; these program development aids will make the programming process partly self-documenting. These programming aids should have a substantial effect on programmer productivity; on the average, the time required to write and test a program should be reduced by half or better. This assumes, however, that the programmer is working in the structured form which the software is designed to accept.

Software Cost

The trend toward separate pricing of software should continue. The operating system is not expected to be software priced, largely because (as discussed above) it will have fewer functions and be less visible to the user. The other varieties of software discussed above will be separately priced, however. The prices will vary by function and by level of computer system for which they are designed, but for the large multiprocessor system, 1985 software prices are forecast to be as follows:

Data Management System	$60,000
Language Processor (each)	$12,000
System Management Complex	$60,000
Message Control Program	$50,000

These are generally higher than prices for equivalent products today, because of their greater value and complexity (the data management and system management software will often dominate the user's interaction with his computer). Separate prices for program development aids are not shown, because they will probably be bundled with the compilers.

COMMUNICATIONS

Controllers

Small computers and terminals will usually be provided with a limited degree of communications control capability, since the great majority will be connected to communication lines at least part of the time, and the cost of incorporating an extra level 1 component processor for the purpose will be insignificant. With the larger monoprocessors and multiprocessors, and perhaps in some cases with miniprocessors used in networks, stand-alone communications controllers or front-end processors will be generally used. The host dependent communications controllers that are now widely used will, in general, be superseded by them. These stand-alone controllers will receive, route, sequence, and account for streams of message traffic of varied kinds independently of the connected host processors. They will have their own disc storage, I/O equipment, and software. Their functions will be essentially the same as those now performed by comparable devices, but their costs are expected to drop dramatically because of the decreased costs of their processors and other components. Table 10 summarizes their expected costs by major component. Costs are shown only for large systems (incorporating redundant cpu's and failsoftness) designed to work primarily with multiprocessors, and for intermediate systems that will work primarily with monoprocessors.

Small systems are not expected to exist, because the small host computers should have a limited degree of intrinsic capability. Message control software will be

TABLE 10
COST FORECASTS FOR COMMUNICATIONS CONTROLLERS

	1974	1977	1985
A. Large systems			
2 CPU's* + 128K memory	$ 80,000	$30,000	$15,000
100-megabyte disc	55,000	22,000	10,000
Line adapters (100)	45,000	25,000	10,000
Host interface	12,000	8,000	2,500
Total	$192,000	$85,000	$37,500
B. Intermediate systems			
CPU* + 16K core	$ 12,000	$ 6,000	$ 3,000
2-megabyte disc	5,000	1,000	100
Line adapters (20)	6,000	4,000	1,500
Host interface	8,000	5,000	2,000
Total	$ 31,000	$16,000	$ 6,600

* Processors include teleprinter control, power supply system, power fail/auto re-start, memory protection, and similar features.

unbundled and priced separately; an estimated software purchase cost for a large system is show in Figure 2 in the software cost section. It is conceivable that the cost of software for communications controllers will become greater than that of hardware.

Networks

Data traffic in the U.S. is expected to continue growing at its recent 35% annual rate continuously through 1985. A variety of new and expanded carrier services will evolve to meet this demand.

The Bell System expects to be serving about 100 major metropolitan areas in the United States with an interconnected digital data service (DDS) by about 1978. We anticipate that the initial point-to-point networking of DDS will be followed by switching digital transmission service before 1985.

The first of several domestic satellite systems commenced operation in early 1974, offering new flexibility to data communications services in terms of routing, capacities, and pricing structure. Western Union's Westar network typifies one approach to domestic satellite systems, wherein large earth stations are looped to users via conventional terrestrial links. A more innovative approach, where small earth stations are placed at the user's operating location, should be implemented in this time period.

The emerging specialized common carriers, such as MCI and Datran, have entered a critical period of development. We expect that at least two of the MCI-type networks will achieve economic viability. However, it will be several years before the form of their unique service offerings is definite.

This expansion of common carrier services is likely to be accompanied by substantial reductions in charges, brought about both by technological improvement and increased competition. Figure 2 forecasts the overall trend of line costs through 1985 for three standard speeds; the average reduction should be about 50% through 1985. (The actual reductions will of course be discontinuous because they will result from specific tariff changes; these are overall trends.)

In addition to acquiring leased or dial-up lines, users will increasingly have the alternative of using packet switching. Packet switching technology was developed specifically to improve data communications services and make possible network performance capabilities suited to the requirements of terminal-to-computer and computer-to-computer communications. Briefly, these capabilities are as follows:

• Rapid response time—packets are transmitted through the network with an average delay of less than a second. The network delay incurred in the establishment of a connection between a terminal and a host is on the order of a second.

• High reliability—multiple transmission paths between packet switching nodes protect against line failures. High reliability at each node can be insured with redundant packet switching equipment.

• Very low error rate—powerful error detection systems insure that transmission errors are detected and corrected before packets are delivered to users, thus providing users with virtually error free data communications.

• Dynamic allocation of transmission capacity—the capacity of a packet switched network is dynamically shared among the nodes so that if any node is momentarily relatively inactive, more transmission capacity is available to all other nodes.

• Charges proportional to traffic volume—a user consumes significant network resources only when he is actually sending or receiving data. Thus, his charges can be based primarily on the quantity of data transmitted rather than on-line holding time, line capacity (bandwidth), or distance, as is the case in communications circuit tariffs.

• Improved transmission facilities—as new transmission facilities are introduced by the carriers, a packet switching network can quickly take advantage of these developments and pass the improvements in cost and/or performance on to the user without any effort on the user's part.

Because these advantages of packet switching will appeal to many users it is expected to become widely available and grow steadily. However, since its growth

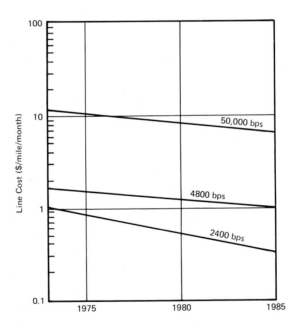

Fig. 2. *The trend of data transmission line costs will be down through 1985, with an average cost reduction of 50% for transmission at each of three standard speeds.*

involves the establishment of extensive networks requiring a great deal of capital, the rate of growth of packet switching services will be slower than demand would permit.

A FINAL WORD

This article includes many generalizations and brief, overall forecasts of product areas that are in fact broad and complex. The data processing industry is heterogeneous, and many products will prosper that vary widely from those forecast here. Nevertheless, at an overall level this article may provide useful guidance to users concerned about tomorrow's products.

CHAPTER 3

MANAGING THE
INFORMATION SYSTEM

The management information systems literature is filled with discussions of planning, organizing, and controlling the direction and operation of information systems. However, before trying to incorporate all of the ideas into one system, the total information requirements of each organization should be carefully analyzed. This chapter considers different philosophies of management as to how the information system should operate, the problems of planning the system, and several control aspects related to the management of the information system.

Tremendous growth in the size and complexity of organizations has made necessary the use of more advanced planning and control techniques by both general management and accountants. With this growth and the introduction of the computer and its related technology, most organizations have undergone structural changes. Heretofore, the problems of design, implementation, operations monitoring, and control of computerized systems were unknown to most organizations; therefore, management had to make the necessary changes to maintain control over the organization.

In "Managing the Crises in Data Processing," Nolan discusses six stages of data processing growth and the problems related to each stage. With growth comes management headaches, and several problem areas and possible solutions are outlined in the article. One of the most important things that managements need to know is the actual stage of growth that their companies are in and the problems that accompany different growth stages. Nolan provides identifying benchmarks of each stage and discusses proper guidelines for action in managing each stage.

One of the structural changes that has greatly affected the organization in general, and the accountant in particular, is the move toward greater decentralization. The cumulative and permanent effects of computerized data processing on the organization are in many instances unclear and sometimes questionable. For the accountant the impact is definite but the advantages and disadvantages are unclear. The shift from one structure to the other influences internal reporting practices and in many cases causes major changes in basic managerial and cost accounting systems.

Initially the introduction of the computer into an organization has been for the purpose of substituting mechanized data processing for manual processing. With this change the accountant can easily cope; but with the advanced utilizations of the computer the accountant must be properly trained to accept and understand the new role of accounting. To improve the accountant's understanding of his or her changing role as the organizational structure changes, a knowledge of the underlying concepts of centralization and decentralization is necessary.

The above problems are addressed by Fried in "Centralization: 'To Be or Not to Be'." He begins by discussing the reasons for both centralization and decentralization. Because the philosophy of management may differ between how management operates the business and how the computer system needs to be operated, the author concentrates his discussion on the problems of coordination and organizational options. Change is traumatic and the organization should not undertake structural change without careful planning and strong incentives. Just because there is an organizational option is not reason enough to make changes in structural design. Almost every attempt at structural change generates advocates and opponents for every option, and the likelihood of satisfying everyone is impossible. It is essential to remember that most proposals for organizational change have political overtones, and the final selection must be based on sound reasoning after weighing the advantages and disadvantages of all proposals.

As organizations become more complex their managements are forced to develop formal plans and methods for the information system. Improving and formalizing the concepts of planning are difficult for most organizations and McFarlan, in "Problems in Planning the Information System," addresses ways to make planning easier. The author advocates manageable planning and provides an outline of the factors that an organization must consider in developing its planning. He also examines several administrative structures that have worked well in large organizations.

After carefully studying 15 companies, McFarlan and his associates have determined the characteristics that they believe constitute good planning practices. This article discusses several of their findings starting with the factors that induce a company to begin formalized planning. Next, the author presents the elements of good planning and the interaction that must take place for effective planning to become a reality. Also, McFarlan briefly examines planning as it relates to centralization and decentralization. Lastly, two cases are used to illustrate the basic principles of planning and to point out possible strengths and weaknesses.

Unlike many writers who provide general concepts of planning, McFarlan has not only described the basics of planning but also has shown in detail what good plans should consist of and how planning relates to other management areas. Also, the realism of the two cases provides the reader with something practical rather than just another theoretical approach to planning.

Another important aspect of managing the system involves the allocation of computer costs to internal users. In "Controlling the Costs of Data Services," Nolan develops seven steps that organizations can undertake to design an effective charge-out system. His idea is to develop an allocation system where more control over costs can be placed with those who use data services and therefore hold the users accountable for their computer service costs.

In the companies that he studied, Nolan found most methods of charging computer services to be unacceptable to the service users. Because of the unhappy users many organizations are formalizing the allocation of computer service costs. Nolan has studied these formalized systems and found that they, too, have problems and communications breakdowns between managers and data processing. Hopefully the plan that he proposes will solve many of these problems and enable computer service cost allocation methods to operate more smoothly in the future.

The design, implementation, and management of computer systems cannot be conducted on an unplanned, unsound basis. The complex assemblage of computers, people, and systems—along with their related costs—are such that effective systems management cannot be performed without considering the needs of the total information system. More and more modern organizations are looking for a new generation of managers just as they change generations of computers. If today's manager does not join this new generation through education and retraining, he cannot survive in the modern organization. And, it is equally important to remember that accountants, who are generally considered a part of the total management team, must also change with the changing organization.

Managing the Crises in Data Processing

RICHARD L. NOLAN

The member of the corporation's steering committee did not mince words:

> I'm telling you I want the flow-of-goods computer-based system, and I am willing to pay for it. And you are telling me I can't have it after we have approved your fourth running annual budget increase of over 30%. If you can't provide the service, I'll get it outside. There are now reliable software companies around, and my people tell me that we should take seriously a proposal that we received from a large minicomputer vendor.

The reply of the vice president of information services was not well received:

> I'm at the edge of control. It isn't any longer a question of financial resources. My budget has grown from $30 million in 1975 to over $70 million in 1978. The technology is getting ultracomplex. I can't get the right people fast enough, let alone provide suitable space and connections to our sprawling computer network.

On returning to his office, the vice president knew that the steering committee member would be going ahead with the minicomputer. There was no way that the corporate technical staff could provide the flow-of-goods functions for the money or within the time frame that the minicomputer vendor had promised. Something was not right, even though he could not put his finger on it.

The vice president mused at the irony of it all. Five years ago he was brought in to set up a corporate computer utility after a similar period of poorly understood growth (that growth had been the undoing of his predecessor). Now key questions were being asked about a similar growth pattern of the data processing (DP) budget, and he did not have the answers. He wished he did!

The plight of the vice president of information services is not singular. The rapid growth in DP services that many companies experienced in the mid- to late 1960s is occurring again in numerous companies. The resurgence is confusing.

The senior managements of some of these companies thought that the DP control structures put in place during the 1970s, such as chargeout, project management, and consolidation of computing activities under tight budgetary control, would contain any future budget growth. Nevertheless, the annual DP budget growth rates are exceeding 30%. Further, just the annual budget *increments* are equal to the total size of the budgets four or five years ago. The confused top executives of these companies are searching for answers to what underlies this growth. Is it good? Will it stop? What are the limits?

The answers are not obvious, but a probing of the status of the DP activities in different companies and of the current technological environment sheds light on the situation and provides insights into the management actions that are needed to prepare for and manage the growth.

SIX STAGES OF GROWTH

Studies I have made during the 1970s of a series of companies—3 large corporations early in this decade, 35 companies several years ago, and then a large number of IBM customer concerns and other corporations since then—indicate the existence of six stages of growth in a company's DP function. These stages are portrayed in *Exhibit I*.

Exhibit I. SIX STAGES OF DATA PROCESSING GROWTH

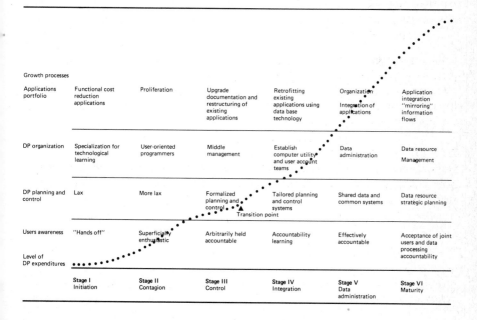

Growth processes	Stage I Initiation	Stage II Contagion	Stage III Control	Stage IV Integration	Stage V Data administration	Stage VI Maturity
Applications portfolio	Functional cost reduction applications	Proliferation	Upgrade documentation and restructuring of existing applications	Retrofitting existing applications using data base technology	Organization Integration of applications	Application integration "mirroring" information flows
DP organization	Specialization for technological learning	User-oriented programmers	Middle management	Establish computer utility and user account teams	Data administration	Data resource Management
DP planning and control	Lax	More lax	Formalized planning and control Transition point	Tailored planning and control systems	Shared data and common systems	Data resource strategic planning
Users awareness	"Hands off"	Superficially enthusiastic	Arbitrarily held accountable	Accountability learning	Effectively accountable	Acceptance of joint users and data processing accountability
Level of DP expenditures						

The scheme shown in this exhibit supersedes the four-stage concept I described in HBR in 1974.[1] The four stages described then continue to be valid, but the experience of recent years reveals a larger and more challenging picture.

This exhibit shows six stages of DP growth, from the inception of the computer into the organization to mature management of data resources. Through mid-stage 3, DP management is concerned with management of the computer. At some point in stage 3, there is a transition to management of data resources. This transition involves not only restructuring the DP organization but also installing new management techniques.

To understand the new picture, one must look at the growth in knowledge and technology, at organizational control, and at the shift from computer management to data resource management. I will consider each of these topics in turn.

Burgeoning of Knowledge

Organizational learning and movement through the stages are influenced by the external (or professional) body of knowledge of the management of data processing as well as by a company's internal body of knowledge.

The external body of knowledge is a direct response to developments in information technology. It is concerned with developments in the theory of DP management as well as with the collective documented experiences of companies. The internal body of knowledge, however, benefits from the external body of knowledge but is primarily *experiential*—what managers, specialists, and operators learn firsthand as the system develops.

It is important to realize how greatly DP technology spurs the development and codification of an external, or professional, body of knowledge. For this reason a company that began to automate business functions in 1960 moved through the stages differently from a company that started to automate in 1970 or 1978. The information technology is different, and the extent of professional knowledge on how to manage the DP technology is much greater in the latter years. Not only is the external body of knowledge more sophisticated, but the information technology itself is more developed.

Control & Slack

Organizational learning is influenced by the environment in which it takes place. One possible environment is what might be called "control"; a second might be called organizational "slack," a term coined by Richard M. Cyert and James G. March.[2]

---

[1] See my article written with Cyrus F. Gibson, "Managing the Four Stages of EDP Growth," HBR January-February 1974, p. 76.

[2] Richard M. Cyett and James G. March, "Organizational Factors in the Theory of Oligopoly," *Quarterly Journal of Economics,* February 1956, p. 44.

In the *control* environment, all financial and performance management systems—including planning, budgeting, project management, personnel performance reviews, and chargeout or cost accounting systems—are used to ensure that DP activities are effective and efficient. In the *slack* environment, though, sophisticated controls are notably absent. Instead, incentives to use DP in an experimental manner are present (for example, systems analysts might be assigned to users without any charge to the users' budgets).

When management permits organizational slack in the DP activities, it commits more resources to data processing than are strictly necessary to get the job done. The extra payment achieves another objective—nurturing of innovation. The new technology penetrates the business's multifunctional areas (i.e., production, marketing, accounting, personnel, and engineering). However, the budget will be looser, and costs will be higher. Management needs to feel committed to much more than just strict cost efficiency.

The balance between control and slack is important in developing appropriate management approaches for each stage of organizational learning. For example, an imbalance of high control and low slack in the earlier stages can impede the use of information technology in the organization; conversely, an imbalance of low control and high slack in the latter stages can lead to explosive DP budget increases and inefficient systems.

Exhibit II shows the appropriate balance of control and slack through the six stages. In stage 3 the orientation of management shifts from management of the computer to management of data resources. This shift, associated with introduction of the data base technology, explains the absence of entries in the computer columns after stage 3.

Exhibit II OPTIMUM BALANCE OF ORGANIZATIONAL SLACK AND CONTROL

Stages	Organizational slack		Control		
	Computer	Data	Computer	Data	Objective of control systems
Stage 1	Low		Low		
Stage 2	High		Low		Facilitate growth
Stage 3	Low	Low	High	Low	Contain supply
Stage 4		High		Low	Match supply and demand
Stage 5		Low		High	Contain demand
Stage 6		High		High	Balance supply and demand

Shift in Management Emphasis

In stage 2 more and more senior and middle managers become frustrated in their attempts to obtain information from the company's computer-based systems to support decision-making needs. *Exhibit III* helps to explain the root of the problem. The exhibit is based on a fictional corporation that represents a kind of composite of the organizations studied. The spectrum of opportunities for DP equipment is called the "applications portfolio."

The triangle illustrates the opportunities for cost-effective use of data processing to support the various information needs in the organization. Senior management predominantly uses planning systems, middle management predominantly uses control systems, and operational management predominantly uses operational systems. At every level there are information systems that are uneconomic or unfeasible to automate, despite managers' desires for faster and better data.

In stage 1 in this organization, several low-level operational systems in a functional area, typically accounting, are automated. During stage 2 the organization encourages innovation and extensive application of the DP technology by maintaining low control and high slack. While widespread penetration of the technology is achieved by expanding into operational systems, problems are created by inexperienced programmers working without the benefit of effective DP management control systems. These problems become alarming when base-level systems cannot support higher-level systems—in particular, order processing, production control, and budgetary control systems. Maintenance of the existing, relatively poorly designed systems begins to occupy from 70% to 80% of the productive time of programmers and systems analysts.

Sometime in stage 3, therefore, one can observe a basic shift in orientation from management of the computer to management of the company's data resources. This shift in orientation is a direct result of analyses about how to put more emphasis, in expanding DP activities, on the needs of management control and planning as opposed to the needs of consolidation and coordination in the DP activities themselves. This shift also serves to keep data processing flexible to respond to management's new questions on control or ideas for planning.

As the shift is made, executives are likely to do a great deal of soul searching about how best to assimilate and manage data base technologies. The term "data administration" becomes common in conferences, and there is much talk about what data administration controls are needed.

But there is little effective action. I believe there is little action because the penetration of the technology is obviously low at its inception, and a combination of low control and high slack is the natural balanced environment to facilitate organizational learning. However, at the same time the seeds are being sown for a subsequent explosion in DP expenditures.

Stage 3 is characterized by rebuilding and professionalizing the DP activity to give it more standing in the organization. This stage is also characterized by

Exhibit III APPLICATIONS PORTFOLIO LATE IN STAGE II

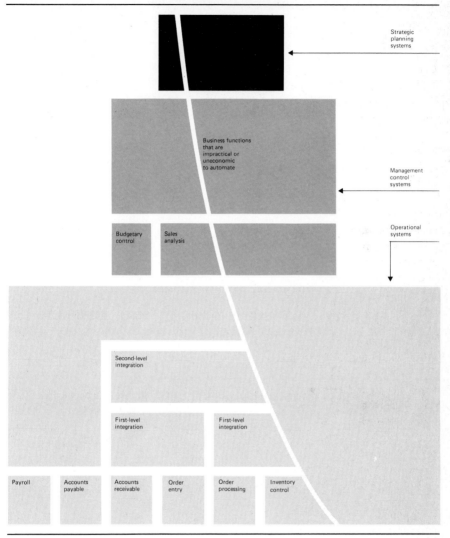

Note: An example of first-level integration is a purchase order application that uses order processing and inventory status information. An example of second-level integration is a vendor payment application that uses accounts payable and purchasing information.

initial attempts to develop user accountability for the DP expenditures incurred. Usually these attempts take the form of chargeouts for DP services. Unfortunately, both the conceptual and technical problems of implementing user accountability lead to confusion and alienation; real gains in accountability are not made. Nevertheless, the trends of DP charges in user budgets are rarely reversed.

Consequently, during stage 3 the users see little progress in the development of new control systems while the DP department is rebuilding, although they are arbitrarily held accountable for the cost of DP support and have little ability to influence the costs. Even the most stalwart users become highly frustrated and, in a familiar phrase, "give up on data processing."

Explosive Growth

As stage 3 draws to a close, the DP department accomplishes its rebuilding and moves the data base and data communication technologies into several key application areas, such as order entry, general ledger, and materials requirements planning. In addition, the computer utility and network reach a point where high-quality services are being reliably provided to the users. When these accomplishments are realized, a subtle transition into stage 4 takes place.

Just when users have given up hope that data processing will provide anything new, they get interactive terminals and the various supports and assistance needed for using and profiting from data base technology. Already they have benignly accepted the cost of DP services. Now, with real value perceived, they virtually demand increased support and are willing to pay pretty much whatever it costs. This creates DP expenditure growth rates that may be reminiscent of those in stage 2, rates one may have thought would not be seen again.

It is important to underscore the fact that users perceive real value from data base applications and interactive terminals for data communication. In a recent study of one company with more than 1,500 applications, I found that users ranked their data base and interactive applications as far and away more effective than users of conventional or batch technology ranked their applications. This company has been sustaining DP expenditure growth rates of about 30% for the past four years. More important, the users of the new applications are demanding growth to the limits of the DP department's ability to expand.

The pent-up user demand of stage 3 is part of the reason. But a more important part of the reason is that the planning and control put in place in stage 3 are designed for *internal* management of the computer rather than for control of the growth in use of it and containment of the cost explosion. *Exhibit IV* shows the typical pattern of starting and developing internal and external (that is, user-managed) control systems. Late in stage 4, when exclusive reliance on the computer controls proves to be ineffective, the inefficiencies of rapid growth begin to create another wave of problems. The redundancy of data complicates the use of control and planning systems. Demands grow for better control and more efficiency.

Exhibit IV GROWTH AND MATURATION OF DATA PROCESSING PLANNING AND CONTROL

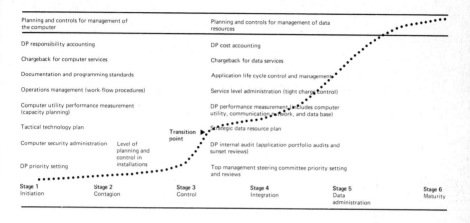

Planning and controls for management of the computer				Planning and controls for management of data resources		
DP responsibility accounting				DP cost accounting		
Chargeback for computer services				Chargeback for data services		
Documentation and programming standards				Application life cycle control and management		
Operations management (work-flow procedures)				Service level administration (tight charge control)		
Computer utility performance measurement (capacity planning)				DP performance measurement includes computer utility, communication network, and data base)		
Tactical technology plan		Transition point		Strategic data resource plan		
Computer security administration	Level of planning and control in installations			DP internal audit (application portfolio audits and sunset reviews)		
DP priority setting				Top management steering committee priority setting and reviews		
Stage 1 Initiation	Stage 2 Contagion		Stage 3 Control	Stage 4 Integration	Stage 5 Data administration	Stage 6 Maturity

In stage 5, data administration is introduced. During stage 6, the applications portfolio is completed, and its structure "mirrors" the organization and the information flows in the company.

IDENTIFYING THE STAGE

How can executives determine what stage of development their corporate data processing is in? I have been able to develop some workable benchmarks for making such an assessment. Any one of the benchmarks taken alone could be misleading, but taken together these criteria provide a reliable image. I will describe some of the most useful benchmarks so management can gain a perspective on where it stands and on what developments lie down the road. For a visual portrayal of the benchmarks, see *Exhibit V.*

It is important to understand that a large multinational company may have divisions simultaneously representing stages 1, 2, 3, 4, and perhaps 5 or even 6. However, every division that I have studied has its DP concentrated in a particular stage. Knowledge of this stage provides the foundation for developing an appropriate strategy.

First–level Benchmarks

The first step is to analyze the company's DP expenditure curve by observing its shape and comparing its annual growth rate with the company's sales. A sustained growth rate greater than sales indicates either a stage 2 or 4 environment. Then, analyze the state of technology in data processing. If data base technology has been introduced and from 15% to 40% of the company's computer-based applications

Exhibit V BENCHMARKS OF THE SIX STAGES

		Stage 1 Initiation	Stage 2 Contagion	Stage 3 Control	Stage 4 Integration	Stage 5 Data administration	Stage 6 Maturity
First-level analysis	DP expenditure benchmarks.	Tracks rate of sales growth.	Exceeds rate of sales growth.	Is less than rate of sales growth.	Exceeds rate of sales growth.	Is less than rate of sales growth.	Tracks rate of sales growth.
	Technology benchmarks.	100% batch processing.	80% batch processing. 20% remote job entry processing.	70% batch processing. 15% data base processing. 10% inquiry processing. 5% time-sharing processing.	50% batch and remote job entry processing. 40% data base and data communications processing. 5% personal computing. 5% minicomputer and microcomputer processing.	20% batch and remote job entry processing. 60% data base and data communications processing. 5% personal computing. 15% minicomputer and microcomputer processing.	10% batch and remote job entry processing. 60% data base and data communications processing. 5% personal computing. 25% minicomputer and microcomputer processing.
Second-level analysis	Applications portfolio.	There is a concentration on labor-intensive automation, scientific support, and clerical replacement.		Applications move out to user locations for data generation and data use.		Balance is established between centralized shared data/common system applications and decentralized user-controlled applications.	
	DP organization.	Data processing is centralized and operates as a "closed shop."		Data processing becomes data custodian. Computer utility established and achieves reliability.		There is organizatinal implementation of the data resource management concept. There are layers of responsibility for data processing at appropriate organizational levels.	
				◀ Transition point			
	DP planning and control.	Internal planning and control is installed to manage the computer. Included are standards for programming, responsibility accounting, and project management.			External planning and control is installed to manage data resources. Included are value-added user chargeback, steering committee, and data administration.		
Level of DP expenditures ▶	User awareness.	Reactive: End user is superficially involved. The computer provides more, better, and faster information than manual techniques.		Driving force: End user is directly involved with data entry and data use. End user is accountable for data quality and for value-added end use.		Participatory: End user and data processing are jointly accountable for data quality and for effective design of value-added applications.	

are operating using such technology, the company is most likely experiencing stage 4.

In the light of International Data Corporation's research on the number of companies introducing data base management systems technology in 1977 (shown in *Exhibit VI*), I believe that roughly half of the larger companies are experiencing stage 3 or 4. This is further corroborated by evidence that 1978 saw the largest annual percentage growth in the total DP budgets of U.S. companies—from $36 billion to an estimated $42 billion, or a 15½% increase.

As shown in *Exhibit VI*, about 55% of IBM installations in 1979 will have data base technology, compared with only about 20% in 1976. I feel that this means the explosive stage 4 in DP expenditures can be expected in the next two to five years in most companies; the increases may be somewhat moderated by continuance of

Exhibit VI DATA BASE MANAGEMENT SOFTWARE INSTALLED AND PROJECTED TO BE INSTALLED ON IBM MEDIUM- TO LARGE-SCALE COMPUTERS IN THE UNITED STATES

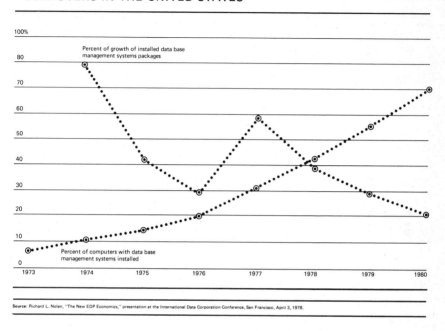

Source: Richard L. Nolan, "The New EDP Economics," presentation at the International Data Corporation Conference, San Francisco, April 3, 1978.

the impressive technological advances that have improved prices and equipment performance.

Second-level Benchmarks

The second step is to focus on the four growth processes shown in *Exhibit V*. Each major organizational unit of the company, such as a subsidiary, division, or department, should be listed. Then the growth processes associated with each organizational unit should be identified. For example, a decentralized subsidiary generally has all four growth processes, from expansion in the applications portfolio to an increase in employees' awareness of DP potentials and functions (see the left-hand side of *Exhibit V*). However, a division using the services of a corporate computer utility is likely to have only two of the growth processes—expansion in the applications portfolio and in user awareness.

Next, identify the stage (see the bottom of *Exhibit V*) of each of the growth processes associated with the organizational unit. Use growth as an example in the applications portfolio. The approach used for this process is similar to that for any of the processes. The procedure is as follows:

1. Define the set of business functions for the organizational unit that represents cost-effective opportunities to apply DP technology. I call this the "normative

applications portfolio." It represents the business functions that would be receiving DP support if the company had achieved stage 6 maturity. *Exhibit VII* portrays such a scheme.

2. Taking each function in turn, indicate for each set of systems the support that data processing gives to the function in the organization. Ask, "What is it doing for our business?" I suggest doing this by shading the space for the function on the normative applications portfolio; use a ten-point scale to shade the function at 10%, 40%, 80% or whatever amount seems appropriate. Looking at all the shaded functions as a whole, judge the level of support given the system as a whole.

3. Then, match the support given the system as a whole with the benchmarks shown to the right of *Exhibit VII*. For instance, 80% support of operational systems, 20% support of management control systems, and just a faint trace of support for strategic planning systems would show the organization to be at stage 3.

4. Next, look for matches and mismatches between DP investment and the key functions that contribute to the company's return on investment or profitability. For example, if the company's business is manufacturing, and if half of the DP system investment goes to support accounting, a red flag is raised. The possibility of a mismatch between expenditure and need should be investigated.

After the functional assessment, one should conduct a technical assessment of the applications. The technical assessment gets at the concern of whether the DP activity is using current technology effectively. Benchmarks used include individual system ages, file structures, and maintenance resources required.

Again using a scheme like that described for *Exhibit VII*, compare the support given by data processing to the different corporate functions with the technical assessment. Are the DP systems old, or are the file structures out of date, or are there other shortcomings indicating that up-to-date technology is being neglected? Such neglect may be the result of managerial oversight, of a shortsighted desire to make a better annual profit showing, or of other reasons. In any case, it means that a portion of the company's assets are being sold off.

During the definition and assessment of the applications portfolios for a company, a DP "chart of accounts" is created. The business functions identified in the applications portfolio are the "objects of expenditures." Creating the chart of accounts is an important step in achieving the level of management sophistication required to effectively guide this activity through stages 4 and 5 and into the stage 6 environment.

So much for the applications portfolio analysis. Using the same sort of approach, management can turn next to the other growth processes shown in *Exhibit V* for second-level analysis. When the analysis is completed, management will have an overall assessment of the stage of the organization and of potential weaknesses in its ability for future growth.

If complete analyses of this type are made for all important organizations—divisional and functional—of the company, management will have a

Exhibit VII INVESTMENT BENCHMARKS FOR DP APPLICATIONS

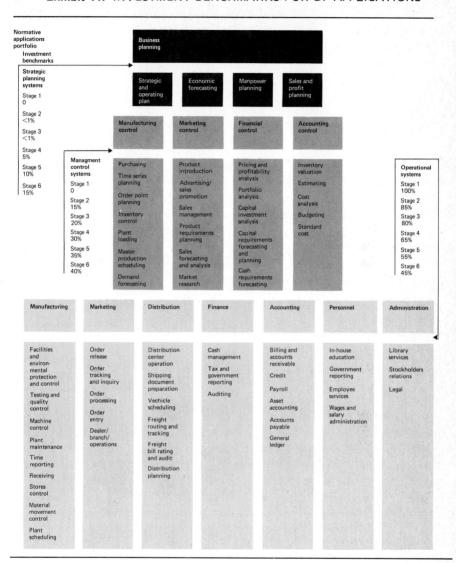

Exhibit VIII ONE COMPANY'S STAGE ANALYSIS

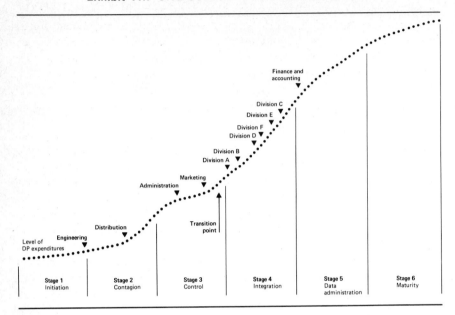

corporate-wide profile. *Exhibit VIII* is an example. Such a profile provides the foundation for developing an effective DP strategy.

GUIDELINES FOR ACTION

In most sizable U.S. corporations, data processing is headed for an extremely rapid growth in the next five years. This growth is not necessarily bad; in fact, I believe that if the growth can be managed, it will be the most cost-effective growth experienced to date. Here are five guidelines for managing the growth successfully.

1. Recognize the Fundamental Organizational Transition from Computer Management to Data Resource Management

With the introduction of data base technology in stage 3, an important shift in emphasis occurs—from managing the computer to managing the company's data resources. Obviously, this transition does not occur all at once. It appears first in the analysis of the late stage 2 applications portfolio and is a result of the requirement to restructure it so that applications can be tied together efficiently.

The transition also becomes apparent during the implementation of controls. Difficulties with chargeout systems that are computer-oriented cause management searches for alternative ways to achieve user accountability. This often leads to the conclusion that the user can be accountable for the functional support, but data processing must be accountable for management of shared data.

The key idea is to recognize the importance of the shift in management emphasis from the computer to data and then to develop applications and planning and control systems to facilitate the transition. Applications should be structured to share data; new planning and control systems should be data-oriented.

2. Recognize the Importance of the Enabling Technologies

The emerging information technologies are enabling companies to manage data economically. It is important to emphasize the word *economically*. What companies did only a few years ago in establishing large central DP utilities is no longer justifiable by economic arguments. Data resource management changes the economic picture.

Data base and data communication technologies are important from an organizational standpoint. Sprawling DP networks are enabling new approaches to management control and planning. We can now have multidimensional control structures such as function (e.g., manufacturing, marketing, and finance), product, project, and location. Managers and staff can be assigned to one or more of the dimensions. Through shared data systems, senior management can obtain financial and operating performance reports on any of the dimensions in a matter of hours after the close of the business day, month, quarter, or year.

Last, but not least, developments in on-line terminals, minicomputers, and microcomputers are opening up new opportunities for doing business at the operational level. Airline reservation systems, for example, no longer stand alone in this area; we now can include point of sale (POS) for the retail industry, automated teller terminals (ATMs) for the banking industry, and plant automation for the manufacturing industry.

3. Identify the Stages of the Company's Operating Units to Help Keep DP Activities on Track

A basic management tenet is: "If you can't measure it, you can't manage it." The applications portfolios of a company provide data processing with a chart of accounts. In the past, management lacked a generic and meaningful way to describe and track a DP activity—that is, to locate it in relation to the past and future. However, there is now a generic and empirically supported descriptive theory of the evolution of a DP activity—the stage theory. One can use this theory to understand where the company has come from, which problems were a result of weak management, and which problems arose from natural growth. More important, one can gain some insight into what the future may hold and then can try to develop appropriate management strategies that will accomplish corporate purposes.

4. Develop a Multilevel Strategy and Plan

Most DP departments have matured out of the "cottage industry" era. They have reached the point where they are woven into the operating fabric of their companies. There are many documented cases of the important impact that a computer failure of mere hours can have on a company's profitability.

Nevertheless, many DP departments continue to hold on to the cottage industry strategy of standing ready to serve any demands that come their way. This can have a disastrous effect when stage 4 begins to run its course. The extent and complexity of corporate activity make it impossible for data processing to be "all things to all users." Consequently, decisions will have to be made on what data processing will be—its priorities and purposes; when, where, and whom it will serve; and so on.

If the DP management makes these decisions without the benefit of an agreed-on strategy and plan, the decisions are apt to be wrong; if they are right, the rationale for them will not be adequately understood by users. If users do not understand the strategic direction of data processing, they are unlikely to provide support.

Development of an effective strategy and plan is a three-step process. *First*, management should determine where the company stands in the evolution of a DP function and should analyze the strengths and weaknesses that bear on DP strategies. *Second*, it should choose a DP strategy that fits in with the company's business strategy. And *third*, it should outline a DP growth plan for the next three to five years, detailing this plan for each of the growth processes portrayed in *Exhibit V*.

It is important to recognize that the plan resulting from this three-step process is, for most companies, an entry-level plan. Thus the plan cannot and should not be too detailed. It should provide the appropriate "blueprint" and goal set for each growth process to make the data processing more supportive of the overall business plan. It should also be a spark for all those in DP activities who want to make their work more significant and relevant to corporate purposes.

5. Make the Steering Committee Work

The senior management steering committee is an essential ingredient for effective use of data processing in the advanced stages. It provides direction to the strategy formulation process. It can reset and revise priorities from time to time to keep DP programs moving in the right direction.

From my observation, I think that the steering committee should meet on a quarterly basis to review progress. This would give enough time between meetings for progress to be made in DP activities and would allow the committee to monitor progress closely. Plan progress and variances can make up the agenda of the review sessions.

Centralization: "To Be or Not To Be?"

LOUIS FRIED

PROBLEMS ADDRESSED

First National of N.Y. Decentralizes

Citing major cost savings, First National City Bank has launched what amounts to a massive decentralization effort with its computer operations.

The bank, the second largest in the country, will reportedly replace two IBM 370/165s with six 145s and a host of small computers. The current FNCB data processing operation costs the bank roughly $2.8 million a year. The new system would run about half that, John L. Hughes, a bank vice president, estimates.

FNCB reportedly will rely heavily on Interdata 8/32s because they combine COBOL, ITAM, OS/MT, and a multitasking operating system. The small computers will tie into the six 145s which will replace the 165s in mid-1976. Several other major financial institutions are also rumored to be looking into decentralization efforts, and one is reportedly on the verge of signing a major contract with a mini manufacturer.

The above news article is another indicator of the continuing effort to find an optimum solution to the "centralization versus decentralization" controversy. Similar articles, claiming substantial savings, have appeared in the past and will appear in the future. Savings will be claimed for centralizing operations as well. (A vast project for centralizing all computer operations of North American Rockwell Corporation has been completed within the last two years.)

As examples proliferate on both sides, concerned managers ask, "What is the answer?" The question should be, "Is there an answer?" This portfolio is intended to explore the latter question. It is most appropriate to start this analysis by examining the objective reasons for both strategies of EDP organization.

REASONS FOR CENTRALIZATION

Economy of Scale

The reason most frequently used for centralization of operations is economy of scale. This economy results from several factors:

1. Decentralized small computers may have unused capacity. Centralization on a large computer could eliminate the cost of such unused capacity.

2. Individual small computers may be overloaded, generating pressure for upgrading equipment or purchasing expensive service bureau time. Centralization on a large computer could absorb this overload against the unused capacity of other small computers.

3. In terms of floor space, electricity, air conditioning, and other facility costs, a single large installation is less costly than multiple smaller installations.

4. The number of support personnel (operators, systems programmers, etc.) is lower for a large installation than for multiple small installations.

5. A single large installation would require fewer management and staff personnel than multiple smaller installations.

6. A large computer is more cost effective than a small computer. This is normally the strongest argument advanced for economy of scale. It is derived from "Grosch's Law," advanced in the early 1950s. H. R. Grosch suggested that the performance of a computer increases as the square of its cost. That is to say, a computer that costs twice the amount of another should deliver four times the processing power. (Of course, the reverse is implied also. One larger computer could do the work of four smaller machines at half the cost of the four.)

Kenneth Knight tested Grosch's suggestion on the IBM 360 series using two different instruction sets, one scientific and one a commercial mix.[1] He discovered that economies were even greater than those predicted by the law, especially for scientific work. (See Figure 1.)

Sophistication of Applications

Large computers have other advantages beyond economy of scale. Higher internal speed, greater primary storage, and higher channel capacity may make practical certain applications that are not feasible on smaller equipment. In some cases, though it is technically possible to operate an application on a small computer, doing so would absorb a major part of the computer's capacity.

Some examples might include scientific computation, data base management systems, and the maintenance of, and access to, hierarchically structured files for manufacturing systems. In such cases, the application would justify the larger capacity computer, which would, in turn, justify the elimination of smaller computers in the organization in order to utilize the excess capacity of the large machine.

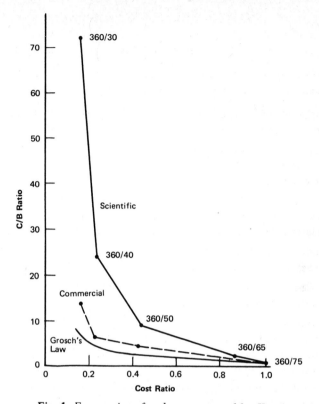

Fig. 1 *Economies of scale as measured by Knight*

The trend toward increasing the use of on-line access to large data base systems further emphasizes the need for a central operation that can provide this access to a common file to users throughout the organization. A decentralized operation is inherently incapable of providing this service.

Quality of Systems Development

Empirical evidence lends weight to several reasons for centralizing the systems development and programming functions. Centralization permits design and use of common data bases (as indicated above) as well as common standards for data entry and input validation. It can also enhance the ability to utilize development and project control techniques that result in specific benefits to the organization. Some of these benefits include the ability to:

1. Implement a data dictionary, saving considerable time in research for system modification.

2. Establish and enforce systems documentation standards to ensure future maintainability of systems and programs.

3. Regulate standards for user documentation, reinforcing the ability to achieve the optimum benefits of the system.

4. Establish and review proper programming techniques to minimize inefficient use of computer facilities.

5. Evaluate development projects from an overall organization perspective, including establishing priorities, conducting cost/benefit analyses, etc.

6. Avoid redundant development of similar systems for different divisions of the organization.

7. Apply good project control techniques, ensuring that projects are completed on time and within estimated cost.

In addition, there are substantial differences between the abilities of large and small installations to attract and retain highly qualified technical personnel. The smaller installation will frequently suffer a higher turnover rate as talented individuals outgrow the opportunities available.

The retention of highly qualified personnel provides the centralized group with the capability to apply a higher level of expertise to the solution of problems. This personnel can then provide a greater range of alternative solutions to problems for evaluation by management, resulting in a lower cost of development, operation, and future maintenance of the systems. Furthermore, a lower turnover rate aids in reducing both maintenance costs and risk exposure on systems.

Martin Solomon[2] has taken a "negative approach" by outlining the deficiencies of smaller installations. He indicates that smaller installations cannot provide the same quality of work for the following reasons:

1. Limited supply of competent personnel.

2. Loss of continuity due to turnover.

3. Lack of task specialization.

4. Lack of standard procedures.

5. Inadequate documentation.

6. Inability to integrate data and application.

7. Lack of professional EDP management.

8. Lack of exciting, employee-attracting work.

9. Lack of cross-fertilization.

10. Inability to direct overall use of computing.

Control of EDP Expense

There remain reasons for centralization that do not properly fit the general areas previously explored. Most of these involve controlling the cost of EDP on an organization-wide basis; they include the following.

1. Decentralized installations are difficult to audit for operation or project development efficiency, effectiveness, and conformity to overall organization standards. They may, therefore, be less visible (and perhaps more expensive) than centralized installations.

2. Smaller installations generally do not have personnel with the skills and experience necessary to perform a good job of equipment selection. They may rely on simply ordering from the current vendor or the largest vendor of equipment. Frequently, the *equipment salesman* will develop the specifications.

3. Smaller installations generally do not have the negotiating power or experience necessary to develop favorable contracts with hardware and software vendors. So-called "national accounts," centrally controlled, frequently contract at better terms and prices than individual divisions could manage.

4. Centralization reduces the cost and improves the quality of personnel training. One current example is the use of video-assisted instruction by larger organizations.

5. Smaller installations generally lack sufficient overview to perform adequate advance planning. This may result in unexpected requirements for equipment or development.

6. Decentralization tends to obscure management's vision into the total cost of EDP for the entire organization. Some of the costs of decentralized data processing functions may be recorded in other organizational components (e.g., manufacturing or accounting). It is difficult for top management to apply measures of cost (such as EDP cost as a percentage of sales) or effectiveness to a decentralized EDP function.

REASONS FOR DECENTRALIZATION

As part of the continuing discussion that is almost as old as the computer industry, there have been as many reasons advanced for decentralization as for centralization. However, in contrast to the arguments for centralization, which center around *efficiency*, the arguments for decentralization center around *effectiveness*.

Economies

Until recently, there had been little attempt to argue that decentralization of general-purpose computers offered anything but added cost. In the last few years, with the advent of the minicomputer, a potential for savings has developed.

A single-purpose mini, programmed for a specific application, is extremely inexpensive. Furthermore, if it is used as an office machine, it does not require the operator or programming and technical support of a general-purpose computer. Some minicomputers can provide on-line inquiry, saving the cost of telecommunications for this type of service. The high cost of telecommunications, the overhead associated with large general-purpose computers, and the potential for under-utilizing the capacity of a large centralized installation combine to mitigate the case against decentralization.

Sophistication of Applications

It is frequently proposed that the applications developed for a centralized operation are far more complex and costly than those required to meet divisional needs. This results from the attempt to meet the needs of all divisions in a single common application. A version of Parkinson's Law seems to be applied in a large installation—applications grow to take advantage of all available capability and capacity.

A major problem that results is that maintenance to the system for one division could potentially affect all divisions. Similarly, if the central computer is disabled, all divisions are adversely affected. Whereas the decentralized installation has only two areas of vulnerability—software and hardware—the centralized installation presents the divisional user with several, including:

1. Central computer hardware.
2. Central computer software.
3. Communications lines (and/or mail and delivery services).
4. Local RJE or terminal hardware.

Not only are the risks increased, but centralization forces divisions into a common mold that may be inappropriate for their needs. The specific hardware required for one user may be different than that required by another. These different needs could be satisfied with far less complexity and cost by smaller installations.

The centralized installation also creates a contention for machine time between users. Several jobs running concurrently on a single machine may delay response time to all users and, invariably, create competition for priority of service.

Quality of Systems Development

Proponents of decentralization argue convincingly that local analysts are more attuned to local needs. They acquire an in-depth knowledge of divisional operations, managerial preferences, and organizational strengths and weaknesses. This enables them to establish requirement specifications and to design systems that are optimally suitable for the local user. The local analyst can also respond more quickly to the emergencies and changes in priorities of local management. In contrast, setting priorities in a centralized environment places the division manager in contention with other users for the central systems development resources.

The closer association between the analyst and user also means that the user would become better educated in regard to the benefits and limitations of EDP. The user would also have tighter control of EDP personnel and the quality of their work in relation to the perceived needs.

Control of EDP Expense

Even though most centralized installations allocate their costs to users according to the resources used, the division manager feels little responsibility for the total cost of EDP. The salaries paid to central personnel, the overhead rates, the choice of equipment, the time spent on projects, and the share of resources used all seem to be out of the division manager's control. As a result, the allocations are viewed as "paper dollars." The manager's only incentive is to obtain as much service as he can from the centralized installation. In the long run, this drives up the cost of the installation. In contrast, if the EDP resource is local, the division manager has direct insight into all the elements of cost and a direct incentive to control those costs.

EDP ORGANIZATIONAL DESIGN

The initial organization of the EDP function is rarely planned. It begins where the need is first perceived—at corporate headquarters for corporate accounting, or at a major division headquarters for accounting or manufacturing applications. Even computers installed for scientific purposes have been partially diverted to business applications. From these random beginnings, an organizational form for the EDP function grows within the firm.

In the 1950s and early 1960s, the options were limited. If data processing was required at a divisional location, an EDP facility was installed. If cost prohibited multiple installations, or if the firm could afford the time necessary to mail or ship data input and reports, the firm established a central EDP facility at headquarters.

By the late 1960s technical options in the form of data transmission capabilities began to appear. Innovative EDP organizations recognized the potential for either centralization or decentralization inherent in data communications. Given the opportunity to implement alternatives, all that was needed was motivation—and motivations existed in four areas:

- Type of corporate organization.
- Economic considerations.
- Service considerations.
- Political considerations.

Types of Organization

A 1968 survey of 108 large manufacturing companies indicated that 91 percent of the companies which were organizationally decentralized had computer facilities similarly divisionalized. In the same survey, 57 percent of the centralized companies were found to have decentralized computer facilities.[3] Since that time, there may have been some change to this apparent correlation. In the 1968 booming business environment, divisions with substantial decision-making autonomy created their own EDP resources. As the economic crunch of the 1970s extended, however, many decentralized companies emphasized stricter management of controllable expenses.

An obvious target (often as great as two to three percent of sales) was EDP expenditures. As a result, while many other aspects of company operation remained decentralized, tighter control was exercised on EDP. This contributed to some emphasis on centralization of EDP to achieve better corporate visibility and control. Nevertheless, a significant correlation probably remains between the form of the EDP organization, the form of the corporate decision-making structure, and the size of the company and its divisions.

Economic and Service Considerations

While these considerations have been addressed separately in the first two sections of this portfolio, they are frequently linked to any analysis of the EDP organization.

In describing the stages of EDP growth, Gibson and Nolan entitle the third stage "formalization"—the point at which the initial explosive growth of EDP in an organization is over, there is a moratorium on new applications, and the emphasis is on control. It is at this point that the issue of centralization versus decentralization arises.

> ...because the company reaches a turning point in the way it uses the resource. As the EDP function evolves from the early cost-reduction applications of initiation and early growth toward projects aimed at improving operations, revenues, and the quality of unprogrammed and strategic decisions, the influence of the computer will begin to move up and spread out through the organization. The function may truly be called MIS instead of EDP from this stage forward.[4]

Part of the rationale for combining the economic and service considerations is the fallacy of isolating EDP cost from the other operating costs of the organization. Improvements in the level of service to users may result in cost-saving efficiencies or profit-making effectiveness far in excess of the EDP cost differential achieved by one EDP organizational method over another. In other words, the company must accept the principle of suboptimization of certain functions in order to achieve overall optimization of company operations.

These concepts were summarized very effectively by Robert B. White, Executive Vice President of First National City Bank, in an address before a financial systems marketing seminar conducted by NCR Corporation.[5] In describing the thinking behind the decentralization program referenced at the beginning of this portfolio, Mr. White cited the following points in regard to systems designed for the large-scale multiprogramming computer:

- Such an approach is machine-efficient and people inefficient.

- This approach tends to require that systems which homogenize user requirements be developed.
- The approach, because it is based on the principle of "economy of scale," militates against the ability of the manager to solve the small-scale problems, wherein most of his short-term cost and quality opportunities lie.
- Functional systems tend to erect barriers that hinder the accountability system on which most business organizations are based.
- This approach encourages (indeed, demands) the optimization of specific functions, usually the data processing activity, at the expense of all other functions when the issue is really optimization of the complete system.

In regard to using large-scale computers, White points out that:

- The large-scale computer assumes a level of business understanding that most businesses today simply do not possess.
- The long lead-time needed to integrate systems in order to take advantage of the sheer scale of these computers is out of all proportion to business needs.
- It is often necessary to practically rebuild our buildings to establish facilities for the large-scale computers.
- Basically, we end up grasping for technical solutions to what are fundamentally business problems.

While these views represent a justification for a decentralized approach and the use of minicomputers located at the user site, there is considerable merit in the arguments. There is even greater merit in the consideration of EDP and non-EDP costs together. Depending upon immediate circumstances, the combination of these factors could serve to justify moves toward either centralization or decentralization on the basis of total economic and service factors.

Political Considerations

It would be foolish to assume that organizational, economic, and service considerations are always made in an objective, dispassionate manner. This is probably the exception, rather than the rule.

Almost every attempt at reorganization brings forth advocates for each position. Vested interests and territorial imperatives are challenged. Larger divisions making a greater contribution to corporate profits may push for decentralization of EDP to extend their autonomy of operation. Smaller divisions may "gang up" to oppose decentralization, viewing it as a threat to their ability to obtain a share of the more sophisticated centralized resources.

The incumbent members of an existing EDP organization may fight reorganization proposals that threaten their positions or reduce their authority. Divisions may claim that they obtain inadequate service. Corporate management may protest that it will lose control and the ability to coordinate efforts and direct priorities based on the greatest return to the overall organization. In fact, almost all of the other considerations may become weapons in the political struggle.

It is essential to remember that any proposal for organizational change will become political; that even if the best decision is reached, it will not be reached in a completely rational and objective manner. Because of political factionalism, the final decision must be made at the highest organizational level (chief operating executive) to assure the maximum opportunity for success.

THE PROBLEMS OF EDP COORDINATION

A critical concern of corporate management is control of EDP in the areas of cost, use of resources, and effectiveness. Therefore, regardless of the form of EDP organization, most companies feel that a top EDP executive is required at the corporate level. This executive's minimal responsibilities include coordination of EDP activities between divisions and corporate headquarters, overall planning and monitoring of EDP costs and resources, ensuring effective use of resources, and providing technical advice to top management. These responsibilities may be examined by viewing the specific functions in terms of planning and control.

Planning

The prerequisite to control is planning. To this end, it is necessary to provide corporate management with overall annual and long-range plans. These involve:

1. Maintaining a concise description of the current status of EDP systems, hardware, personnel, and costs.

2. Gathering corporate and divisional systems requirements and priorities.

3. Developing, in coordination with users, an annual systems plan that is consistent with the resources available, to accomplish the desired projects.

4. Reviewing the systems plan for potential impact on hardware capacity and staffing.

5. Advising top management of the alternatives available for achieving planned objectives.

The plans must be developed with consideration of recent trends in the EDP field which impose constraints or add complexity to the system design function. For example, constraints arise through the use of common systems by several divisions, through the need for divisional systems to interface with corporate systems, and through the use of large standardized data bases.

The complexity and variety of solutions available in hardware, software, and telecommunications make overall system design more difficult. The range of responsibilities includes: remote job entry to a centralized computer, intelligent terminals, distributed processing on small- or medium-sized computers, specialized applications on single-purpose minicomputers, and the development of networks for communications and processing, to name a few.

This is further complicated by the acquisition of equipment from various vendors and by the rent, lease, or purchase options—an almost bewildering proliferation of alternatives that leads to the need for control.

Control

The tasks relating to control are considered necessary in either form of organization. They include:

1. Monitoring budgets and performance against budgets for all EDP activities.
2. Reviewing and approving the purchase of equipment, software, and outside services.
3. Applying management guidelines to the selection of major projects (in terms of cost/benefit analysis and return on investment).
4. Establishing and maintaining standards for operating procedures, project development, programming methods, and documentation.
5. Auditing progress and performance on major projects.
6. Maintaining a specialized staff to provide services (such as technical advice on hardware, communications, or sophisticated systems or applications software) to the applications development or operating groups throughout the company.

The strength of these control functions is contingent upon the management style of the corporation's top executives. A strong top executive who desires centralized control of EDP costs and use of resources may impose this type of control through the corporate EDP executive, even if the EDP functions are decentralized. On the other hand, even a centralized EDP function probably will not work well if the top executive desires divisional autonomy in the selection and operation of systems.

ORGANIZATIONAL OPTIONS

The range of options for organizing the EDP function can best be analyzed by recognizing that the systems development and operation functions are not constrained to take identical organizational paths. In fact, a matrix of options exists that may be illustrated by Figure 2.

This diagram simply indicates that there are a large number of possible organization structures and combinations that may be viable. Since every possible combination cannot be examined, this portfolio concentrates on the more obvious alternatives for operations and systems development.

EDP Operations

Distributed input and control Techniques of this type have existed since the beginning of commercial data processing. In its simplest form, distributed input and

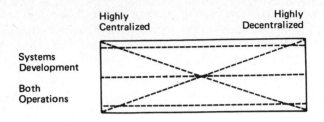

Fig. 2 *EDP organizational options*

control means that the user has the responsibility for controlling input and converting input to machine-readable form. Users may have their own data entry equipment (keypunches or key-to-magnetic media) or may contract the work to outside vendors.

This approach has several advantages.

1. The user feels more responsibility for, and "ownership" of, the system.
2. Data entry costs are not a part of the EDP organization's budget.
3. The EDP control costs are lowered when users control input and validate output.
4. Data entry problems can be corrected by direct user involvement.
5. Personnel costs may be reduced by using data entry employees for clerical and control tasks at the user site.

Disadvantages may be:

1. Higher equipment costs due to decentralization and the resultant inability to fully utilize equipment capacity.
2. Depending on the size of the installation, additional supervisory employees may be needed.

Some developments during the last few years have made this approach increasingly attractive. Data communication techniques have reduced the time of transmitting the data before and after processing. On-line and key-to-disc data entry permit extensive editing and validation of data prior to processing. (This not only results in quick correction of data locally, but frequently saves the cost of processing incorrect or incomplete data.) Where central computer capacity is available, on-line data entry also makes the resultant files immediately ready for processing or can provide for on-line update of data bases.

Distributed processing This has become a new "buzzword" in the EDP industry. Very simply, it means that data is processed at separate computer installations which transmit data to each other. The following excerpts from a recent article illustrate one approach to distributed processing.

SAN FRANCISCO. The Bank of America has developed and is now implementing a distributive processing system to meet its requirement of having current information on more than 10 million accounts accessible around the clock from more than 1,000 statewide branch locations.

This approach became inevitable, according to John D. Foster, senior systems consultant, three years ago when a feasibility study showed a single integrated large-scale data base system wouldn't handle that kind of load with the reliability the bank had to have.

. . . the hardware modules are linked through standard communications interfaces, simplifying the transfer of information among the specialized processors and the end-users. Beyond that, all parts of each system are duplicated to protect the bank against failure anywhere in the system, Foster said.

The number of files, the size of the corporate data base, the volume of activity, and the time constraints were cited by Foster as factors that ruled out the single, large mainframe approach.

. . . the bank also foresaw a hazard in depending on a single mainframe, even if software could be found to support the required workload. "If that computer decided to take a lunch break, we'd be in a real jam. But a 'hot' standby large-scale computer was an expensive solution," Foster added.

. . . each of these segmented distributive systems could communicate with all the others, so when an inquiry or transaction against a different part of the data base came in, it would be handled automatically.

The linkage extends between the bank's two data centers—one here and one in Los Angeles—as well as between systems in the individual centers, Foster noted.

. . . initially, these systems are intended to support inquiries and data capture on checking and savings accounts. Close to 4 million transactions must be posted to the 10 million accounts overnight, and these are handled by a mainframe-based batch processing system, he explained.

In its turn, the batch system passes a copy of the updated data base to the distributive systems each morning so the inquiries and transactions coming in that day are matched against current information.

COMPUTERWORLD, March 8, 1976

Bank of America personnel call this a distributive system because the entire data base is still retained for batch processing on central mainframes, but the processing work of inquiry and transaction posting is distributed.

It becomes obvious that there are also permutations of the technique which can fall into the general classification of distributed systems. These may include partially or completely distributed data bases.

One company maintains its inventory records through the use of mini-computer-based on-line systems in all locations. Summarized inventory status is periodically transmitted to corporate headquarters for updating central files. All invoicing, order entry, and inventory-related accounting is done on the mini-computer locally.

Some of the advantages of distributed processing are:

1. "Safety in numbers." The entire operation is not dependent on one main computer. Down-time affects only the immediate local operation.
2. Users feel greater system responsibility and believe the system is more responsive to their demands.
3. Distributed processing costs may not be substantially greater than remote job entry costs since the central installation may be able to operate with a less powerful computer.

Disadvantages include:

1. There may be less corporate visibility into local operations.
2. Divisions may tend to build up their own data processing departments and move to larger equipment.

Remote job entry (RJE) This is a well-established processing method that permits use of a central computer (or time on a service bureau computer) by a local station having tape or card input/output devices, and a printer.

Some advantages are:

1. Speed of transmitting input and output.
2. Extending the use of existing central computer capability at low cost.
3. User feelings of increased system responsiveness.

Some disadvantages are:

1. Users can create or modify central programs from the RJE terminal. This reduces control over the program library.
2. Heavy RJE use can force the central installation into larger equipment. Users are difficult to control.
3. Since the RJE terminal provides all the capability of a large computer, users may tend to develop their own data processing department.

Systems Development Options

Since the extreme ends of the centralization/decentralization spectrum are well known and have been explored earlier in this portfolio, this section will address several variations in use.

User group liaison In almost all EDP organizations, this is a continuing problem that seems to have no solution without additional cost to the company. Two solutions that do seem to work are:

1. Assignment of a person with EDP experience to a division staff. Unless the EDP organization is lucky enough to have an analyst familiar with the user

division and its problems (and can spare the analyst), it is difficult to find someone with knowledge of both worlds. This leaves two options: transfer an analyst from the EDP group (or hire one) and train that person in the needs of the division; or create an "internship" program whereby a person is transferred to the EDP organization for 18 months to two years, after acquiring a thorough working knowledge of the user area. He/she is then transferred back to the user staff after he/she gains programming and analysis training and experience. The writer has used both techniques with substantial success.

2. Assignment of analysts within the EDP organization as "account managers" to specialize in the needs of, and communication with, a particular division or user function. While this method provides greater control by the EDP group, experience seems to indicate that it does not satisfy the user as well emotionally.

Decentralized analysis This method has been recommended as a way of improving user satisfaction while retaining the benefits associated with centralized design and programming. In this concept, the user maintains a staff of analysts who define system requirements, establish user priorities, participate in acceptance testing, and direct users in implementation.

An American Management Association research study performed in 1968 indicated that large corporations tend to encourage divisions to maintain their own systems staffs while the programming staff is located with the hardware.[6] Several other authorities in the EDP field indicate that this seems to be a frequently selected organization pattern.

Some advantages of this method are:

1. User control of the staff permits local direction, flexibility, and assignment of priorities.
2. Analysts are more responsive to the user who is their "boss."
3. Analysts become thoroughly familiar with user problems, personnel, and requirements.
4. Analysts protect the interests of the user.
5. Acceptance testing prior to implementation may be more rigorous.
6. User project managers may enhance visibility and control of EDP costs.

Disadvantages include:

1. Smaller staffs are more vulnerable to turnover and less likely to have technical expertise in certain areas.
2. Corporate documentation and design standards are more difficult to maintain.
3. Selection of projects may easily deviate from corporate return-on-investment guidelines.

4. Friction between the divisional analysts and central programmers and analysts may result from conflict over design criteria.

5. Control of applications design as it affects the economic utilization of hardware is difficult to maintain.

6. Divisions tend to invent their own solutions to problems rather than use corporate-wide systems. This adds substantially to all EDP costs.

Decentralized analysis and programming This method emphasizes many of the above advantages and disadvantages. Those advantages relating to user responsiveness are enhanced. However, acceptance testing and cost control of projects may suffer. The disadvantages relating to maintaining standards and system redundancy tend to become more intense.

Combinations

Combining features of centralization and decentralization is another alternative available once it is realized the hardware and the systems development function are not necessarily coupled. For example:

1. Centralized hardware with decentralized analysis, or analysis and programming.

2. Centralized analysis and programming of distributed small (or mini) computers.

3. Organization by application, with corporate-wide systems centralized, and exclusive division systems decentralized either with hardware alone, or with hardware and development.

REACHING A DECISION

Change is traumatic and the average organization is well advised to avoid it unless it is well justified. For this reason, an EDP manager should look carefully into the question of organizational change before acting. In fact, one key question should be raised before any detailed analysis is performed: *Why is the centralization versus decentralization issue being raised at all?*

If the answer is that the issue is politically motivated (and it frequently is), the manager should attempt to resolve, by means other than organizational change, those factors that created or influenced the political motivation. This can save the time and cost of performing the studies and may avoid the cost of change.

If the issues are in the realm of service, effectiveness, and cost, they must be addressed as "real" issues. It is then necessary to balance the requirements of the divisions against those of the overall corporation in terms of these issues and corporate control of standards, resource utilization, and return on investment.

To resolve the issues, the manager must determine all the appropriate questions or considerations for both the EDP organization and the company, and apply certain weighting factors to a range of positive-through-negative answers. The resulting matrix will permit an objective evaluation.

In this evaluation, initial attention should be paid only to developing proposed alternative organizational designs and comparative costs, since the exposure of the latter to top management may resolve the question. If, however, the top executive is primarily service-oriented rather than cost-oriented, this may not accomplish the task. Each EDP manager must determine the organizational and management climate of his individual corporation.

The following list, developed by Harvey Golub, provides an excellent foundation for the list of questions that the EDP manager must answer.[7]

Computer Operations

1. How many installations are too small or too large to enjoy economies of scale in consolidation?
2. Are some installations growing so rapidly that consolidation could avoid continual equipment conversions?
3. What communications costs may occur as a consequence of geographic dispersion and movement to interactive and on-line systems?
4. How many different kinds and configurations of equipment, languages, and operating systems are in use?
5. Is it possible to level the workload through consolidation—during a day and over longer periods?
6. Can backup be better provided in consolidated centers?
7. Does centralization allow better control over access to confidential files?
8. Will the organization agree on some degree of commonality?
9. What flexibility now exists in modifying configurations?
10. Can currently employed space be used by other parts of the organization?
11. Can the staff be separated?
12. How many programs must be rewritten?
13. How many programs must be redesigned because of such factors as extensive operator intervention?
14. How dispersed are the users of existing decentralized centers?
15. What business risks would be incurred through consolidation?
16. Should centers be organized by application, organizational unit, or along geographic lines?
17. How competent are the current managers?
18. What quality of service are users now receiving?

Systems Development

1. What opportunities exist for developing common systems?
2. Which functions receive strong central guidance now and, therefore, offer opportunities for commonality?

3. What variation now exists in levels of sophistication?

4. Do we now have adequate quality and quantity of staff?

5. If more than one business exists, how similar or dissimilar are they?

6. Have we grown by acquisition?

7. Do management people typically transfer among divisions?

8. Do we have a strong central philosophy; is ours an operating or a holding company?

9. Do we often add or spin off parts of the business?

10. Are managers familiar with the systems?

11. Is a great deal of missionary and basic educational work needed?

12. Have we purchased duplicate packages?

13. Is there a strong central thrust to management planning, control, and reporting systems?

14. Are users satisfied with their systems?

15. Do the systems meet standards of performance in control and efficiency?

16. Is there an opportunity for one division to learn from another?

17. How much travel would be entailed with any option?

18. Are personnel needs in balance over short periods?

19. Can specialists be efficiently shared?

Planning and Control Functions and Decision Authorities

1. Do centers plan well?

2. Are sound equipment acquisition and financing arrangements employed?

3. Do new projects meet basic ROI and other selection criteria?

4. Are programming, documentation, and control standards in use?

5. Are purchased packages an important component of costs?

6. Do opportunities exist to share or move hardware?

7. Do line managers require external support?

8. How competent are the staffs?

9. Are projects inordinately late or over budget?

10. Are total expenditures well out of line with general industry experience?

11. Does corporate headquarters have a substantial data processing requirement?

RECOMMENDED COURSE OF ACTION

Organizational change should not be undertaken without substantial motivation. The organizational mode of EDP must be congruent with the company's management style, organizational design, corporate objectives, and user needs—with the advantages and disadvantages of each mode assessed in light of the above. Both experience and research indicate that the following conclusions are applicable to a large majority of EDP installations:

1. Centralization of computer facilities is usually desirable since it provides greater capacity, permits more sophisticated applications, and costs less than other approaches.

2. Benefits of centralized programming generally outweigh those of the decentralized approach when considered in the overall corporate context.

3. Systems analysis functions can be performed effectively in either the central or user organization, but, if the centralized approach is used, the user group liaison position becomes extremely important.

In conclusion, there is no easy answer or "one best way" to organize the EDP function. Although, as experience is gained, there may emerge common guidelines for certain industries of given size and geographic distribution, at this point each company must determine the proper solution for itself.

REFERENCES

1. Knight, Kenneth, "Evolving Computer Performance, 1962–1967," *Datamation,* January 1978.

2. Solomon, Martin, "Economics of Scale and Computer Personnel," *Datamation,* March 1970.

3. Dean, Neal, "The Computer Comes of Age" *Harvard Business Review,* January–February 1968.

4. Gibson, C.F. and R.L. Nolan, "Managing the Four Stages of EDP Growth," *Harvard Business Review,* January–February 1974.

5. Reported in *Automatic Data Processing Newsletter,* Volume XIX, November 25 and December 8, 1975.

6. Reichenbach, R. and C. Tasso, "Organizing for Data Processing," *AMA Research Study 92,* 1968.

7. Golub, H., "Organizing Information System Resources: Centralization vs. Decentralization," *The Information Systems Handbook,* edited by F.W. McFarlan and R.L. Nolan, Dow Jones, Irwin, IL, 1975, p.70.

Problems in Planning the Information System

F. WARREN McFARLAN

As computer applications have multiplied in size and complexity over the past decade, the task of managing a company's computer-based resources has become tough and intricate. To maintain good managerial control over this activity, companies are beginning to develop formal plans and formal planning methods for their computer-based information systems (CBIS's).

This development is well justified. Recent field work shows that companies that formally plan their CBIS's have more *effective* CBIS's than companies that do not. A recent study by McKinsey and Company demonstrates this; the pertinent data are given in the insert on page 187, "McKinsey study on effective users."

Also a recent study of my own fully corroborates this finding. My associates and I visited 15 companies that use CBIS's extensively and have a reputation for using them effectively. We interviewed key executives, other users, and EDP personnel in these companies (a) to determine firsthand how effective their systems are, and (b) to analyze the planning processes behind the systems. (See *Exhibit I* and the ruled insert on page 188, "What is 'Effectiveness'?").

By comparing each company's approach to CBIS planning with its effectiveness as a user of CBIS's, we have reached certain hard conclusions on what constitutes good planning practice in this area today. In this article I should like to sketch this kernel of good practice step by step. To do this, I shall proceed as follows:

- Discuss the pressures, both external and internal, that induce a company to plan formally. (These pressures define the parameters of the planning process and of the formal, or written, plan itself.)
- Exhibit the elements of the planning process in a diagram showing how they ought to interact.

Exhibit I PROFILE OF COMPANIES STUDIED

	Number of companies
Sales volume	
Under $200 million	2
$200 million to $499 million	1
$500 million to $999 million	1
$ billion to $1.9 billion	9
$2 billion and over	2
Number of EDP personnel	
Under 100	3
100–499	3
500–999	3
1,000 and over	6
Industry	
Government agency	3
Aerospace	2
Electronics	3
Paper	2
Insurance	1
Oil	2
Railroads	1
Utilities	1

- Summarize my conclusions on the relations that ought to exist between a company's CBIS planning effort and its corporate planning.
- Next, briefly analyze the critical issue of centralization versus decentralization of divisional CBIS facilities within a company. (This issue bears heavily on organization and corporate planning.)
- Finally, present two examples of effective CBIS planning which, although they are widely different, serve to illustrate basic principles by both their strengths and weaknesses. (In a sense, these two examples define the range of possibilities of contemporary information systems planning.)

Of course, the *full* range of planning possibilities is still undefined because this field is very new and evolving fast. Only one company of those we examined had been planning its CBIS systematically for as long as four years.

In general, CBIS planning today is at roughly the same stage of development as corporate planning was in 1960. As a refinement and elaboration, CBIS has naturally lagged behind. The same interest and enthusiasm that attended corporate planning a decade ago attends CBIS planning now, as well as a parallel confusion about how to approach the task.

Every company we visited had sweated with this confusion, and each had experienced enormous changes in its planning processes over the past three or four years. For example:

Three years ago, one multibillion-dollar company completely exhausted its thoughts about the future of its EDP activities in three pages of project names and weak documentations of schedules and costs.

Currently its formal plan is 150 pages long, and is substantively and qualitatively superior to the earlier one in every critical dimension. Its statements of goals and estimates of manpower and facilities needs two years hence are the result of intensive, detailed analysis, and, as such, are worthy of considerable attention.

This company has gone through a learning process that is paying off today in the remarkable effectiveness of its information systems.

PRESSURES TO PLAN

Learning to plan is never easy, but the general conclusions we have drawn from the experience of the pioneering companies in our sample may make it easier to understand how to structure the CBIS planning process and to define the senior manager's role in it.

Let us first look at the pressures that make it so attractive—indeed, necessary—for a company to plan in this area.

Technical Improvements

Because technological change in hardware and software occurs so rapidly, both company staff and consulting groups should hold regular, coordinated reviews of replacement and improvement options to identify significant shifts in cost/performance relationships and develop contingency plans to handle them. A planning system provides a focus for ensuring that this is done.

Also, the lead time for acquiring new equipment is often long, and once acquired, a new piece of equipment must be thoroughly integrated with a company's existing configuration. This integration task is frequently so complex that integration procedures dictate the timing and sequence of acquisitions.

Together, lead time and integration considerations demand that a company plan with an extended time horizon—four years, in one company studied.

At the present time, this particular company has seven decentralized, "stand alone" computer installations, all within a 100-mile radius. They are all medium-sized, and the company is using equipment from two computer vendors.

The company plans first to phase out the equipment of one vendor and then to install two large central processing units (CPU's) at existing locations 15 miles apart. The medium-sized equipment at the other five locations will be converted to remote terminals for batch processing. Once installed, the two new CPU's will be connected for multiprocessing, and finally, a third large CPU will be added to the network within 50 miles of the other two.

MCKINSEY STUDY ON EFFECTIVE USERS

In 1968 McKinsey & Company conducted a study of the computer systems employed in 36 major companies. The sample was designed to cover a wide range of sizes and types of industry, as shown in *Table A*. McKinsey then ranked the companies on three criteria—measurable return on the computer investment, range of meaningful computer applications, and the CEO's assessment of the computer effort—and divided them into "more successful" and "less successful." The results are shown in *Table B*.

TABLE A
BREAKDOWN OF COMPANIES IN THE MCKINSEY STUDY

	Number of companies		Number of companies
Sales volume		Industry	
Under $200 million	6	Airlines	2
$200 million to $499 million	5	Apparel	1
$500 million to $999 million	10	Chemical	8
$1 billion to $1.9 billion	9	Feed	3
$2 billion and over	6	Forest products	1
		Insurance	3
Computer outlay as a percent of sales		Machinery	6
		Paper	1
Under 0.25%	7	Petroleum	3
0.25%–0.49%	7	Primary market	2
0.50%–0.99%	14	Railroads	1
1.0%–1.99%	7	Textiles	1
2% and over	1	Transportation equipment	4

TABLE B
RANKING OF THE STUDY COMPANIES

	More successful users	Less successful users
Companies that plan EDP activities and audit results against plan	9	3
Companies that plan EDP but do not audit results	7	3
Companies that neither plan EDP nor audit results	2	12

WHAT IS *EFFECTIVENESS*?

The 15 companies in the study sample are a diverse group of heavy EDP equipment users. The size of their annual EDP management and hardware expenditures ranges from $2 million to $22 million; the size of their system and programming groups varies from 50 to more than 300 men. *Exhibit I* describes other characteristics of these important users. In our interviews in each of these companies, we focused on the scope of its EDP applications, its current approach to planning, and the overall *effectiveness* of its EDP activity.

Measuring effectiveness of information systems in such a wide variety of contexts is a complex task, and necessarily is heavily subjective. Still, we tried to give objective recognition to the following factors:

The comparative quality of a company's applications in its own critical problem areas—In my view, an application is successful if it is demonstrably profitable, in money or intangible benefits.

The level of service and support furnished by the central computer staff—The best criterion for judging this is user satisfaction.

The innovativeness of the applications—The managerial excellence of a company's basic data flows and management reporting systems is a much more reliable yardstick here than sheer technological sophistication (which might be reflected in extensive real-time system simulation, linear program modeling, etc.).

The competence of the company's professionals—A specialist is best evaluated by his experience, the depth of his background, and his potential for assuming key leadership positions in other, highly progressive organizations.

The tautness, efficiency, and reliability of the EDP operations.

For maximum effectiveness, then, a superior professional group would devise clever, straightforward, up-to-date applications for the areas in which a company needs them most, and keep the data flowing on schedule to the satisfaction of every user in the company.

On these dimensions, we found 10 of the 15 companies highly effective—of these, 9 engaged in serious CBIS planning. Of the 5 marginal ("somewhat effective") companies, 2 engaged in serious CBIS planning. These figures themselves demonstrate the correlation between planning and effectiveness.

Company management states that laying out this particular technical plan has dramatically increased the effectiveness of its developing applications and its short-term decisions on hardware acquisitions.

Volatile environment As new products appear, as the laws change, as mergers and spinoffs take place, the priorities a company assigns to its various applications are likely to change as well. Some low-priority or new applications may become critically important, while others previously thought vital may diminish in significance.

This volatility places a real premium on building a flexible framework within which such change can be managed in an orderly and consistent fashion. Hence recognizing it is vital to planning an effective CBIS.

In a similar vein, every information systems plan is built around very specific assumptions about the nature and rate of technological evolution. If this evolution occurs at a different rate from the one forecasted (as is often the case), then major segments of the plan may have to be reworked.

For example, if the present speed of access to a 10-million-character file were suddenly increased by one order of magnitude with no change in cost, most of the plans we have seen in use would have to be seriously revised, with dramatic reshufflings of priorities and applications structures. And such an increase is by no means farfetched.

Some executives choose to interpret this volatility as a pressure *against* planning. One installation manager stated that while his superiors required him to plan three years ahead, this single factor of technological uncertainty made it impossible for him to estimate realistically more than one year in advance. He said he goes through the long-range planning process as an elegant ritual that makes his superiors happy, without any personal conviction that his output is meaningful.

However, this narrow view of the effective time horizon for CBIS planning was certainly not common among the companies studied. The great majority of those interviewed feel that in this area it is now more effective to work from plans with multiple-year horizons, even though these plans must be revised unexpectedly from time to time, than to try to manage without them. They perceive a difference between revising from an established base and constantly improvising from scratch.

Manpower Scarcity

The scarcity of trained, perceptive analysts and programmers, coupled with the long training cycles needed to make them fully effective, has been the chief factor restraining CBIS development in the companies we studied. To circumvent this restraint, planning is definitely necessary.

An excellent illustration of this appeared in a company whose main business is information systems of a specialized kind—its major product is financial services. The company's primary EDP applications, on which its whole product structure is highly dependent, are intricate financial programs requiring the largest available computers.

When I visited this company, a new, sophisticated set of financial services, deemed significant and potentially very profitable by the executive vice president, had recently been developed in rough outline form. Bringing these services on-stream meant extensive systems design and programming—so extensive that, after a careful review of existing EDP operations, management concluded that this new product could not be operational for 4½ years. Independent consultants subsequently confirmed this estimate.

This estimate assumed that the company would devote 4 of its best analyst-programmers to the job, plus 10 assistants. Assistants could not be spared from regular operations, however, and hence would have to be recruited from outside.

The main reason for such a long preparation was this: the complexity of creating the new service package and the difficulty of consolidating it with existing applications was so great that a new assistant, even one with a strong financial background, would need to pass through a two-year training cycle before he could be fully effective on the project.

Management considered that even this relatively modest rate of recruitment would reduce departmental efficiency on necessary maintenance and developmental work, since senior analysts would have to spend more time than formerly on training and less on developmental work.

The company decided to proceed with the introduction of the new services, but, because of the hiring and training problem, the process is proving very painful and difficult. Planning it earlier would have made it easier. Planning it now, step by step, to make every move count, is smoothing the process somewhat. In general, the scarcity of critical manpower and the length of training cycles make formal planning in this field a virtual necessity.

Scarcity of Corporate Resources

Another critical factor that induces companies to plan is the limited availability of precious company resources, both financial and managerial.

CBIS development is merely one of many strategic investment opportunities for a company, and cash invested in it is often obtained only at the expense of other areas. In most of the companies surveyed the EDP budget is charged directly against earnings. Hence this is a matter of intense interest and a critical limiting factor for new projects in companies under profit or cost pressure.

One must also mention the scarcity of EDP managers available within any given company. Companies' inability to train sufficient project leaders and supervisors has significantly restrained CBIS development. As a result, companies have delayed implementing various valuable applications.

In one case, a company needed to install new systems for message switching, sales reporting, and production scheduling, all at the same time, while maintaining service levels on other existing applications. This simply could not be managed with the company's thin group of skilled project leaders.

Together with the difficulty of hiring qualified people "off the street," the problem of juggling these resource restrictions has stretched the necessary CBIS planning horizon to three or even five years in the companies studied.

Planning as resource drain Even within the EDP area, of course, assigning a man to planning diverts dollars away from system and program development. The extent to which financial resources can be effectively and profitably diverted to planning is still very much a question.

For example, of the companies studied, the one with the heaviest commitment to planning has assigned only 1.5% to 2.0% of its total information service group to planning as a fulltime activity. This may not be a sound yardstick, however, because a major part of its planning task is done by executives, project leaders, and analysts as part of their own general responsibilities; the company has made no attempt to estimate the total size of its aggregate planning effort.

Four organizations studied are quite concerned about the wisdom of establishing a planning group as such, regardless of the contribution it could make. As a highly visible overhead item, the group would be vulnerable to sharp budget cutbacks during periods of economic stress, and these companies realize that this effort would seriously compromise the quality of their CBIS planning. They feel the better strategy is to needle planning in as a component of many people's jobs, thus ensuring the continuity of the effort, albeit at some cost in reduced effectiveness.

Legitimate competitor for funds In general, therefore, these companies are aware of the connection between formal CBIS planning and CBIS effectiveness, and such planning certainly is becoming a serious, legitimate competitor for budgeting funds and managerial personnel.

One company that has chosen to set up an independent planning department has recognized the difficulty and complexity of the task of managing CBIS planning by pulling together a full description of the planning manager's function. This is shown in *Exhibit II*. This manager's department consists of six full-time planners, and many of the company's other 880 analyst programmers and EDP employees are actively involved in its work.

The reader will recognize many of the items in the manager's job description as parameters defined by the pressures to plan which I have been discussing. Before I go on to the details of the written plans themselves, I should mention one additional pressure of great importance.

Trend to Systems Integration

Systems design is currently evolving in the direction of integrated arrays of program packages. Failure to recognize and plan for interdependency and coordination of different packages can lead to major reprogramming in the future or, worse still, to complete revision of a system that cannot accommodate new requirements.

To install a new personnel information system in one major utility, for example, six pieces of information had to be added to the employee's master record used in the payroll system (among other places). The original system design was not structured to accommodate this type of change; consequently, 50 programs had to be patched, requiring 6 months of straight time and 2½ man-years of effort.

Because of the inordinate expense incurred in accommodating these changes, the company inaugurated a systematic effort to plan its CBIS two months later.

Exhibit III indicates the various factors that must be creatively consolidated in the planning process:

- The evolving technology—the state of the art, forecasts of hardware and software improvements, and external computer utility resources.

- The company's EDP resources—its CBIS support base and the resources associated with it.
- The company as a working whole—its organizational structure, resources and capabilities outside the EDP area, its market opportunities, and its strategic planning.

Exhibit II JOB DESCRIPTION OF A PLANNING MANAGER

POSITION TITLE: Manager of Divisional EDP Planning

REPORTS TO: Manager of Divisional EDP Department

WHO REPORTS TO: Controller

SUMMARY:

Develops and maintains a divisionwide, short-range operating plan and long-range strategic plan by which to optimize the return on the investment of resources in information processing systems. Provides planning guidance and direction to EDP division management to maintain consistency of EDP planning and implementation with the overall objectives of the division.

PRIMARY TASKS:

1. To develop and maintain, in consort with operations personnel, short- and long-range objectives and plans for systems to obtain maximum cost/effectiveness both in the EDP function and in the division facilities it services.

2. To help corporate planning management integrate EDP objectives and plans developed at the division into general corporate objectives; and to help corporate planning management optimize cost/effectiveness.

3. To see that resources allocated to the EDP function are adequate for maintaining a rate of technical progress that will enhance the division's competitive position.

4. To see that resources allocated to the EDP function are directed to objectives that will result in maximum return to the division.

5. To review all proposals and requisitions for consistency with established short- and long-range plans.

6. To develop planning techniques and documentation methods that minimize planning effort and maximize planning utility.

7. To review performance evaluations and identify the causes of differences between plans and achievement.

8. To revise plans as dictated by division information requirements.

9. To keep abreast of developments in information technology so objectives and plans of the division reflect the latest advances in the field.

Exhibit III INFORMATION SYSTEMS PLANNING PROCESS

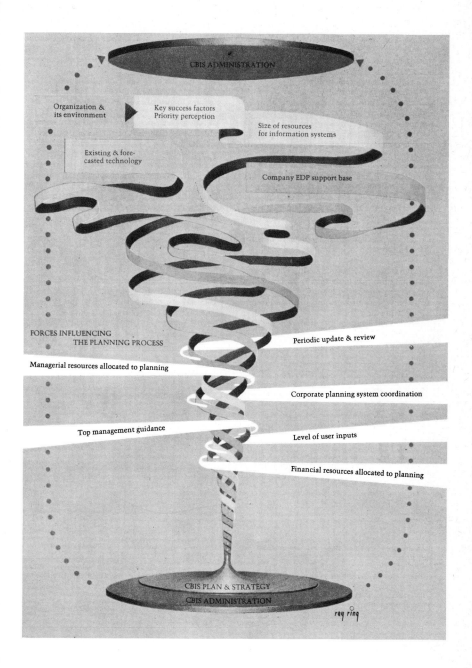

The dynamic model in this exhibit is in some ways similar to that presented by Professor Zani in his recent article, "Blueprint for MIS."[1] However, Zani's point of view and my own differ in the following dimensions:

- I stress the need for a formal, periodic planning process as the driving mechanism which ensures that a company's CBIS will evolve as a viable entity. In a sense, Zani seems more concerned about covering all possible variables; I am more concerned with establishing an analytic process.

- I stress the importance of scanning the technological environment to ensure that new concepts are identified, and, when appropriate, assimilated.

- I distinguish sharply between CBIS planning and administration. When a company's CBIS plan and strategy have been formulated, as at the bottom of *Exhibit III*, the administrative function takes over to make them operational. This administrative implementation naturally augments the company's systems support base (shown at the top of the exhibit); but this administrative function is essentially distinct from the planning function because the two have essentially different missions.

THE WRITTEN PLAN

The most significant factors differentiating the companies that are effective CBIS users from those that are not are the quality and content of their written plans. An outline of overall plan contents taken from the actual documents appears in *Exhibit IV*, but it is important to distinguish the following as the key features of the sound plan:

- The sound plan defines a 2- to 4-year time horizon, with detail declining in the later years. Most of the effective plans specify considerable detail concerning project features, manpower needs, and hardware timing requirements for the first year and then grow more general in format for each succeeding year.

- It embodies a series of detailed descriptions of specific projects. These descriptions include goals and economic analyses for the projects, the projects' aggregate manpower requirements by skills categories, its hardware time requirements for program testing and ongoing operation, and gross project flow charts, accompanied by whatever volume of supporting material is necessary. This last is usually considerable.

- It states a strategy for CBIS development and a broad conceptual scheme for the "final form" of the CBIS. These statements are invariably general in nature; they are loosely related to substantive action proposals and loosely coordinated with the other components of the plan.

---

[1] *HBR* November–December 1970, p. 95.

Exhibit IV THE CONTENTS OF A CBIS PLAN

A. Introduction
1. Summary of major goals, a statement of their consistency with corporate goals, and current state of planning vis-à-vis these goals.
2. Summary of aggregate cost and savings projections.
3. Summary of manpower requirements.
4. Major challenges and problems.
5. Criteria for assigning project priorities.

B. Project identification
1. Maintenance projects, all projects proposed, and development projects.
2. Estimated completion times.
3. Manpower requirements, by time period and job category.
4. Computer capacity needed for system testing and implementation.
5. Economic justification by project—development costs, implementation costs, running costs, out-of-pocket savings, intangible savings.
6. Project control tools.
7. Tie-ins with other systems and master plans.

C. Hardware projections (derived from projects)
1. Current applications—work loads and compilation and testing requirements.
2. New applications—work loads and reruns.
3. Survey of new hardware, with emphasis on design flexibility which will allow the company to take full advantage of new developments in hardware and in software.
4. Acquisition strategy, with timing contingencies.
5. Facilities requirements and growth, in hardware, tape storage, offices and supplies.

D. Manpower projections (derived from projects)
1. Manpower needed by month for each category.
   a. General—management, administrative, training, and planning personnel.
   b. Developmental—application analysts, systems designers, methods and procedures personnel, operating system programmers, and other programmers.
   c. Operational—machine operators, key punchers/verifiers, and input/output control clerks.
2. Salary levels, training needs, and estimated turnover.

E. Financial projections by time period
1. Hardware rental, depreciation, maintenance, floor space, air conditioning, and electricity.
2. Manpower—training and fringe benefits.
3. Miscellaneous—building rental, outside service, telecommunications, and the like.

There is considerable concern within the companies about the utility of this section of the plan. On many dimensions, executives feel that the overall plan is best conceived as a sophisticated project management system that ensures effective use of resources, and hence it may be best not to try to state final objectives in too detailed a form.

• It develops a detailed exposition of future hardware and physical facility requirements. Specific pieces of equipment are identified, along with the optimum timing for their arrival, estimated usage rates, and so forth. These requirements have been systematically developed from existing work levels, new project plans, and specific assumptions concerning overall increases in activity. Software packages such as SCERT, which translates specific program descriptions into estimated running times and hardware requirements, are frequently used to assist in these analyses.[2]

• It includes technology forecasts that name assumptions about the pace of change in EDP hardware and software and assess their impact on the company's information systems activity. The sophistication of these forecasts varies widely.

• It also includes aggregate forecasts of future manpower and training levels, estimates of manpower requirements by job classification, employee turnover rates, and other like factors. These are derived from each specific project.

These key factors, once again, reflect the primary pressures to plan.

Naturally, the precise content, form, and quality of a company's CBIS plan are strongly molded by some additional factors, one of the most important of which is the quality of the company's corporate long-range planning. Top management participation and the planning structures used are also important.

Relation to Corporate Planning

We found a strong correlation between a company's ability to develop an effective CBIS planning process and the maturity and scope of its corporate planning process.

Four of the companies studied went so far as to postulate a formal relationship between the two planning activities, corporate and CBIS. The two activities are connected in the company budgets, of course, but the real relationship between them is far more meaningful than a mere formal budgetary connection would suggest. In fact, one company took its CBIS manager directly from its long-range planning department.

When this relationship is a strong one, it appears to contribute three concrete advantages:

1. The CBIS group is made explicitly aware of overall company objectives. This helps it develop priorities realistically.

---

[2] SCERT is a product of COMPRESS, Inc., of Washington, D.C.

2. In the reverse direction, a strong relationship helps executives in other areas to know and understand the goals and targets of the CBIS group. (Incidentally, this wider publicity and exposure enhance the commitment of EDP personnel at all levels to their work.)

3. Perhaps most important, the corporate planning group's expertise can be transferred to the CBIS planning and administrative groups.

These advantages can help to combat a very real communication problem. In one organization, for example—a large, successful bank—no one in the corporate planning department had ever spoken to, or even knew the name of, anybody in the CBIS group. The problems of planning are generic, to some extent, and it is a pity to isolate CBIS planning groups from experienced corporate planners if these are available.

Where no planning expertise is available, on the other hand, the company that is contemplating a CBIS should beware. The controller of one company I visited was particularly proud of his new budget system, the company's first in the 110 years of its existence. The company employed 50 analysts and programmers in its ordinary applications; but, not too surprisingly, its written plan consisted only of 3 pages of project titles. The EDP manager discoursed at great length on his company's CBIS plan for the future, but, while his verbal virtuosity impressed me, I could not help wondering if any vestige of the planning document would survive the next couple of months.

It seemed to me that this management was expecting too much from too little too soon. Developing a formal CBIS plan is a slow process; a company benefits from a secure base of planning skills and attitudes in the organization.

Relation to Top Management

Like corporate planning itself, CBIS planning stands a better chance of getting off the ground if the chief executive backs it personally. Also, the closer information systems activity is to the CEO, the more emphasis is placed on planning it formally.

Those organizations in which two or more layers of management lay between the CBIS department and the CEO ranked lower in effectiveness and planning ability. In this respect our findings are consistent with Neal J. Dean's.[3]

Structures Used for CBIS Planning

Of the 15 companies studied, 9 use a well-defined, formal planning structure to write and update their plans annually. This structure for creating and revising plans is laid out either as a series of operating procedures or as a corpus of job descriptions, or both.

---

[3] "The Computer Comes of Age," HBR January–February 1968, p. 83.

There is, of course, wide variation among these nine companies, with respect to the specific methods used to develop plans and decide what personnel shall be involved at each stage of plan development. One large organization has gone so far as to print a 250-page manual that details the working procedures, reporting formats, and groups participating at each stage—committees, dates, printout formats, and the like are all well defined.

In another organization, judged equally effective as a user of CBIS, the EDP manager prepares the annual plan, consulting with a steering committee and with users throughout the company as he thinks necessary. This organization is small in size, and the manager has a genuine user orientation and excellent communication skills; so this informal procedure is entirely workable.

But in all nine cases, in addition to existing formal structures for planning, the companies have installed special informal procedures—safety valves, really—to accommodate unusual needs or circumstances arising during the year. Overall, the structures are characterized by flexibility and responsiveness, their primary function being to provide a framework for managing change, rather than to create iron-clad documents to be administered regardless of consequences.

I shall have more to say about structures and their flexibility and responsiveness as these are reflected in two examples of CBIS planning. Before presenting these examples, however, I wish to discuss the critical issue of centralized versus decentralized planning of companywide CBIS. An understanding of this issue will help the reader to appreciate the examples.

CENTRALIZED PLANNING

In the companies in the sample, planning tends to be done on a decentralized basis around local computer centers or islands of automation. Companywide coordination between different centers is generally very weak, except when there is only one major computer center in the organization; this is particularly true when there is any significant geographic separation between computer centers within a company.

For example, in one electric equipment manufacturing company with $500 million in sales and 16 divisions, there is a very strong tradition of centralized financial control. All divisions use the same chart of accounts and standard procedures manual, and these materials can be altered only on direct instruction from corporate headquarters.

But, at the same time, IBM 360/25's and 30's and 40's are scattered through the divisions, and the EDP managers of the various divisions have little (if any) contact with one another. During my group's research, for example, it was discovered that no less than six of these installations were currently working to develop the same production scheduling applications. Parallel design teams in competition often produce a better result than an individual team, but with six groups competing, the company had obviously reached the point of diminishing returns. Some centralized coordination was obviously required.

Another large company has three EDP installations, each budgeted in excess of $10 million. The only formal communication and coordination between these installations is a really quite informal two-day meeting of eight to ten of the installation managers every three months. The key topics discussed in these meetings are:

- Salary and wage guidelines.
- Projects to develop classification standards for operators, programmers, and analysts.
- Joint purchase contracts and standards for items such as tapes and discs, for which economies of scale are obviously available.
- Systems to measure computer-room performance more accurately.
- Procedures for sharing reports on the failure rates of machine components.
- Limited joint development of program packages. (Development of operating systems was felt to be a particularly appropriate topic for discussion.)
- Company hardware capabilities and personnel capabilities for specific studies.
- Evolving hardware technology and its implications.

Other companies in the survey also focused primarily on these topics, which, as a group, surely represent the bare minimum for planning CBIS administration and growth. They cover some basic operations, but do not touch the "big picture" at all.

In general, I sense, the companies realize this. More than half strongly expressed the sentiment that much more centralization of CBIS planning is desirable.

Attractiveness of Multiprocessing

In part, this desire for centralization is a consequence of companies' growing awareness of the new multiprogramming and multiprocessing environment, in which it is eminently feasible to connect a large central computer via telephone lines to remote batch-processing facilities. Many companies now have several medium-sized computers at discrete locations. The idea of turning them in for a central-control computer facility is becoming more and more attractive, for the following reasons:

- Large-machine economies mean more computation per dollar expended.
- Software development can be coordinated to serve several installations.
- Hardware-software planning and development can be more sophisticated.
- Integrating the data files from many discrete locations into a single file structure makes more data available for companywide use.
- There is a critical mass of programming and development activity that a company must reach before it can attract truly competent analysts. Large-machine installations are much more likely to achieve this critical mass than small or medium-sized installations.

Such arguments apply more readily to companies having several small, geographically proximate installations than to companies having two or three massive installations in which economies of scale have already been achieved.

Some companies, however, even among those for which multiprocessing should be attractive, are resisting the trend toward centralization, apparently because they either fear the task of managing a very large installation or are concerned that a centralized system will not be responsive to local needs. Companies that fear decreased responsiveness argue that poor communications with local management might warp application priorities and structures.

Thus, when to centralize and how rapidly to centralize are points that are far from clear. (They are now the subject of ongoing research.) For example, economies of scale are extremely complex to calculate when a company contemplates consolidating two installations, each with a budget in excess of $15 million.

One company studied, in exactly this position, decided *not* to consolidate, describing the situation as one in which a reverse critical mass would be created—i.e., one that would create more disadvantages than advantages. On the other hand, other companies in closely similar situations have decided to proceed with consolidation, and have been glad they did so.

More work and research in the area may produce guidelines on when and how fast to centralize, but we found overwhelming evidence that companies are tending toward consolidation. This trend increases the need for, and the payoffs from, central CBIS planning.

TWO COMPANIES' METHODS

To draw the foregoing analysis together and give the reader some feeling for the diversity of approaches a company can take to integrate the process of CBIS planning with its other operations, I present two case examples: one, a division of a major aerospace company, and the other, an international manufacturer of electrical and mechanical equipment. Both have sales in excess of $2 billion annually.

In Aerospace

This company division has been active in CBIS planning for four years. With respect to this relatively long planning history, it is significant that the division's information systems manager spent a large part of his early career working in the company's corporate planning department.

The division's CBIS operation is budgeted in excess of $20 million a year and has nearly 1,000 employees. For all practical purposes, it is completely independent of any other EDP activities of the company, all of which are a considerable distance away. *Exhibit V* indicates the principal groups involved in the division's CBIS activity.

Exhibit V FRAMEWORK OF CBIS ACTIVITY IN A MAJOR AEROSPACE COMPANY

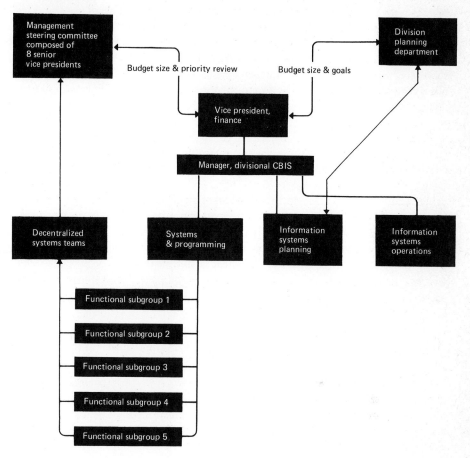

The following points about the exhibit are particularly relevant to the planning process:

1. *A top management steering committee guides the overall process of budgeting and setting priorities.* Composed of eight vice presidents, this steering committee meets once a month to review progress and priorities. It continually faces the job of making broad policy for a very technical area, the underlying complexities of which are largely foreign to its members. Installed by the company, abandoned as unworkable, and then reinstated because of a sharp disruption in communication, this group serves primarily as a safety valve for pressures of extreme dissatisfaction from divisional users.

The same basic feature is present in 12 of the 15 companies studied; it ensures the participation of and guidance from the top.

2. *"Decentralized systems teams" link the vice presidential steering committee with the functional subgroups.* This is the key organizational mechanism in this division, so far as CBIS planning and administration are concerned. The EDP department is not laid out to correspond with its array of activities and systems. Rather, over one third of the division's analysts are on the staffs of the eight vice presidents and report directly to them, instead of reporting to the information systems manager. These staff members work both on special projects of particular interest to the vice presidents and on regular projects, where they join with departmental information systems analysts to form the so-called decentralized systems teams.

As members of these teams, their role is to communicate the peculiar needs and requirements of regular projects to the vice presidential level, and to assure the vice presidents that the system designs created for these regular projects are adequate.

A small fraction of the decentralized team members have come originally from the information systems department. The great majority, however, have been either hired directly into the functional department to fill this special role or transferred from some non-EDP position within the division and then trained. Division personnel judge this to be an extremely effective arrangement.

3. *The existence of an information systems planning department.* This department of five people is directly responsible for coordinating and implementing the process of formal planning. The job description of the manager of this department is the one given in *Exhibit III*; that exhibit provides insight into the scope of his responsibilities and the vital task of the group—to ensure that the planning process is carried out in a timely and apt fashion.

4. *The influence of a strong bottom-up planning process.* CBIS planning begins in the five subgroups of the systems and programming area. Working alone, or in conjunction with the analysts from the various vice presidential staffs and with user-managers, as they see fit, the members of these five subgroups have the basic responsibility for putting together a two-year plan.

They then forward these plans to the information systems planning department, which coordinates them and begins to integrate them, matching costs against available budget dollars. The manager of divisional CBIS and the vice president for finance participate in this process.

Within the divisional CBIS framework, there are three main issues to be resolved. The first is the degree of involvement vice presidents should undertake and how they can provide meaningful guidance to the CBIS activities as they evolve. By the time the consolidated plan is passed up to them through the levels, all the basic decisions have been made, in a very real sense, and it is most difficult for them to reverse this momemtum and make substantive changes. As the company uses this framework, then, the real challenge is to find means to bring the vice presidents into the planning process in a meaningful way, given the enormous time pressures under which these men labor.

Second, the planning horizon currently being used is under fire. At present the period is two years, and in the startup stages of planning (which are still in the recent past) this relatively close horizon made sense because it cut the planning job down to manageable proportions. But today the company can handle a more extended horizon, and there is considerable pressure to extend it by one year. It takes about 4½ years for this company to develop a new aircraft, and both the steering committee and the EDP department realize the desirability of extending the planning horizon toward this ideal limit.

Third, the divisional CBIS activity is isolated from similar activity elsewhere in the company. There is only limited coordination with the other company EDP centers, and it is possible that opportunities are being lost through not sharing hardware-software expertise and not working out joint applications.

On balance, however, this department provides an example of a highly organized, comprehensively planned organism built around a major computer installation.

In International Manufacturing

A quite different picture is presented by a major international manufacturing company.

Operating in over 60 countries, with the equipment of 6 different computer manufacturers, the company has an annual hardware rental bill which runs to nearly $100 million. More than 95% of this is spent in its 40 largest installations.

Until two years before our research project, these installations developed largely independently of one another. Concerned with rising aggregate costs of the company's CBIS activities, top management founded a control group, staffed from corporate headquarters, that was split 50-50 between personnel with user orientations and personnel with technical strengths. This group's role is currently threefold.

First, the group must approve acquisition of any hardware renting for more than $2,000 per month. When such an acquisition is contemplated, a feasibility study must be prepared and submitted to this group, which then draws on its knowledge of the hardware at other company installations and evaluates the economic justification presented in the study to make its decisions. The company feels that this mechanism has significantly improved its technical decisions by bringing a quality of expertise to bear on them that was simply not possible before.

Second, and more to the point of this article, the group has installed, and now monitors, a formal planning system. Each division is required to submit a two-year CBIS plan to headquarters under the signature of the vice president in charge of the division. This procedure forces senior division management to review plans in detail, a fact that has produced startling results in several instances.

In one case, when division CBIS management presented its proposed plan to senior division management, the vice president made the startling discovery, about 15 minutes into the presentation, that the document, which represented one man-year's worth of work, had been prepared under a completely different set of assumptions about division goals from those contained in the division's strategic plan. Needless to say, it was resoundingly rejected, and there ensued a period of considerably closer relations between the headquarters control group and the division CBIS management.

As of now the group has developed standard procedures specifying plan format and contents to guide the individual division in preparing its plan. This guidance will hopefully improve the overall quality of the different divisions' efforts, which has varied widely in the past.

Third, the group visits at least once a year with the manager of each division's CBIS operation, either at corporate headquarters or at the division's offices. This helps extend the already strong informal contacts of the headquarters group with the individual installations, and enables it to monitor continually for opportunities for joint efforts between different installations.

This particular corporation does not have a geographical "home base" hardware facility to build on because its applications are diffused worldwide. Hence, in the foreseeable future it is unlikely to find physical consolidation an appropriate goal.

Rather, the company has found it effective to develop a planning and control structure that rations scarce technical expertise in hardware in a particularly efficient fashion, facilitates communication about EDP operations and goals between its far-flung divisions, and coordinates these divisions' EDP activities.

These two examples show that the nature of the CBIS plan and the structure that creates it must be tailored to company needs. The items covered by a CBIS plan are relatively constant, since the pressures to plan are relatively omnipresent, but they can and must be dealt with in a fashion that meets specific company operating requirements. The range of possible planning structures is clearly very great.

KEY ISSUES FOR THE FUTURE

Information systems planning is still in an early stage of development in most organizations, and numerous critical issues must still be clarified—especially the following.

1. *What are the comparative benefits of the top-down and bottom-up approaches to planning?*

The effective organizations studied to date have been primarily oriented to the bottom-up approach. With this approach, different interest groups, both inside and outside the EDP department, lobby for specific projects. As these groups and their projects achieve formal recognition from above, they are assigned priorities and receive more or less formal supervision to ensure optimum resource utilization.

The main difficulty of the bottom-up approach is that top management does not actively participate in structuring the projects themselves or the general plan that grows out of them. Thus the real challenge in this area appears to be how to channel top management guidance into the planning process right from the start.

2. *What level of detail can be meaningfully incorporated in plan formation?*

The more complex plans now include flow charts and time estimates for computer runs (made via SCERT or similar packages). But for no significant projects are there comfortable guides either for assessing the appropriate level of detail for current-year plans or deciding how rapidly this level should decline for ensuing years.

3. *What should the time horizon of a sound plan be?*

The effective companies believe it is appropriate to prepare detailed plans for one to two years, with additional statements for two to six years that encompass general goals, objectives, manning levels, and hardware strategy. Still, in all cases there is uncertainty concerning the appropriateness of these horizons and a desire to rethink them. Executives stated that a short horizon had been used to reduce the setup work required to develop an adequate initial plan, and that they intend to place more emphasis on the long-range aspects in the future.

4. *How should a company scan for outside EDP services?*

Service organizations offer specialized data bases, statistical services, time-sharing services, and special program packages. Traditionally, coordination between company CBIS's and outside service has been minimal; flexible integration of the two may become a watchword in the future.

Additionally, the two companies studied that included outside services in their information systems planning feel that they thereby stimulated a broad, thorough review of such activities and the potential benefits which they might contribute, and that this review was in itself a great benefit.

Controlling the Costs of Data Services

RICHARD L. NOLAN

Without exception, the companies that I have studied for the past four years have found it difficult to make their transfer-pricing, or "charge-out," systems for data processing services understandable to the managers who use them.

The root of this problem is not the inherent technical complexity of computer technology—it is a historical error made in the management of data processing. To date, we have designed our DP management systems around the *computer* instead of the *data*. Consequently, chargeout systems have been designed to hold the manager who uses the data accountable for computer-related resources such as processing time, main memory time and space, and input/output accesses.

However, the user works with output units, such as invoices processed, inventory reports, and production schedules. Thus the user is forced to somehow translate input and processing charges into the information for which he or she receives value. Only then can he take appropriate control and be held accountable. In a sense, what is being asked of the user is analogous to asking a car buyer to make a decision on several automobiles by being given a bill of materials on the different types of cars. The car buyer makes the decision on information such as performance of a V-8 versus the economy of a six-cylinder engine; the convenience of an automatic versus manual transmission; economy, safety, and wear of radial versus belted tires, not on kilos of steel, cast iron, and rubber.

Take, for example, this all too common vignette. On July 1, the vice president of marketing had just received his third monthly bill for his department's use of the order entry system. The bill he received is shown in *Exhibit I.*

Although he did not understand the detail of the bill (for example, he had no idea what CPU, kilobytes, and EXCP stand for), he felt that it was way too much. In fact, the charge represented a good 25% of his budget. He also knew from the president's recent memorandum that he was now accountable for these expenses.

Exhibit I DATA PROCESSING SERVICES BILL

Resource	Use	Charge per unit	Total
Elapsed time on computer (minutes)	243,000	$0.04	$ 9,720
CPU (seconds)	2,430,000	0.0167	40,500
Kilobytes (1K memory/minute)	14,515,000	0.0016	23,220
EXCP (I/O accesses)	105,000,000	0.0002	21,000
Total due			$94,440

So he picked up the telephone and made an appointment to talk with his newly appointed "data processing coordinator."

Management's experience with data processing had followed the pattern of many other companies. After starting out in the early 1960s by automating payroll, the company had experienced extremely rapid growth in its DP budget as applications were developed for almost all parts of the business. The order entry system was one of the early applications.

It was close to a disaster when the revised estimate of development costs skyrocketed from $100,000 to $275,000 with less than half of the originally promised capability. Nevertheless, the marketing department stuck with it, and the costs were treated as corporate overhead. The bugs were shaken out by 1967, and the system was gradually expanded to the point where the vice president of marketing said that the company couldn't carry on business without it.

A year ago, management had become concerned with ever-rising DP expenses and seemingly declining performance, as maintenance problems with existing applications seemed to have gotten out of hand. Therefore, the company centralized data processing under a new vice president of information services, and there was a general consensus that users should be held accountable for the services they were using. With the support of the president, the vice president of information services had his staff design a system for charging out all costs on the basis of resources used to support the various applications. He also established data-processing coordinators for each major user group.

It was in this context that the vice president of marketing opened the meeting with his data processing coordinator:

"Although I really don't understand this bill, it has to be too high. Order entry cost us less than $30,000 per month before the computer system was installed. Not only is the $94,400 too high, even taking inflation into account, but the cost has varied from $78,000 to $104,000 in the three short months that the chargeout system has been in effect. How is a manager supposed to plan in such a volatile environment?"

"You are absolutely right about the variance," the coordinator responded. "It is due partly to the volume of orders processed and due partly to the upgrade in the computer operating system software last month. We have also incurred technical difficulty in measuring kilobyte minutes in an MVS operating system environment. You see we have a "meg" of main memory, but with virtual memory software we have a lot more. Our problem in charging equitably is one of. . . ."

The vice president didn't understand this explanation and felt that he was getting the same waffle treatment that he had come to expect from data processing. Somewhat irritated, he said he didn't give a damn about the technical problems but wanted the bill to be reduced by 25%.

The coordinator reminded him that the information services division was only a service department and that it was the vice president's responsibility to provide the guidance for making such cuts. He then asked him what component of the bill he would like to attack: CPU seconds, elapsed time, kilobytes, or EXCPs?

At this point, the vice president of marketing became very angry. Shoving the coordinator out the door with instructions not to come back, he got the president on the telephone: "I'm strapped. Data processing is charging me for services that are essential, and I can't do anything about the cost. When I try to get down to how to control the costs, all I get is technical gibberish. . . ."

DESIGN FOR CHARGEOUTS

Data services have become much too important to companies to be left to technicians. Management must devote the time necessary to understand data processing's current and future impact on the business so that it can provide the guidance that both data processing and users need.

In a sense, the chargeout systems that I have studied have been attempts to provide this guidance. Unfortunately, many of them were built on shaky DP accounting systems and implemented without a clear understanding of what was expected from the user.

As a result, both DP management and users became frustrated. The extent and intensity of the frustration are reflected in the vignette. The vice president of marketing was confused about what actions he should take to be accountable, and what the control rationale was. Another dysfunctional result is that the user gets too involved in the operational details of data processing.

One manager told me, "I now demand internal reports from data processing to check up on just how well they are running their operation."

How can a company develop an effective chargeout system? Obviously, no one system can work for all companies since the needs of companies vary tremendously. However, I think that one good approach to designing an effective system is to follow these seven steps:

1. Assess the overall status of data processing services within the company.
2. Sort out how data processing is organized.
3. Evaluate capacity of accounting systems to support a DP management control system.
4. Assess current chargeout approach.
5. Develop chargeout system objectives and strategy.
6. Develop implementation goals and milestones.
7. Implement and review.

Let's look at each of these seven chargeout system steps in turn.

Assess Status of Data Services

The search for alternatives begins with a careful analysis of the characteristics of a company's industry and management philosophy. For example, managements of companies in high technology industries, such as electronics and aerospace, are more tolerant and understanding of technical complexities than managements of companies in service industries, such as insurance and banking. Also, managements of companies with sophisticated budgeting and financial controls are more receptive to similar systems for data processing. The general rule is that management control systems for data processing cannot be significantly more advanced than the management control systems used for the company as a whole.

Management's next task is to determine the status of its services. What I call the "stage process audit" is a useful way to structure this analysis.[1] Based upon the status of the applications portfolio, data processing organization, control mechanisms, and user awareness, an organization's data services can be thought of as being in one of four stages: initiation, contagion, control, or integration. *Exhibit II* shows the attributes for each of these stages. This detailed audit provides the foundation for tailoring the design of a control system.

A frequent mistake in designing an effective system is to impose sophisticated controls upon organizational units that are not "ready." The organizational unit is not ready if controls hinder its operation or if personnel cannot clearly see the relevance of the controls to their problems.

For example, one user in my study was charged for programming services that he did not fully understand because a new on-line system was being developed. Nevertheless, he was asked to make judgments on the resource commitments being made on the project, as well as to accept an accountability for those judgments even though the development process was largely out of his hands.

---

[1] See my article, "Managing the Computer Resources: A Stage Hypothesis," *Communications of the ACM,* July 1973, p. 300.

Exhibit II STAGE PROCESS AUDIT CRITERIA

Criteria	Stage I: Initiation	Stage II: Contagion	Stage III: Control	Stage IV: Integration
DP organization				
Objective	Get first application on the computer	Broaden use of computer technology	Gain control of data processing activities	Integrate data processing into business
Staffing emphasis	Technical computer experts	User-oriented system analysts and programmers	Middle management	Balance of technical and management specializations
Structure	Embedded in low-functional area	Growth and multiple DP units created	Consolidation of DP activities into central organizational unit	Layering and "fitting" DP organization structure
Reporting level	To functional manager	To higher level functional manager	To senior management officer	VP level reporting to corporate top management
User awareness				
Senior management	Clerical staff reduction syndrome	Broader applications in operational areas	Crisis of expenditure growth. Panic about penetration in business operations	Acceptance as a major business function. Involvement in providing direction
User attitude	"Hands-off". Anxiety over implications	Superficially enthusiastic. Insufficient involvement in applications design	Frustration from suddenly being held accountable for DP expenditures	Acceptance of accountability. Involvement in application, budgeting, design, and maintenance
Communication with DP	Informal. Lack of understanding	Oversell and unrealistic objectives and schedules. Schism develops	Formal lines of communication. Formal commitments. Cumbersome	Acceptance and informed communication. Application development partnership
Training	General orientation on "what is a computer"	Little user interest	Increase in user interest due to accountability	User seeks out training on application development and control
Planning and control				
Objective	Hold spending at initial commitment	Facilitate wider functional uses of computer	Formalize control and contain DP expenditures	Tailor planning and control to DP activities
Planning	Oriented toward computer implementation	Oriented toward application development	Oriented toward gaining central control	Established formal planning activity
Management control	Focus on computer operations budget	Lax to facilitate applications development activity growth	Proliferation of formal controls.	Balanced formal and informal controls
Project management	DP manager responsibility	Programmer's responsibility	Formalized system. DP department responsibility	Formalized system tailored to project. DP and user/management joint responsibility
Project approval and priority setting	DP manager responsibility	Multi-functional managers. First in, first out	Steering committee	Steering committee. Formal plan influence
DP standards	Low awareness of importance	Inattention	Importance recognized. Activity aggressively implemented	Established standards activity. Published policy manuals
Application portfolio				
Objective	Prove value of computer technology in organization	Apply computer technology to multi-functional areas	Moratorium on new applications. Consolidate and gain control of existing applications	Exploit opportunities for integrative systems. Cost-effective application of advanced technology
Application justification	Cost-savings	Informal user/manager approval	Hard cost savings. Short-term payout	Benefit/cost analysis. Senior management approval

Sort Out the Organization Structure

Although many companies for the most part have centralized their data processing, there are usually pockets of activities still embedded within the organization that have not been dislodged.

The question of what constitutes an effective organization is complicated by wide disagreement on which activities should be centralized, even when they are only broadly categorized into systems development and operations. The majority of DP personnel I interviewed agreed that operations should be centralized, at least enough to support the specialists necessary to run and maintain the computer facility. However, proponents of minicomputers believe decentralization is preferable. The main disagreement concerns the location of systems development personnel, even though for the 18 research sites studied, 90% of the central DP departments had programmers and 60% had systems analysts—and over half of the user organizations had programmers and systems analysts.

Organizing data processing becomes even more complex and difficult when activities are sorted into maintenance, data entry, batch processing, on-line services and processing, and telecommunication facilities.

A study of an organization's structure will expose irrational locations for various data processing activities. The majority of these locations can probably be changed; others may have to be viewed as constraints in the short run.

Even when an irrational structure cannot be altered, the structure must be understood because almost every control action taken for the central DP group will also affect the splinter groups.

For example, in one company I studied, the corporate data processing department decided to charge users the full cost of providing services. The divisional data processing department charged less than full costs because occupancy and employee benefits were excluded from the calculation of costs. The effect of the corporate decision was to shift users to the divisional data processing facility, even though the best interests of the company were not served. If these responses are anticipated, systems may be designed to avoid dysfunctional relationships between the central and splinter groups, as well as between corporate and divisional management.

Evaluate Capacity of Accounting System

Since accounting systems provide the foundation for management control, management control can only reflect the quality of the accounting system. As shown in *Exhibit III*, a logical progression exists in the development of the accounting systems, from after-the-fact, object-of-expenditure control to budgetary control responsibility center, by program (or job), and by quantitative measure of output units.

Although all 18 companies studied had developed meaningful classifications for expenditures—that is, charts of accounts—4 companies still had not integrated the DP chart of accounts into the company's general ledger system. In addition, the DP accounting systems were of varying quality, which influenced their reliability.

The development of data processing accounting systems is initially an accounting problem rather than a data processing problem because basic accounting concepts are most important. Unfortunately, this need for accounting skills does

Exhibit III EVOLUTION OF ACCOUNTING AND CONTROL SYSTEMS

Stages I and II	Stage III		Stage IV
General ledger	Budgeting	Usage	User orientation

Direct expenses

Indirect expenses

Cost centers

Units of work

Transaction by account

Budget by account

By cost center

By job

Control of accounts

Control by responsibility center

Cost per unit of work by cost center (rates)

Control by planned vs. actual

Volume and efficiency variance analysis

Volume and efficiency user variance analysis

Variance by user responsibility center

Variance by accounts

Variance by DP responsibility center

not seem to be fully recognized in the beginning. Over half of the companies studied reported that their technical personnel played the dominant role in designing the initial accounting systems. Systems analysts and programmers were usually assigned this task on the assumption that their technical skills were needed to measure computer system resource usage. Rather quickly, however, it became apparent that the real problems were accounting problems concerning responsibility centers, costing, and allocating costs to responsibility centers. Accounting personnel then would be brought into the project.

Cost centers, too, seemed to have evolved from the existing structure of the data processing department rather than from an analysis of basic DP functions. Consequently, organizational changes often have a detrimental effect on control. In addition, costs are not consistently categorized by type—direct, indirect, and overhead.

These fundamental problems seriously hindered the effective design, implementation, and administration of the chargeout systems. Simply stated, you cannot build a sophisticated control system on a sandy foundation of weak accounting systems.

Assess Current Chargeout Approach

A useful chargeout system communicates to managers the consequences of their decisions concerning use of services. Cost responsibility will tend to motivate users to employ the resources more effectively and efficiently. Four criteria can be used for determining the usefulness of a chargeout system—understandability, controllability, accountability, and cost/benefit incidence. *Exhibit IV* shows the criteria and questions for determining the maturity of the chargeout system.

As shown in *Exhibit IV,* chargeout systems initially are directed at high-level managers. Summary data processing bills are sent to divisional controllers without much information on the charges being conveyed to end users. With maturity, the chargeout systems become more sophisticated and permit detailed bills to be sent directly to low-level users. It is important that the chargeout system evolve through successive phases so that users and DP managers can learn how to interpret and use the information. It is especially important that the means for accountability be coordinated with the expectations for accountability.

After assessing the status of the existing chargeout system, management's next objective is to develop a strategy that will increase the maturity (and effectiveness) of the chargeout system at an appropriate pace for the major user groups. It is likely that several chargeout strategies may be required for the different user groups.

Develop Objectives and Strategy

In the companies I studied, objectives for the chargeout systems were rarely articulated. Or, if they were articulated, the objectives were often narrowly defined short-term goals. For example, eight of the companies stated that their chargeout system objective was to allocate data processing costs. No mention was made of providing the cost information to users that they needed to make effective decisions about services. In other words, using data accounting systems to allocate costs for financial reporting and budgeting purposes should not be confused with chargeout. Chargeout brings the user into the realm of control and accountability.

Exhibit IV CRITERIA FOR CHARGEOUT SYSTEMS

Understandability:
To what extent can the manager associate chargeout costs to the activities necessary to carry out his or her tasks?

Attributes:
High—Manager can associate costs with functions and determine variables accounting for costs.
Medium—Manager can roughly associate costs with functions, but cannot directly determine major variables accounting for costs.
Low—Manager cannot associate costs with functions.

Controllability:
To what extent are charges under the control of the user?

Attributes:
None—No control. The manager has no influence on acceptance or rejection of the charges. These decisions are made at a higher level.
Indirect—Through communication with others, such as divisional or departmental controllers that receive charges, the manager can influence the charges.
Direct/arbitrary—Charges are allocated directly to the manager, but his decision is to either accept or reject the application charges. Little information is provided on controllable versus noncontrollable data processing costs.
Direct/economic—Charges are directly charged in a manner that allows the manager to make decisions that actually reduce controllable data processing costs.

Accountability:
Are costs and utilization of computer-based systems included in performance evaluation of the user?

Attributes:
None—Not included in performance evaluation.
Indirect—Included indirectly in performance evaluation; costs can be related to user, but not done routinely.
Direct—Included directly in periodic user-performance evaluation.

Cost/benefit incidence:
Does the user responsible for task accomplishment also receive the chargeout bill?

Attributes:
Yes.
No.

In my opinion, the absence of a clear statement of objectives or an excessively narrow statement was the single most troublesome factor inhibiting chargeout system effectiveness. Consequently, systems were not well thought out, but were designed to provide minimal information for accounting, or to support other management tools such as project management systems.

Chargeout objectives should be stated in terms of desirable results for user accountability. Examples of such objectives include:

- Make managers aware of the economic (full absorption) costs of data processing services provided to them.
- Make managers responsible for the economic costs of services they use.
- Motivate managers to make decisions about the use of data processing on the basis of the direct costs of providing the services.
- Charge costs in understandable volume units to facilitate data processing capacity planning.
- Charge costs in a manner to facilitate manager product (service) pricing.

Each of these examples specifies a particular result, and taken together they imply the design of a system much broader than one that simply charges for computer services. Alterations in organization structure, budgeting, and performance review and measurement are often necessary. Once management has articulated an appropriate set of objectives, it should formulate a strategy to achieve them that takes into account the necessary changes in organization and administrative practices.

Develop Implementation Goals

The stage audit I discussed earlier provides an idea of how advanced a company is in respect to data processing. It also specifies a long-term objective.

Keeping in mind that a great deal of difficult organizational changes are required to first synchronize the status of the applications portfolio, organization, control system, and user awareness, and second, to progress through the advanced stages, management can lay out short-run goals and a schedule for longer term goals. A common mistake is to go too fast or to attempt to leap-frog a stage. It is important to remember that learning at all levels within the organization is involved in progressing through the stages.

The more detailed analysis of the organization's chargeout status and specification of management control objectives provide the groundwork for establishing short-run and long-run goals. These goals should be realistic in terms of schedule and sequence. In addition, they should be initially tailored to the individual user groups with the long-term goal of progressing toward a common chargeout system for the entire organization or, at least, a common chargeout system for each of the major divisions.

Implement and Review

The data processing department should never take it upon itself to implement a management control and chargeout strategy. Implementation of the strategy will have far-reaching effects on the overall management control system of the company, as well as immediate effects on users. It is clear that managers must be able to evaluate information system alternatives since it is the development and operation of *their* applications that will determine what the costs will be. The chargeout system effectively brings the user into control by matching costs and benefits by responsibility center. Of course, there are complicating factors where applications serve several users in more than one responsibility center.

High-level steering committees play a crucial role in providing a forum for shaking down and ratifying a management control and chargeout strategy. Just as important as ratification is management's agreement on implementation goals and schedules. Organizational changes associated with a realistic strategy will inevitably result in some conflict and disagreement. To constructively negotiate through obstacles that arise, management needs to have a plan or road map on direction and destination.

The steering committee, or some type of quarterly review board, should ensure that the organization maintains progress. In addition to its role of approval and guidance, such a group provides a source of commitment that is necessary for successful management control programs.

THE FUTURE

The 18 companies that I studied are at the forefront of data processing. Their DP organization charts, trends, and plans provide a glimpse of future organization structures and control systems. The extensive incorporation of data-base technology is the most important trend, leading toward a structure that facilitates data-oriented management.[2]

For example, one of the more advanced companies had explained especially well the role of data-base technology in this orientation. The company used a facsimile of *Exhibit V* to compare the traditional computer-oriented accountability scheme with the data-oriented accountability scheme for two applications: an order entry system and an inventory control system. Traditionally, both the definition of data (inventory part numbers, reorder points, customers) and function (the way an order is processed) is contained in the application, using programming languages such as COBOL or PL/1. Chargeout is based on the computer-related resources used, and the user is held accountable for both data and function.

But data-base technology enables management to separate function from data. As a result, users can be held directly accountable for function, and data processing can be held directly accountable for management of the company's data resources.

This company envisions a chargeout system including both simplified user bills and data processing bills from users. In other words, data would be purchased from functional groups that originate them, as well as from outside sources. In

---

[2] See my article "Computer Data Base: The Future Is Now," *Harvard Business Review,* September–October 1973, p. 98.

responding to requests from users, data processing would provide value-added services by combining, processing, and distributing data. The users would be charged for the cost of the data plus the value-added services of processing them. The value-added concept solves a basic problem of current chargeout systems; it provides a quid pro quo for those who bear the costs of collecting the data but who are not the end-users.

The rapid development of data-base technology will most likely lead to specialized components for data management. *Exhibit VI* shows the three main components: data, processing, and control.

To start with, current processing systems will be relieved of data management functions and will be designed to carry out value-added functions of combining, mutating, and distributing data. Both the data and processing systems will incorporate large-scale and mini/micro-computer technologies.

This division of functions will then lead to a separate control system to facilitate specialized management necessary to account, bill, schedule, monitor, and

Exhibit V COMPARISON OF TRADITIONAL COMPUTER-ORIENTED ACCOUNTABILITY WITH DATA-ORIENTED ACCOUNTABILITY

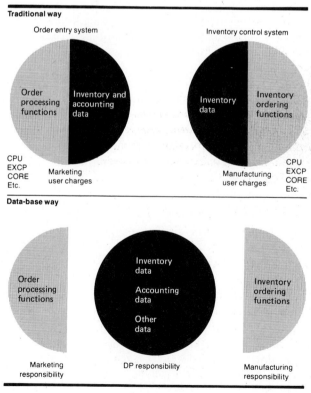

Exhibit VI COMPONENTS OF FUTURE DATA
SERVICES INSTALLATION

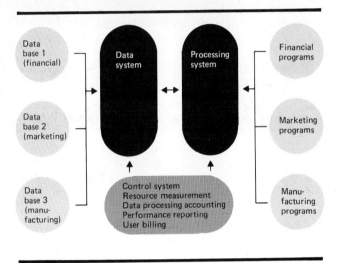

control the efficiency of the company's data processing installation. Although this control component is at present at a rudimentary state, one manufacturer has already entered the market and has delivered such systems to the Social Security Administration and the General Electric Company.

The impact of the evolving data processing installation is distinctly visible on several of the organization charts of the companies I studied. One of the first signs is the incorporation of data administration positions. Data administration separates the management of data from the development of user applications. Another sign is the emergence of the controller position. This position is created to recognize the need for more formal management of data processing, as well as to cope with the need for bringing about effective user accountability. *Exhibit VII* shows my projected organization chart for the future data processing installation.

IN SUMMARY

The role and position of data processing has now taken sufficient form to mount effective management programs to fit it into the modern organization. It is clear that organizations progress through stages of maturity for data processing management and the next apparent stage is to establish three separate functions for this management.

In order for it to better control these functions, it is important that top management first understand the natural shift from computer management to data management. This shift cannot and will not take place overnight. It is, and for each organization will be, a gradual shift beginning with the incorporation of data-base technology and an elaboration of control systems.

Exhibit VII FUTURE DATA SERVICES ORGANIZATION

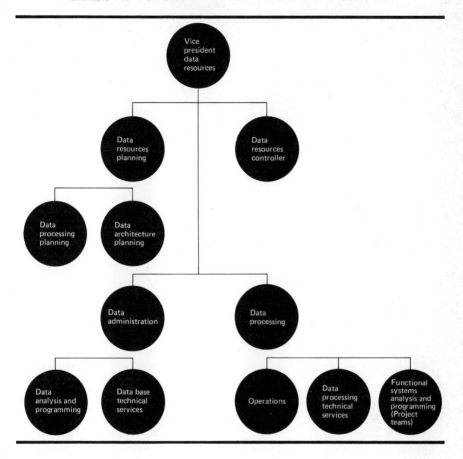

Next, top management needs to realize that an effective chargeout system is essential if those who use data processing are to be in control and held accountable for the services they receive. It is the users that ultimately justify and obtain the potentially lucrative returns from the company's investment in data processing.

It is this simple fact that should determine top management's orientation and decisions concerning data processing.

CHAPTER 4

SYSTEMS ANALYSIS, DESIGN AND IMPLEMENTATION

The material presented in this chapter is probably not what most readers would expect. While accountants must know something about this topic they do not necessarily need to be experts in analysis, design, and implementation. Therefore, the readings chosen for this chapter present several controversial topics relating to the design and implementation of systems which hopefully will stimulate accountants to be more aware of the problems and solutions of these aspects of information systems.

The first article, entitled "Chief Executives Define Their Own Data Needs," by Rockart, addresses the problem of who determines the information needs of an organization. He offers a brief synopsis of four ways of determining executive information needs and discusses the relative strengths and weaknesses of each. The article focuses on the critical success factors approach as being highly effective in helping define information needs. A discussion of actual interview results is used to show the excellent response that has been received from the critical success factors method. An example of how the method works illustrates how seven critical success factors were applied to a particular problem.

A uniquely titled article by Ackoff, "Management Misinformation Systems," is the next reading in the chapter. He first presents his idea of the five commonly made assumptions of systems designers. It is then argued that none of these is justified except in rare cases and most of them lead to major inefficiencies in the resulting systems. To overcome these assumptions the author suggests that a management information system should be developed which encompasses the control system of the organization. A method for designing such a system is proposed and an example follows which illustrates its advantages. However, the author warns that unless the system has the support and involvement of management, it or any other system will fail.

Because of Ackoff's strong criticism of many generally accepted assumptions of systems design, several counterarguments soon appeared in the literature. The third article in this chapter, by Rappaport, "Management Misinformation Systems—Another Perspective," extends the discussion of the Ackoff article by elaborating on the five assumptions discussed in the preceding article. While Rappaport agrees with the assumptions, he does not agree with the criticisms and/or justifications given by Ackoff. The reader's appreciation for the difficulty in designing efficient systems should be increased after reading both of these articles. Although not everyone is expected to agree, the underlying needs and assumptions of systems design must have general acceptance before progress can continue toward meeting the needs of today's organizations.

The utopian concept of a total management information system is quite misleading, according to Dearden in "MIS Is a Mirage." Another area of professional disagreement is addressed in this article. Every organization has a system but the type of system varies with every organization. Many organizations refer to their system as a total management information system and it is with this concept that Dearden takes exception. He begins the article by labeling such a total system as "absurd" and gives his reasoning for the characterization. After providing sufficient evidence for the unworkability of total information systems he recommends several practical steps for improving and revamping currently existing systems.

As Dearden suspected in the closing remarks of his article, his stand on the total information system concept caused heated debate. The next reading in this chapter is a selection of "Letters to the Editor" from the *Harvard Business Review*. The theme of most of the responses centers around the validity of a total approach to systems design. Although there was some support for Dearden's philosophy, most of the responses were critical of his views. This reading includes both sides of the argument and should leave the reader with a basis for attempting to resolve the dilemma in his own mind.

Much has been written (and argued) about the kinds of systems that organizations should use in their operations. The next article, by Paretta, entitled "Designing Management Information Systems: An Overview," discusses not the kind of system that is needed, but the methods available for designing the information flows for a system. This article provides a general background that will enable systems designers to develop and refine systems in terms of the organization's changing needs and available resources. Besides a discussion of the alternative approaches to systems design, the author reviews how the various approaches evolved and how each design method can be identified with an organization's given stage of development. Next, the design philosophy is discussed within the context of its inherent limitations, and the problems of risk associated with each approach are evaluated. Three different models are presented in the article, with a compromise model selected as the best approach. By being aware of the strengths and weaknesses of alternative design methodologies, management should be better prepared to select the system that best fits their needs within their financial and environmental constraints.

Systems analysis, design, and implementation causes many arguments among both theoreticians and practitioners. One primary reason for such disagreement is that every organization has different characteristics and needs, and no single system exists which can satisfy the information requirements of every organization. While systems development activities may take place in any size and type of organization, it is important to remember that every undertaking must be well-planned, be supported by management, and include the involvement of those who are going to be the major interactors with the system.

Chief Executives Define Their Own Data Needs

JOHN F. ROCKART

He could have been the president of any one of a number of successful and growing medium-sized companies in the electronics industry. He had spent the previous day working to salt away the acquisition of a small company that fitted an important position in the product line strategy he had evolved for his organization. Most of this day had been spent discussing problems and opportunities with key managers. During both days he had lived up to his reputation of being an able, aggressive, action-oriented chief executive of a leading company in its segment of the electronics field.

Unfortunately, the president had chosen the late afternoon and early evening to work through the papers massed on his desk. His thoughts were not pleasant. His emotions ranged from amusement to anger as he plowed through the papers. "Why," he thought, "do I have to have dozens of reports a month and yet very little of the real information I need to manage this company? There must be a way to get the information I need to run this company!"

In effect, he was expressing the thoughts of many other general managers—and especially chief executive officers—whose needs for information are not as clearly determined as are those of many functional managers and first-line supervisors. Once one gets above the functional level, there is a wide variety of information that one might possibly need, and each functional specialty has an interest in "feeding" particular data to a general manager. As in this case, therefore, a massive information flow occurs. This syndrome is spelled out with differing emphases by the recent comments of two other chief executives:

> The first thing about information systems that strikes me is that one gets too much information. The information explosion crosses and criss-crosses executive desks with a great deal of data. Much of this is only partly digested and much of it is irrelevant. . . .[1]

---

[1] Interview with Anthony J.F. O'Reilly, president of H.J. Heinz Co., *M.I.S. Quarterly*, March 1977, p. 7.

I think the problem with management information systems in the past in many companies has been that they're overwhelming as far as the executive is concerned. He has to go through reams of reports and try to determine for himself what are the most critical pieces of information contained in the reports so that he can take the necessary action and correct any problems that have arisen.[2]

It is clear that a problem exists with defining exactly what data the chief executive (or any other general manager) needs. My experience in working with executives for the past decade or more is that the problem is universally felt—with individual frustration levels varying, but most often high.

In this article, I will first discuss four current major approaches to defining managerial information needs. Next, I will discuss a new approach developed by a research team at MIT's Sloan School of Management. Termed the "critical success factor (CSF) method," this approach is being actively researched and applied today at the MIT center. Finally, I will describe in detail this method's use in one major case as well as provide summary descriptions of its use in four other cases.

CURRENT PROCEDURES

In effect, there are four main ways of determining executive information needs—the *by-product* technique, the *null* approach, the *key indicator* system, and the *total study* process. In this section of the article, I will offer a brief synopsis of each of these and discuss their relative strengths and weaknesses.

By-product Technique

In this method, little attention is actually paid to the real information needs of the chief executive. The organization's computer-based information process is centered on the development of operational systems that perform the required paperwork processing for the company. Attention is focused, therefore, on systems that process payroll, accounts payable, billing, inventory, accounts receivable, and so on.

The information by-products of these transaction-processing systems are often made available to all interested executives, and some of the data (e.g., summary sales reports and year-to-date budget reports) are passed on to top management. The by-products that reach the top are most often either heavily aggregated (e.g., budgeted/actual for major divisions) or they are exception reports of significant interest (e.g., certain jobs now critical by some preset standard). All reports, however, are essentially by-products of a particular system designed primarily to perform routine paperwork processing.

Where the information subsystem is not computer-based, the reports reaching the top are often typed versions of what a lower level feels is useful. Alternatively,

---

[2] Interview with William Dougherty, president of North Carolina Bank Corporation, *M.I.S. Quarterly*, March 1977, p. 1.

they may be the ongoing, periodically forthcoming result of a previous one-time request for information concerning a particular matter initiated by the chief executive in the dim past.

Of the five methods discussed herein, the by-product approach is undoubtedly the predominant method. It leads to the welter of reports noted in the introductory paragraphs of this article. It has the paper-processing tail wagging the information dog.

The approach is, however, understandable. Paperwork must be done and clerical savings can be made by focusing on automating paper-processing systems. It is necessary to develop this class of data processing system to handle day-to-day paperwork. However, other approaches are also necessary to provide more useful management information.

Null Approach

This method is characterized by statements that might be paraphrased in the following way: "Top executives' activities are dynamic and ever changing, so one cannot predetermine exactly what information will be needed to deal with changing events at any point in time. These executives, therefore, are and must be dependent on future-oriented, rapidly assembled, most often subjective, and informal information delivered by word of mouth from trusted advisers."

Proponents of this approach point to the uselessness of the reports developed under the by-product method just noted. Having seen (often only too clearly) that (1) the *existing* reports used by the chief executive are not very useful, and (2) he, therefore, relies very heavily on oral communication, advocates of this approach then conclude that all computer-based reports—no matter how they are developed—will be useless. They look at inadequately designed information systems and curse all computer-based systems.

Proponents of the null approach see managerial use of information as Henry Mintzberg does:

> . . . it is interesting to look at the content of managers' information, and at what they do with it. The evidence here is that a great deal of the manager's inputs are soft and speculative—impressions and feelings about other people, hearsay, gossip, and so on. Furthermore, the very analytical inputs—reports, documents, and hard data in general—seem to be of relatively little importance to many managers. (After a steady diet of soft information, one chief executive came across the first piece of hard data he had seen all week—an accounting report—and put it aside with the comment, "I never look at this.")[3]

To some extent, this school of thought is correct. There is a great deal of information used by top executives that must be dynamically gathered as new situations

---

[3] See Henry Mintzberg, "Planning on the Left Side and Managing on the Right," *HBR,* July-August 1976, p. 54.

arise. And, most certainly, there are data that affect top management which are not computer-based and which must be communicated in informal, oral, and subjective conversations.

There are, however, also data that can and should be supplied regularly to the chief executive through the computer system. More significantly, as I will note later on, it is also important to clearly define what informal (*not* computer-based) information should be supplied to a top executive on a regular basis.

Key Indicator System

A clear contender today for the fastest growing school of thought concerning the "best" approach to the provision of executive information is the key indicator system. This procedure is based on three concepts, two of which are necessary and the third of which provides the glamour (as well as a few tangible benefits).

The first concept is the selection of a set of key indicators of the health of the business. Information is collected on each of these indicators. The second concept is exception reporting—that is, the ability to make available to the manager, if desired, only those indicators where performance is significantly different (with significance levels necessarily predefined) from expected results. The executive may thus peruse all the data available *or* focus only on those areas where performance is significantly different from planned.

The third concept is the expanding availability of better, cheaper, and more flexible visual display techniques. These range from computer consoles (often with color displays) to wall-size visual displays of computer-generated digital or graphic material. A paradigm of these systems is the one developed at Gould, Inc. under the direction of William T. Ylvisaker, chairman and chief executive officer. As *Business Week* reports:

> Gould is combining the visual display board, which has now become a fixture in many boardrooms, with a computer information system. Information on everything from inventories to receivables will come directly from the computer in an assortment of charts and tables that will make comparisons easy and lend instant perspective.
>
> Starting this week Ylvisaker will be able to tap three-digit codes into a 12-button box resembling the keyboard of a telephone. SEX will get him sales figures. GIN will call up a balance sheet. MUD is the keyword for inventory.
>
> About 75 such categories will be available, and the details will be displayed for the company as a whole, for divisions, for product lines, and for other breakdowns, which will also be specified by simple digital codes.[4]

At Gould, this information is displayed on a large screen in the boardroom, and is also available at computer terminals. The data are available in full, by exception, and graphically if desired.

---

[4] "Corporate 'War Rooms' Plug into the Computer," *Business Week*, August 23, 1976, p. 65.

As in most similar key indicator systems I have seen, the emphasis at Gould is on financial data. Daniel T. Carroll, reporting on Gould's system in mid-1976, described the system's "core report."[5] The report, available for each of Gould's 37 divisions, provides data on more than 40 operating factors. For each factor, current data are compared with budget and prior year figures on a monthly and year-to-date basis. The report, as noted by Carroll, is ever changing, but its orientation toward "profit and loss" and "balance sheet" data, as well as ratios drawn from these financial data, is evident.

Total Study Process

In this fourth approach to information needs, a widespread sample of managers are queried about their total information needs, and the results are compared with the existing information systems. The subsystems necessary to provide the information currently unavailable are identified and assigned priorities. This approach, clearly, is a reaction to two decades of data processing during which single systems have been developed for particular uses in relative isolation from each other and with little attention to management information needs. In effect, this approach was developed by IBM and others to counter the by-product method previously noted.

The most widely used formal procedure to accomplish the total study is IBM's Business Systems Planning (BSP) methodology. BSP is aimed at a top-down analysis of the information needs of an organization. In a two-phase approach, many managers are interviewed (usually from 40 to 100) to determine their environment, objectives, key decisions, and information needs. Several IBM-suggested network design methods and matrix notations are used to present the results in an easily visualized manner.

The objectives of the process are to develop an overall understanding of the business, the information necessary to manage the business, and the existing information systems. Gaps between information systems that are needed and those currently in place are noted. A plan for implementing new systems to fill the observed gaps is then developed.

This total understanding process is expensive in terms of manpower and all-inclusive in terms of scope. The amount of data and opinions gathered is staggering. Analysis of all this input is a high art form. It is difficult, at best, to determine the correct level of aggregation of decision making, data gathering, and analysis at which to work.

Yet the top-down process tends to be highly useful in most cases. The exact focus of the results, however, can be biased either toward top management information and functional management information or toward paperwork processing, depending on the bias of the study team. I have not seen a BSP study that gives

---

[5] Daniel T. Carroll, "How the President Satisfies His Information Systems Requirements," published in *Society for Management Information Systems Proceedings,* 1976.

priority to top executive information in the study's output. The design, cleaning up, and extension of the paper-processing information network is too often the focus of the study team.

Each of the four current procedures just discussed has its advantages and disadvantages. The by-product technique focuses on getting paperwork processed inexpensively, but it is far less useful with regard to managerial information. It too often results in a manager's considering data from a single paperwork function (e.g., payroll) in isolation from other meaningful data (e.g., factory output versus payroll dollars).

The null approach, with its emphasis on the changeability, diversity, and soft environmental information needs of a top executive, has probably saved many organizations from building useless information systems. It, however, places too much stress on the executive's strategic and person-to-person roles. It overlooks the management control role of the chief executive, which can be, at least partially, served by means of routine, often computer-based, reporting.[6]

The key indicator system provides a significant amount of useful information. By itself, however, this method often results in many undifferentiated financial variables being presented to a management team. It tends to be financially all-inclusive rather than on-target to a particular executive's specific needs. The information provided is objective, quantifiable, and computer stored. Thus in the key indicator approach the perspective of the information needs of the executive is a partial one—oriented toward hard data needs alone. More significantly, in its "cafeteria" approach to presenting an extensive information base, it fails to provide assistance to executives in thinking through their real information needs.

The total study process is comprehensive and can pinpoint missing systems. However, it suffers, as noted, from all of the problems of total approaches. There are problems concerning expense, the huge amount of data collected (making it difficult to differentiate the forest from the trees), designer bias, and difficulty in devising reporting systems that serve any individual manager well.

NEW CSF METHOD

The MIT research team's experience in the past two years with the critical success factors (CSF) approach suggests that it is highly effective in helping executives to define their significant information needs. Equally important, it has proved efficient in terms of the interview time needed (from three to six hours) to explain the

---

[6] Management control is the process of (a) long-range planning of the activities of the organization, (b) short-term planning (usually one year), and (c) monitoring activities to ensure the accomplishment of the desired results. The management control process thus follows the development of major strategic directions that are set in the strategic planning process. This definition roughly follows the framework of Robert N. Anthony, *Planning and Control: A Framework for Analysis* (Boston: Division of Research, Harvard Business School, 1965).

method and to focus attention on information needs. Most important, executive response to this new method has been excellent in terms of both the process and its outcome.

The actual CSF interviews are usually conducted in two or three separate sessions. In the first, the executive's goals are initially recorded and the CSFs that underlie the goals are discussed. The interrelationships of the CSFs and the goals are then talked about for further clarification and for determination of which recorded CSFs should be combined, eliminated, or restated. An initial cut at measures is also taken in this first interview.

The second session is used to review the results of the first, after the analyst has had a chance to think about them and to suggest "sharpening up" some factors. In addition, measures and possible reports are discussed in depth. Sometimes, a third session may be necessary to obtain final agreement on the CSF measures-and-reporting sequence.

Conceptual Antecedents

In an attempt to overcome some of the shortcomings of the four major approaches discussed earlier, the CSF method focuses on *individual managers* and on each manager's *current information needs*—both hard and soft. It provides for identifying managerial information needs in a clear and meaningful way. Moreover, it takes into consideration the fact that information needs will vary from manager to manager and that these needs will change with time for a particular manager.

The approach is based on the concept of the "success factors" first discussed in the management literature in 1961 by D. Ronald Daniel, now managing director of McKinsey & Company.[7] Although a powerful concept in itself for other than information systems' thinking, it has been heavily obscured in the outpouring of managerial wisdom in the past two decades. It has been focused on and clarified to the best of my knowledge only in the published work of Robert N. Anthony, John Dearden, and Richard F. Vancil.[8]

Daniel, in introducing the concept, cited three examples of major corporations whose information systems produced an extensive amount of information. Very little of the information, however, appeared useful in assisting managers to better perform their jobs.

To draw attention to the type of information actually needed to support managerial activities, Daniel turned to the concept of critical success factors. He stated,

> . . . a company's information system must be discriminating and selective. It should focus on "success factors." In most industries there are usually three to

---

[7] See D. Ronald Daniel, "Management Information Crisis," *HBR*, September-October 1961, p. 111.

[8] See Robert N. Anthony, John Dearden, and Richard F. Vancil, "Key Economic Variables," in *Management Controls Systems* (Homewood, Ill.: Irwin, 1972), p. 147.

six factors that determine success; these key jobs must be done exceedingly well for a company to be successful. Here are some examples from several major industries:

- In the automobile industry, styling, an efficient dealer organization, and tight control of manufacturing cost are paramount.

- In food processing, new product development, good distribution, and effective advertising are the major success factors.

- In life insurance, the development of agency management personnel, effective control of clerical personnel, and innovation in creating new types of policies spell the difference.[9]

Critical success factors thus are, for any business, the limited number of areas in which results, if they are satisfactory, will ensure successful competitive performance for the organization. They are the few key areas where "things must go right" for the business to flourish. If results in these areas are not adequate, the organization's efforts for the period will be less than desired.

As a result, the critical success factors are areas of activity that should receive constant and careful attention from management. The current status of performance in each area should be continually measured, and that information should be made available.

As *Exhibit I* notes, critical success factors support the attainment of organizational goals. Goals represent the end points that an organization hopes to reach. Critical success factors, however, are the areas in which good performance is necessary to ensure attainment of those goals.

Daniel focused on those critical success factors that are relevant for *any* company in a particular industry. *Exhibit I* updates Daniel's automobile industry CSFs and provides another set of CSFs—from the supermarket industry and a nonprofit hospital.

As this exhibit shows, supermarkets have four industry-based CSFs. These are having the right product mix available in each local store, having it on the shelves, having it advertised effectively to pull shoppers into the store, and having it priced correctly—since profit margins are low in this industry. Supermarkets must pay attention to many other things, but these four areas are the underpinnings of successful operation.

Writing a decade later, Anthony and his colleagues picked up Daniel's seminal contribution and expanded it in their work on the design of management control systems. They emphasized three "musts" of any such system:

The control system *must* be tailored to the specific industry in which the company operates and to the specific strategies that it has adopted; it *must* identify the "critical success factors" that should receive careful and continuous

---

[9] Daniel, "Management Information Crisis," p. 116.

management attention if the company is to be successful; and it *must* highlight performance with respect to these key variables in reports to all levels of management.[10]

While continuing to recognize industry-based CSFs, Anthony et al. thus went a step further. They placed additional emphasis on the need to tailor management planning and control systems to both a company's particular strategic objectives and its particular managers. That is, the control system must report on those success factors that are perceived by the managers as appropriate to a particular job in a particular company. In short, CSFs differ from company to company and from manager to manager.

Exhibit I HOW ATTAINMENT OF ORGANIZATIONAL GOALS IS SUPPORTED BY CSFs

Example	Goals	Critical success factors
For-profit concern	Earnings per share	**Automotive industry**
	Return on investment	Styling
	Market share	Quality dealer system
	New product success	Cost control
		Meeting energy standards
		Supermarket industry
		Product mix
		Inventory
		Sales promotion
		Price
Nonprofit concern	Excellence of health care	**Government hospital**
	Meeting needs of future health care environment	Regional integration of health care with other hospitals
		Efficient use of scarce medical resources
		Improved cost accounting

Prime Sources of CSFs

In the discussion so far, we have seen that CSFs are applicable to any company operating in a particular *industry*. Yet Anthony et al. emphasized that a management control system also must be tailored to a particular *company*. This must suggest that there are other sources of CSFs than the industry alone. And, indeed, there are. The MIT team has isolated four prime sources of critical success factors:

---

[10] Anthony, Dearden, and Vancil, "Key Economic Variables," p. 148.

1. Structure of the particular industry As noted, each industry by its very nature has a set of critical success factors that are determined by the characteristics of the industry itself. Each company in the industry must pay attention to these factors. For example, the manager of *any* supermarket will ignore at his peril the critical success factors that appear in *Exhibit I*.

2. Competitive strategy, industry position, and geographic location Each company in an industry is in an individual situation determined by its history and current competitive strategy. For smaller organizations within an industry dominated by one or two large companies, the actions of the major companies will often produce new and significant problems for the smaller companies. The competitive strategy for the latter may mean establishing a new market niche, getting out of a product line completely, or merely redistributing resources among various product lines.

Thus for small companies a competitor's strategy is often a CSF. For example, IBM's competitive approach to the marketing of small, inexpensive computers is, in itself, a CSF for all minicomputer manufacturers.

Just as differences in industry position can dictate CSFs, differences in geographic location and in strategies can lead to differing CSFs from one company to another in an industry.

3. Environmental factors As the gross national product and the economy fluctuate, as political factors change, and as the population waxes and wanes, critical success factors can also change for various institutions. At the beginning of 1973, virtually no chief executive in the United States would have listed "energy supply availability" as a critical success factor. Following the oil embargo, however, for a considerable period of time this factor was monitored closely by many executives— since adequate energy was problematical and vital to organizational bottom-line performance.

4. Temporal factors Internal organizational considerations often lead to temporal critical success factors. These are areas of activity that are significant for the success of an organization for a particular period of time because they are below the threshold of acceptability at that time (although in general they are "in good shape" and do not merit special attention). As an example, for any organization the loss of a major group of executives in a plane crash obviously would make the "rebuilding of the executive group" a critical success factor for the organization for the period of time until this was accomplished. Similarly, while inventory control is rarely a CSF for the chief executive officer, a very unusual situation (either far too much or far too little stock) might, in fact, become a high-level CSF.

Like Organizations, Differing CSFs

Any organization's situation will change from time to time, and factors that are dealt with by executives as commonplace at one time may become critical success factors at another time. The key here is for the executive to clearly define at any point in time exactly those factors that are crucial to the success of his particular organization in the period for which he is planning.

One would expect, therefore, that organizations in the same industry would exhibit different CSFs as a result of differences in geographic location, strategies, and other factors. A study by Gladys G. Mooradian of the critical success factors of three similar medical group practices bears this out.[11] The medical group practices of the participating physicians were heterogeneous with regard to many of these factors. Each group, however, was well managed with a dynamic and successful administrator in charge.

Mooradian defined the CSFs through open-ended interviews with the administrator of each group practice. She then asked the managers to define their critical success factors and to rank them from most important to least important. Finally, to verify the factors selected, she obtained the opinions of others in the organization.

Exhibit II shows the adminstrators' key variables for the three group practices, ranked in order as perceived by the managers of each institution. It is interesting to note that several of the same variables appear on each list. Several variables, however, are unique to each institution. One can explain the difference in the CSFs chosen by noting the stages of growth, location, and strategies of each clinic:

Exhibit II CRITICAL SUCCESS FACTORS FOR THREE MEDICAL GROUP PRACTICES

	Clinic # 1	Clinic # 2	Clinic # 3
Most important	Government regulation	Quality and comprehensive care	Efficiency of operations
	Efficiency of operations	Federal funding	Staffing mix
	Patients' view of practice	Government regulation	Government regulation
	Relation to hospital	Efficiency of operations	Patients' view of practice
	Malpractice insurance effects	Patients' view of practice	Relation to community
	Relation to community	Satellites versus patient service	Relation to hospital
		Other providers in community	
Least important		Relation to hospital	

---

[11] Gladys G. Mooradian, "The Key Variables in Planning and Control in Medical Group Practices," unpublished master's thesis (Cambridge, Mass.: MIT, Sloan School of Management, 1976).

- The first medical group is a mature clinic that has been in existence for several years, has a sound organization structure, and has an assured patient population. It is most heavily concerned with government regulation and environmental changes (such as rapidly increasing costs for malpractice insurance), which are the only factors that might upset its highly favorable status quo.

- The second group practice is located in a rural part of a relatively poor state. It is dependent on federal funding and also on its ability to offer a type of medical care not available from private practitioners. Its number one CSF, therefore, is its ability to develop a distinctive competitive image for the delivery of comprehensive, quality care.

- The third clinic is a rapidly growing, new group practice, which was—at that point in time—heavily dependent for its near-term success on its ability to "set up" an efficient operation and bring on board the correct mix of staff to serve its rapidly growing patient population.

In looking at these three lists, it is noticeable that the first four factors on the mature clinic's list also appear on the other two lists. These, it can be suggested, are the all-encompassing industry-based factors. The remaining considerations, which are particular to one or the other of the practices but not to all, are generated by differences in environmental situation, temporal factors, geographic location, or strategic situation.

CSFs at General Manager Level

To this point, I have discussed CSFs strictly from the viewpoint of the top executive of an organization. Indeed, that is the major focus of the MIT research team's current work. It is, however, clear from studies now going on that CSFs, as might be expected, can be useful at each level of general management (managers to whom multiple functions report). There are significant benefits of taking the necessary time to think through—and to record—the critical success factors for each general manager in an organization. Consider:

- The process helps the manager to determine those factors on which he or she should focus management attention. It also helps to ensure that those significant factors will receive careful and continuous management scrutiny.

- The process forces the manager to develop good measures for those factors and to seek reports on each of the measures.

- The identification of CSFs allows a clear definition of the amount of information that must be collected by the organization and limits the costly collection of more data than necessary.

- The identification of CSFs moves an organization away from the trap of building its reporting and information system primarily around data that are "easy to collect." Rather, it focuses attention on those data that might otherwise not be collected but are significant for the success of the particular management level involved.

- The process acknowledges that some factors are temporal and that CSFs are manager specific. This suggests that the information system should be in constant flux with new reports being developed as needed to accommodate changes in the organization's strategy, environment, or organization structure. Rather than changes in an information system being looked on as an indication of "inadequate design," they must be viewed as an inevitable and productive part of information systems development.

- The CSF concept itself is useful for more than information systems design. Current studies suggest several additional areas of assistance to the management process. For example, an area that can be improved through the use of CSFs is the planning process. CSFs can be arrayed hierarchically and used as an important vehicle of communication for management, either as an informal planning aid or as a part of the formal planning process.

Let me stress that the CSF approach does not attempt to deal with information needs for strategic planning. Data needs for this management role are almost impossible to preplan. The CSF method centers, rather, on information needs for management control where data needed to monitor and improve existing areas of business can be more readily defined.

ILLUSTRATIVE CSF EXAMPLE

Let us now turn to an example of the use of this approach. The president referred to at the start of this article is real. He is Larry Gould, former president of Microwave Associates, a $60-million sales organization serving several aspects of the microwave communication industry.[12] When he first looked carefully at the "information" he was receiving, Gould found that some 97 "reports" crossed his desk in a typical month. Almost all were originally designed by someone else who felt that he "should be receiving this vital data."

However, the reports provided him with virtually nothing *he* could use. A few gave him some "scorekeeping data," such as the monthly profit statement. One or two others provided him with bits and pieces of data he wanted, but even these left major things unsaid. The data were either unrelated to other key facts or related in a way that was not meaningful to him.

The concept of critical success factors sounded to him like one way out of this dilemma. He therefore, with the MIT research analyst, invested two two-and-a-half-hour periods in working through his goals, critical success factors, and measures. First, he noted the objectives of the company and the current year's goals. Then, he went to work to assess what factors were critical to accomplish these objectives.

---

[12] Since this was originally written, Gould has assumed the position of chairman of the board at M/A-COM, Inc., a holding company of which Microwave Associates is a subsidiary.

Factors and Measures

The seven critical success factors Gould developed are shown in *Exhibit III,* along with from one to three prime measures for each factor (although he also developed some additional measures). The reader should note that this specific set of CSFs emerged only after intensive analysis and discussion. At the end of the first meeting, nine factors were on Gould's list. By the end of the second meeting, two had been combined into one, and one had been dropped as not being significant enough to command ongoing close attention.

Exhibit III CSFs DEVELOPED TO MEET MICROWAVE ASSOCIATES' ORGANIZATIONAL GOALS

Critical success factors	Prime measures
1. Image in financial markets	Price/earnings ratio
2. Technological reputation with customers	Orders/bid ratio
	Customer "perception" interview results
3. Market success	Change in market share (each product)
	Growth rates of company markets
4. Risk recognition in major bids and contracts	Company's years of experience with similar products
	"New" or "old" customer
	Prior customer relationship
5. Profit margin on jobs	Bid profit margin as ratio of profit on similar jobs in this product line
6. Company morale	Turnover, absenteeism, etc.
	Informal feedback
7. Performance to budget on major jobs	Job cost budgeted/actual

Most of the second interview session centered on a discussion of the measures for each factor. Where hard data were perceived to be available, the discussion was short. Where softer measures were necessary, however, lengthy discussions of the type of information needed and the difficulty and/or cost of acquiring it often ensued. Yet convergence on the required "evidence" about the state of each CSF occurred with responsible speed and clarity in each case. Some discussion concerning each CSF and its measures is perhaps worthwhile. Consider:

1. Image in financial markets Microwave Associates is growing and making acquisitions as it seeks to gain a growth segment of the electronics industry. Much of the company's growth is coming from acquisitions. Clearly, the better the image on Wall Street, the higher the price-earnings ratio. The measure of success here is clear: the company's multiple vis-à-vis others in its industry segment.

2. Technological reputation with customers Although Microwave Associates has some standard products, the majority of its work is done on a tailor-made, one-shot basis. A significant number of these jobs are state-of-the-art work that leads to follow-on production contracts. To a very large extent, buying decisions in the field are made on the customer's confidence in Microwave's technical ability. Sample measures were developed for this CSF. The two measures shown in this exhibit are at the opposite extremes of hard and soft data. The ratio of total orders to total bids can be easily measured. While this hard measure is indicative of customers' perception of the company's technical ability, it also has other factors such as "sales aggressiveness" in it.

The most direct measure possible is person-to-person interviews. Although this measure is soft, the company decided to initiate a measuring process through field interviews by its top executives. (Other measures of this CSF included field interviews by sales personnel, assessment of the rise or fall of the percentage of each major customer's business being obtained, and so forth.)

3. Market success On the surface, this CSF is straightforward, but as shown by the measures, it includes attention to *current* market success, as well as the company's progress with regard to significant *new* market opportunities (e.g., the relative rate of growth of each market segment, opportunities provided by new technology, and relative—not just absolute—competitive performance).

4. Risk recognition in major bids and contracts Because many of the jobs accepted are near or at the state of the art, controlling the company's risk profile is critical. As noted in the exhibit, a variety of factors contribute to risk. The measurement process designed involves a computer algorithm to consider these factors and to highlight particularly risky situations.

5. Profit margin on jobs When profit center managers have low backlogs, they are often tempted to bid low to obtain additional business. While this procedure is not necessarily bad, it is critical for corporate management to understand the expected profit profile and, at times, to counter lower-level tendencies to accept low-profit business.

6. Company morale Because of its high-technology strategy, the company is clearly heavily dependent on the esprit of its key scientists and engineers. It must also be able to attract and keep a skilled work force. Thus morale is a critical success factor. Measures of morale range from hard data (e.g., turnover, absenteeism, and tardiness) to informal feedback (e.g., management discussion sessions with employees).

7. Performance to budget on major jobs This final CSF reflects the need to control major projects and to ensure that they are completed on time and near budget. Adverse results with regard to timeliness can severely affect CSF #2 (technological perception), and significant cost overruns can similarly affect CSF #1 (financial market perception). In general, no single job is crucially important. Rather, it is the *profile* of performance across major jobs that is significant.

Reports and Subsystems

Given the foregoing CSFs and measures, the next step was to design a set of report formats. This step required examination of both existing information systems and data sources.

For the soft, informal, subjective measures, this process was straightforward. Forms to record facts and impressions were designed so as to scale (where possible) perception and highlight significant soft factors.

For some of the hard computer-based measures, existing information systems and data bases supplied most of the necessary data. However, in every case—even where *all* data were available—existing report forms were inadequate and new reports had to be designed.

Most important, however, two completely new information subsystems were needed to support the president's CSFs. These were a "bidding" system and a vastly different automated "project budgeting and control" system. (Significantly, each of these subsystems had been requested many times by lower-level personnel, who needed them for more detailed planning and control of job bidding and monitoring at the product-line manager and manufacturing levels.) Subsequently, these subsystems were placed at the top of the priority list for data processing.

In summarizing the Microwave case, it is clear that the exercise of discovering information needs through examination of the chief executive's critical success factors had a number of specific benefits. All of the seven general advantages of the CSF method for information systems development previously noted applied to some extent. However, the importance of each of these varies from organization to organization. At Microwave, the most striking advantages were:

• The conscious listing (or bringing to the surface) of the most significant areas on which attention needed to be focused. The process of making these areas *explicit* provided insights not only into information needs, but also into several other aspects of the company's managerial systems.

• The design of a useful set of *reports* to provide the information needed for monitoring ongoing operations at the executive level. (There clearly were other data needed—i.e., for developing strategy, dealing with special situations, and so on.) The CSF route, however, focused on the data needed for the ongoing "management control" process, and this need was significant at Microwave.

• The development of *priorities* for information systems development. It was clear that information needed for control purposes by the chief executive should have some priority. (It also highlighted priorities for other management levels.)

• The provision of a means of hierarchical *communication* among executives as to what the critical factors were for the success of the company. (Too often, only goals provide a major communication link to enhance shared understanding of the company and its environment among management levels.) This hierarchical approach provided another—and we believe more pragmatic and action-oriented—means of communication. At Microwave, there is a current project aimed at developing and sharing CSFs at the top four management levels.

OTHER CASE EXAMPLES

The critical success factors developed in four other cases provide useful additional background for drawing some generalizations about the method and executive information needs. These CSFs are arrayed in *Exhibit IV*.

Major Oil Company

The chief executive of this centralized organization responded quickly and unhesitatingly concerning his critical success factors. His goal structure was oriented toward such traditional measures as increasing return on investment, increasing earnings per share, and so forth. Yet he felt there were two major keys to profitability in the future. One was to improve relationships with society as a whole and with the federal government in particular. The other was the urgent need to provide a broader base of earnings assets in petroleum-shy future decades.

As a result of this view of the world, the CEO had initiated major programs to develop new ventures and to decentralize the organization. To facilitate the acquisition process, emphasis was placed on cash flow (liquidity) as opposed to reported earnings. In addition, prime attention was given to understanding and improving external relationships.

All of these efforts are reflected in the company's critical success factors shown in *Exhibit IV*. Progress in each of these areas is monitored weekly. CSFs #1, #3, and #4 are reported on with regard to both actions taken and the appropriate executive's subjective assessment of results attained. Liquidity measures are provided by computer output. New venture success is now assessed by a combination of hard and soft measures.

Store Furnishings Manufacturer

This midwestern company has three major product lines. The largest of these is a well-accepted but relatively stable traditional line on which the company's reputation was made (product line A). In addition, there are two relatively new but fast-growing lines (B and C). The president's preexisting information system was a combination of monthly financial accounting reports and several sales analysis reports.

The president's critical success factors directly reflected the changing fortunes of his product lines. There was a need to concentrate on immediate foreign penetration (to build market share) in the two "hot" lines. At the same time, he saw the need to reassess the now barely growing line on which the company was built three decades ago.

Exhibit IV CSFs IN FOUR CASES

Chief executive of a major oil company	President of a store furnishings manufacturer	Director of a government hospital	Division chief executive of an electronics company
1. Decentralize organization.	1. Expand foreign sales for product lines B and C.	1. Devise method for obtaining valid data on current status of hospital operations.	1. Support field sales force.
2. Improve liquidity position.	2. Improve market understanding of product line A.	2. Devise method for resource allocation.	2. Strengthen customer relations.
3. Improve government/business relationships.	3. Redesign sales compensation structure in three-product lines.	3. Manage external relationships.	3. Improve productivity.
4. Create better societal image.	4. Improve production scheduling.	4. Get acceptance of concept of regionalization by all hospital directors.	4. Obtain government R&D support.
5. Develop new ventures.	5. Mechanize production facilities.	5. Develop method for managing regionalization in government hospital group.	5. Develop new products.
	6. Strengthen management team.	6. Strengthen management support, capability, and capacity.	6. Acquire new technological capability.
		7. Improve relationship with government department central office.	7. Improve facilities.
		8. Meet budgetary constraints.	

Equally significant, whereas direct selling had been the only feasible mode for the traditional line, the new lines appeared to respond heavily to trade advertising to generate both leads and, in some cases, direct-from-the-factory sales. Because margins are relatively tight in this competitive industry, one factor critical to the company's success with this new product structure, therefore, was a redesign of the sales compensation structure to reflect the evidently diminished effort needed to make sales in the new lines.

A similar need for cost-consciousness also dictated attention to the CSFs of production scheduling efficiency and productivity improvements through the increasing mechanization of production facilities. Finally, strengthening the management team to take advantage of the opportunities presented by the new product lines was felt to be critical by this president.

The analysis of CSFs in this case indicated a need for two major changes in formal information flow to the president. Subsequently, a far more meaningful production reporting system was developed (to support CSF #4), and a vastly different sales reporting system emphasizing CSFs #2 and #3 was established.

Government Hospital

The CSFs for the director of a government hospital reflect his belief in the need for his organization to radically restructure itself to adapt to a future health care environment perceived as vastly different. He believes that his hospital and his sister government agency hospitals must provide specialized, cost-conscious, comprehensive health care for a carefully defined patient population. Moreover, this care will have to be integrated with that provided by other government hospitals and private hospitals within the region of the country in which his hospital exists.

The director's critical success factors are thus, as shown in *Exhibit IV*, concerned primarily with building external links and managing cooperation and resource sharing within the set of eight government agency hospitals in his region. The director is also concerned with the development of adequate data systems and methods to manage effective and efficient use of scarce medical resources.

The organization currently has only minimal management information—drawn in bits and pieces from what is essentially a financial accounting system designed primarily to assure the safeguarding and legal use of government funds. The director's desire to get involved in a CSF-oriented investigation of management information needs grew from his despair of being able to manage in the future environment with existing information.

The MIT research team is currently conducting a study involving CSF-based interviews with the top three levels of key managers and department heads in the hospital. Their information needs are heavily oriented toward external data and vastly improved cost accounting.

Major Electronics Division

This decentralized electronics company places return-on-investment responsibility on the top executive of a major division. His first two CSFs indicate his view of the need for an increasing emphasis on marketing in his traditionally engineering-oriented organization. As *Exhibit IV* shows, his CSFs #3, #6, and #7 are oriented toward the need for more cost-effective production facilities.

Equally important is his attention to new product development (CSF #5) in a fast-moving marketplace. In conjunction with this, CSF #4 reflects his view that a healthy portfolio of government R&D contracts will allow a much larger amount of research to be performed, thereby increasing the expected yield of new ideas and new products. Thus he spends a significant share of his time involved in the process of assuring that government research contracts are being avidly pursued (although they add relatively little to his near-term bottom line).

Efforts to improve the information provided to this division manager have revolved primarily around making more explicit the methods of measuring progress in each of these CSF areas. More quantitative indexes have proved to be useful in some areas. In others, however, they have not improved what must be essentially "subjective feel" judgments.

SUPPORTIVE CSF INFORMATION

Previously, I discussed the advantages (both general and specific to one case) of using the CSF process for information systems design. Additionally, some important attributes of the types of information necessary to support the top executive's CSFs can be drawn from the five examples. Consider:

• Perhaps most obvious, but worth stating, is the fact that traditional financial accounting systems rarely provide the type of data necessary to monitor critical success factors. Financial accounting systems are aimed at providing historical information to outsiders (e.g., stockholders and others). Only very occasionally is there much overlap between financial accounting data and the type of data needed to track CSFs. In only one of the companies studied was financial accounting data the major source of information for a CSF, and there for only one factor. However, the need for improved *cost* accounting data to report on CSFs was often evident.

• Many critical success factors require information external to the organization—information concerned with market structure, customer perceptions, or future trends. Approximately a third of the 33 CSFs in the five examples fit this description. The data to support these CSFs are not only unavailable from the financial accounting system but, in the majority of cases, are also unavailable as a by-product of the organization's other usual day-to-day transaction-processing systems (e.g., order entry, billing, and payroll). The information system must therefore be designed, and the external information consciously collected from the proper sources. It will not flow naturally to the CEO.

- Many other CSFs require coordinating pieces of information from multiple data sets that are widely dispersed throughout the company. This is perhaps best noted in the Microwave case, but it is a recurrent feature in all companies. This situation argues heavily for computer implementation of data base systems that facilitate accessing multiple data sets.

- A small but significant part of the information concerning the status of CSFs requires subjective assessment on the part of others in the organization, rather than being neatly quantifiable. About a fifth of the status measures at the companies studied require subjective assessment. This is significant managerial data, and top executives are used to these soft but useful status measures.

(However, it should be noted, many more of the measures at first devised were subjective. It takes considerable work to find objective measures, but in more instances than originally perceived, suitable objective measures are available and can be developed.)

- Critical success factors can be categorized as either the "monitoring" or the "building" type. The more competitive pressure for current performance that the chief executive feels, the more his CSFs tend toward monitoring current results. The more that the organization is insulated from economic pressures (as the government hospital was) or decentralized (as the oil company was becoming), the more CSFs become oriented toward building for the future through major change programs aimed at adapting the organization to a perceived new environment.

In all cases that I have seen thus far, however, there is a mixture of the two types. Every chief executive appears to have, at some level, both monitoring and building (or adapting) responsibilities. Thus a great deal of the information needed will not continue to be desired year after year. Rather, it is relatively short-term "project status" information that is needed only during the project's lifetime. Periodic review of CSFs will therefore bring to light the need to discontinue some reports and initiate others.

Management
Misinformation Systems

RUSSELL L. ACKOFF

The growing preoccupation of operations researchers and management scientists with Management Information Systems (MIS's) is apparent. In fact, for some the design of such systems has almost become synonymous with operations research or management science. Enthusiasm for such systems is understandable: it involves the researcher in a romantic relationship with the most glamorous instrument of our time, the computer. Such enthusiasm is understandable but, nevertheless, some of the excesses to which it has led are not excusable.

Contrary to the impression produced by the growing literature, few computerized management information systems have been put into operation. Of those I've seen that have been implemented, most have not matched expectations and some have been outright failures. I believe that these near- and far-misses could have been avoided if certain false (and usually implicit) assumptions on which many such systems have been erected had not been made.

There seem to be five common and erroneous assumptions underlying the design of most MIS's, each of which I will consider. After doing so I will outline an MIS design procedure which avoids these assumptions.

GIVE THEM MORE

Most MIS's are designed on the assumption that the critical deficiency under which most managers operate is the *lack of relevant information.* I do not deny that most managers lack a good deal of information that they should have, but I do deny that this is the most important informational deficiency from which they suffer. It seems to me that they suffer more from an *over abundance of irrelevant information.*

This is not a play on words. The consequences of changing the emphasis of an MIS from supplying relevant information to eliminating irrelevant information is considerable. If one is preoccupied with supplying relevant information, attention

---

Copyright © 1967 by the Institute of Management Sciences, *Management Science* (December 1967), pp. B147–B156. Reprinted by permission.

245

is almost exclusively given to the generation, storage, and retrieval of information: hence emphasis is placed on constructing data banks, coding, indexing, updating files, access languages, and so on. The ideal which has emerged from this orientation is an infinite pool of data into which a manager can reach to pull out any information he wants. If, on the other hand, one sees the manager's information problem primarily, but not exclusively, as one that arises out of an overabundance of irrelevant information, most of which was not asked for, then the two most important functions of an information system become *filtration* (or evaluation) and *condensation*. The literature on MIS's seldom refers to these functions let alone considers how to carry them out.

My experience indicates that most managers receive much more data (if not information) than they can possibly absorb even if they spend all of their time trying to do so. Hence they already suffer from an information overload. They must spend a great deal of time separating the relevant from the irrelevant and searching for the kernels in the relevant documents. For example, I have found that I receive an average of forty-three hours of unsolicited reading material each week. The solicited material is usually half again this amount.

I have seen a daily stock status report that consists of approximately six hundred pages of computer print-out. The report is circulated daily across managers' desks. I've also seen requests for major capital expenditures that come in book size, several of which are distributed to managers each week. It is not uncommon for many managers to receive an average of one journal a day or more. One could go on and on.

Unless the information overload to which managers are subjected is reduced, any additional information made available by an MIS cannot be expected to be used effectively.

Even relevant documents have too much redundancy. Most documents can be considerably condensed without loss of content. My point here is best made, perhaps, by describing briefly an experiment that a few of my colleagues and I conducted on the OR literature several years ago. By using a panel of well-known experts we identified four OR articles that all members of the panel considered to be "above average," and four articles that were considered to be "below average." The authors of the eight articles were asked to prepare "objective" examinations (duration thirty minutes) plus answers for graduate students who were to be assigned the articles for reading. (The authors were not informed about the experiment.) Then several experienced writers were asked to reduce each article to 2/3 and 1/3 of its original length only by eliminating words. They also prepared a brief abstract of each article. Those who did the condensing did not see the examinations to be given to the students.

A group of graduate students who had not previously read the articles were then selected. Each one was given four articles randomly selected, each of which was in one of its four versions: 100%, 67%, 33%, or abstract. Each version of each article was read by two students. All were given the same examinations. The average scores on the examinations were then compared.

For the above-average articles there was no significant difference between average test scores for the 100%, 67%, and 33% versions, but there was a significant *decrease* in average test scores for those who had read only the abstract. For the below-average articles there was no difference in average test scores among those who had read the 100%, 67%, and 33% versions, but there was a significant *increase* in average test scores of those who had read only the abstract.

The sample used was obviously too small for general conclusions but the results strongly indicate the extent to which even good writing can be condensed without loss of information. I refrain from drawing the obvious conclusion about bad writing.

It seems clear that condensation as well as filtration, performed mechanically or otherwise, should be an essential part of an MIS, and that such a system should be capable of handling much, if not all, of the unsolicited as well as solicited information that a manager receives.

THE MANAGER NEEDS THE INFORMATION THAT HE WANTS

Most MIS designers "determine" what information is needed by asking managers what information they would like to have. This is based on the assumption that managers know what information they need and want it.

For a manager to know what information he needs he must be aware of each type of decision he should make (as well as does) and he must have an adequate model of each. These conditions are seldom satisfied. Most managers have some conception of at least some of the types of decisions they must make. Their conceptions, however, are likely to be deficient in a very critical way, a way that follows from an important principle of scientific economy: the less we understand a phenomenon, the more variables we require to explain it. Hence, the manager who does not understand the phenomenon he controls plays it "safe" and, with respect to information, wants "everything." The MIS designer who has even less understanding of the relevant phenomenon than the manager, tries to provide even more than everything. He thereby increases what is already an overload of irrelevant information.

For example, market researchers in a major oil company once asked their marketing managers what variables they thought were relevant in estimating the sales volume of future service stations. Almost seventy variables were identified. The market researchers then added about half again this many variables and performed a large multiple linear regression analysis of sales of existing stations against these variables and found about thirty-five to be statistically significant. A forecasting equation was based on this analysis. An OR team subsequently constructed a model based on only one of these variables, traffic flow, which predicted sales better than the thirty-five variable regression equation. The team went on to *explain* sales at service stations in terms of the customers' perception of the amount of time lost by stopping for service. The relevance of all but a few of the variables used by the market researchers could be explained by their effect on such perception.

The moral is simple: one cannot specify what information is required for decision making until an explanatory model of the decision process and the system involved has been constructed and tested. Information systems are subsystems of control systems. They cannot be designed adequately without taking control in account. Furthermore, whatever else regression analyses can yield, they cannot yield understanding and explanation of phenomena. They describe and, at best, predict.

GIVE A MANAGER THE INFORMATION
HE NEEDS AND HIS DECISION MAKING WILL IMPROVE

It is frequently assumed that if a manager is provided with the information he needs, he will then have no problem in using it effectively. The history of OR stands to the contrary. For example, give most managers an initial tableau of a typical "real" mathematical programming, sequencing, or network problem and see how close they come to an optimal solution. If their experience and judgment have any value they may not do badly, but they will seldom do very well. In most management problems there are too many possibilities to expect experience, judgment, or intuition to provide good guesses, even with perfect information.

Furthermore, when several probabilities are involved in a problem the unguided mind of even a manager has difficulty in aggregating them in a valid way. We all know many simple problems in probability in which untutored intuition usually does very badly (e.g., What are the correct odds that 2 of 25 people selected at random will have their birthdays on the same day of the year?). For example, very few of the results obtained by queuing theory, when arrivals and service are probabilistic, are obvious to managers; nor are the results of risk analysis where the managers' own subjective estimates of probabilities are used.

The moral: it is necessary to determine how well managers can use needed information. When, because of the complexity of the decision process, they can't use it well, they should be provided with either decision rules or performance feed-back so that they can identify and learn from their mistakes. More on this point later.

MORE COMMUNICATION MEANS BETTER PERFORMANCE

One characteristic of most MIS's which I have seen is that they provide managers with better current information about what other managers and their departments and divisions are doing. Underlying this provision is the belief that better interdepartmental communication enables managers to coordinate their decisions more effectively and hence improves the organization's overall performance. Not only is this not necessarily so, but it seldom is so. One would hardly expect two competing companies to become more cooperative because the information each acquires about the other is improved. This analogy is not as far fetched as one might suppose. For example, consider the following very much simplified version of a situation I once ran into. The simplification of the case does not affect any of its essential characteristics.

A department store has two "line" operations: buying and selling. Each function is performed by a separate department. The Purchasing Department primarily controls one variable: how much of each item is bought. The Merchandising Department controls the price at which it is sold. Typically, the measure of performance applied to the Purchasing Department was the turnover rate of inventory. The measure applied to the Merchandising Department was gross sales; this department sought to maximize the number of items sold times their price.

Now by examining a single item let us consider what happens in this system. The merchandising manager, using his knowledge of competition and consumption, set a price which he judged would maximize gross sales. In doing so he utilized price-demand curves for each type of item. For each price the curves show the expected sales and values on an upper and lower confidence band as well. (See Figure 1.) When instructing the Purchasing Department how many items to make available, the merchandising manager quite naturally used the value on the upper confidence curve. This minimized the chances of his running short which if it occurred, would hurt his performance. It also maximized the chances of being overstocked but this was not his concern, only the purchasing manager's. Say, therefore, that the merchandising manager initially selected price P_1 and requested that amount Q_1 be made available by the Purchasing Department.

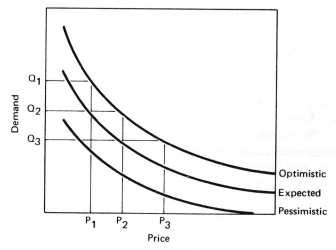

Fig. 1 *Price-demand curve*

In this company the purchasing manager also had access to the price-demand curves. He knew the merchandising manager always ordered optimistically. Therefore, using the same curve he read over from Q_1 to the upper limit and down to the expected value from which he obtained Q_2, the quantity he actually intended to make available. He did not intend to pay for the merchandising manager's optimism. If merchandising ran out of stock, it was not his worry. Now the merchandising manager was informed about what the purchasing manager had done so he adjusted his price to P_2. The purchasing manager in turn was told that the merchandising manager had made this readjustment so he planned to make only Q_3 available. If this process—made possible only by perfect communication between departments—had been allowed to continue, nothing would have been bought and nothing would have been sold. This outcome was avoided by prohibiting communication between the two departments and forcing each to guess what the other was doing.

I have obviously caricatured the situation in order to make the point clear: when organizational units have inappropriate measures of performance which put them in conflict with each other, as is often the case, communication between them may hurt organizational performance, not help it. Organizational structure and performance measurement must be taken into account before opening the flood gates and permitting the free flow of information between parts of the organization. (A more rigorous discussion of organizational structure and the relationship of communication to it can be found in [A].)

A MANAGER DOES NOT HAVE TO UNDERSTAND HOW AN INFORMATION SYSTEM WORKS, ONLY HOW TO USE IT

Most MIS designers seek to make their systems as innocuous and unobtrusive as possible to managers lest they become frightened. The designers try to provide managers with very easy access to the system and assure them that they need to know nothing more about it. The designers usually succeed in keeping managers ignorant in this regard. This leaves managers unable to evaluate the MIS as a whole. It often makes them afraid to even try to do so lest they display their ignorance publicly. In failing to evaluate their MIS, managers delegate much of the control of the organization to the system's designers and operators who may have many virtues, but managerial competence is seldom among them.

Let me cite a case in point. A Chairman of a Board of a medium-size company asked for help on the following problem. One of his larger (decentralized) divisions had installed a computerized production-inventory control and manufacturing-manager information system about a year earlier. It had acquired about $2,000,000 worth of equipment to do so. The Board Chairman had just received a request from the Division for permission to replace the original equipment with newly announced equipment which cost several times the original amount. An executive "justification" for so doing was provided with the request. The Chairman wanted to know whether the request was really justified. He admitted to complete incompetence in this connection.

A meeting was arranged at the Division at which I was subjected to an extended and detailed briefing. The system was large but relatively simple. At the heart of it was a reorder point for each item and a maximum allowable stock level. Reorder quantities took lead-time as well as the allowable maximum into account. The computer kept track of stock, ordered items when required and generated numerous reports on both the state of the system it controlled and its own "actions."

When the briefing was over I was asked if I had any questions. I did. First I asked if, when the system had been installed, there had been many parts whose stock level exceeded the maximum amount possible under the new system. I was told there were many. I asked for a list of about thirty and for some graph paper. Both were provided. With the help of the system designer and volumes of old daily reports I began to plot the stock level of the first listed item over time. When this item reached the maximum "allowable" stock level it had been reordered. The system designer was surprised and said that by sheer "luck" I had found one of the few errors made by the system. Continued plotting showed that because of repeated premature reordering the item had never gone much below the maximum stock level. Clearly the program was confusing the maximum allowable stock level and the reorder point. This turned out to be the case in more than half of the items on the list.

Next I asked if they had many paired parts, ones that were only used with each other; for example, matched nuts and bolts. They had many. A list was produced and we began checking the previous day's withdrawals. For more than half of the pairs the differences in the numbers recorded as withdrawn were very large. No explanation was provided.

Before the day was out it was possible to show by some quick and dirty calculations that the new computerized system was costing the company almost $150,000 per month more than the hand system which it had replaced, most of this in excess inventories.

The recommendation was that the system be redesigned as quickly as possible and that the new equipment not be authorized for the time being.

The questions asked of the system had been obvious and simple ones. Managers should have been able to ask them but—and this is the point—they felt themselves incompetent to do so. They would not have allowed a handoperated system to get so far out of their control.

No MIS should ever be installed unless the managers for whom it is intended are trained to evaluate and hence control it rather than be controlled by it.

A SUGGESTED PROCEDURE FOR DESIGNING AN MIS

The erroneous assumptions I have tried to reveal in the preceding discussion can, I believe, be avoided by an appropriate design procedure. One is briefly outlined here.

1. Analysis of the Decison System

Each (or at least each important) type of managerial decision required by the organization under study should be identified and the relationships between them should be determined and flow-charted. Note that this is *not* necessarily the same thing as determining what decisions *are* made. For example, in one company I found that make-or-buy decisions concerning parts were made only at the time when a part was introduced into stock and was never subsequently reviewed. For some items this decision had gone unreviewed for as many as twenty years. Obviously, such decisions should be made more often; in some cases every time an order is placed in order to take account of current shop loading, underused shifts, delivery times from suppliers, and so on.

Decision-flow analyses are usually self-justifying. They often reveal important decisions that are being made by default (e.g., the make-buy decision referred to above), and they disclose interdependent decisions that are being made independently. Decision-flow charts frequently suggest changes in managerial responsibility, organizational structure, and measure of performance which can correct the types of deficiencies cited.

Decision analyses can be conducted with varying degrees of detail, that is, they may be anywhere from coarse to fine grained. How much detail one should become involved with depends on the amount of time and resources that are available for the analysis. Although practical considerations frequently restrict initial analyses to a particular organizational function, it is preferable to perform a coarse analysis of all of an organization's managerial functions rather than a fine analysis of one or a subset of functions. It is easier to introduce finer information into an integrated information system than it is to combine fine subsystems into one integrated system.

2. An Analysis of Information Requirements

Managerial decisions can be classified into three types:

(a) Decisions for which adequate models are available or can be constructed and from which optimal (or near optimal) solutions can be derived. In such cases the decision process itself should be incorporated into the information system hereby converting it (at least partially) to a control system. A decision model identifies what information is required and hence what information is relevant.

(b) Decisions for which adequate models can be constructed but from which optimal solutions cannot be extracted. Here some kind of heuristic or search procedure should be provided even if it consists of no more than computerized trial and error. A simulation of the model will, as a minimum, permit comparison of proposed alternative solutions. Here too the model specifies what information is required.

(c) Decisions for which adequate models cannot be constructed. Research is required here to determine what information is relevant. If decision making cannot be delayed for the completion of such research or the decision's effect is not large enough to justify the cost of research, then judgment must be used to "guess" what information is relevant. It may be possible to make explicit the implicit model used by the decision maker and treat it as a model of type (b).

In each of these three types of situation it is necessary to provide feedback by comparing actual decision outcomes with those predicted by the model or decision maker. Each decision that is made, along with its predicted outcome, should be an essential input to a management control system. I shall return to this point below.

3. Aggregation of Decisions

Decisions with the same or largely overlapping informational requirements should be grouped together as a single manager's task. This will reduce the information a manager requires to do his job and is likely to increase his understanding of it. This may require a reorganization of the system. Even if such a reorganization cannot be implemented completely what can be done is likely to improve performance significantly and reduce the information loaded on managers.

4. Design of Information Processing

Now the procedure for collecting, storing, retrieving, and treating information can be designed. Since there is a voluminous literature on this subject I shall leave it at this except for one point. Such a system must not only be able to answer questions addressed to it; it should also be able to answer questions that have not been asked by reporting any deviations from expectation. An extensive exception-reporting system is required.

5. Design of Control of the Control System

It must be assumed that the system that is being designed will be deficient in many and significant ways. Therefore it is necessary to identify the ways in which it may be deficient, to design procedures for detecting its deficiencies, and for correcting the system so as to remove or reduce them. Hence the system should be designed to be flexible and adaptive. This is little more than a platitude, but it has a not-so-obvious implication. No completely computerized system can be as flexible and adaptive as can a man-machine system. This is illustrated by a concluding example of a system that is being developed and is partially in operation. (See Figure 2.)

The company involved has its market divided into approximately two hundred marketing areas. A model for each has been constructed as is "in" the computer. On the basis of competitive intelligence supplied to the service marketing manager by marketing researchers and information specialists he and his staff make policy decisions for each area each month. Their tentative decisions are fed into the computer which yields a forecast of expected performance. Changes are made until the expectations match what is desired. In this way they arrive at "final" decisions. At the end of the month the computer compares the actual performance of each area with what was predicted. If a deviation exceeds what could be expected by chance, the company's OR Group then seeks the reason for the deviation, performing as much research as is required to find it. If the cause is found to be permanent the computerized model is adjusted appropriately. The result is an adaptive man-machine system whose precision and generality is continuously increasing with use.

Finally it should be noted that in carrying out the design steps enumerated above, three groups should collaborate: information systems specialists, operations researchers, *and managers*. The participation of managers in design of a system that is to serve them assures their ability to evaluate its performance by comparing its

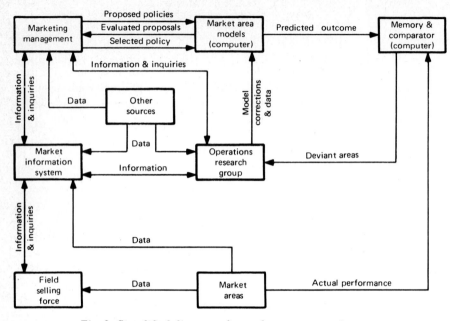

Fig. 2 *Simplified diagram of a market-area control system*

output with what was predicted. Managers who are not willing to invest some of their time in this process are not likely to use a management control system well, and their system, in turn, is likely to abuse them.

REFERENCE

A. Sengupta, S. S., and Ackoff, R. L., "Systems Theory from an Operations Research Point of View," *IEEE Transactions on Systems Science and Cybernetics,* Vol. 1 (November, 1965), pp. 9–13.

Management Misinformation Systems— Another Perspective

ALFRED RAPPAPORT

An identification and critical examination of the assumptions made by designers of management information systems is particularly timely. Russell L. Ackoff attempted to do just that in his article, "Management Misinformation Systems" (*Management Science,* December 1967). He identified five common assumptions underlying management information systems design and proposed that these assumptions are unwarranted in many (if not most) cases and lead to major deficiencies in the resulting systems. The purpose of this letter is to examine briefly these assumptions (given in italics) and the supporting illustrations presented in the Ackoff article.

1. The critical deficiency under which most managers operate is the lack of relevant information. Ackoff contends that managers suffer more from an over abundance of irrelevant information than they do from lack of relevant information. This is followed by the suggestion that information be filtered (evaluated) and condensed to reduce the information overload to which managers are subjected. In the face of seemingly endless pages of computer print-outs, book-size requests for equal expenditures, and other forms that consume unnecessary hours of managers' time, suggestions leading to filtered and/or condensed information are likely to be greeted with enthusiasm. This does however raise another important issue: What are the useful limits to filtration and condensation?

Just as processing leading to information overload is not in the best interests of the organization, indiscriminate filtration and "over-condensation" can likewise lead to non-salutary results. For example, consider the case of major capital investment proposals originating from various divisions of a company. Assume that book-size capital expenditure proposals are now condensed for headquarters to a single listing of proposed projects (with brief descriptions) and ranked according to some criterion function such as internal rate of return. The headquarters group has two basic options available: (1) accept the divisional estimates; or (2) make a subjective adjustment to compensate for estimated divisional bias. Neither of these alternatives is very comforting since there is no compelling basis for choice except perhaps assessing past behavior which may be neither instructive nor relevant. Here then is clearly a case of "over-condensation" since the report received by headquarters cannot be used to make an intelligent appraisal of the proposals competing for scarce resources since information about the uncertainty underlying key market and cost variables is not available. "Over-condensation" can occur even if risk analysis techniques are actually employed in a company.

In brief, the undesirable state of "over-condensation" is reached when the decision maker no longer has a sound basis for judging the validity of transmittal information.

Filtration has potential as an effective adjustment in the face of information overload. The key question is: where in the system should "filtration decisions" be made? If these decisions were initiated largely at the lower levels of the organization one might question the limited perspective underlying the decisions. Filtration decisions made at the highest level of the organization, however, offer little or no relief from information overload. The relevant strategy then is a function of the confidence that executives have in the filtration decisions made by managers at lower levels.

To illustrate this in context of the capital expenditure analysis example, consider the set of projects enumerated by the divisions for review by the headquarters group. This set consists only of those projects proposed for adoption and excludes projects rejected at the divisional level. Hence, the information presented to headquarters was indeed filtered. If there are no serious conflicts between the way divisions and headquarters perceive organizational objectives and their attitudes toward risk are identical, then the filtered list of projects is in all probability justified. In the overwhelming majority of cases, where the ideal headquarters-divisional relationship does not exist, it would seem to be more appropriate to ask divisions to enumerate their total set of project opportunities with "accept" or "reject" recommendations for each. (Even in this situation divisional managers would undoubtedly filter certain projects, but the potential for filtering is decreased.)

In summary, while managers can often make reasonable adjustments to compensate for information overload, overfiltration and condensation tend to accentuate the biases of lower-level managers and provide the executive decision maker with an inadequate basis for making necessary adjustments. The relevant information for managers is somewhere on the continuum between over-filtration-and-condensation, and information overload. I contend that the basic assumption that "the critical deficiency under which most managers operate is the lack of relevant information" remains unchallenged.

2. The manager needs the information that he wants. Ackoff argues that the conditions for a manager to know what information he needs are rarely satisfied. The principal problem here is that the decision maker's own conception of an appropriate decision model to fit a specific situation is generally not well developed. I would fully subscribe to Ackoff's subsequent plea for an active collaboration among information systems specialists, operations researchers, and managers in the various stages of system design as the best available strategy for overcoming this deficiency.

The respective roles of the operations researcher-information specialist and manager can be illustrated in the context of the service station problem presented by Ackoff. I would envision the main thrust of the manager's responsibility to be, first, to recognize occasions for making decisions and, then, to frame appropriate questions in light of the decisions to be made. The manager in the major oil company, for example, finds it necessary to make decisions concerning locations of future service stations. An appropriate criterion may be sales or profit maximization subject to certain technological and management-imposed constraints. The manager clearly wants information about future sales potential for alternative service-station locations. *And the manager needs the information that he wants.*

While the task of enumerating relevant variables for forecasting equations should be conducted jointly by the operations researcher and manager, in most situations it would be reasonable to expect that model choice and refinements are largely the domain of the operations researcher. The choice of a statistical forecasting model in this case or any model in the more general case calls for the exercise of careful judgment on the part of the operations researcher. Problem type, relative importance of the problem, time available before decision must be made, and expected degree of utilization of model results by decision makers all qualify as strategic considerations in choosing among alternative models. Finally, the information specialists should present the results to the manager in an easily understood form, without resorting to either information overload or over-condensation.

3. If a manager has the information he needs his decision making will improve. Ackoff points out that because of the complexity of the decision process, managers oftentimes cannot use information well. To support this contention, Ackoff suggests that most managers furnished with an *initial* tableau of a typical mathematical programming, sequencing, or network problem are unlikely to come close to an optimal solution. While one certainly would not want to argue with the validity of this proposition, its relevance to the main argument must be questioned. Specifically, I would submit that to furnish a manager with an initial tableau *is to furnish him with data, not information.* (The decision is explained by Adrian M. McDonough in his book, *Information Economics and Management Systems:* "The term 'data' is used here to represent messages that can be available to the individual but which have not as yet been evaluated for their worth in a specific situation. . . . 'Information' is used here as the label for *evaluated data* in a specific situation. . . . a given message may remain constant in content and yet, under this approach change from data to information when it is put to use in making a decision.") The fact that managers cannot easily convert data to information underlies the very need and justification for developing management decision models. If managers could independently iterate from an initial to a final tableau, the simplex and other related algorithms would become redundant and unnecessary. In the Ackoff case, the manager is not provided information until the results appearing in the final tableau are communicated to him. At that juncture we can only hope that his decision making will improve.

In brief, then, Ackoff's illustration fails to invalidate the assumption that if a manager has the information he needs his decision making will improve, because the decision maker was not provided with the *information* he needed. Perhaps, a more interesting and significant question to ask is: to what extent does the information the manager really needs (e.g., final tableaus) improve decision making?

4. Better communication between managers improves organizational performance. It is true that better communication between managers does not necessarily improve organizational performance. Ackoff's example involving a purchasing and a merchandising department in a department store illustrates this point. I believe it is important to emphasize, however, that the origin of the problem described does not lie in the communication, but instead in the conflicting measures of performance used to judge the two departments. Ackoff thus has properly established that interdepartmental communication among departments with conflicting measures of performance may not only be of doubtful value, but may actually work counter to the best interests of the organization as a whole. However, the proposition that well-conceived interdepartmental communication enables managers to coordinate their decisions more effectively when appropriate, nonconflicting measures of performance are present was not invalidated.

5. A manager does not have to understand how an information system works, only how to use it. Ackoff's challenge to the notion that a manager need not understand how an information system works, only how to use it, is particularly significant. It is difficult to debate the merits of this assumption without a more detailed agreement concerning the degree of understanding Ackoff would require of managers. The best available evidence of intent can be gleaned from the case study presented.

A computerized production and inventory control system was discovered to be costing the company almost $150,000 per month more than the former manual system. Most of this was attributed to excess inventories. Apparently, a major cause of unreasonable inventory accumulation was a program error which confused the maximum allowable stock level and the reorder point. To suggest that the manager understand the information system to a point where he would detect the programming error seems neither reasonable in an organizational plan nor an economical use of the manager's time. Indeed, to argue for understanding and analysis by managers at this level of detail is legitimate cause for cries of "information overload." A more constructive approach would suggest that a manager should have developed techniques and guidelines using exception reporting for discovering a situation where an "improved" system costs $150,000 more than its unglamorous predecessor. Perhaps even more importantly the manager would be well advised to develop a more reliable system for hiring better systems designers.

While I agree with Ackoff that "no management information system should ever be installed unless the managers for whom it is intended are trained to evaluate and hence control it rather than be controlled by it," my agreement is within the context explained above. To insist upon *detailed* systems design knowledge by managers as a prerequisite for new management information systems is tantamount to calling for an information systems moratorium or at minimum a significant reduction in research and progress in the field.

MIS Is a Mirage

JOHN DEARDEN

Some years ago I expressed the opinion that "of all the ridiculous things that have been foisted on the long-suffering executive in the name of science and progress, the real-time management information system is the silliest."[1]

I no longer believe this statement is true. We now have something even sillier: the current fad for "*the* management information system," whether it is called the Total System, the Total Management Information System, the Management Information System, or simply MIS.

I certainly do not mean to suggest that a company does not need good management information systems—nothing could be further from the truth. But the notion that a company can and ought to have an expert (or a group of experts) create for it a single, completely integrated supersystem—an "MIS"—to help it govern every aspect of its activity is absurd.

For many businessmen, it is probably inconceivable that the lofty phrases and glittering promises surrounding the MIS conceal a completely unworkable concept. Yet this is exactly what I propose to demonstrate—that a company that pursues an MIS embarks on a wild-goose chase, a search for a will-o'-the-wisp.

Let me first try to explain what I understand by the "MIS concept" and examine its alleged advantages, and then show why the concept is unworkable. Then I shall be in a position to recommend some practical remedies for defective management information systems, which certainly constitute a real problem for executives today.

CONFUSION BETWEEN TERMS

It is difficult even to describe the MIS in a satisfactory way, because this conceptual entity is embedded in a mish-mash of fuzzy thinking and incomprehensible jargon. It is nearly impossible to obtain any agreement on how MIS problems are to be

---

[1] "Myth of Real-Time Management Information," *HBR*, May-June 1966, p. 123.

analyzed, what shape their solutions might take, or how these solutions are to be implemented. This confusion makes it very difficult to attack the concept, because no matter what assumptions a critic makes about the nature of the MIS approach, a proponent can always reply that *his* use of the term is different from others'.

But there is a common thread which runs through the various uses of the term, a thread that at once unifies but also subverts the MIS literature. This thread is the computer-based information system.

Computer-based Activity . . .

Wherever the MIS is discussed, it is almost invariably stated that a management information system does not necessarily require a computer and that many forms of management information are not computer-based.

Yet, if one looks at what is actually being discussed, he quickly discovers that the term "MIS" is used, essentially, to stand for "computer-based information systems." For example, a recent article in *Business Week* read as follows:

> [Some], concerned that systems analysts are . . . a "mixed bag" whose training and knowledge are a hit-or-miss proposition, are convinced that management information systems (MIS) is *the* emerging field in business administration. Both Wharton and MIT have tailored programs especially for systems specialists, but no school has gone further than the University of Minnesota, whose B-school now offers MS and PhD degrees in management information systems and has launched an MIS research center. Since the center's opening three years ago, MIS Director Gordon B. Davis and his staff have worked to develop 12 new systems-related courses—from on-line, real-time systems to a seminar on software. In addition, the program's 50 MS and 22 PhD candidates spend a good portion of their time alone and in teams at work on actual computer problems in industry.[2]

It seems evident to me that MIS education as described here is principally education in computer-based information systems.

It is vital to note, first of all, that the information generated by this kind of system does not include a great deal of the information that is most important to management—especially, important *qualitative* information. Second, a specialist group that develops such a system is usually responsible for implementing only one part of any of a company's individual management information systems—namely, that part that interfaces directly with the computer. For example, such a group has little (if anything) to do with specifying the nature of an accounting and financial control system, although it may be responsible for the computer programming this system employs.

My conclusion, therefore, is that such a group has little impact on most of the information supplied to management, particularly at upper levels. Consequently, it is ridiculous to say that it creates (or *can* create) a total management information system.

---

[2] June 5, 1971, p. 96.

... vs. MIS

To the extent that MIS refers only to company information systems that use a computer base and to the extent that everyone understands this limitation, I have no serious quarrel with the trend to MIS; it is vital that management tightly control its computer-based information systems, and in general the so-called MIS groups seem designed to guarantee a tight rein to management.

In my experience, however, such a limited definition of MIS is *not* what advocates of this approach to information systems mean when they use the term. They intend something novel and far more global, some entity that can provide revolutionary benefits we cannot derive from the traditional approach. Walter Kenneron suggests this definition of the MIS:

> A management information system is an organized method of providing past, present and projection information relating to internal operations and external intelligence. It supports the planning, control and operational function of an organization by furnishing uniform information in the proper time-frame to assist the decision-maker.[3]

This is approximately what I perceive most people to mean by MIS. And if this definition seems grandiose, I can only remark that "*the* management information system" describes a grandiose idea. If the definition were less global in its scope, it would not measure up to the term. If, for example, one were to limit the definition to the context of a company's financial accounting programs, he would have to speak of the *financial* MIS of the company, rather than its general MIS.

However, in practice, no such limitations are intended. Kenneron's inclusive definition of the MIS approach is quite consistent with the nearly universal benefits claimed for it.

THE MIS APPROACH

Given this inclusive definition, how is management to apply it? In other words, how should management think about the problem of setting up an MIS?

Fundamental Assumptions

First, it appears that if management wishes to subscribe to the theory of the MIS, it must make up its mind to accept two fundamental (if highly questionable) assumptions that are quite different from traditional ones made in this area:

1. Management information is a subject for study and specialization. That is, it is sufficiently homogeneous so that a set of principles and practices can be established for evaluating all management's information needs and satisfying them. In short, the MIS approach attacks all the problems of management information as a whole,

---

[3] "MIS Universe," *Data Management,* September 1970.

rather than by individual areas, such as finance and marketing. This homogeneity is a necessary assumption, since without it there is no reason why general solutions to a management's information requirements can be found.

2. The systems approach can and should be used in analyzing management's information requirements. Proponents claim the systems approach is necessary for mastering the sprawl of requirements and for synthesizing the general MIS solution. (I shall have more to say about the systems approach later.)

Diagnosis and Development

Once management has accepted these two assumptions, it can begin to develop an MIS program. As the theory goes, there seem to be two techniques for setting to work:

• Management can hire an MIS expert to act as a superconsultant to the president of the company. This expert studies the types of problems that the president must solve, the decisions that he must make, and so forth, and recommends methods for satisfying the president's total information requirements. He then drops to lower levels of management and provides the same services there.

In general, the expert depends on others to implement his recommendations. For example, the controller becomes responsible for changing the cost accounting system in the way the consultant recommends.

• Management can create a staff department that reports to the top. This group is responsible for the company's computer-based systems but also provides the same type of diagnoses and evaluations as the superconsultant.

The staff group, unlike the consultant, usually has responsibility for implementation.

ITS ALLEGED ADVANTAGES . . .

Under this approach, then, either a single person or a group of persons is responsible for developing and overseeing the construction of the entire management information system. The concentration of authority and responsibility in the hands of systems experts supposedly creates a number of significant advantages:

• Experts schooled in the MIS "discipline" can analyze management's information needs more effectively than can the people traditionally responsible for satisfying them. Moreover, these experts can better determine which techniques will best meet these needs.

• Because the MIS is developed as a unified, single system, rather than as a number of separate systems, it is completely coordinated and completely consistent.

• Information needs are determined from the top down. Hence the top will be in better control; the frequent practice of letting lower management decide what information will pass upward is eliminated.

- The company reduces its direct information costs by eliminating systems. Also, the MIS itself is cheaper to run because it has been designed by information experts who know the most economical means for satisfying management's information needs.

- Since one expert or group is responsible for the system, management's desire that the system be kept up-to-date can readily be satisfied.

In short, the proponents promise, experts can design an MIS that is more effective, more efficient, more consistent, and more dynamic than the haphazard aggregate of individual systems a company would otherwise employ.

These are impressive advantages that any manager would enjoy, and doubtless this approach was developed to solve the real problems of poor information that have been plaguing management with increasing frequency. The growing complexity and the pace of change of modern business, especially in the last ten years, have surely made many information systems obsolete and many more inadequate for present tasks.

Equally, the last ten years have seen the extensive development of information technology, management science, and systems analysis—a development that has been accompanied by rapid growth in the number of experts working in information systems.

To some—that is, the proponents of MIS—it seemed logical to centralize the development and control of information systems in the hands of these experts. After all, the problems that beset information systems have been the result of change and growth, they reasoned; and these problems could perhaps be solved by using the new information technology that had been developing simultaneously.

Several companies have tried this approach, and many people currently advocate it. In spite of its apparent logic, however, I know of no company in which it has worked out. This fails to surprise me because, as I have already implied, I believe the whole MIS approach is fundamentally fallacious.

... & ITS REAL FALLACIES

There are four fallacies and one serious misconception inherent in the MIS approach as I have described it. The fallacies are these:

- Management information is sufficiently homogeneous so that it can be made an area of specialization for an expert.

- If the different information systems ordinarily used by a company are developed separately, the resulting management information system will necessarily be uncoordinated and therefore inefficient and unsatisfactory.

- The "systems" approach is a new boon to business administration.

- It is practicable to centralize the control over a company's entire management information system.

The misconception is this: The specialist expertise that creates a good logistics system for a company can extend its talents into the broad domain of general company activity and create a general management information system.

There is no reason to suppose an MIS group can actually do this—in fact, there is good reason to think it cannot.

Let me refute these errors one by one.

1. The true MIS expert does not and cannot exist.

A complete management information system consists of such a huge assortment of different types of activities that no man can possess a broad enough set of special skills to apply to even a small proportion of them. Consider the skills required to build any one of these individual information systems.

The financial accounting and control system: This includes preparation of financial statements, development of budgets and long-range plans, analyses of capital investments, publication of product costs, and so forth.

Traditionally, the controller is responsible for all these financial subsystems; with respect to the financial information systems, he plays the role that the MIS expert is supposed to play in the general management information systems. In complementary fashion, the MIS expert must have a thorough understanding of the controller's systems function.

The logistics information system: This system controls the flow of goods from the purchase of raw materials to the physical distribution of the finished products. Next to the financial control system, it is probably the most comprehensive information system in the typical manufacturing business.

A logistics system normally consists of several subsystems of varying degrees of independence. For example, there could be distinct systems for different product lines. Within each product line, furthermore, there could be subsystems for procurement, production scheduling, finished goods, inventory control, and so forth, and still others for plant utilization and expansion. Depending on its industry, a company has a larger or smaller number of complex, interrelated logistics information subsystems.

The critical point to note here is that the logistics information system is almost completely different from the financial information system. In point of fact, most of the skills needed to develop financial information systems are of no use in developing logistics information systems and vice versa. Even the user relationships are different. In building a financial information system, the controller develops a system that provides information for management outside the finance function, whereas logistics information is normally developed and used by the people directly concerned with logistics.

Furthermore, logistics subsystems frequently have little in common with each other, so that an expert in one type of subsystem might not be able to transfer his expertise to a different type. For example, there may be little or no similarity between a procurement information system and a finished-goods distribution system.

Like the financial system, the logistics information system or subsystem is a job for a specialist.

The marketing information systems: Like the two systems just described, the marketing information system can also consist of a number of subsystems. A company may maintain separate product lines; and within a product line, it may maintain further subsystems for advertising and sales promotion, short-term sales forecasting, long-term sales forecasting, product planning, and so forth.

Again, the critical point is this—a marketing information system is almost completely different from the other two systems. Consequently, expertise in either or both of the other systems would be of limited value in developing a marketing information system and vice versa.

Legal services, industrial relations, and public relations: One of the major purposes of each of these staff functions is to provide top management with specialized information different from that provided by any other staff office and different from that provided by the three information systems previously described.

R & D reporting: The information system management requires in this area is distinct from all others, and expertise in these other areas offers limited help in developing an R & D information system.

In short, except in the small company (which probably needs only simple systems), there are several information systems that have very few similarities and many wide differences. Consequently, it makes no sense to regard the processes of developing and implementing these several management information systems as consititufing a single and homogeneous activity.

I conclude that few, if any, individuals have the training to call themselves experts in management information systems. Indeed I believe it is much more practical to teach the new information technology to the functional experts than to teach information technologists functional specialties. After all, the man who could master all the functional specialties—the true MIS expert—would have to be an intellectual superman; and hence he does not and cannot exist except, perhaps, as a very rare exception.

If an MIS can be implemented at all, it can only be implemented by a staff group, and one of considerable size.

2. Coordinated systems for functional areas can be developed without a "total system approach."

"Unless you develop the MIS as a single, integrated system, all you will get is a bunch of unrelated, uncoordinated, ineffective systems." If I have heard this statement once, I have heard it a hundred times and it still is not true.

I have seen many systems that have intricate interfaces with one another and that are still efficient and effective. In the automobile industry, for example, the development of a new model car involves many functions—styling, engineering, product planning, finance, facility planning, procurement, and production scheduling. Each functional unit develops its internal information system for controlling its part of the operation; in addition, at each interface, the functional units exchange the information necessary to maintain coordination between them.

If an information system is ineffective, the cause is very likely to be the incompetence of the people responsible for it, *not* the absence of the general MIS approach. In this connection I might quote William M. Zani:

> Most companies have not conceived and planned their management information system with any significant amount of attention to their intended function of supporting the manager as he makes his decisions.[4]

Zani goes on to suggest a new approach to developing an MIS as a solution to this situation. My solution would be to make some personnel changes, because anyone who fails to design an information system for its users is incompetent.

Such incompetence is very prevalent. I have seen dozens of companies where management is not receiving half the relevant accounting information that could be made available if the financial information system had been properly designed in the first place. And although I am not sufficiently expert in other types of information systems to know whether the same situation exists there, I have no reason to believe accounting is worse than the others.

To assert that such problems as these result from the independent development of different information systems, rather than from sheer and ordinary incompetence, is simply ridiculous—and to recommend the "MIS cure" is even more ridiculous. To ensure that a company has efficient information systems which are well coordinated with one another, management need only bear down on the personnel in the various functional areas who are responsible.

3. "The systems approach" is merely an elaborate phrase for "good management."

There are many definitions of the systems approach, but the following is representative:

> The systems approach to management is basically a way of thinking. The organization is viewed as an integrated complex of interdependent parts which are capable of sensitive and accurate interaction among themselves and with their environment.[5]

What does this mean? It took me some time to figure it out.

When the systems approach first appeared in the literature, I had a great deal of difficulty understanding the concept; and my confusion increased until I started asking people this question: "What would an executive do differently if he were to adopt the systems approach in place of the traditional one?"

Without exception, the replies I received made assumptions about the traditional approach that simply are not valid. For example, some assumed that the executive perceives his organization as static; others, that he fails to consider the

---

[4] "Blueprint for MIS," *HBR*, November-December 1970, p. 95.

[5] Spyros Makudakis, "The Whys and Wherefores of the Systems Approach," *European Business*, Summer 1971.

interaction of related variables. In other words, the replies were predicated on an incompetent, even a stupid, executive.

Thus I concluded that the alleged advantages of the systems approach really result from the difference between an adequate and an inadequate manager. If you doubt this, I invite you to ask the question I did the next time you hear someone champion the systems approach to management.

It is therefore not surprising that good managers follow the systems approach, because this approach is merely the ancient art of management. Would a competent business executive plan a major expansion program without considering the sources and timing of funds, the availability of people, the possible reactions of competitors, and so forth? Certainly not. And he would consider them in relation to one another.

My conclusion, then, is that the systems approach is precisely what every good manager has been using for centuries. The systems approach may be new to science and to weapons acquisition, but it is certainly not new to business administration.

At this point, let me summarize briefly. First, an MIS would have to be developed by a *group* composed of experts in the various types of information systems used by management. This must be so because the possibility that a single individual will be expert in *all* types of information is remote. Second, the approach taken by the MIS group would be approximately the same as that taken by any competent and expert manager working in one of the functional information systems.

How, then, does the MIS approach differ from the traditional approach to information systems?

The only difference I can see is that a company's management information system would be the responsibility of one centralized group; whereas, traditionally, the information systems experts have been located in the various functional areas. This brings me to the last fallacy—that such centralization is practicable.

4. Centralizing the control of a company's information systems in a staff group creates problems that are insoluble; therefore it is simply not feasible.

It is theoretically possible to assemble a staff MIS group that is sufficiently large and diversified to have expertise in all the formal information systems described earlier—marketing, manufacturing (logistics), finance, and so forth. But to organize this group properly, the company should appoint an executive vice president for information to supervise the work of the group—that is to say, the systems of the staff vice presidents, the controller, the logistics information group, the marketing information group, and so forth. But what would this accomplish? Let me ignore the fact that no sane manufacturing or marketing executive would delegate the responsibility for his information system.

One result might be that this executive vice president for information would promote better coordination between functional areas. On the other hand, of course, the problems of coordination would drastically increase in the manufacturing and marketing areas because the responsibility for the information systems had been separated from the people who hold the line responsibility. And in any event, simply having all of the information groups, including the MIS group, report to a single executive would hardly change the *approach* to developing information systems. Thus the special value of the MIS approach is still obscure.

In short, it seems to me that if any of the MIS people are competent to tell the functional experts what to do, they should be in the functional area. I see no logical way to centralize the responsibility for all the management information systems.

Significant Misconception

If the MIS approach is as fallacious as I believe it to be, how has it been able to maintain even a superficial credibility?

The answer, as I have hinted earlier, is this: the early success of information technology in renovating logistics systems has been so great that there is a natural inclination to try the same methods on the company information systems as a whole.

This misconception has evolved in a natural enough way. Responsibility for a logistics system has traditionally been divided among several executives—e.g., in purchasing, in manufacturing, and in marketing. This divided responsibility has often resulted in poor coordination throughout the system. Furthermore, the people responsible for the system have often been old-fashioned in their methods and relatively unskilled in information techniques. Thus a vacuum has frequently existed with respect to the responsibility for a company's logistics information system into which the burgeoning information technology has moved easily and successfully.

However, as we have seen, there is no reason to suppose that the principles of information technology used so successfully in the logistics area can be generalized to apply to the other management information systems within a company or to the management information system considered as a whole.

Thus, when a group of experts has completed its overhaul of the logistics system, it will *not* be in a position to attack the financial, marketing, or any other system. First, the group will not have the specialist expertise required. Second, the type of problems the group may have found in the logistics area will almost certainly not exist in other areas if the staffs in these other areas are competent. Third, there will be no responsibility vacuum as in the logistics area; the MIS group will not be in a position to take over by default.

If you have any doubt about the validity of these statements, I suggest that you examine the kinds of things that any MIS group is doing. Outside of the routine computer systems, you will almost certainly find them concerned basically with parts of the *logistics* information system only.

ROOTS OF POOR INFORMATION

So far this article has been quite negative. Now I should like to suggest some positive actions to mitigate the information crisis, if it can be called that. Before I propose these actions, however, it is appropriate to review the causes of management information problems.

As I have pointed out, the principal cause of poor information systems is that we have put incompetent or ineffective people in charge of these systems.

The secondary causes are somewhat more complicated.

Growing Use of Computers

Computers and computer-related systems activites have been growing very rapidly, and currently the cost of these activities has become very significant in many companies. In spite of large expenditures, however, the quality of the information available to management appears unimproved.

One reason is, of course, that some computer installations are not run effectively. Another is that the computer-based information systems have been oversold; management has been led to expect much more than it has received. In other words, management's dissatisfaction with its information occurs, not from any deterioration in its information systems, but from its inflated expectations.

Interface Conditions

Individual systems change and improve at different rates, and this creates problems at the interfaces between them. For example, operations research techniques, used in modern logistics systems, require much more sophisticated cost accounting information than traditional cost accounting techniques can generate. Problems can also occur at the interface between production and marketing, because production-scheduling techniques are frequently much more sophisticated than the techniques ordinarily used in market forecasting.

In general, the benefits of advanced techniques may be largely lost where they are dependent on primitive ones. (To some extent, of course, the problem of proper coordination at the interfaces reflects the competency of the staff involved. Other things being equal, only an incompetent would use an advanced technique whose effectiveness would be undermined by inadequate support.)

Rapidity of Change

Many companies are changing very rapidly, and it is necessary that their information systems keep pace. In some companies, information systems are *not* keeping pace. To some extent, this is caused by the inability of the staff personnel traditionally responsible for information systems to react to change. After all, many people who were once perfectly adequate in a relatively static situation become ineffective in a dynamic situation.

Greater Management Challenge

Management must always operate with insufficient information. And frequently, the more important the decision, the greater the uncertainty. In many areas the truth of these statements is becoming more salient because, while the role of management is becoming more complex, the new information technology is not helping significantly.

For example, I have spent many years working on control systems for decentralized companies. The problems of control in such companies today are much more difficult than they were ten years ago—increases in size, complexity, and geographical dispersion have made control much more difficult. Yet the new information technology has been of little help in this area, simply because the problems of controlling decentralized divisions do not lend themselves to computerized or mathematical solutions.

Accordingly, it is important to realize that part of our information crisis results from the nature of the present business environment. We shall simply have to live with it. This does not mean, of course, that we should not continue trying to improve the situation.

TOWARD REAL SOLUTIONS

Any company that believes it is facing genuine management information problems and wants to solve them should consider the following measures:

1. Place competent people in each of the formal information systems.

To my mind there is no question that incompetency is the leading cause of problems in many management information systems. Hence the obvious answer is to retrain or replace the incompetents.

2. Examine the interfaces.

This is best done in connection with system evaluation, and the examination should focus on these evaluative questions:

- Is there adequate communication between individual groups at all important interfaces?

  The executive might bear in mind formal techniques such as scheduled meetings and formal agreements.

- Does each group involved in an interface know enough about the other interfacing systems to do its job effectively?

  This is a question of education. For example, cost accountants should know enough about company operations-research models to be sure these models are providing correct information; or, at the very least, they should be able to explain to the OR group the relevant limitations of the information their group can supply. On the other hand, the OR people should know enough about cost accounting to ask for the right type of data and to appreciate the limitations in the data they receive.

  But although this is principally a matter of education, it may well be that some staff members are not intellectually capable of handling interface requirements, and they may have to be replaced.

3. Examine the logistics system.

Originally many logistics systems were organized for manual data processing and have never been changed. Equally, the procurement, production, and distribution functions typically report to different executives, and consequently no one is formally responsible for the logistics information system. Since it is here that computers and information technology are most applicable, management should evaluate its logistics area and, where appropriate, reorganize it and make a staff unit, responsible for its logistics information system, report to the company officer who directs the logistics system itself.

4. Organize a central computer group for systems control.

Computer use will continue to expand, and it is vital that management maintain central control over computers and computer-based information systems.[6] Such a group should be responsible for overseeing all computer-related work—for long-range planning, coordination, and control of all computer acquisitions and applications. In addition, it should be responsible for coordinating computer-based systems and might even undertake the systems and implementation work in a situation where several organization groups use the same data base.

Most companies already have such groups. Some are even called "MIS groups," although, in reality, they have authority only over computer-related work.

5. Create an administration vice president, if one does not already exist.

I recommend the creation of an office to which the following report:

- The controller.
- The treasurer.
- The computer and systems group.
- The legal office.
- The industrial relations office.
- Other offices for company relations (that is, public and governmental).
- Organization planning.

The marketing, manufacturing, and R & D groups would continue to be independent. Such an office has several advantages:

- It provides better control over the staff activities. The increasing number of staff operations, together with their increasing specialization, has made it nearly impossible for the president to exercise real control here. An administrative vice president can exercise much more effective control over the size and direction of these activities.

- It provides a practical alternative to locating the computer and systems group in the controller's office. An administrative vice president can provide effective supervision and, at the same time, maintain an objectivity that a controller often finds difficult because of his involvement with specific computer applications.

---

[6] See Warren F. McFarlan, "Problems in Planning the Information System," *HBR*, March-April 1971, p. 75.

- It allows the company to handle miscellaneous projects easily—for example, an evaluation of a functional information system or an analysis of the formal information entering the president's office. To take care of nonrecurring or particularly pressing information systems problems, frequently the best arrangement is to organize temporary task forces that report to the administrative vice president.
- It simplifies the process of coordinating staff offices.

However, I would not make the administrative vice president or the offices reporting to him responsible for the *entire* management information system. Marketing, manufacturing, and R & D would all be responsible for their own information systems. Also, the different activities reporting to his office would develop their information systems in relative independence except where interface communications are in question.

QUESTIONS FOR MY CRITICS

Inevitably, I shall be accused of setting up a straw issue in this article and then demolishing it.

If the MIS approach really embraces only computer-based information systems or centralized logistics systems, then I *have* set up a straw issue. No harm has been done, however, because I have at least clarified the meaning of "MIS."

But I cannot believe the concept is meant to embrace only this. I have done my best to discover what the MIS approach really is, through talking with its proponents and studying its literature; and this article honestly represents my best understanding.

If I am correct in believing that the approach pretends to embrace more than computerized systems and logistics, then I have *not* set up a straw issue. And those who doubt my conclusions, negative as these may be, would be wise to ask themselves the following questions before they take up the pen of protest:

- Which information systems are to be included in the MIS?
- What kinds of experts are to be included in an MIS group, and what training shall they have?
- Where is this group to fit into the corporate organization? In particular, what will happen to the staff groups from the controller's office, the legal department, the marketing research department, and so forth?
- What authority is the MIS group to have? Is it to have authority to design and implement systems, or is it to serve in an advisory function only?
- What can this group accomplish that cannot be better accomplished by placing information specialists under functional groups?

Arguing the viability of the MIS approach is pointless unless answers to these questions are set forth clearly. And the clearer the answers, I believe, the more transparent the MIS mirage.

Discussion of
"MIS Is a Mirage"

Professor Dearden, in his article, "MIS is a Mirage" (January-February 1972), correctly anticipated that his critics would accuse him of setting up a straw issue and then demolishing it. We believe that he has done just that—and thereby marred some otherwise well-conceived advice to management. He quite correctly cautions against wild fancies of MIS advocates. He also raises some provocative questions that help to clarify important issues about information systems and their implementation.

Our quarrel with Dearden stems from his description of an MIS as perceived by practitioners in the field. Dearden states that MIS advocates take the view that the only acceptable MIS is a unified, single system that is completely coordinated and completely consistent. Such an MIS is indeed a mirage—but one created by his own misconceptions about the nature of an MIS.

Competent practitioners do not set out to design a totally integrated MIS. They rightly view the MIS—or whatever name one chooses to use—as composed of a collection of subsystems. In some cases a considerable degree of integration exists among these subsystems; but in most cases the subsystems are only loosely coupled or largely independent. The issue is one of degree.

While Professor Dearden emphasizes the dissimilarities that exist among various subsystems of an MIS, we prefer to focus on their similarities. This rather subtle distinction can lead to major differences in the way one tackles the task of implementation.

A person who dwells on dissimilarities often fails to exploit what commonness exists. He tends to rely on piecemeal implementation carried on in relative isolation. He relies primarily on persons with functional skills rather than persons having generalized MIS skills.

Those of us who take the other viewpoint look for ways to handle the interdependencies and commonness that exist among subsystems. Our differences with Professor Dearden hinge on the issue of whether we can expect an MIS practitioner to acquire generalized skills that allow him to take a relatively global view of the

Reprinted by permission from *Harvard Business Review*, "Letters to the Editor" (May-June 1972), pp. 22–31.

system. Persons having these skills are certainly not in plentiful supply, but they certainly exist—and in growing numbers. An MIS depends heavily, in our view, on an organization's ability to hire and retain at least a few practitioners with such skills.

Although a well-designed MIS that exploits current technology is likely to differ in many ways from most existing MIS, it will certainly not be entirely computer-based, totally integrated, operating in real-time, and serving all levels of management with equal facility. It is highly misleading to imply that MIS practitioners aim at such gee-whiz systems; it only serves to reinforce the limited perspective of the hairy-chested school of managers who cannot see any significant role of the computer beyond routine data processing.

James C. Emery

As a goad to stimulate MIS thinking, Mr. Dearden's article is excellent. It also provides a good example of how an apparently conscientious researcher can be led astray when he works within a poorly conceived framework. Since this is exactly the type of error that Dearden places on the MIS designer, it is interesting to note that he himself has fallen into the same trap.

. . . As for Mr. Dearden's "Questions for my critics," the answers are simple though they are not easily achieved.

What management information systems should be included?

All information systems should be included in an MIS; if not, we have the ridiculous situation of a sales department whose performance is measured by gross sales, a production department whose performance is measured by units and costs, and a company that is measured by profits. As any executive knows, here we have a case of separate information systems in which both the production and sales departments can be reaching performance highs while the company is going bankrupt. Integration of information systems is a must and, for all of Mr. Dearden's protestations, he should realize the *interfacing* of subsystems is one sign of a total systems approach.

What experts should be included?

The MIS is in part every manager's job. If there is a special group, its task should be to help the system users define and learn to use the MIS improvements. The "experts" should understand the department they are helping, but, in addition, they should understand decision analysis, the economics of information value, systems theory, and information systems.

Where should the group be located?

This "group" should not fit into the organization. Its members should infiltrate the organization. Its task is to improve the company's information system and this includes improving the data flow, updating the concept of "what the job or business is all about," creating "games" so that managers can learn new decision making habits and in other ways help coordinate and stimulate the development of the people in the system and the equipment-based data feedback systems.

What authority should the group have?

The MIS group should work for the CEO and have unlimited authority—but it should never use it. Any information or decision analyst knows that you can move an elephant faster by loosing a mouse than by pulling on his trunk.

Why not place the experts under a functional group?

If the information and decision analysts are placed *under* functional groups, they will be used to optimize the functional group. It is unlikely that the company will benefit from the resulting suboptimization of functional groups. The task is to improve the company—not its respective parts (this . . . is fully explained in systems theory).

In summary, if Mr. Dearden's MIS article is a mirage or a straw man set up to stimulate discussions about MIS—Bravo! But, if he really believes what he wrote—for shame, Mr. Dearden, you should know better and, further, you should not blame the MIS concept for the fact that you have discovered that some MIS designers are incompetent.

Robert H. Long

Author's reply: I would like the *HBR* reader to examine carefully Long's answers to my five questions. These answers disclose precisely the fuzzy thinking and unworkable concepts that I had in mind when I wrote the article.

First, Long would include *all* information systems in his MIS. Since he places no limit whatsoever on what his MIS includes, I can only conclude that he is talking about all information systems whether formal or informal, whether past or future, whether written, oral, or visual. Such an all-encompassing concept includes just about everything that goes on within a firm. Long is equally global and equally vague about what experts should be included, "The MIS is part of every manager's job." So far he has included about everything and everybody in management in his concept.

Next, in answer to the question, "Where should the group be located?" he achieves what must be the ultimate in confusion. His group would "infiltrate" the organization. Since they include all managers who are responsible for all information, one wonders who will be the "infiltrators" and who will be the "infiltratees." Finally, Long would give the MIS group (at this point he seems to have forgotten that it is *all* managers) "unlimited authority" which, of course, they will not use.

This is exactly the type of thinking that my article was aimed at and I thank Long for demonstrating this. If I had quoted anything like this in my article, I certainly would have been accused of setting up straw issues.

John Dearden

. . . My reaction to the article can best be summed up by saying that I was pleased to find Mr. Dearden's thinking on the impracticality of a Total Management Information System and his recommendations regarding real solutions to systems problems very closely paralleling our own thinking and actions here at Chrysler Corporation. . . .

John J. Riccardo

The "Questions for my critics" presented by Professor Dearden will serve as a valuable basis for planning for his supporters. A critical approach is essential at this early stage for all deeply involved in using information resources to support management decision making. These questions represent an important contribution to better information systems planning and evaluation.

. . . Companies that plan and provide intensive senior management leadership achieve much higher returns from all forms of management technology. They also set and attain higher standards for competence and performance, a point strongly made by Professor Dearden. In recent years, this emphasis has produced a relatively high turnover among information systems directors, with men having technical competence being replaced by men having broad general management competence.

Ercole Rosa

Designing Management Information Systems: An Overview

ROBERT L. PARETTA

Perhaps the most common misconception about management information systems is the notion that there exists a single, general approach to systems design that is sufficiently broad to meet the needs of all firms regardless of their size, industrial setting or stage of development. All too often firms are encouraged by sellers of computer equipment to implement a management information system whose scope and design philosophy are beyond both current and foreseeable needs. When designing an information system, the client is frequently so enraptured by the data manipulation features of the elaborate hardware that important questions of technical, operational and economic feasibility go unanswered. If the client falls into this trap, an unfortunate sequence of events is set in motion that is all too common in firms today.

It begins with top management's becoming overly cautious after suffering a costly and disappointing experience with some highly touted form of "advanced" management information system that failed to live up to expectations. Thus sensitized, management tends to delay needlessly the implementation of subsequently recommended systems improvements because of the fear of repeating earlier mistakes, even though such refinements may be warranted. The result is the familiar cycle of management information systems development that is characterized by either excesses or deficiencies.

While the CPA is often not brought into the decision process early enough to have any positive impact in guiding policy in the area of management information systems, he nevertheless has a responsibility to help his clients resist the temptation to leap into the computer age in pursuit of the "ultimate" information system without first conducting a rigorous cost-benefit analysis. Clients must be reminded that each new systems refinement must be justified in terms of the firm's changing needs and available resources.

This article attempts to provide the CPA with a general background that will enable him to advise his clients in this regard (1) by examining some of the more commonly encountered alternative approaches to management information systems design; (2) by showing how the various approaches evolved and how each design can be identified with a firm's given stage of development; (3) by demonstrating what each design philosophy has to offer within the context of its inherent limitations; and (4) by pointing out the safest course for clients to follow in order to achieve implementation of systems improvements when they are called for.

APPROACHES TO MANAGEMENT INFORMATION SYSTEMS DESIGN

To understand how the various approaches to management information systems design relate to the stages of a firm's development, a look into the past will be useful. Systems design philosophies have developed through an evolutionary process beginning with the simple accounting systems of the 19th century when accountants were primarily concerned with measuring an entrepreneur's income and wealth. Though used to a certain extent as aids to planning and control, the income statements and balance sheets produced by these systems were used mostly for obtaining credit. Other kinds of decision making information were gathered informally, as needed, through personal observation by the owner.

SIMPLE MULTI-FLOW MODELS

As commercial activity expanded in the 20th century, businessmen found it difficult to keep pace with the growing number of increasingly complex and diverse decisions they had to make. Soon they realized that it was possible neither to be everywhere at once to observe the facts as they occurred nor to remember all the data to which they had been exposed. In addition, decision making in a business environment subject to increased competition, government regulation and public ownership required a range of skills beyond the capacity of most individual managers. Specialists were needed in functional areas like finance, marketing, production and personnel. A first step toward solving these problems, therefore, was to delegate decision making responsibility to subordinates, but delegation alone was not enough.

Knowledge within each specialized area grew rapidly. It soon became apparent that something more than traditional accounting statements and personal observations were required to meet the demands of the new kinds of planning, operating and control decisions that specialization and decentralization helped to create. In the course of performing their tasks, therefore, individuals within each functional area took the initiative and began independently to gather and file the data they thought were relevant to them. The result was an information system composed of many spontaneously developed, unrelated, task-oriented subsystems geared toward specialized kinds of jobs such as accounts receivable, payroll, inventory control and purchasing.

Naturally, there was much firm-wide duplication of data gathering and storage (multi-flow data), but it nevertheless marked the first time that firms began to think in terms of formal information systems with an overall managerial emphasis beyond traditional accounting reports. In fact, it was not long before the phrase "management information system" began to appear in the literature as a label for those kinds of comprehensive information systems that attempted to provide managers throughout the firm with the information they needed to make decisions.

IMPROVED MULTI-FLOW MODEL

The emergence of the management information systems concept owed much to the technological developments in electronic data processing equipment, which permitted the volume, frequency and dependability of information flows to increase to levels not possible with less sophisticated clerical operations. As the computer's capabilities continued to improve, management began to group the activities and files (data banks) of the numerous independent, task-oriented subsystems into larger elements or modules within the context of the broad functional areas in the firm (finance, marketing, production, etc.), thereby reducing some of the duplication of effort found in the simple multi-flow model.

Characteristically, data were processed separately by each functional module over various periods of time, the data being updated at different intervals (batch processing). Data storage made extensive use of magnetic tape, which had to be mounted and sequentially searched before information could be made available.

Though an improvement over the task-oriented model, and widely adopted in practice, this functionally oriented approach still did not overcome the weakness inherent in all multi-flow systems. Maintaining a set of independent subsystems (even though their number is reduced by modularization) still means that the same information often enters the information system more than once and is subsequently stored in a variety of subsystem data banks. The result is wasteful duplication in data processing and storage, placing an unnecessary strain on physical and human resources. Furthermore, redundant data (assumed to be identical when entering the system) are in many cases quite different because of the lack of uniform measurement schemes as well as diverse classification criteria used in the individual subsystems. Consequently, an overall system emerges that produces inconsistent data output, which hinders coordination and analysis. The absence of connecting links between the independent subsystems perpetuates this condition by both hampering the reconciliation of multi-stored data and inhibiting the merging of sets of data contained in the numerous data banks—two activities that are so necessary for effective planning and control.

Finally, since multi-flow systems develop from the bottom up, the implicit assumption persists that those who make the decisions are best qualified to know what information is relevant. In many cases this may be so, but as a decision process becomes more complex and less understood, managers tend to search for more information to explain it. Not sure of what to look for, they often attempt to play it "safe" by requesting "everything."[1] Groping for relevant information in this way, however, needlessly burdens the information system with useless data, much of it of an internal, historical nature. As the firm grows, its need for additional information forces an expansion in the size and scope of the functional subsystems. All the above problems then become more acute, and multi-flow models begin to lose their appeal.

THE SINGLE–FLOW MODEL

An approach to information systems design that offers an interesting theoretical alternative for dealing with the problems of multi-flow models is the single-flow model. Though not without practical problems, it has as its focus a single integrated data bank where centrally processed bits of relevant data (internal and external, historical and forecasted) are entered into the system only once. The data are updated as events occur (real-time processing) and are stored in the computer, where information is available to the decision maker on request (on-line storage).[2]

The most obvious advantage of this approach is the complete elimination of the redundancy problem that plagued the multi-flow models. By doing away with the costly duplication of data processing equipment and personnel, a more efficient allocation of the firm's resources is possible. Unifying independent subsystems into a single, integrated system centrally controlled by a group of information specialists also fosters coordination among the operating elements in the firm, for it provides a decision making orientation that cuts across functional lines. Last, it is argued that on-line, real-time processing can improve control over operations by decreasing the feedback cycle. "Red" variances from the budget can be reported as they occur, rather than at the end of some arbitrary period as is done in multi-flow models where batch processing is used.

In the 10 years since it was first talked about, the single-flow approach has been identified by a wide assortment of labels. Listed alphabetically, they include

- Fundamental information system.
- Integrated data processing (IDP).
- Integrated information system.
- Integrated management information system.
- Management information system (MIS).[3]

---

[1] Russell L. Ackoff, "Management Misinformation Systems," *Management Science,* December 1967, p. 149.

[2] Alfred L. Bauman, Jr., "Single Information Flow Philosophy," *Data Processing Year Book* (American Data Processing, 1963); and A. F. Moravec, "Basic Concepts for Planning Advanced Electronic Data Processing Systems," *Management Services,* May-June 1965, pp. 52–60.

[3] Has this meaning only when abbreviated (MIS).

- Total information system (TIS).[4]
- Total integrated system.
- Unified information system.

To minimize confusion, the term "single-flow" will continue to be used in this article.

DISENCHANTMENT WITH THE SINGLE–FLOW MODEL

Despite the wealth of theoretical arguments put forward in the literature in support of the single-flow approach to information systems design, acceptance by business firms in the real world has been something less than enthusiastic. A recent survey sponsored by the National Association of Accountants discovered that "no totally integrated management information systems were found in the firms studied nor were there serious plans being made for such systems in the near future."[5]

Schoderbek and Schoderbek have observed: "The number of firms that have attempted complete integration of information (often with the computer manufacturer's warranties and vows of assistance) only to experience absolute failure is not insignificant."[6]

Chambers points out with reference to single-flow information systems: ". . . as far as I know, no one has yet developed and implemented a total information system."[7] . . . [It] is something which I think most people, or at least those who have been in MIS for any length of time, have discarded."[8]

In the light of these current findings, one might well ask why a concept which seems to offer so many advantages should be cast aside. Why have attempts to implement single-flow information systems ended in disaster? What new things have been learned about this approach that were previously not known or ignored?

No doubt some of the failure of the single-flow approach to take root in practice can be traced to organizational resistance to change. Change moves an individual

---

[4] The term "total information system" is without doubt the most overworked in all the information systems literature. It has been used so often, in such a variety of contexts, to describe systems from the most elementary to the most complex that its meaning is now entirely without precision.

[5] Neil C. Churchill, John H. Kempster and Myron Uretsky, *Computer-Based Information Systems for Management: A Survey* (NAA, 1969), p. 139.

[6] Peter P. Schoderbek and Steven E. Schoderbek, "Integrated Information Systems— Shadow or Substance?" *Management Adviser,* November-December 1971, p. 31.

[7] Chambers uses the term "total information system" in this case to mean a system based on the single-flow approach.

[8] John C. Chambers, "Total Versus Modular Information Systems: Empirical Experience in Finance and Personnel," in *Management Information Systems for the 1970's,* Robert D. Smith (ed.) (Kent, Ohio: Center for Business and Economic Research, Kent State University, 1970), p. 47.

from a state of known risks and alternatives to a state of uncertainty. The uncertainty associated with change can produce specific job-related fears to the extent that personnel block or even sabotage new programs. Naturally, anyone in danger of being displaced by information systems improvements is going to fight implementation regardless of the benefits that would accrue to the firm as a whole. Even those who are certain to be retained by the firm will resist change because of the fear that a reduction in personnel will mean uncompensated increases in their workloads. Fears can also arise when personnel are unsure of their abilities to adjust to new job demands created by information systems refinements. When this sort of resistance to change builds in an organization, distrust is generated, rapport between systems designers and operating personnel ends and modifications to existing systems are doomed from the start.

Although some of the reluctance to embrace the single-flow approach is related to these behavioral problems, the major obstacles are the astounding costs and practical problems of implementation. The adoption of a single-flow approach requires a great deal of highly sophisticated storage and input/output equipment. On-line real-time capability means expensive use of very costly random access devices and remote terminals, which involves large financial commitments at the initial stage of implementation. Many firms may neither have nor be willing to risk such enormous amounts of capital on new, untested systems.

While the costs of single-flow systems are all too real in the short run, the benefits can be elusive. Developing a centrally controlled, integrated data bank involves a good deal of advance planning and coordination in order to isolate user needs and match them to information sources for each decision center in the firm. Such activity implies supporting a staff of operations and systems specialists who determine system specifications after careful investigation and analysis. Of course this will take a good deal of time. Large-scale acquisition and installation of sophisticated computer hardware will entail expensive training of personnel in its use, an additional investment in time. The global nature of the single-flow system makes small problems in the system hard to locate and correct, adding further to delays. When all these things are considered, operational lead time for a single-flow system could take several years. The magnitude of the information flows of some large firms may be so overpowering as to make implementation unfeasible at any time, given the current state of the art.

While the practical problems may someday be overcome, there are theoretical weaknesses in the single-flow design as well. First, it can be argued that the creation of a "single, completely integrated supersystem" is absurd because it assumes management information to be sufficiently homogeneous to permit a single set of principles to handle problems for the firm as a whole rather than by individual functional area.[9] Centralizing control of the information system in a separate group

---

[9] John Dearden, "MIS Is a Mirage," *Harvard Business Review*, January-February 1972, pp. 90–99.

of information specialists can be dangerous, too, because centralization removes control from the hands of those who make the decisions and could lead to less rather than more coordination. Second, while it is a popular belief that increasing the frequency of information flows will improve a manager's performance, it can be demonstrated that on-line real-time information may not always do so, even when it is supplied at zero marginal cost.[10] For example, in cases where the decision input is highly unstable, raising the rate of information flow tends to increase the probability that a message sent to a decision center will contain data that are not representative of the events being observed. This could transmit a false signal to the manager, causing him to take action where none is appropriate. This can prove harmful to the firm when the cost of taking the wrong action is high, compared with the cost of not acting and waiting for more information.

THE MIXED-FLOW MODEL: A COMPROMISE

Multi-flow and single-flow models represent opposite ends of the information systems design spectrum, each having sets of limitations. Most knowledgeable management information systems professionals seem to favor an approach that offers a compromise between these two extremes, the "mixed-flow" approach, which draws from the strengths of both while avoiding many of their individual weaknesses.[11] In practice it has been widely accepted by firms.

Where functional information subsystems handle large amounts of similar internal and historical data (finance, personnel, etc.), they can be integrated quite readily by creating a single data base to include information common to the participating subsystems, where it will be stored and processed centrally. This will enhance coordination, planning and control. For subsystems that contain diverse kinds of external and forecasted data (R & D, market research, etc.), integration of data would serve little purpose because it would neither contribute materially to reducing data file redundancy nor foster more coordination. With unrelated subsystems, therefore, separate data bases are recommended. On-line real-time data flows are supplied only in those cases where they are justified by decision needs and are economically feasible.

CONCLUSIONS

Approaches to information systems design have evolved over the years, each new one trying to correct deficiencies in the one that preceded it. The discussion in this article has centered around only a few discrete points along a continuum of alternative approaches in management information systems design (multi-, mixed- and

---

[10] Robert L. Paretta, "The Frequency of Information Flows: A Misunderstood Variable," *Management Adviser,* July-August 1974, pp. 46–49.

[11] Also known as the "functional data base" approach.

single-flow). In practice many hybrid systems will be found. The point to be remembered is that no one model exists which has universal applicability. Each model must be matched against a firm's changing needs dictated by its stage of development and available resources.

In advising clients, what has to be emphasized is that funds committed to a formal information system represent a use of scarce resources. If limited resources are to be optimally allocated, the expected acquisition and operating costs of a new system must be matched against the benefits it is expected to provide. Only when the expected marginal benefits are greater than the expected marginal costs should more complex systems be introduced. As long as there are backlogs of operationally sound systems improvements which have passed the cost-benefit test, movement in the direction of higher order systems should be supported until some budgetary constraint is reached.

Clients must be reminded, however, that very real risks are present when this movement occurs too rapidly. Many firms have experienced unpleasant results in their attempts to jump too quickly from multi-flow task-oriented systems to integrated single-flow decision-oriented systems. Upgrading an information system using this kind of "go for broke" thinking is valid only if the client is prepared to accept the risk of incurring the kinds of large scale economic and organizational shocks that historically have occurred with such frightening regularity. It is generally believed to be less costly in the long run to introduce systems improvements gradually in a series of smaller, more manageable segments. Developing an advanced information system within this kind of "building block" framework tends to minimize many of the problems that are traditionally encountered during the implementation phase:

1. Behavioral problems would certainly be reduced. Resistance to change will always be present, but if change takes place over time, it will be less perceptible and personnel will be better able to adjust to it.

2. If implementation is accomplished in separate segments, users' information needs can be more carefully analyzed and specified. The matching of information flows to user requirements is critical to the success of all information systems work. For routine kinds of decisions this process is fairly straightforward, but often the more complex decisions must be observed for a time before they can be fully understood.

3. Introducing systems improvements in stages reduces economic risks because it is achieved in more manageable financial increments. When problems are encountered, fewer resources are at stake, and alterations to the system's scope and design can more readily be made to meet the demands of new situations. This is especially important in the uncertain economic environment we face today.

By being aware of the strengths and weaknesses of alternative design philosophies, as well as some general management information systems principles, the CPA will be better prepared to help his client choose the system he needs, can afford and can get functioning with the fewest operational difficulties.

CHAPTER 5

INFORMATION
SYSTEMS AND
INTERNAL CONTROL

In earlier chapters, several of the readings briefly touched on the problems of internal control and the computer. This chapter focuses attention on internal control weaknesses and computer abuses. While most information systems textbooks cover the important control aspects of computer systems, the emphasis on specific abuses is often treated lightly. Therefore, a need exists to examine more closely the basic fundamentals of where, how, and why computer abuses take place.

Internal control procedures vary among different computer systems but several studies indicate that the best control for the big frauds appears to be improved management reporting systems. By making management aware of all transactions related to the computer system, the exception-reporting concept can greatly improve the detection of questionable activities. In most computer systems the improvements in exception reporting may begin with the operations procedures. Especially when financial processing is being performed, this phase seems to be a primary control element. Based on many actual case evaluations the point of entry is where most financial fraud begins, and a system of reporting input exceptions can improve the detection of unauthorized activities.

In most organizations the management information system encompasses a total control system in the sense that it embraces all aspects of the organization. The need for total control should be obvious after reading the article by Allen, "The Biggest Computer Frauds: Lessons for CPAs." In this article Allen presents a summary and analysis of most of the large publicly documented computer fraud cases. His study of 150 major cases of computer fraud is one of the most comprehensive to date. After analyzing these cases he discusses how it was possible to determine the major control weaknesses which seemed to invite each fraudulent scheme. The most popular methods of computer manipulation are presented and analyzed according to broad financial and organizational areas. His analysis also includes such information as: job position of perpetrator, average financial loss, and type of organization. To enable management to evaluate and improve the management information system it is important to know the characteristics of fraudulent activities, most of which Allen has presented in this article. Although his article enumerates the areas of weaknesses surrounding the computer which all management should be aware of, he concludes by warning that the biggest frauds are still to be revealed— and he knew about "Equity Funding"!

After recognizing that computer frauds do exist it is important to turn our attention to the prevention and control of such activities. The next two articles address this area primarily by discussing the different types of controls that can be implemented in a computerized system. Thorne, in "Control of Computer Abuses," reports the results of a survey of 160 computer related crime cases. From the data collected, six abuse characteristics of computer installations were categorized and subsequently analyzed for necessary control applications. On the basis of these six broad abuse characteristics, Thorne delineates the control features necessary to provide reasonable assurance that undetected fraud does not occur.

Davis, in "EDP Control Means Total Control," focuses on the internal control related aspects of computerized systems. His discussion includes the major control features of documentation, application, organizational independence, and the audit trail. Throughout the article the integration of each major computer control element into the overall control scheme of the organization is emphasized.

A different problem of fraud and fraud detection is discussed in "Management Fraud: The Insidious Specter," by Sayer et al. Management fraud has been found in a variety of forms and the authors discuss such problems as: where it takes place, the type of people involved, and the type of activities which are susceptible to such fraud. From their experiences they present eight reasons why management frauds take place. A lengthy discussion of the symptoms of management fraud provides enlightenment as to the conditions which often point to financial manipulation. Lastly, the authors present several management measures that top management and/or company directors should install to control and prevent management fraud.

To relate the importance of computer controls to external auditors we have included the Mason and Davies article, "Legal Implications of EDP Deficiencies." While the courts have seldom found it necessary to relate the auditor's legal responsibilities to the area of electronic data processing systems evaluations, the authors discuss such a situation in Adams v. Standard Knitting Mills, Inc. They elaborate on the facts of the case and the issues decided by the court. Lastly, they analyze the implications of the case on future audit engagements where computer systems are deficient but overlooked by the auditors. It is the implications of such a legal case that provide the justification and need for all accounting students to become familiar with the control aspects of computer systems. Whether internal or external auditor, data supplier, or information user, persons involved in all accounting related functions must accept responsibility for their share of computer control.

Because computer frauds are, unfortunately, an activity in American business, it is important for accountants to be aware of all possible types of computer related fraud. By studying the fraud cases presented in this chapter the reader can gain an appreciation of the many variations of computer abuses. This chapter also includes the more important control features that are available to management, with which the accountant must become familiar. If accountants fail to get involved in this area, the last article should provide insight as to what the result may be.

The Biggest Computer Frauds: Lessons for CPAs

BRANDT ALLEN

Today no one argues that computers are "fraud-proof" as some did a decade ago, but there is still much disagreement as to what comprises computer fraud, where it begins and how to prevent it. As a result, the activities of accountants and auditors as they relate to computers and computer security systems often lack direction and focus. Because of the increased incidence of computer frauds, auditors can no longer consider them of concern only to law enforcement agencies. Now the entire accounting profession must be alerted to the proliferation of these crimes and must understand how to recognize them and how to inform management of ways to prevent them.

This article analyzes most of the publicly documented computer fraud cases detected to date with special emphasis on the major ones. The latter include those that were long running, were difficult to detect, produced large losses and are representative of frequently detected schemes. Through analysis, it has been possible to determine the major control lapses that seem to invite such schemes. Through analysis, we're also able to speculate about the major undetected computer frauds and where they may turn up.

This analysis focuses on 150 major cases that have been publicized, excluding many others where the data was skimpy. For purposes of this article, computer fraud is defined as any defalcation or embezzlement accomplished by tampering with computer programs, data files, operations, equipment or media, and resulting in losses sustained by the organization whose computer system was manipulated. In most instances, this would encompass all activities in the computer department as well as those departments that directly enter or prepare computer input. Excluded are thefts of computerized information, use of computer time for personal gain, alteration of computer records for nonfinancial gain and schemes where the employer was not the victim. These excluded schemes cover instances where the records of credit bureaus, license agencies and property registers were altered to defraud credit grantors and others dependent on these records. Also eliminated are unusual cases like *Equity Funding* or *Computer Payroll and Accounting Services, Inc.,* where the service bureau owner absconded with the payroll funds of his client companies.

PREVENTION NECESSARY

As will be seen from the analyses of the computer fraud cases subsequently described in this article, such fraud can often be prevented by a tight system of internal control. Later analyses of these cases will show that certain areas of internal control are weak and in need of improvement. As a result, the CPA should give special attention to the following areas:

1. Transaction controls. The most important area for improvement seems to lie in tightening controls over the generation and flow of input transactions. In all the big cases, perpetrators were able to add bogus transactions or to alter others. Computer users need to perfect means to ensure that all transactions are subject to controls and that the controls are tight. Obvious problem areas, such as adjusting entries and error corrections, should be designed to be controlled by persons other than those responsible for the entries.

2. Rigorous audits. Auditors must give increased attention to the causes of inventory losses. It seems clear that many of the disbursement and inventory frauds were conducted in an environment of large, continuing inventory losses. It appears that the growing crime problem has established the expectation of inventory shrink in many organizations. Inventory frauds or disbursement frauds flourish in this climate; not only does it reduce the organization's diligence but it also tends to foster fraud ideas. Where losses run to the hundreds of thousands or even millions of dollars per year, additional inventory controls and investigations are warranted and can probably be cost justified.

3. Improved responsibility reporting. The most effective internal control for the big cases seems to be improved management reporting systems to alert others to possible fraudulent transactions. Buyers should receive recapitulations of orders placed, received, paid and canceled by time period, by vendor and by type of item. Adjustments and corrections should be highlighted in special management reports. All expense entries should be reported to authorizing management in sufficient detail and clarity to enable the executives to spot unauthorized charges.,

4. Program controls. In a well-run computer department, neither programs judged to be critical nor those that access critical programs or data collections are accepted for use in the computer center until they have been subject to independent verification. Once so accepted and approved, they are placed in secure file storage and are available for use only according to schedule. At any time, internal audit can verify that the current program version being used is the one approved for use. All program changes must go through the same sequence.

5. *File controls.* Every computer user must have a file librarian responsible for the security of all critical program and data files. No files should be released to computer operations except as scheduled. Monitors are necessary to ensure that files are used according to the approved schedule and that all deviations are investigated.

6. *Place EDP house in order.* Even today many computer centers are run on a crisis basis with few controls, poorly designed systems and unaudited and unauditable software. In too many organizations, edit tests and input controls are relaxed when backlogs grow. Program patches are made in desperation with no review or control. In such an environment it would not be surprising to find computer fraud, and such was the situation in the cases in this study. In one case, the data files and programing systems were in such bad shape that direct file changes were made repeatedly in order to correct errors. This made it easy for the dishonest employee to make certain other "corrections" to effect his scheme without arousing suspicion. In my opinion, the auditor who discovers a chaotic, poorly controlled data center in his review of internal control is in trouble. He can hardly proceed without additional, and sometimes exhaustive, verification, but it is in just such situations that the additional review is so difficult to perform. The auditor can do a great service for his client and for himself by working to reduce the "management by crisis" conditions found in many computer rooms.

TYPE OF SCHEME

The 150 cases were first sorted into categories by type of scheme and victim organization. In examining Figure 1 we observe that accounting and inventory control fraud involves average losses of $1.3 million, the largest in the corporate category. Schemes based on fraudulent payments account for almost 40 percent of the cases involving corporations. Fraudulent payments to creditors average $324,000 while fraudulent payments to corporate employees average a $139,000 loss per case. Fraudulent payments in corporations are made to employees (payroll), to other individuals (usually pension or insurance claims) or to creditors or suppliers (disbursements). Losses average well over $100,000 per case. Disbursement frauds are the most costly, primarily because they are more difficult to detect and thus continue longer. Disbursement frauds also are more complex and can be understood and planned by only a few in the company, usually members of management.

In banks and savings institutions, the payment frauds are, with one exception, manipulations of withdrawals. Ordinarily, these involve attempts to withdraw funds from inactive or dormant accounts or efforts to prevent the processing of a check by rendering the MICR (magnetic ink character recognition) codes unreadable. By their very nature, these schemes usually are detected quickly by auditing procedures or internal controls. In one atypical case, however, where check processing was blocked on a customer account resulting in a $6.8 million loss, a bank officer was in collusion with an officer of the client company and was in a position to hide the discrepancy in the reconciliation of the bank's account with the regional Federal Reserve Bank.

Type of fraud	Corporation	Bank/savings and loan	State and local government	Federal government
Payments to employees	$ 139 (4/8)	$ 3 (1/1)	$ 14 (3/4)	$33 (22/29)
Payments to other individuals	133 (2/4)	—	487 (6/9)	
Payments to creditors	324 (5/5)	252** (8/12)	—	56 (25/30)
Accounting/ inventory control	1,300 (10/10)	195 (10/12)	*(–/1)	
Collections/deposits	43 (2/6)	157 (8/9)	—	—
Billings	6 (2/6)	—	—	—
Miscellaneous	* (–/2)	—	* (–/2)	—
Average loss totals	$ 621 (25/41)	$193 (27/34)	$329 (9/16)	$45 (47/59)

* Amount of loss unknown.

** One case of $6.8 million deleted from figures to avoid distortion.

Note: The average loss figure is based upon x cases out of y total cases in that category where (x/y) is shown just to the right of the average. Losses in some cases were unavailable or were eliminated for other reasons.

Fig. 1 *Average losses in computer frauds ($000's)*

Frauds shown as payments to other individuals for state and local governmental agencies were for welfare payments, unemployment insurance and job corps programs.

In summary, in most types of organizations automated systems that pay money from the organization to suppliers, employees and others are the most troublesome.

All the cases in the accounting/inventory control category shown in Figure 1 are based on changes made in accounting and subsidiary records without an immediate change in physical assets or cash payout. Several of the corporate cases had the same pattern: inventory clerks or managers entered fraudulent transactions into computerized inventory systems; this, in effect, deleted items from inventory or assigned responsibility for the items to someone or someplace else. Then items would be stolen, bringing the physical count into line with inventory records. In the bank and savings and loan cases, various schemes were employed. The simplest schemes were thefts from inactive accounts accomplished by transferring funds to accounts of the perpetrators. Several other cases involved crediting perpetrators' accounts while charging the offset to various expense and adjustment accounts. In one case, service charges to customers were overbilled, with the overage flowing into the programer's account.

In cases involving the manipulation of incoming funds, the number of cases and size of losses for corporations were less significant. There are several reasons for this. Most corporations can and do exercise tight control over customer remittances; the process is more easily audited. Payments to a firm are generally made by check and are not easily cashed. Manipulations of receivables or deposits, the so-called "lapping schemes," require constant attention and manipulation of accounts. These schemes are also risky; the stolen amount is always hidden in the accounts, awaiting detection. In only two cases was there a potential for large losses. In each instance, the perpetrators had discovered how to permanently eliminate the receivables from the accounts through unauthorized adjustment of entries. In certain corporate receivables frauds, the billings were manipulated—and reduced—before the basic sales transactions were recorded in the accounts.

The analysis revealed a significant number of deposit frauds in banks, which yielded much higher average losses. The basic scheme is really the same as that for receivables collection in a corporation: deposits intended for one account are pocketed or credited to another; then the former is made good later by diverting another deposit intended for still another account. Also in this category are check-kiting schemes where deposit tickets or records were altered so that uncleared deposits could be immediately withdrawn.

It's probably misleading to draw any conclusions from the fact that corporations had the largest average fraud losses per case, because only the major cases are publicized. No doubt there were many smaller detected computer frauds in corporations that were simply settled by dismissal; it's the bigger cases that are brought to court and thus reported. Banks, on the other hand, probably report a much higher percentage of their fraud cases because they're federally regulated, insured and required to report their losses. As in corporations, possible computer frauds in state and local governments appear to be under-reported and the losses understated.

METHODS OF COMPUTER MANIPULATION

Figure 2 and Figure 3 illustrate how the computer system was manipulated. Several things are clear from these tabulations. Manipulation of transactions is by far the most frequent method: adding unauthorized transactions, such as phony purchase orders and warehouse receipts in the case of disbursement frauds; altering transactions, such as posting deposits or payments on account to some other account; or not processing a transaction at all, such as payments on long term certifications of deposit. Sometimes a combination of methods is used, as in the cases of pension fraud where a termination triggered by a death notice is not processed (transaction deleted) and then an address change (unauthorized transaction added) is used to channel the payments to the schemer.

Schemes involving direct charges to master files by the use of utility programs or direct terminal entry via file maintenance were found less frequently. In several cases, transactions had to be added or altered in order to accomplish the file change.

I classified these schemes as file changes if a one-time, unauthorized transaction resulted in a recurring fraudulent activity, such as the misappropriated pension payments. If an unauthorized transaction had to be added each time a fraudulent activity was triggered, this was classified as a transaction, even though the effect of the transaction was to change a master file.

Method of computer manipulation	Corporation	Bank/savings and loan	State and local government	Federal government
Transactions added	16	9	9	{ 48
Transactions altered	8	12	—	
Transactions deleted	3	4	—	—
File changes	5	3	5	—
Program changes	6	8	—	—
Improper operation	4	—	1	—
Miscellaneous, unknown	4	1	1	11
Totals	46	37	16	59

Note: Case totals do not add up to 150 because some are classified in more than one category.

Fig. 2 *The victims of computer frauds*

Method of computer manipulation	Payments to employees and other individuals	Accounting/ inventory control/ disbursements	Billings/ collections/ deposits	Miscellaneous
Transactions added or altered	40	44	17	—
Transactions deleted	2	3	2	—
File changes	6	3	1	2
Program changes	2	7	5	—
Improper operation	4	1	—	—
Miscellaneous, unknown	2	11	2	2
Totals	56	69	27	4

Note: Totals do not add up to 150 because some cases are classified in more than one category.

Fig. 3 *The schemes used in computer frauds*

Direct manipulation of master files can be difficult to prevent because of the difficulty of establishing file maintenance and change controls:

In one case, a programer/systems analyst used his ability to make direct changes to master files to change the price on items he was purchasing just before the billing run; later he'd return the price to its correct condition. In another, a programer transferred funds from inactive accounts to his own and his associates' by using a utility program and by carefully making all switches within a file control block. The change was made between the end of one quarter and the beginning of another, further compounding the auditor's detection problem.

Computer frauds caused by program changes or patches have been discovered in only a few cases. This method has been used to hide overdrafts on checking accounts, to accumulate fractional cents on interest calculations, to skip over accounts at billing time in order to inflate service charges and to mispost accounting transactions fraudulently. Computer users appear to be particularly vulnerable to program patches, as can be seen in the following recent case:

A programer at a large savings and loan association attempted what could have been the perfect computer fraud. At this institution, the on line teller terminal accessed only a temporary customer file during the day; after all tellers had balanced out, the day's transactions were posted to the permanent files and the temporary file was then refreshed for the following day's business. This two-file system was used for security reasons and is the preferred approach for advanced, on line systems. The programer had patched the program so that any withdrawals against his personal account, when posted to the permanent file, would be actually charged to an inactive account. On the following day he would remove his withdrawal slip from the documents sent to the computer center from the branches and substitute one drawing on the inactive account. With the program patch removed, it would have been impossible for auditors to discover the perpetrator. Fortunately, the scheme never got off the ground; the programer erred in keying the inactive account number on his first effort. He was caught the next day.

Frauds caused by improper computer operation were almost always payroll frauds, where extra checks were printed or where unauthorized use of computer terminals was employed to enter fraudulent payroll data, thus leading to excessive payments.

UNDETECTED COMPUTER FRAUDS

One cannot help inferring that a significant amount of fraud and embezzlement goes undetected. Since so many cases are uncovered only by chance or because the perpetrator simply gives up or makes a stupid mistake, one may well conclude that most fraud goes undetected. I believe this is true for computer fraud as well. Furthermore, it's possible to determine the most likely undetected cases simply by applying the pattern of noncomputer-related frauds to computer users. Other cases appear probable, considering the buying, selling, employment or functional activities of various types of organizations.

First, it should be clear that a large number of undetected computer frauds simply follow the patterns found in these detected cases. Thus, there is much undetected corporate inventory and disbursements fraud, much undetected welfare fraud in federal, state and local government agencies and many undetected funds transfers in banking institutions. Theft from inactive accounts in savings institutions is a good case in point. This scheme was the most frequently reported in this analysis, and yet many more probably go undetected. Officers of such institutions depend heavily on the computer to block attempted withdrawals from dormant accounts, yet this control can easily be circumvented by the computer thief. Long running dormant account thefts can easily be masked by blocking or diverting quarterly statements and then sending adjusted statements in their places. Beyond this, my guesses as to undetected schemes are the following:

1. Pension frauds. There were a couple of cases in this study where pension payments were discovered being made in the names of deceased individuals. But the number of pensioners in this country, the number of pension-paying organizations and the ease of the scheme suggest that computerized pension fraud in the United States is a hidden problem of major significance. There are probably thousands of deceased pensioners on computer files whose monthly checks are being diverted to white collar criminals.

2. Inventory and disbursement frauds in state and local governments. Disbursement and inventory frauds were found to be big problems for automated systems in corporations and federal government agencies; the same must be true for state and local governments, but no cases of this type were found in my collection. It seems clear that they weren't included because they haven't been detected, perhaps because auditing of these agencies is not as thorough. When you consider the number of state and local governments in existence, the amount of purchasing they do and the size of their inventories, this must be considered another hidden problem.

3. Insurance claims fraud. From the cases to date it might be concluded that there is no computer-related fraud in insurance companies. This can't be so. The nature of the business in this industry is money collecting, investing and paying; there are many individual accounts, many transactions, a high degree of automation, the dollar magnitude is high and much of the industry depends primarily on good faith—such as medical insurance claims processing. Few industries have such a high potential for computer fraud and so few detected cases to date.

4. Corporate billing frauds. While there were a few detected cases of this type in my collection, the total was surprisingly small considering the vast amount of billing activity in the corporate sphere. The large number of employees who have access to billing transactions and the ease of manipulation suggest that much fraud here goes undetected, particularly that effected by deleting, blocking or altering transactions.

5. Federal government program frauds. If the results of this survey can be believed, there have been no dishonest computer programers in the federal government. This hardly seems possible. Considering the potential for abuse in such agencies as the Department of Health, Education and Welfare, the Department of Defense, the Internal Revenue Service and the Agriculture Department and in programs such as revenue sharing, it may be concluded that a significant number of payment frauds generated by unauthorized program patches go undetected in the federal government.

6. *Loan frauds in commercial banks.* Commercial banks, as opposed to savings institutions, also appear surprisingly clean in this survey. For many reasons, the chances of operating successful funds transfers are lower for demand accounts than for savings accounts, but the opportunities for loan frauds are greater in commercial banks. It seems impossible that computer-assisted loan frauds are not a giant problem for commercial banks. My guess is that many are out there waiting to be detected.

PERPETRATORS' JOB POSITIONS

Some of the most interesting observations to be made from computer fraud cases come from looking at the job positions of the perpetrators. As shown in Figure 4, there was much collusion, particularly in those cases initiated by data entry personnel. Line 1 of Figure 4 should be read as follows: There were 15 cases involving data entry personnel; 4 of these acted alone; 5 colluded with 1 other employee, 1 colluded with 2 others and 3 with more than 2 employees; 1 colluded with a nonemployee and 5 colluded with at least 3 nonemployees; the average loss per case for those 4 employees working alone was $8,000 and it was $727,000 per case for all cases in this category.

Job position of primary perpetrator	Total	Perpetrator alone	Inside			Outside			Average loss (thousands)	
			1	2	>2	1	2	>2	Alone	Total
1 Data entry/terminal operator	15	4	5	1	3	1	–	5	$ 8/	$ 727
2 Clerk/teller	16	11	3	1	1	2	–	1	37/	58
3 Programer	15	10	4	1	–	3	–	1	20/	53
4 Officer/manager	21	18	–	3	–	–	–	1	274/	314
5 Computer operator	9	5	–	2	1	–	1	1	33/	37
6 Other staff	5	4	–	1	–	–	–	–	48/	92
7 Computer operator	5	3	–	–	–	–	–	–		696
8 Unknown	3	–	–	–	–	–	–	–		2,400

Note: All but 4 of the federal government cases were excluded because of missing information in those case descriptions.

Fig. 4 *Average loss, job position of perpetrator, individuals involved*

The distinction between data entry/terminal operators and clerk/tellers is essentially that the latter category deals directly with customers, suppliers and others; the former do not.

The higher the rank or position of the perpetrator, the less likely is one to find collusion; thus, managers were found to work alone much more often than keypunchers or teller operators. Perhaps this is because the higher the rank, the broader the job responsibilities and the greater the knowledge of company operations and controls. Thus, there is less need to collude for purposes of gathering knowledge or to effect frauds via transaction generation, etc. Also, the higher the rank, the greater the loss. For example, officers and managers, working alone, stole $274,000 on the average, whereas other staff took $48,000 and clerk/tellers $37,000.

Something of a surprise was the fact that the computer specialists were caught taking much less when working alone than were nonspecialists; operators took $33,000, programmers averaged $20,000 and data entry personnel only $8,000. It seems that ordinary managers and clerks have learned to use the computer to steal much more readily than have the computer specialists.

The anomaly of the $727,000 average loss per fraud perpetrated by data entry personnel and cohorts is explained by the nature of the cases here. Several were large welfare frauds, one with over $2.5 million of fraudulent payments to bogus recipients, and several others were large inventory frauds. The cases in this category come as close to being "organized crime" situations as any observed in this project. The majority of deceptions by "unknown" perpetrators or outsiders were inventory frauds; one of these apparently involved organized crime.

The perpetrator was considered an "outsider" if he is unknown and could have conducted the scheme without specialized knowledge or access.

For example, an unknown person or group stole over $2 million from New York banks by depositing bogus checks designed so they could never clear the bank's computer. The checks were printed as if they were drawn on a New York bank, but with a California bank's MICR encoding. The checks were ping-ponging back and forth between New York and California well after the normal clearance time; by then, the funds had been withdrawn.

Comparison of the perpetrator's job position with the method used to manipulate the computer system confirms that the majority of the schemes involve employee actions very similar to those of his job position: data entry personnel and tellers manipulated transactions and programers manipulated programs as shown in Figure 5. Management, staff and computer operators engaged in several types of schemes, but the majority involved tampering with input transactions.

Comparison of perpetrator's job position and type of scheme yielded little pattern in the data. All types of employees operated payroll, disbursement and accounting/inventory frauds. About all that can be said from the analysis was that just about anyone could be involved in a fraud scheme.

Figure 6 suggests differing degrees of control in different types of organizations. Corporate computer frauds were perpetrated by all types of employees from officers to keypunchers. In banks and savings and loan associations, the primary fraud position was one of management; branch managers and teller supervisors were frequently responsible for the crimes. In state and local governments, the primary job position involved data entry; here again, most of these cases were welfare frauds where bogus recipients or payments were simply added to the transaction flow at the time of computer input.

Job position	Trans-actions added	Trans-actions altered	Trans-actions deleted	File changes	Program changes	Improper operation	Miscel-laneous unknown
1 Data entry/terminal operator	9	4	–	1	–	–	1
2 Clerk/teller	9	6	–	1	–	–	–
3 Programer	–	–	–	–	14	–	1
4 Officer/manager	8	4	3	1	3	1	1
5 Computer operator	1	4	–	1	–	3	–
6 Other staff	1	–	1	1	–	–	2
7 Outsider (nonemployee)	3	1	–	–	–	–	1
8 Unknown	–	1	–	2	–	–	–

Note: All but 4 of the federal government cases were excluded because of missing information in those case descriptions.

Fig. 5 *Job position of perpetrator, method of manipulation*

Job position	Corporation	Bank/ savings and loan	State and local government	Federal government	Total
1 Data entry/ terminal operator	6	2	6	1	15
2 Clerk/teller	6	4	3	3	16
3 Programer	7	7	1	–	15
4 Officer/manager	7	12	2	–	21
5 Computer operator	3	5	1	–	9
6 Other staff	4	–	1	–	5
7 Outsider (nonemployee)	2	3	–	–	5
8 Unknown	2	1	–	–	3

Note: All but 4 of the federal government cases were excluded because of missing information in those case descriptions.

Fig. 6 *Job position of perpetrator, type of victim*

AN OUNCE OF PREVENTION

Many of the fraud cases cited here could have been prevented by a revision of the company's organizational structure. Employees should be given positions that do not conflict or overlap with the responsibilities of others in the organization. And all employees should be consistently observed and reviewed to prevent opportunities to commit fraud.

Separation of responsibility. Perhaps half the fraud cases summarized in this article would have been impossible had separation of responsibility in data processing been practiced and enforced. In many of these cases, employees who had no responsibility for transactions were still able to generate, tamper with or delete them. Separation of responsibility in a computer environment means separation of the following functions:

1. Input data generation.
2. Input control.
3. Computer operation.
4. Programing and maintenance.
5. Output control.
6. Data, program file control (librarian).

It is essential that programers not have access to input transactions, real data or program files and that they not operate the computer. Computer operators must not be able to change programs or gain access to data files except according to job scheduling, and they should not be able to enter or change input data. In keeping with time-honored auditing principles, certain responsibilities should be kept separate and controls or checks are necessary to make sure that data is not manipulated as it is generated and processed.

Employee surveillance. Bankers have always tried to monitor the financial situations of their employees—and for good reason. All computer users should realize that all data center employees and particularly those managers and staff who work with the data center should be closely supervised. All systems where employees or associates have personal accounts (banks, insurance companies, brokerage houses, etc.) should be given special attention.

THE BIGGEST DETECTED COMPUTER FRAUDS

From the 150 computer fraud cases included in this survey, 15 were selected and are listed in Figure 7 as "the biggest." These cases all involved schemes that ran for more than a year, were operated by employees of the victim organization and are typical of the schemes discovered to date. Excluded from this list are half a dozen cases each with losses greater than $1 million. They were not included because they ran less than a year, the victim was not the employer or the fraud methodology was atypical.

Case	Summary	Amount (thousands)	Time frame (years)	Type of scheme	Computer manipulation	Fraudulent debit	Job position of primary perpetrator	Number of perpetrators inside/outside	Means of detection
1	Accountant at west coast department store set up phony vendors, purchases and vouchers.	$ 100	1.3	Disbursements	Unauthorized transactions added	Inventory	Accountant	1/-	Suspicious bank employee
2	Claims reviewer at insurance company prepared false claims payable to friends in a manner that would be paid automatically by the computer.	$ 128	4	Fraudulent claims paid	Unauthorized transactions added	Expense	Claims clerk	1/22	Error made by greedy associate
3	Clerk at storage facility entered false information to computerized inventory system to mask theft of inventory. Shipments then made without billing.	$ 4,000	6	Inventory/billing	Input transactions altered	Inventory	Computer terminal operator	1/13	Physical inventory shortage detected in audit
4	Warehouse employees manipulated computerized inventory system through unauthorized terminal entries to mask inventory thefts.	$ 200	1.5	Inventory	Unauthorized terminal entries	None (inventory records changed as to location)	Warehouse employee(s)	"Several"	Suspicious wife of store manager
5	Accountant at metal fabricating company padded payroll, thereby extracting funds for own use.	$ 100	3	Payroll	Unknown	Expense	Accountant	1/-	IRS investigation
6	Officer of London bank stole funds from inactive customer accounts.	$ 290	5	Account transfers	Unauthorized addition and alteration of transactions	Customer accounts (liability)	Computer liaison officer	1/-	Unknown
7	Bank employee misused on line banking system to perpetrate large lapping fraud including unrecorded transactions, altered transactions and unauthorized account transfers.	$ 1,400	3	Lapping	Transactions altered, added and withheld	Customer accounts (liability)	Teller supervisor	1/-	Gambling activities uncovered by police raid
8	Manufacturing company manager who had designed and installed automated accounting system used it to steal.	$ 1,000	2	Disbursements (also billings fraud)	Transactions altered (also unauthorized transactions)	Inventory (also expense)	Operations manager	1/1	Suspicious associate
9	Customer representatives of large public utility, together with outside associate, erased customer receivables using computer error correction codes; received kickback from customer.	$ 25 (probable losses much greater)	2	Accounts receivable—collections	Unauthorized transactions	Expense (adjusting entry)	Customer service representative	2/1	Suspicious bank employee together with expanded type of scheme
10	Clerk in department store established phony purchases and vouchers paid to friend's company.	$ 120	3	Disbursements	Unauthorized transactions	Inventory	Accounts clerk	1/1	Suspicious associate
11	Organized crime ring operated check-kiting fraud between two banks using computer room employees who altered deposit memos to record check deposits as available for immediate withdrawal.	$ 900	4	Kiting (float fraud)	Transactions altered	(Timing)	VP-computer systems (also assistant branch manager)	2/3	Bank messenger failed to deliver checks on time
12	Accountant at large wholesaler established phony vendors through computerized accounting system that he operated.	$ 1,000	4	Disbursements	Unauthorized transactions	Inventory	Controller	1/-	Gave up
13	Officer of brokerage house misappropriated company funds through computer system that he controlled.	$ 277	3	Account transfers	Unauthorized transactions	Revenue account (interest earned)	VP-computer systems	1/-	Unknown
14	Partner at brokerage house transferred funds from firm's accounts to his own.	$ 81	3	Account transfers	Unauthorized transactions	Expense (via adjusting entry)	Partner-head of computer system	1/-	Unknown
15	Director of publishing subsidiary manipulated computer system to add false sales and block recording of accounts payable—all to improve operating results, thereby securing a position on board of directors.	$11,500	"Several years"	Padded sales (also unrecorded expense)	Program alterations (also file changes)	Receivables	Director of subsidiary	5/-	Unknown

Fig. 7 *Long running computer frauds*

The most important observation to be made from these cases is that they are common. None are creatures of the computer; they have all been tried before. Four of the cases were disbursement frauds where bogus vendors, together with the supporting details, were set up and paid. Four cases were of the "fund transfers through the accounts" type, all in financial institutions where the perpetrator's and his accomplices' accounts appeared as liabilities; the others were of different types. Thus, in terms of scheme type, the biggest computer frauds are all old wine in new bottles. The technology may be random access and hexadecimal, but the scheme itself should be as familiar to the auditor as debits and credits.

A surprise is the variety of the job positions of the perpetrators; it appears that big frauds can be conducted from almost any job position but the higher the position of responsibility, the greater the prospects for fraud. The one job position conspicuously absent from the big cases was that of computer programer. Perhaps these people are not as dangerous as had been feared; but it's also possible that the reverse is true. This is a good illustration of the problem of working from detected cases—we have no way of correcting for sample bias. In this situation, we know nothing about currently successful embezzlers. One thing that the perpetrators throughout the biggest cases have in common is that each had a thorough understanding of the functional operation of the computer system. Of the 15 cases, 1 involved a man who had designed and installed the computer system, 4 were conducted by managers of computer departments and all others were frequent users of the system.

One big surprise in this tabulation was that all but one of the cases were effected by manipulation of transactions, mostly by unauthorized transactions being added to the input stream. Another was the paucity of cases detected by ordinary audit—1 case out of 15. Most were uncovered by suspicious associates and employees of related parties, such as banks. Again, this is probably misleading. No doubt many schemes were detected by internal audit or external review or were thwarted by internal controls and were never publicized. Thus, long running schemes must necessarily have escaped ordinary audit.

Auditors should be particularly interested in the conclusions about the biggest computer frauds drawn from the column labeled "fraudulent debit." In every accounting-based fraud, a trace or "footprint" of the fraudulent transaction is left in the accounts. In almost every case, it is the debit that should be the focus of internal control or the base of fraud detection. For example, disbursement frauds result in bogus debits to inventory or, in some cases, expense accounts; payroll debits are to expense accounts; and theft from dormant or inactive accounts in banks include fraudulent debits to customer accounts. The key to long running frauds is in the identification of unauthorized debit entries. In the 15 biggest cases, these entries form a definite pattern: 6 were to inventory or receivables, 3 were to expense, 2 were adjusting entries to revenue and 2 were to customer accounts (liabilities). Two involved schemes other than manipulation of accounting entries. These cases became big because these debits were such that detection by management was seriously impaired: inventory shortages were probably considered part of normal shrink, expenses were to those accounts where additional charges wouldn't be easily spotted (payroll, claims expense in an insurance company, interest expense at brokerage houses or revenue adjustments that appeared to be correcting entries). In reviewing automated accounting systems, the auditor would do well to establish a clear idea of the debit entries most likely to be fraudulently used.

CONCLUSION

The first time I assembled a set of computer fraud cases, I was struck by the incompetency of most of the embezzlers who had been discovered.[1] Since the computer provided such a high degree of fraud potential, I wrote at that time "I can't help wondering what the really clever people are doing" with the computer. I still wonder; I think the biggest computer frauds are still to be revealed.

APPENDIX

Five sources were used to collect cases for this article:

1. Annual reports, magazine articles and newspaper clippings.

2. Case files of the Stanford Research Institute. Donn B. Parker of the SRI allowed me to examine his case files, which have been established, in part, through research sponsored by the National Science Foundation.

3. Case files of the U.S. General Accounting Office. These cases are described in *Computer-Related Crimes in Federal Programs*, GAO Report FGMSD-76-27, April 27, 1976. Walter Anderson of the GAO's Financial and General Management Studies Division provided further details of these cases short of identifying the agencies and individuals involved.

4. Case files of the Federal Bureau of Investigation. Summaries of closed cases with individual and institutional identification removed were obtained from the FBI.

5. My own files from previous research and consulting projects.

While I am indebted to these organizations and individuals for their cases and assistance, I alone am responsible for the summaries, analyses and speculations contained in this article.

---

[1] Brandt Allen, "Computer Fraud," *Financial Executive,* May 1971, p. 38.

Control of Computer Abuses

JACK F. THORNE

By the end of 1974, 100,000 computers will be utilized in the United States. With these computers taking over very sensitive functions, where opportunity for gain by unauthorized acts traditionally exists, each computer is a potential tool for fraud or embezzlement. This statement is substantiated by some recent cases including the $300,000 Long Island and Pittsburgh Westinghouse embezzlement, the $1 million Los Angeles Telephone Company equipment theft, the $1.5 million New York Union Dime Bank embezzlement and the $300 million Equity Funding insurance fraud.[1] Although much has been written concerning this situation, research is needed (1) to determine the characteristics of computer facilities most vulnerable to fraud or embezzlement and (2) to indicate control features which will prevent or detect these acts.

The first phase of this research was completed at Stanford Research Institute under a National Science Foundation grant.[2] This project included an analysis of 160 recorded case histories involving crime and unauthorized activities within computer systems. From this analysis six major characteristics of the installations were discerned:

1. The computer system is used for financial processing applications including payroll, accounts payable and receivable and storage and maintenance of files of financial data.

2. Among the employees, there is more loyalty to each other than to the employer.

3. The organization does not separate sensitive job functions and lacks dual control of important tasks.

---

[1] Donn B. Parker and Susan Nycum, "The New Criminal," *Datamation,* January 1974, p. 57.

[2] Donn B. Parker, *Computer Abuse,* a report of research on computer abuse made under a National Science Foundation grant, California: Stanford Research Institute, 1973.

4. The system services and physical facilities are available to some employees during nonworking hours and without supervision.

5. Computer programs, including the operating system, are not under modification control, and ownership is not sufficiently displayed or otherwise established.

6. Disgruntled employees are not identified and removed from sensitive jobs.

This article is the result of the second phase of the needed research—an analysis of these characteristics and a delineation of control features necessary to provide reasonable assurance that undetected fraud or embezzlement does not occur.

During the analysis of these characteristics, the significance of the interrelationships of the various control features became apparent. The following analysis relates the characteristics to their controls. Controls discussed in relation to one characteristic are not repeated with other characteristics except for emphasis. However, Exhibit 1 depicts the interrelationships of all controls to their related characteristics.

Computer system used for financial processing applications. In most situations, operations procedures seem to be the key control element relating to this characteristic. First, these procedures should be formalized. They should be documented in manual form. Second, the operations staff should be aware of these procedures and their relevancy to the successful operation of the system. Orientation for new employees and regular training sessions for all personnel are necessary. Third, these procedures should be designed not to hinder the staff but to provide for orderly operations that can be supervised.

The operations staff should be aware of the personnel who have need to access the computer and the supervision which should be provided for such personnel. All programer activity in the computer room should be under the supervision of operations personnel. The operations log should reflect all programs and data used. Finally, all user-programer activity in the computer room should be kept at a minimum and be subject to supervisory approval.

In some unusual situations, certain data or programs may need to be classified as being highly confidential or secret. All such items, except when actually being used, should be stored offline on removable discs, tapes or cards. The storage area should be highly secure. When these programs and data are being processed, all personnel except those authorized to deal with the highly confidential material should be required to leave the computer room. During processing, all remote terminals should be electronically disconnected from the computer. The printing ribbon on any output devices that use an impact printing method, such as a line printer or teletype, should be removed at the end of the job and placed with the programs and data in secure storage. At the end of processing, all of the computer main memory, scratch tapes and discs should be cleared by a program or hardware procedure. Also, procedures should be developed to provide for the disposal of no longer needed output (punched cards, tapes, and discs) associated with highly confidential information. This would include shredding paper output and punched cards, and the magnetic scrambling of tapes and discs. Since adopting the above procedures for

Exhibit 1 INTERRELATIONSHIPS OF CONTROLS TO ABUSE CHARACTERISTICS*

	System used for financial applications	More loyalty among employees than to employers	Nonseparation of job functions and lack of dual control	System available during nonworking hours and without supervision of sensitive	Insufficient control of computer programs	Disgruntled employees not removed from sensitive jobs
1 Staff awareness	P	P	P	P	P	S
2 Proper training	P	P	S	S	S	N
3 Adequate supervision	P	P	P	P	P	P
4 Operations log	P	P	P	P	P	S
5 Programers' activity in computer room controlled	P	S	P	P	P	N
6 Confidential information procedures	P	S	S	N	P	N
7 Personnel reference check	S	P	S	S	S	S
8 Bonding for employees	S	P	S	S	S	S
9 Mandatory vacations	P	P	P	P	S	N
10 Assignment changes	P	P	P	P	S	N
11 Employees' suggestions	N	P	N	N	N	S
12 Separation of basic functions	P	S	P	S	S	S
13 Proper documentation	S	S	P	S	P	N
14 Personnel behavior controls	S	S	P	S	S	P
15 Programs and data controls	P	S	P	P	P	S
16 Output disposal procedures	S	S	P	S	S	N
17 Independent control procedures	P	P	P	P	P	S
18 Acceptance testing procedures	S	S	P	S	P	S
19 Accounting for computer time	P	S	P	P	P	N
20 Data verification	P	S	P	S	S	S
21 Program verification	P	S	P	S	P	S
22 Program changes procedures	P	S	P	S	P	S
23 Restricted access to computer	P	P	S	P	P	S
24 Identification keys	P	P	S	P	P	S
25 Access authorization tables	P	P	S	S	P	S
26 Unlimited access controls	P	P	S	P	P	S
27 Offline storage of sensitive data	S	S	S	S	P	N
28 Data preparation procedures	S	S	S	S	P	N
29 Auditing subsystems	P	P	P	P	P	S
30 Removal of disgruntled employees from sensitive areas	S	S	S	S	S	P
31 Internal auditors	P	P	P	P	P	S
32 External auditors	P	P	P	P	P	S

*P—Primary control
S—Secondary control
N—Negligible control

highly confidential data and programs is expensive and time consuming, a definite need for this level of secrecy must be justified before engaging in such operations.

Among the employees, more loyalty to each other than to the employer. Regardless of the number of safeguards that may be installed, the basic security of a computer installation is no better than the integrity of the employees. Thus, adequately trained personnel are critical to the security of the entire system. Personnel security has three basic aims:

1. To recruit dependable and stable employees.
2. To insure that employees continue to be persons of integrity.

3. To keep before these employees the knowledge that management relies on them—individually—to preserve the integrity of the computer system.

The primary personnel control is the reference check. Usually, it is comparatively easy to ascertain whether the applicant has the experience and educational requirements to equip him for the position. However, it is equally important but usually more difficult, to accurately relate the applicant's past to his job potential. In this area an evaluation of stability and dependability assumes considerable importance. In fact, stability and dependability may well be the most important attributes desired in computer employees.

The second personnel control is bonding for employees in sensitive positions. Two controls designed to prevent an employee from having exclusive and permanent contact with any particular application are mandatory vacations, which are relatively easy to implement, and assignment changes, which sometimes meet resistance from managements who value specialization. However, the staff training aspects of assignment changes can be pointed out to management along with their control benefits.

The key to a successful computer security program is employee awareness. After their recruitment and as an integral part of their training, employees should be continuously advised that management relies on them to preserve the integrity of the computer system. Since a number of outside individuals are involved with the system, such as maintenance technicians, auditors and engineers, it is essential that employees at the installation take the initiative in regulating and controlling the activities of outside individuals. In fact, a definite program should be established, guiding employees and emphasizing to each individual the importance of his role. Employee suggestions for security should be solicited and carefully considered as one aspect of this program. Most employees will accept high standards and abide by regulations if they understand the objectives to be achieved and the methods to be used.

Nonseparation of sensitive job functions and lack of dual control of important tasks. The critical control feature in this area is the separation of the basic data processing functions, which are programing, operations and control. While the possibility exists that an employee may succumb to temptation and alter records to embezzle money, the probability is greatly reduced if controls in the system require the collusion of two or more employees for the embezzlement to succeed.

These control procedures may be classified according to the three basic data processing functions. First, programing procedures are concerned with the design and creation of new computer programs. The development of all programs should be documented according to specified standards. This documentation should be created along with the development of the program rather than after the program is completed. Personnel who write and develop programs according to prescribed specifications should develop these programs up to the point of acceptance testing of the program. At this stage, the program and its associated documentation should be turned over to the personnel responsible for acceptance testing of new programs.

Personnel involved with the development of user programs for a computer system usually have no reason to be in the computer room. Only in very rare instances is the development of a program facilitated by observing the computer running the program.

Second, operations procedures deal with the daily production operations of the computer center. These procedures augment security by ensuring separation of duties among employees and by regulating the interaction of personnel with the machine. The behavior of operations personnel in the computer room should be regulated by these procedures. For example, no eating, drinking or smoking should be allowed in areas around the computer system. Procedures should cover the submission, running and return of programs and data. All programs and data should be controlled in a systematic manner so that the status of each is known at all times.

In order to accomplish this objective, a computer tape library is usually required. Also, procedures should cover the interaction of operations personnel with personnel involved in certain maintenance aspects of the computer. Care must be exercised not to unduly restrict the activities of maintenance personnel since inefficiency and lost time can be the result. However, procedures should provide for the supervision and coordination of their activities in the computer room. The maintaining of an operations log should be specified by these procedures. The individual who is in charge of the computer room should be responsible for maintaining a log that reflects the status of the computer at all times. Finally, operations procedures should dictate the disposal of computer output and punch cards. Examination of discarded output can reveal much information about computer operations. As indicated above, it may be desirable to shred the material before disposal.

Third, control procedures pertain to the testing of programs for validity and accuracy and with controlling the usage of programs. The control personnel should be independent of the computer line management and must have sufficient technical competence to be able to monitor the system operations. Control personnel should have procedures for the exhaustive acceptance testing of new programs and program changes. Without proper verification of program operation, data can be destroyed or incorrect results obtained with a corresponding loss of time and money. Accounting for computer time usage should be a function of the control staff. The amount of computer time taken by each user should be correlated to the task performed by that user. Verification of data and programs is an important function that should be included in the control procedures. Programs can be verified by comparing the copy in use with the original copy, which should be in the possession of the control personnel. Tests of data files should be made for irregularities and verified with data from outside the computer system. Audit trails, if available, should be examined. On a surprise basis, data and programs should be periodically audited to discourage fraud schemes. Finally, control procedures should cover methods for needed program changes. Requests for program changes, either to correct errors or for operational reasons, should go through the control personnel to the personnel in charge of overall system design.

The operating procedures adopted for any given system should be the result of a systematic analysis of the security needs of the individual situation. Procedures should not be so complex and cumbersome that they will be ignored. However, they should attempt to define each employee's role in the total computer system. Procedures that deal with security, such as programer access to the computer, should never be relaxed because of a crisis or training situation. Little rationale exists in setting up procedures only to ignore them when they are needed.

System available during nonworking hours and without supervision. The major control features in this area seem to emphasize the following four elements: physical access to the computer, identification to the system, authorization to data and programs and supervision of operations.

First, physical access to the computer system should be restricted to only those individuals actually involved in the support of computer operations. To maintain good access controls, both to the building and to the computer room proper, it is usually necessary to place responsibility for security on the staff supervisor for each shift. Access should be limited to one or possibly two controlled points, depending on the number of employees and configuration of the computer facility. Unneeded doors may be simply bricked up. But, some fire exits may be necessary in order to comply with local fire safety regulations. Audible alarms should be placed on all fire emergency exits. Physical entry to the computer system may be controlled by a number of methods, such as "badge and buzzer" techniques, mechanical devices (lock systems) and uniformed guards. However, if the computer system includes remote terminals, control of physical access to the system may not be practical.

Second, once the user has physical access to the computer, he must identify himself to the system. This identification is usually done using some kind of alpha-numeric "key" or code word. Personal keys for each individual are preferred over group keys since they are easier to change if there is a risk that some unauthorized person has possession of them. In choosing a safe key, the number of combinations must be so large that there is little risk that someone will hit on a legal key by chance. The key should be selected randomly among all combinations. Since the risk of unauthorized use is larger if it has to be written down, the key should be easy to memorize. It is important that the computer never outputs the keys, especially at the terminal when they are put in. Finally, an alarm should be given as soon as the user of a terminal has made two or three attempts at entering an illegal key. Each alarm must also lead to an investigation into what has happened.

Third, when a user has proved his or her identity to the computer, by checking an authorization table the computer can determine to what data and what program the individual can have access. This authorization should not be access or no access. Full flexibility requires that a person is given different privileges for different kinds of access:

- The right to read a group of data.
- The right to add to a group of data.

- The right to change existing data.
- The right to delete from a group of data.
- The right to execute a program.
- The right to change a program.

The term "group of data" rather than "file" is used above because from a security viewpoint, a person may be allowed access to, for example, only certain fields in each record or only some of the records in a file.

Finally, those having access to the system should always have proper supervision. While theoretically a number of alternatives to supervision do exist, such as a "buddy system" where employees always work in pairs, experience indicates these systems break down and, thus, are not substitutes for supervision.

Insufficient control of computer programs. The programs of most computer systems can be divided into two general groups, operating system software and user software. The operating system software provides common services to all user software, while the user software accomplishes a more specific job such as updating the accounts receivable and computing the payroll.

Two important points should be emphasized about data security and the operating system. First, since the operating system is responsible for the storage and retrieval of data, it logically follows that the operating system can access any data stored on the computer. Thus, individuals familiar with the operating system and having access to or knowledge of certain identification codes can have a free hand with all data stored on the computer system. The personnel involved with maintaining the operating system should be the only people who possess the ability to access the computer system in an unlimited manner. The number of individuals having unlimited access to data stored on the computer system should be controlled. Programers writing user software have no reason to access data other than that data concerned with their projects.

The second point concerning data security and the operating system deals with computer systems that simply cannot offer protection to a user's data. Usually this is due to the lack of sophistication on the part of the hardware or the operating system or both. When protection cannot be offered in the computer system, sensitive data should not be permanently stored in the system itself but should be stored in secure storage elsewhere. For example, removable magnetic discs may be taken out of the computer system when the job is completed.

Manipulation of user programs for fraudulent ends may be divided into two classes: first, the program itself can be altered; second, the input data to the program can be altered. Achieving criminal goals by program modification is attractive, because the manipulation of the program's operation can be performed independent of the input data to the program. The relationships between the various programs greatly determine the level of software security found in the system. For example, verification for cancelled payroll checks might include a periodic audit against an active employee roster to establish the authenticity of the check's payee.

The goal of a secure data processing system design should be to minimize the likelihood of undetected, hence probably successful, criminal manipulation caused by alteration of a single element of that system.

Tests for correctness of input data, performed by the program, can be classified in two general categories. The first type of test is concerned with the detection of accidental errors in the input data; the second type of test is concerned with the detection of deliberate errors in the input data. The major burden for the development of error-free input data must, of necessity, fall upon the procedures used in the data preparation department. Some types of data are amenable to the use of programing techniques such as batch totals and hash totals. For certain critical data fields the use of a check digit can be justified. Additionally, programs can be designed to verify information about input data files such as creation date, last date accessed and file name.

Development of a programing philosophy for the detection of deliberate errors in the input data should be based on the realization that many errors cannot be detected on the individual program level if the input data is altered in a sufficiently skilled manner. Such errors must be detected by the overall design of the data processing system. That is, the auditing function must be designed into the data processing system.

For example, a program can be designed and written to validate functions requested by the input data. To do so, however, requires the availability of validation information to the program, which, in turn, can be utilized to establish the validity of input data.

In conclusion, the success of testing for deliberate input errors depends on the availability of validation data to individual programs. It is up to the system designer to develop a design philosophy which will minimize the likelihood of successful undetected criminal manipulation of the data processing system through the alteration of any single element, program or data file in the system.

Disgruntled employees not identified and removed from sensitive jobs. Disgruntled employees, such as employees who are given notices prior to their discharges, ideally should be completely removed from the computer installation. If this procedure is impractical, they should be physically restricted to an area where there is no sensitivity. One procedure which has proved successful in regard to discharging employees is to have the individuals transferred to a nonsensitive job before they are given their discharge notices.

However, since surveillance procedures such as the buddy system or closed circuit television often prove ineffective in practice, no substitute for the instant removal of disgruntled employees from sensitive areas is available.

CONCLUSIONS

From the above analysis three major conclusions are drawn. First, the major control procedures necessary to prevent or detect computer abuses, which are summarized in Exhibit 1, are neither extraordinary nor, in most cases, expensive to implement.[3] Of these procedures the most critical ones seem to be employee awareness and proper supervision.

Second, in order to have a secured computer system, control considerations must be given during the design phase of implementation. Not only is the adding of controls to a fully developed program expensive, in many cases it is impossible.

Finally, to ensure that the necessary control procedures are included in the design of the system and are functioning throughout the life of the system, the evaluation of the controls must be continuous. This objective can be accomplished through the joint efforts of the system's control personnel, the organization's internal auditors and the corporation's external auditors.

---

[3] While real time, integrated or other advanced computer systems may require new control procedures, the great majority of recorded computer abuses do not involve advanced systems. For a discussion of control procedures for advanced systems, see Jack F. Thorne, "Internal Control of Real-Time Systems," *Data Management,* January 1971, pp. 34–37.

EDP Control
Means Total Control

JAMES R. DAVIS

The installation of an electronic data processing system in a firm affects many people and alters the internal control system, but it does not lessen in any way the need for a strong system of internal control. In any EDP system, weaknesses in internal control provide more opportunities for errors or fraud to go unnoticed, and it is more difficult to establish accountability for them.

CONTROL CHANGES FOR EDP SYSTEMS

It is generally agreed that accounting internal controls are concerned with safeguarding the assets of the firm and assuring the reliability and accuracy of financial information. In the same way, EDP controls must be operative throughout the system, and include any area where a user has contact with data, either through the equipment or external to it. Such controls include:

1. Limiting data access to authorized persons, and then only to the data that are needed.
2. Reporting variances to management on a timely basis in order to initiate corrective actions.
3. Using the controls over processes within the system itself.
4. Implementing those controls that are effective but not so unreasonable that it becomes impossible to live with the system.[1]

In a manual system the accounting department has traditionally been responsible for the accurate postings to ledgers, arithmetical accuracy, and general bookkeeping activities. In an EDP environment, however, traditional functions once vested in the accounting department have now been altered significantly, eliminated, or transferred to the computer. These changes impose greater responsibility on the accounting department, and also on the source and user departments than was necessary in a manual system. Specific measures must now be imposed on the system to control the actions of people at each stage in the flow of data.

The accuracy of a computer eliminates the need for some of the inspection necessary in a manual system, but the lack of human intervention during processing means that some of the control is lost. Unless the system is designed to recognize unintentional errors or deliberate fraud in the data, machine reliability is lessened. Computers cannot think, so they must be programmed to detect unusual transactions that manual inspection traditionally caught. Fortunately, once programmed for error detection, the procedures for these controls may be more comprehensive, effective, and efficient than previous manual controls.[2]

General controls include the primary plan of organization and operation of the EDP activity, the procedures for documenting, reviewing, testing, and approving system, programs and changes, controls built into the equipment and data files, and other data and procedural controls affecting EDP operations. The specific application controls are categorized into the basic areas of input, processing, and output.

DOCUMENTATION

Documentation consists of descriptions of procedures, charts, instructions to employees, flowcharts, and other necessary descriptive materials. Although it is usually costly, documentation is an absolute necessity if the investment in the computer installation is to be protected. Without sound documentation, the system will be highly vulnerable when key individuals leave. Also, the system may become uncontrolled and incapable of being audited by management or outside auditors.

In general terms, documentation serves to provide management with a clear understanding of systems objectives and concepts, and to ensure adherence to company policies. It also serves as a basis for reviewing accounting and internal controls by internal and external auditors, and provides a reference for systems analysts and programmers responsible for maintaining existing systems and programs. Adherence to the ideal of full documentation varies widely in practice because of the time and expense involved in preparing and maintaining the information.

Documentation serves essentially as a communications link between users and the data processing department. If lucid standards of accuracy and schedule requirements are not specified between these groups, one group may often receive blame for problems outside its realm of responsibility. Also, data inaccuracies may result if schedules that affect more than one group are disregarded. The process of preparing documentation also helps to establish lines of communication between those responsible for getting the jobs completed.

Documentation identifies the placement of control elements by enumerating precise duties and responsibilities. Proper documentation provides a means of monitoring changes in the system and makes the process of change easier, because it presents to all concerned parties a concise analysis of the status of data processing at any given time.

Since an EDP system is a complex collection of subsystems, routines, sources of input, volume variations, and output requirements, documentation is crucial for efficient integration of personnel and equipment according to predetermined schedules and data specifications. Documentation aids both management and accounting in evaluating the operating efficiency and effectiveness of the data processing activity by serving as a basis for comparison. It is also invaluable for training new employees and assisting current employees in learning changes in the system.

Documentation must be protected from loss or destruction. Duplicate copies should be stored in a remote location, accessible only by authorized personnel. These duplicate records serve an additional purpose; they enable members of management and internal auditing to make periodic comparisons with current programs to satisfy themselves that no unauthorized or fraudulent changes have been inserted. The usefulness of duplicate documentation to external auditors is readily apparent.

THREE CATEGORIES

Three categories of documentation must be implemented in a system; systems documentation, programming documentation, and operating documentation.

Systems Documentation

Systems documentation should include an English language narrative stating both the overall objectives of the system and subsystems and the applications of the system in relationship to each other. This narrative should be approved by the user groups for whom the output is intended as well as by top management. Because systems documentation requires the involvement of generalists, the English narrative should avoid technical, computer-oriented terminology.

Along with this narrative, a systems flowchart should be prepared to indicate the flow of data through the system, and to indicate the hardware involved. The flowchart, using standard flowcharting symbols, should correlate with the narrative and be supported by procedures manuals for all operations in the system.

Program Documentation

This documentation should contain comprehensive descriptions of the programs on file. It is a valuable tool for developing tests of this system, for discovering where procedural weaknesses exist, and for providing a point of reference for modification in the system.

Documentation for each program should include an English language description of what the program is intended to accomplish, the hardware required to run the program, flowcharts illustrating the logic of the program, and input/output record layouts for various media. Record layouts should include:

1. Details of records, with descriptions of all fields (use standard abbreviations only)
2. Location of decimal points

3. Indication of field sizes

4. Type of data: alpha, numeric, or alphanumeric allowable on each field

5. Data codes describing all possible values of the code and their meanings

6. Header label record conventions to be used

7. Blocking factors to be used

8. Trailer record conventions to be used

9. Special control records, if any.[3]

Descriptions of printed record layouts, rules for special computations, internal and external controls to be checked, instructions for preparing, editing, and controlling data should be included in documentation for each program. Editing and control procedures should include such tests as reasonableness and consistency. Standards for file descriptions and console messages—and their meanings—are also necessary for each program.

Each program's documentation should be a complete unit, avoiding reference to other documents, and written in accordance with predetermined programming specifications. Program listings should be compiled and English language comments added to explain program components. Copies of source and object programs are part of the documentation, and should be stored away from the main computer center as backup files. Remote storage of programs also serves to discourage unauthorized changes to programs—provided the data processing manager, or internal auditor, periodically compares production programs with copies of the originals.

Program modifications should be approved in writing by the data processing manager and documentation should be updated. Those modifications should then be tested in a manner similar to testing a new program. Test data should include all valid combinations of data as well as data designed to violate control procedures. Thorough modification testing should be monitored by nonsystems personnel and should include the following:

1. Mock data designed to violate the edit and other controls of the system

2. Large doses of "live" transaction data as an assurance check on the comprehensiveness of the mock data

3. "Control answer" violations of the system, with proper followup of variations from controlled answers

4. Tests of more than one cycle of the same program in order to verify its updating capability, and "string tests" of the entire system to verify program compatibility from input, through processing programs, to reporting.[4]

Operating Documentation

Operating instructions, the third category of documentation, should include systems flowcharts, console display explanations, actions to be taken for special conditions, restart procedures, and output disposition. Instructions for data input/output should include media preparation instructions, logging procedures, conversion of raw data into machine readable form, verification instructions, storage of raw data after input to the system, and review of the output, such as batch control checks.

Operating instructions should be legible, and located near the console. To make sure that the instructions are actually being used, the data processing manager should observe operations during working hours, and conduct a periodic review to check for adequate updating of the documentation. Illustration of forms and layouts, and samples of outputs are also a part of this documentation. If machine readable input is prepared by source departments, easily understood procedures manuals must be written for them, since they most likely will have little knowledge of data processing procedures.

APPLICATION CONTROLS

Application controls primarily concern input, processing, and output. The consistency and integration of a system demand valid data handling techniques at every point. Input is typically the weakest link in the processing chain, and many experts consider the manipulation of input data as probably the easiest way to perpetrate fraud. Because fraudulent data may be indistinguishable from legitimate data, the input devices must be carefully controlled. If an unintentional error is made in the initial recording of the data, it may easily pass through the entire system without detection. It may also be transferred to other departments for processing; consequently, there must be control over the interdepartmental movement of data as well. Since a single transaction can affect many files, and eventually output, controls over input must assure both valid input data and proper program posting in specific files.

While data is entering the computer, well-designed data editing functions ensure that only valid data are processed and that unacceptable data are flagged for correction or removal. Some of the more important controls during processing include: sequence check, character check, reasonableness and limit tests, completeness checks, and digit checks. Also, tests of logical transaction combinations provide control over such items as equality of debits and credits. A list of acceptable transaction combinations should be incorporated in the computer program to process accounting data. The inputs of each transaction transmitted for processing are jointly tested against the acceptable transaction combinations, and only transactions with account coding corresponding to that contained in the computer program are accepted for processing.

When errors are detected during a run, good internal control requires established procedures for follow-up and correction. In handling errors:

1. Overall control of good data plus error data must be maintained
2. Reconstruction of the error record from the source data must be possible
3. The rules on resubmission of corrected records must be clearly defined
4. Overall controls must be reestablished after correction runs.[5]

The ability of the computer system to measure itself is a most powerful internal control tool. It reports who is doing what, for how long, how and when. This information may be reported continuously by the console log or stored, analyzed, and reported periodically. This console log is examined by a control group within the data processing department. Actual run times recorded by the console log are compared with predetermined time standards. Halt conditions and machine malfunctions recorded by the console log are also investigated by the control group. This group also records the progress of batches through the department, from initial receipt logging through each step in the processing to final disbursement of output. Persons receiving output also aid in control if they screen output carefully and compare it with control totals maintained in the source department. If the organization is small and does not have the personnel to segregate data processing duties, greater reliance is placed on the controls exercised by source departments. These controls include scrutiny of output processed by the computer, custody and access to assets restricted from the data processing department, and independent reconciliation of accounting controls.

ORGANIZATIONAL INDEPENDENCE

However reliable the input of a system, the effectiveness of controls are reduced if, as in a small manual system, one employee prepares input and also had custody of the assets, or if any one employee is in a position to prepare input and control the program processing it. The following guidelines on the separation of responsibilities are generally accepted:

1. The data proprietor (a functional group in the firm which originates data) determines classification of data, establishes individual needs for access to data, and propriety of data.
2. The installation manager handles data from the functional group according to classification, administers accessibility on local or remote basis, and conducts periodic reviews of operational security under his control.
3. The data processing security administrator monitors the data processing security program, acts as the focal point for security matters, is involved in the security aspects of new applications, and conducts training programs.[6]

Unless the system is large enough to justify separation of the duties, the data processing manager will probably act as the security administrator as well. Within the data processing department, development, operating, and control activities should be separated. In a very small system, however, complete separation may not be practical or possible, but authority should be delegated in such a way that no individual is responsible for the complete processing of any transaction. No one person should have the access necessary to both initiate and conceal errors or irregularities in the normal course of his duties.

LEVELS OF CONTROL

Data controls are determined by two groups in the firm: top management of the organization and data processing management. Top management's overall responsibility for data processing includes authorization of major systems additions or changes (evaluated in terms of expected cost and benefits), and post-installation review of actual cost and effectiveness of systems projects. Management should monitor project proposals and evaluate the reasons for any deviations from projections. The assessment of performance on the post-installation review will aid in evaluating future systems requests. Top management has the responsibility for employing data processing personnel and for reviewing the organization and control practices of the data processing department. Top management also evaluates performance by comparing actual costs, delays in schedules, and error rates with expected levels of performance.

Within the overall structure of the firm, the EDP group should be functionally independent in its relationship to other operating departments. By separating responsibilities, the EDP group operates as a service department to all other functions in the firm.

Although a firm may have sound personnel policies, data processing managers may practice psychological methods, even though disfunctional, that serve to create an atmosphere of security. This can be done most effectively by making the employees aware of their security responsibilities through education and training, and by making sure the department manager observes security rules. The manager should also be sure that employee morale is kept high by informing them of company policy on a regular basis and by including key employees in decisions that may affect their jobs.

AUDIT TRAIL

Compared to a manual system, the EDP system's source documents and visible historical records are easier to alter or eliminate. In a manual system, the audit trail consists of journals, ledgers, and workpapers that permit the auditor to trace transactions through the system. In an EDP system, however, form, content, and accessibility of records frequently make it difficult to follow a transaction completely through the system.

In computer processing, audit trails are readily lost in the collection and summarization of data. Source documents may be filed in a manner that makes subsequent retrieval difficult, or source documents may not exist in an on-line system. The ledgers may be kept in a non-traditional manner, the data access may be limited to magnetic media, and print-outs may consist only of exceptions. Therefore, providing for the audit trail by keeping a record of transactions as they occur may be difficult to achieve. A detailed file could be maintained by printing daily proof listings of each day's transactions, or it might be kept by printing a transactions journal showing detailed transactions for each active account over a short period of time. It might also be kept by assembling all transactions on a journal tape. This tape could then be fed into an audit program, which would extract the transactions for selected accounts and print them in such a way that the accountant or auditor could analyze the status of an account, transaction by transaction.

Another important, but often overlooked, device to help ensure the effectiveness of internal controls is the review of the system and its operation by the internal auditor. The added dimension of having an independent staff, unrelated with designing or operating the system, review the existing procedures, greatly enhances overall system control.

CONCLUSION

It is evident that computer processing systems require many kinds of controls for efficient and effective operation. Along with the basic controls covering input, processing, and output, there must also be controls that cover the general operations of the system. Each major control element must be integrated into the overall control scheme of the computer operation. For a particular operation, control elements should be selected so that they complement each other for the greatest possible benefit.

REFERENCES

[1] Melvin Bund, "Security in an Electronic Data Processing Environment," *CPA Journal,* February 1975.

[2] The AICPA has officially recognized the significance of computers in present day accounting methods with the issuance of *Statement on Auditing Standards, No. 3,* "The Effects of EDP on the Auditor's Study and Evaluation of Internal Control." The statement discusses EDP accounting controls in terms of general controls and specific application controls.

[3] Jeffrey D. Green, "Systems Documentation, Internal Control, and the Auditor's Responsibilities," *CPA Journal,* July 1974.

[4] John M. Horne, "EDP Controls to Check Fraud," *Management Accounting,* October 1974.

[5] Foster Brown, "Auditing Control and System Design," *Journal of Systems Management,* April 1975.

[6] Bund, *Op. Cit.,* p. 34.

Management Fraud: The Insidious Specter

LAWRENCE B. SAWYER, ALBERT A. MURPHY, AND MICHAEL CROSSLEY

A corporation executive, poring over his company's financial reports, found a shortage of $1.2 million in the inventory accounts. Inquiries brought no logical explanations, and the executive suspected the variance was more than some colossal blunder.

With no clue as to how it happened or who was responsible, he sent a frantic call to the "insighters,"* consultants who can burrow beneath coverups to unearth elusive answers.

Through quantitative analysis, consultants identified the source of the impropriety. Through interrogation of personnel, they obtained a confession from a trusted manager. And through experience with developing claims under fidelity bonds, they helped the company recoup its losses.

The cause of these losses was management fraud, a form of fraud that goes beyond the narrow legal definition and encompasses all forms of deception practiced by managers to benefit themselves. Much has been written about deception for gain in the private sector, including theft, embezzlement, larceny, and other illegal practices. But deception by managers—people in positions of trust—is more often concealed than revealed. Its victims usually cover it up to avoid the adverse effects of publicity.

But it exists. It is a cancer spreading through many companies across the entire spectrum of business. Thus, there is an urgent need for management fraud to be placed under the spotlight of public scrutiny to show:

- where it takes place
- what forms it takes
- what reasons are behind it
- what to do when it occurs

* Refers to Insight Services, an investigative consulting service organization which specializes in uncovering frauds.

- what its symptoms are
- how to control it

WHERE MANAGEMENT FRAUD TAKES PLACE

Management fraud can be found wherever managers have the opportunity and the need to better their purses or their status through deception. The opportunity lies largely in the fiduciary position that managers have in the organization. They command belief and respect, their motives are rarely questioned, and their explanations are rarely disputed. Their respected roles as profit center managers—heads of autonomous units—place them above suspicion. They are often immune to the ordinary checks and balances imposed on their subordinates.

In decentralized organizations, division presidents, vice presidents, and general managers are vested with relatively absolute authority. They are judged by the central corporate executive groups and by boards of directors in terms of performance. Such performance is generally portrayed in reports and financial statements. And the deceivers' artful imaginations have little difficulty making red appear black.

The deception can continue for years. It survives where there is no thorough-going surveillance. It goes on where group vice presidents who visit the decentralized organizations use those visits to make social calls, instead of asking the hard questions. Deception flourishes where there are no top-flight internal auditors to analyze and dissect both operations and reports. And when it finally surfaces, or where suspicions trigger investigations, the harm has already been done, and the miscreant usually moves on to browse in other pastures. The damage they leave behind can be incalculable.

THE FORMS MANAGEMENT FRAUD TAKES

Management fraud masquerades in an infinite variety of guises, many of which have never been penetrated. But enough masks have been ripped away to give some inkling of what lies behind a guileless appearance.

Management fraud has been found in overstatements of inventory to show healthy assets which are, in truth, sickly . . . the acceptance of inferior goods to conceal a tottering cash position . . . delayed key expenditures to increase current profits to the detriment of the long-range survival of the company . . . overstatements of receivables to puff both assets and sales . . . fictitious sales which construct a facade of vigorous business volume . . . and understatements of liabilities to gloss over the financial picture.

Here are some illustrations.*

---

* Murphy and Crossley's experiences during their investigations of management fraud are the sources of these case histories. The names of the companies are, of course, fictitious. Indeed, to insure confidentiality, Insight Services' records contain nothing but unidentifiable summaries of these histories. The summaries do, however, show the patterns that management fraud takes.

Overstatement of Inventory

Company WXYZ, a conglomerate with about $1 billion in sales, arranged to divest itself of a profit center engaged in distributing rolls of sheet metal. The company acquiring the profit center asked for and received a certified statement of inventory on hand. WXYZ's external auditors certified the statement which reported $14 million worth of sheet stock.

But the external auditors had been deceived. Actually, there was a huge inventory shortage. The Accounting Department manager had taken the inventory, determined the exact amount of shortage, and known how much of the records to falsify. His people had prepared inventory tags and delivered them to the external auditors. The auditors had verified the amount of the stock shown on those tags and then deposited them in a box in the conference room they used during the audit. The manager had added spurious tags to the box at night. Because there had been little time to prepare a large number of tags, some of them were made to show rolls of sheet stock weighing as much as 50,000 pounds. He had also substituted new inventory reconciliation lists to tie into the total tags, those both valid and spurious.

After the sale of the division had been consummated, the buyers took their own inventory and found about a $6 million shortage. Understandably irked, they rescinded the sale. After WXYZ took back the profit center, its chief executive officer sent for the "insighters."

In their preliminary survey, these investigative consultants converted $14 million of sheet stock into cubic feet. Then they determined the volume within the warehouse that was supposed to contain it. The warehouse could not even hold that volume of sheet stock; it was far too small. To confirm the discrepancy, the consultants scanned the inventory tags and found the ones showing weights up to 50,000 pounds. They went to the warehouse and examined the fork lift trucks used to move the rolls of sheet stock. Not one of those trucks could possibly lift over 3,000 pounds.

The consultants verified purchases of the material reported in inventory and found that purchase orders supported an inventory of about 30 million pounds. Yet the reported inventory amounted to about 50 million pounds. Obviously, the records had been falsified.

Armed with this information, the consultants started interrogating people. The accounting manager soon confessed he had puffed the value of the inventory to show increased profits. He had felt compelled to do so to meet the wildly optimistic forecasts of the profit center general manager. The consultants' findings resulted in a settlement of nearly $1 million from the external auditing firm because its auditors had failed to detect the spurious tags, and a claim of over $10 million under a fidelity bond.

Acceptance of Inferior Goods

While investigating the inventory problem, the insighters found that fraud was spreading to other areas of the corporate body. For example, another of WXYZ's profit centers found its cash flow reduced to a trickle. Yet appearances had to be maintained for corporate headquarters. So suppliers were put on a 90- to 100-day payment cycle. Understandably, the creditors were less than enthralled, soon became downright unpleasant, and threatened to cut off the flow of supplies.

To placate them, the manager of the profit center agreed to accept material of inferior quality. The material was scrap aluminum. The profit center converted it to aluminum ingots, for parts. The consultants, suspecting a quality problem, had WXYZ's test laboratories, under their direction, analyze these materials. The results proved them to be below the standards set forth in the purchase orders, as well as actually paid for by the profit center.

In addition, the consultants determined the percentage of melt loss—the weight lost as the aluminum is melted and converted into ingots. They'd learned from industry publications: the better the scrap, the lower the loss. They found the melt loss to be 14%. Had the scrap met specifications, only a 6% loss would have resulted.

The consultants were able to support a claim of $1.5 million, under WXYZ's fidelity bond.

Delayed Key Expenditures

The metastasis continued. The insighters also found that a division of Company WXYZ postponed major maintenance so that amounts budgeted for that purpose could be used to purchase productive materials for inventory. The inventory values had been overstated. The inventory on hand was far less than the records showed. To make sure there was enough stock in inventory to satisfy the auditors when they made their counts, the division diverted funds allotted for maintenance to purchases of stock.

The amounts averaged about $250,000 a year for three years. Machinery was rapidly becoming obsolete. Besides, pricing was affected because accurate costs could not be determined from falsified records. As a result, prices were set lower than actual costs.

When the reason surfaced, it sounded like a broken record: the profit center manager wanted to make a good showing. The consultants were able to establish losses totaling $750,000—recoverable under the fidelity bond.

Overstatement of Receivables

In the LMS Corporation, with sales of $500 million, a profit center's general manager evidently had delusions of grandeur. He reported to the corporate group vice president that he could achieve unrealistically high profit goals. The group vice president cautioned that he was overly optimistic. But the profit center manager stubbornly stood his ground. The group vice president, exasperated, finally said, "I still don't think you can meet those figures; but if you insist on telling me you can, I'm going to hold you to them."

When information on the commitment reached the profit center's accounting manager, his blood chilled. He knew the goals could not be met. But he was close to retirement. He feared his boss. And he knew from past experience that his boss never wanted to hear bad news. The goals could not be met honestly. But he could give the appearance of them having been met by "cooking the books."

Receivables under government contract held by the profit center were based on a formula. Formulas can, of course, be manipulated; and that is precisely what the accounting manager did. Despite tests by the external auditors over a period of three years, the fictitious receivables slipped by unnoticed.

A party to the misstatements wrote a letter to the corporate office, admitting to overstatements of receivables totaling $500,000. The audit sparked by the revelation showed overstatements of $3 million. The informer left LMS, and the means by which the management fraud was perpetrated remained a mystery.

So the consultants were called in. They gained an understanding of the company's system, then made detailed comparisons between the general ledger accounts and the profit center's operating reports. The financial records painted a glowing picture. But the facts in the operating reports dulled that glow.

The puffed receivables puffed up sales and gave the illusion of a strong profit center. Also, to make the picture brighter, asset accounts were manipulated to give the appearance of reduced costs. The purpose of this was to reduce assets for certain months, since average assets were the basis on which allocations of corporate overhead were based: the lower the allocations, the higher the profit center's profits.

Until the consultants pointed them out, no one at corporate headquarters had noticed the strange gyrations of the asset accounts.

The fraud was perpetrated to pay for the profit center manager's ego trip. He was assisted in his purpose by a weak accounting manager. Nobody profited personally. But the embarrassment to the company was acute: the annual report, just printed, had to be scrapped. The form 8-K, required by the United States Securities and Exchange Commission if certain "significant events" occurred, told the sorry tale. The profit center's general manager and the accounting manager were both replaced. Their successors helped improve employee attitudes, and saw to it that reports to corporate headquarters contained realistic information to provide a more solid base for corporate reports and planning.

Fictitious Sales

In ABC Company, with sales of $400 million, a profit center had overstated its inventory. Corporate executives were unaware of this, and the profit center wanted to keep it that way. But the overstatements were escalating. The day of reckoning had to come, and the conspirators grew desperate. The managers of finance, sales, and purchasing conceived the idea of allocating fictitious sales of about $500,000 to some of the profit center's top customers to make it appear that this is where the fictitious inventory went. Of course, receivables of like amounts had to be set up. But how to liquidate them? The director of finance, involved in the conspiracy, told the accounting people that payments by these customers were to be received in the purchasing organization (of all places), validated, reported to accounting, and shown as liquidating the receivables. Hence, phony payments of false receivables were used to liquidate fictitious sales.

Corporate management was deceived into thinking that an unprofitable subsidiary was doing well. The deception prevented it from amputating a cancerous member of the body corporate. When ABC's executives finally observed the variances and could get no reasonable explanations, they called on the investigative consultants.

While familiarizing themselves with the profit center's systems, the consultants learned that an assistant controller had recently left the company. They located and questioned him. He admitted he had helped overstate inventory to show fictitious profits. The consultants were able to support a $1 million claim under the fidelity bond.

But the interrogation produced evidence that at ABC, just as in WXYZ, the cancer had metastasized. The consultants therefore analyzed all transactions that looked the slightest bit suspicious. Dozens of these transactions turned out to involve management fraud. In fact, the final claim filed under the bond totaled $9 million, including the $1 million in fictitious sales. One of the fraudulent transactions involved a number of managers who conspired to keep top management in ignorance about a $1 million receivable which was uncollectable. The story follows:

Understatements of Liabilities

One of ABC's customers prepared an unsupported, erroneous journal entry to reduce its liabilities by $1.5 million. The customer needed to show a good financial picture to negotiate a loan, which was duly obtained. The division manager and the financial manager of the ABC profit center involved were fully aware of the customer's shaky financial condition. Nevertheless, they granted the customer a line of credit totaling $1 million. The inducement to do so was a kickback from the customer. The line of credit was used. Later, the customer went bankrupt and ABC Company was left with an uncollectible receivable.

Corporate management inquired about the receivable and the steps leading to its uncollectibility. The division manager, piously affirming that the credit line had been based on certified financial statements, actually produced them. He told a plausible story in exquisite detail to assure his superiors that his judgment had been faultless. He claimed to be simply a victim of the vicissitudes of the marketplace.

Senior management accepted the story; the consultants did not. They charted the events as related by the division manager, showing the dates they were purported to have occurred. Then they went behind the oral statements to the underlying documentation.

It turned out that the customer had indeed submitted certified financial statements to the division manager. But the external auditors who certified the statements had been deceived by the customer's management people. The statement did not represent the true state of affairs. Moreover, the documents showed that the credit and kickback arrangement took place before the statement was received. As a matter of fact, ABC's division issued purchase orders to procure goods for the customer under the line of credit two months before the financial statements had been certified. The consultants were able to support a claim for $1 million under the bond.

THE REASONS BEHIND MANAGEMENT FRAUD

As the examples show, different pressures push managers into deception. These pressures can be internal or external. The manager may have the inner drive to outperform all others, to exceed the performance he or she displayed during the last fiscal year, to beat a rival to a coveted promotion, or to receive a larger incentive bonus. And the manager's grasp may exceed his or her reach. The goals set may be beyond the capacity to achieve.

Similar pressures may come from superiors. Unrealistic goals may be set by centralized management. These goals filter down to subordinate managers who are forced to meet what they had never committed to. And since they cannot achieve these goals fairly, they use deception to give the appearance of meeting them. Here is a summary of some of these reasons behind management fraud, including several already touched on:

1. *Executives sometimes take rash steps from which they cannot retreat.* In one instance, the president of a large conglomerate unthinkingly asserted before a group of financial analysts that profits for the current year would be X dollars a share. The assertion became a company goal. One subordinate manager, carrying his share of the unfair burden placed upon his shoulders, talked the external auditors into writing off an inventory adjustment over a five-year period. The transaction increased the current year's profits. But it caused a distortion in the corporate financial statement, and corporate management was unaware of the deception until it was unearthed by consultants.

2. *Profit centers may distort facts to hold off divestment.* One profit center was running to hard times. Corporate management was looking only at the bottom line, judging the worth of the division by what it brought into the corporate coffers. When the line started turning from black to red, corporate executives started thinking about amputation.

But the division comprised more than numbers and things. It was also made up of people. And they were fully aware that poor performance could bring drastic action; that their jobs, their status, their seniority, and their futures were in jeopardy. The first law of nature is self-preservation. And those with much to lose and the opportunity to protect themselves resorted to "cooking the books" to turn actual red into ostensible black.

3. *Incompetent managers may deceive in order to survive.* Nothing stands still. Ours is a galloping technology. Good managers keep abreast of change; poor ones slip back. In a number of instances the consultants found that what some managers could not produce on merit they spelled out in reports that puffed up their performance in defiance of the facts.

4. *Performance may be distorted to warrant larger bonuses.* Managers in many organizations participate in management incentive plans. The better the performance, the larger the bonus. And, in large organizations, performance is often delineated by numbers in a report. There is a temptation to put the best face on our accomplishments. And if the size of the reward hangs on the size of the reported numbers, and managers feel they can manipulate the numbers without detection, some of them may succumb to temptation.

5. *The need to succeed can turn managers to deception.* Ambition is a worthy trait. It can move ordinary people to do extraordinary things. But when ambition wields an unmerciful whip, and when self-advancement becomes more important than solid accomplishment, some managers will betray their stewardship. To the detriment of reasonable long-range performance, some managers have shown superior short-range performance and then moved on before the long-range effects could catch up with them. Their methods included: inadequate funding of research and development so that the company ultimately lost its share of the market, deterioration of machinery and equipment so that production faltered, and the replacement of good, well-paid people by low-salaried hacks.

6. *Unscrupulous managers may serve interests which conflict.* A manager should be loyal to one master only. That loyalty must never be divided. The chief engineer who requires all potential suppliers of goods to use a testing company he personally owns, the purchasing agent who specifies products only a favored and compliant supplier will produce, the inspector who certifies a low quality supplier for a price— all these contribute to the hiding or falsification of records which will hush the cry of conflict of interest.

7. *Profits may be inflated to obtain advantages in the marketplace.* Financial officers or executives who wish their stock to make a splash in the market or who seek to obtain unwarranted credit lines may inflate profits unfairly. They take this path if they bow to temptation, have the opportunity, and feel they will not be detected. The consultants have found that those who deceive have a supreme contempt for the abilities of those who have the job of detecting improprieties. Many defrauders' belief in their own abilities transcends any fear of detection.

8. *People who control both the assets and their records are in a perfect position to falsify the latter.* When a manager is in a strategic position both to control physical assets and adjust the records of those assets he or she may make off with large amounts and not be detected.

Each of these reasons for deception abounds in the business world. But they sprout only under the rains of opportunity. The shelters against these rains are good business practice, adherence to accepted principles of management, knowledge of what goes on in the corporation, and reports that are independently reviewed. Let corporate executives forget their responsibility to *manage*—a responsibility they dare not delegate—and they reap a bitter harvest.

WHAT TO DO WHEN MANAGEMENT FRAUD OCCURS

An immediate result of management fraud, after it is detected, is the cruel drain on the time and nervous systems of the senior executives or the members of the boards of directors who must cut away the cancer and close up the wound. The cost and the time spent on the cure may far exceed the cost of preventive medicine. All auditors and investigators engaged in fraud cases will recall the pain that top executives experience and exhibit when they find a valued subordinate has betrayed their trust. It is a trauma no executive seeks.

Stockholders have little sympathy for executives who pilot the organization and permit it to founder on the shoals of management fraud. No longer will the courts permit boards of directors to say: "We did not know." The courts sternly rebuke: "You should have known." And to the extent that management fraud proliferates, so will suits against senior management and board members.

Shareholders are not the only ones to exhibit displeasure. Relations with external auditors become strained. Faith in management's assertions evaporates. Auditors' unqualified opinions on the fairness of financial statements are hard to come by. The financial counselor assumes the aspect of an adversary.

The displeasure spills over to employees of the company. They do not feel secure in their positions. The good men and women who can see little future in a fraud-stained company leave. Employee turnover mounts, as do the costs of hiring and training new people. And where perpetrators are not disciplined, the morale of those employees who remain drops badly.

Not only do employees feel distrust. The sensitive marketplace reacts as well. The stock of WXYZ company, for example, dropped two points after the fraudulent condition was reported to the SEC. Considering that more than 100 million shares were outstanding, the impact of the fraud was shattering.

When the specter becomes a hard reality, executive management—in its outrage—may take swift and drastic action. This can be a fatal error. The tendency is to focus on the legal aspects, turn loose the authorities, dismiss the ostensible miscreant, and thus abort a methodical, thorough, productive investigation.

Corporate heads, including the board of directors, should regard the occurrence as a *business problem, not a legal problem.* The latter comes afterward. Key personnel should not be dismissed before the problem is solved. There may be innocents among the guilty. Only a fair investigation can sort them out. And the professional investigator has as great a duty to protect the innocent as to identify the guilty.

Corporate heads should try to minimize losses so they can honestly tell the bonding company they exerted all efforts to prevent any extension of losses and to mitigate damages.

They must look at a broader picture than one which focuses solely on the cancer within the body corporate. They must be concerned with the possible loss of credibility in the marketplace—the assessment that financial analysts will place upon the circumstances. They should be concerned with the premiums on new fidelity insurance and the impact on new coverage. And they should be able to point out to the insurance carrier that the steps taken in the wake of the investigation will ensure that no surprises are in the offing.

They should concern themselves with the disruption of business. Herds of auditors and investigators descending on a profit center can have a devastating effect. Thus, an executive should be assigned to coordinate the efforts of all groups involved in the investigation. These efforts, among others, are as follows:

- *External auditors.* Have them verify financial reports. Request the external auditors to perform a "heavy review," as compared to an audit. Since the matter may result in litigation, the corporate legal staff should arrange to have access to the external auditors' working papers.

- *Internal auditors.* With their more intimate understanding of the organization's systems, internal auditors may be able to supplement the work of the external auditors, analyze operating records and reports—as distinguished from financial records and reports—and support any consultants used, gathering information for them and helping them to analyze data.

- *Legal counsel.* The corporate attorneys should determine the need for disclosure and for compliance with all regulatory requirements. Premature disclosure, before determining for a certainty that fraud exists, may prejudice the company's case and reputation. The attorneys can determine, as a matter of law, when the facts demand disclosure and when disclosure can properly be delayed. The attorneys should also evaluate the legal aspect of recoveries under any fidelity policies, as well as what action may be taken against third parties whose negligence or participation contributed to the difficulties.

- *Outside consultants.* Consultants skilled in the identification of fraudulent acts and in the delicate task of interrogating witnesses can provide the aura of objectivity and neutrality needed to obtain the cooperation of witnesses. They can advise the internal auditors which avenues to explore, what information to obtain and what records to analyze. They can guide the analysis of third-party records— documents submitted by people outside the organization. They can help determine whether those documents are valid, and they can go behind supporting documents to dredge up the whole truth. Also, since they are external to the organization and may never again be seen, they can obtain information an insider might be denied. Strangers on shipboard often exchange intimate confidences. They tell things they would not tell intimates, unburdening themselves freely because they feel certain they will never again see their temporary friends.

THE SYMPTOMS OF MANAGEMENT FRAUD

The "insighters" have identified a set of symptoms that are usually reliable indicators of an improper condition. The symptom is but a surface lesion. The cancerous condition lies below it. But the lesions have to be recognized for what they cover. Here are a few of these indicators, some explanations, and some examples:

1. *Consistently late reports.* Honest reports can usually be issued on time since their purpose is to inform, not deceive. But in order for a deceiver to know where figures need to be plugged, he must analyze the reported data to know just how that data has to be manipulated. These analyses take time. Continuing late reports cry for in-depth analysis, as well as the reasons for the delays.

2. *Managers who regularly assume subordinates' duties.* In ABC Company, a vice president of administration never relinquished the comptrollership function. The nominal comptroller was a flunky. The vice president also overrode the credit manager and acted as warehouse manager. Even worse, he preempted the cash manager's responsibilities and took deposits to the bank. Some of the purported deposits, most of them in cash, were never made to the company's account. An alert Internal Auditing Department might have detected the symptom and done some digging. But the ABC Company, large enough to generate $400 million in sales, apparently did not feel the need for internal auditors.

3. *Noncompliance with corporate directives and procedures.* A chief financial officer of a subsidiary was directed by corporate executives to install a standard cost system. He gave excuse after excuse for the delay. Three years went by while he hid the cost problems that a standard cost system would have exposed.

4. *Managers dealing in matters outside their profit center's scope.* A division manager acted as a broker on products outside his cost center's product line. He needed the cash to hide other manipulations. Such an action should have been an indicator to a corporate manager or internal auditors. But the corporate group executive responsible for the profit center visited it for social calls only; there was no internal audit function. The corporate headquarters relied on the external auditors to ferret out such matters. But the normal financial audit by external auditors is not designed for that purpose.

With respect to the external auditor's responsibility for the detection of fraud, Section 100.05 "Detection of Fraud," of the AICPA's *Statement on Auditing Standards,* November 1972, states as follows:

> In making the ordinary examination, the independent auditor is aware of the possibility that fraud may exist. Financial statements may be misstated as the result of defalcations and similar irregularities, or deliberate misrepresentations by management, or both. The auditor recognizes that fraud, if sufficiently material, may affect his opinion on the financial statements, and his examination, made in accordance with generally accepted auditing standards, gives consideration to this possibility. However, the ordinary examination directed to the expression of an opinion on financial statements is not primarily or specifically designed, and cannot be relied upon, to disclose defalcations and other similar irregularities, although their discovery may result. Similarly, although the discovery of deliberate misrepresentation by management is usually more closely associated with the objective of the ordinary examination, such examination cannot be relied upon to assure its discovery. The responsibility of the

independent auditor for failure to detect fraud (which responsibility differs as to clients and others) arises only when such failure clearly results from failure to comply with generally accepted auditing standards.

5. *Payments to trade creditors supported by copies instead of originals.* One subsidiary had a practice of doctoring the support for payments to its creditors. Some of the payments were supported with original invoices but with copies of the receiving memos. Others were supported with the original receiving memos but duplicate invoices. The duplicates and the originals were artfully mixed so as to avoid a pattern which might have alerted the external auditors. The company employed no internal auditors. Because of the clever mixture of originals and copies, and in the absence of the deterrent effect of competent internal auditors, duplicate payments and kickbacks flourished.

6. *Negative debit memos.* At one profit center, credit memos were generated by the computer. When financial officers wished to write off a credit memo, they would generate a negative debit memo. The external auditors were dutifully provided with all credit memos. They were not made aware of the debit memos.

7. *Commissions not in line with increased sales.* In one corporation, sales skyrocketed. But most of the increase was the result of cranking fictitious contracts into the computer. At the same time commissions to salesmen were valid and accurate. The sales and the commissions were supposed to be interrelated. So the picture was there for anyone to see. The "insighters" plotted the pattern somewhat as follows:

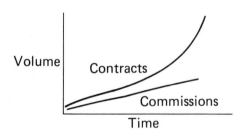

In all the cases encountered by the "insighters," the symptoms were there. The indicators could be plotted and the data behind them could be verified. An alert internal auditing group should be able to determine the types of indicators needed for top management surveillance. Many internal auditors have been able to counsel management on the kinds of information which should raise eyebrows and spark the hard questions. Here is an example which illustrates how an internal auditor used quantification to focus on problem areas:

In one corporation with a large number of sales outlets, an internal auditor was responsible for the audit of about 35 such outlets. Each outlet was required to submit monthly reports which showed the results of operations for the period.

The internal auditor, mathematically literate, determined the mean of the 35 net profits or losses and the standard deviations from that mean.

He found that in 90% of the sales outlets whose performance results fell minus two or more standard deviations below the mean, irregularities could be found. Conversely, when performance results were "too good"—on the high side of the mean—problems could be found in accounting errors, overstated inventories or, in rare cases, manipulation.

The theory was tested by other internal auditors within the company. And when the director of internal auditing was convinced of its reliability, he presented the formula to the executives responsible for the sales outlets so they would know where to focus their attention.

HOW TO CONTROL MANAGEMENT FRAUD

The cornerstone in the structure designed to control management fraud is an environment created by the organization's policymakers. It is an environment that fosters morality and high business ethics. Let sharp practices flourish at the top— income smoothing, lavish entertainment, bribes to officials—and the seeds for management fraud are sown.

Senior management must also understand that the manager of a profit center has autonomy and opportunity. The greater the freedom, the easier it is to fall into temptation. Without constricting managers so that imagination and innovation are squeezed out of them, the systems should provide checks and balances and reports that cause flares to streak across the corporate sky if improprieties are practiced. Some of the control measures which executive managers should install are:

• Establish standards—budgetary and statistical—and investigate all material deviations.

• Use quantitative and analytical techniques (time series analyses, regression and correlation analyses, and random sampling) to highlight aberrant behavior. Develop indicators—such as space used, time required, weight limitations imposed, usage and output compared. Where possible, develop management information systems that supply the data needed for such analyses.

• Compare performance with industry norms, as well as with the performance of comparable profit centers within the organization.

• Identify critical process indicators: melt loss in smelting, death loss in feed lots, rework in manufacturing and assembly, and gross profit tests in buy-sell or retail operations.

• Analyze carefully performance that looks too good, as well as performance that does not meet standards.

• Establish a professional Internal Auditing Department. Provide it with a charter—signed by the chief executive officer and approved by the audit committee of the board of directors—which gives it independence of the activities it audits, guarantees objectivity, authorizes the periodic review of *all* operations, and demands the appropriate consideration of all deficiency findings and audit recommendations. Fund the internal audit function from the corporate budget; do not charge any of its costs to subsidiary organizations as direct expense; and staff the function with personnel of high calibre. Place it in a position within the corporation that makes it directly responsible to the chief executive officer, yet grants it access to the audit committee of the board. Establish a policy of engaging or terminating the chief internal auditor only with the approval of the audit committee. And have the Internal Auditing Department's work periodically audited by external auditors.

Clearly, internal auditors, no matter how sound their expertise or how broad their charter, cannot be insurers against fraud. They can no more be such a guarantor than the attorney can insure his clients against all litigation or the doctor can insure his patients against all illness. The ways of villains are infinite and those of the auditors all finite. As the learned Justice Lopes once said (*In re Kingston Cotton Mill Co.* (No. 2) [1896] 2 Ch. 279, 288), "The auditor is a watchdog, not a bloodhound." But the ubiquitous, ever-watchful internal auditor can be a powerful deterrent and a restricter of opportunities through appraisal of the systems of internal controls, and by focusing on the risk areas and danger points in the enterprise.

SUMMARY

The uninspected inevitably deteriorates. People in complete authority have the opportunity to manipulate the facts for their own gain with little possibility of detection. When the pressures to improve performance push them beyond their abilities, they may resort to management fraud.

Nobody has developed a sure way of preventing or detecting fraud. But executive management can go a long way toward deterring it.

Top management can emphasize publicly that honest dealings are the company's way of life. And by its own actions it can show commitment to that principle. It can visit outlying profit centers to inspect and to ask pointed questions, rather than merely fly in and fly out after a social meeting. It can insist on reports that are timely, accurate, and meaningful; it can see to it that those reports are independently verified—somebody, periodically, must go behind the numbers. It can develop ratios, comparisons, and other indicators that point an unerring finger at aberrations.

Executive management and the audit committee of the board should rely on the external auditor for audits, not for fraud protection. But they should expect the external auditor to perform professional work, done in accordance with generally accepted accounting standards.

Executive management and the board can establish and support a professional internal auditing staff which has access to all operations, is independent of the activities it reviews, will audit all significant management reports, and is empowered to insist on answers to its questions and appropriate consideration of its recommendations.

At the same time, both executive management and the audit committee must understand that internal auditors are staff, not line. They advise; they do not manage. The operating manager must be looked to for planning, organizing, directing, and controlling the activities for which he or she is responsible. The internal auditor is responsible for reporting on how well those functions are being carried out and where deficiencies need correcting.

Finally, when fraud is suspected, executive management should call in the experts, make no rash moves, and from the start treat the matter as a business—not a legal—problem.

Legal Implications of EDP Deficiencies

JOHN O. MASON, JR.
AND JONATHAN J. DAVIES

While the legal relationship between public accountants and financial statement users has been in a constant state of flux, the courts seldom have found it necessary (or desirable) to comment on the auditor's legal responsibilities in the examination of electronic data processing systems. In the recent case of *Adams v. Standard Knitting Mills, Inc.,*[1] (*Standard Knitting Mills*), the federal court saw fit to break this legal silence, and thus, defined the basic legal responsibilities of those engaged in audits of computer-based accounting systems.

This article takes a three-step approach toward analyzing the ramifications of the *Standard Knitting Mills* case. The first section of the article presents a brief description of the facts that served as the basis of the litigation. The second section presents a discussion of the various legal issues decided by the court. The final section speculates on the effects that this decision will have on auditing practices. This three-step analysis provides the auditor with a base of information for a proper assessment of the legal responsibilities inherent in the provision of audit services where EDP is involved (as well as having implications for the reporting of internal control weaknesses in any accounting environment).

BASIC FACTS OF THE LITIGATION

In 1969, Chadbourn, Inc., engaged its auditor, Peat, Marwick, Mitchell & Co. (PMM & Co.), to prepare a proxy statement for filing with the Securities and Exchange Commission in connection with the proposed acquisition of *Standard Knitting Mills, Inc.* (Standard). The proxy statement that was subsequently prepared failed to accurately report two situations which Standard stockholders later alleged to be material in relation to the merger decision.

The first of these inaccuracies concerned the ability of Chadbourn to pay dividends and redeem capital stock. In the preparation of the proxy statement, PMM & Co. noted at several different times that existent loan agreements contained severe restrictions with respect to all Chadbourn *capital* stock. Yet, the footnotes actually included in the audited financial statements indicated that these restrictions applied only to *common* stock. On realizing that the dividend and redemption restrictions also applied to the preferred stock that they had accepted under the merger agreement, Standard stockholders filed suit contending that PMM & Co. had violated generally accepted auditing standards and thus seriously misled them.

The second proxy statement inaccuracy (and the more generally significant one) concerned certain weaknesses in the Chadbourn *system of internal control.* While PMM & Co. did realize that several deficiencies and serious defects did exist in the Chadbourn EDP system, the proxy statement submitted to Standard shareholders made no mention of these problems.

In litigating this matter, Standard shareholders argued that PMM & Co.'s failure to disclose significant information about internal control weaknesses in the Chadbourn EDP system seriously impaired their ability to make informed judgments about the proposed merger transaction. Thus, the plaintiffs argued that PMM & Co. had again violated generally accepted auditing standards by failing to implement full and accurate disclosure.

ISSUES DECIDED BY THE COURT

Since the *Standard Knitting Mills* case was predicated upon inaccuracies contained in a proxy statement filed with the Securities and Exchange Commission, the plaintiffs contended that liability should be imposed under Commission Rules 10(b)-5[2] and 14(a)-9[3]. In determining the applicability of these rules to this specific fact situation, the court embarked upon an analysis of several major factors that it considered prerequisites to the existence of such legal responsibility.

The first of the prerequisite factors to be dealt with by the *Standard Knitting Mills* Court was that of materiality. If the defendants were to be held legally responsible for violations of Federal Securities Law, it would have to be proven that the inaccuracies contained in the proxy statement were material.

Traditionally, a decision of the materiality of a particular fact is a judgment issue which centers around whether a reasonable man would have assigned significance to that fact in making his ultimate decision.[4] With respect to the EDP problems existent at Chadbourn, the *Standard Knitting Mills* Court concluded:

> The EDP deficiencies at Chadbourn were of such pervasive nature and importance that their existence did, or at a minimum, could have significantly affected the entire operation of Chadbourn and would therefore most directly relate to matters contained in the financial statements.[5]

Thus the court reasoned that PMM & Co.'s failure to reveal significant EDP weaknesses constituted a misstatement of a material fact.

The second legal issue to be dealt with by the court was that of duty. Unless it could be shown that the public accountants had a legally enforceable responsibility to the third party proxy statement users, the imposition of liability for pecuniary losses would be precluded.

While the common law approach to such a legal question is directly dependent upon the existence of privity of contract or some similar state of plaintiff-defendant relationship,[6] the institution of the Securities Acts in the early 1930s did away with many such restrictions. In the *Standard Knitting Mills* case, the court agreed that an adequate degree of legal responsibility did exist by saying:

> PMM & Co. had full knowledge of Standard shareholders' reliance on PMM & Co. representations contained in the financial statements. In such a situation, PMM & Co. owed the Standard shareholders, including plaintiffs, the duty to perform and conduct the audit with due care and to observe and comply with applicable auditing standards. At a minimum, that was PMM & Co.'s duty to plaintiff . . .[7]

Beyond this basic statement of the facts inherent in the *Standard Knitting Mills* case, the court commented on the general duties of public accountants by saying, "Additionally, an accountant owes a duty to the public to be independent of his client and to report *fairly* the facts before him."[8] This broad statement of the court's perception of the accounting function not only established the existence of the prerequisite degree of responsibility, but also implied a legal precedent which if later applied, would impose a degree of legal duty on the public accountant that has seldom, if ever, been sought by the courts.

The last major legal determination to be made by the *Standard Knitting Mills* court concerned the existence of scienter, or intent, on the part of the defendants. In March 1976, the Supreme Court ruled that proof of a defendant's intent to deceive was prerequisite to the imposition of liability under many of the provisions of the 1934 Securities Exchange Act.[9] Therefore, if PMM & Co. were to be held legally responsible under Rules 10b-5 and 14a-9, the prerequisite degree of intent would have to be proven.

With respect to PMM & Co.'s failure to adequately describe the EDP weaknesses existent in the Chadbourn system, the court concluded:

> Defendant's agents documented Chadbourn's numerous EDP defects at the time of the 1969 audit and approximately one year later some corrections had been made but a considerable number of deficiencies still remained—yet defendant did not feel obligated to report this to plaintiffs. Finally, with full knowledge of Chadbourn's EDP and other internal weaknesses, defendant conducted its 1969 audit as though Chadbourn was as sound as a dollar used to be—clearly deviating from GAAP, GAAS and the provisions of PMM & Co.'s own audit manual. The court finds and holds the proof in this case clearly established that, with the knowledge defendant possessed prior to, during and after the 1969 audit compared against the content of the PMM & Co.'s 1969 Chadbourn financial statement, defendant acted willfully, with intent to "deceive" and "manipulate and in reckless disregard for the truth."[10]

Thus, the court interpreted PMM & Co.'s failure to fully disclose all available financial information as evidence of an intent to mislead the users of the proxy statement.

The decisions of the *Standard Knitting Mills* court with respect to materiality, duty and scienter opened the door to third party liability under the provisions of the Securities Exchange Act. The imposition of such a degree of legal responsibility on those involved in EDP system audits should have several significant effects on members of the public accounting profession.

IMPLICATION FOR THE AUDITING PROFESSION

If not reversed on appeal, the decision in *Standard Knitting Mills* is likely to stir as much controversy and comment as that of the recent *Hochfelder* case. From the standpoint of the members of the auditing profession, *Standard Knitting Mills* may mark the most painful crisis since the *Continental Vending* case[11] of the late sixties. Clearly, the *Standard Knitting Mills* decision will have a multidimensional effect on auditing standards, accounting principles and the manner in which they both are applied.

Perhaps the most significant lesson to be learned from *Standard Knitting Mills* will deal with the process known as "auditing around the computer." For years the accounting profession has circumvented many of the problems associated with audits of computer-based systems by relying upon an "informal understanding" that the ultimate extent of review and testing applied to an EDP system may vary as other optional audit procedures are applied.

Yet, while some practicing accountants were relying on this "informal understanding," the profession as a whole was moving toward more rigorous standards for EDP audits. In "Statement on Auditing Standards Number 1," the profession concluded that the auditor's study of internal control should produce:

1. A knowledge and understanding of the procedures and methods prescribed, and

2. A reasonable assurance that they are in use and operating as planned, regardless of the type of system employed by the firm for accounting purposes.[12]

The *Standard Knitting Mills* Court's firm adherence to professionally espoused auditing standards is exemplified by its conclusion that, "in areas of internal control . . . especially EDP . . . PMM & Co. violated the second . . . and third standard(s) of audit field work."[13] Such a conclusion, when combined with the court's rejection of any "real world" distinction between "accounting" and "administrative" controls,[14] clearly indicates that the professional accountant will soon be forced to place more emphasis on EDP controls when carrying out his audit function.

A second, and more puzzling, aspect of the *Standard Knitting Mills* case lies in the area of financial disclosure. While the accounting profession has generally felt that the audit opinion alleviated the need for statements about specific matters, the *Standard Knitting Mills* court reasoned that in this particular instance, *the EDP and internal control weaknesses* of Chadbourn were so *significant* as to *warrant specific disclosure.* In presenting this argument for full financial disclosure, the court reasoned:

> No experienced accounting firm can report a company's financial position today and ignore what it may be tomorrow. This is especially true when as in this instance, the accountant has knowledge of adverse information and conditions which obviously may significantly jeopardize the client company's future performance. . . [15]

The court's implication of such a full disclosure doctrine could easily introduce a strange twist to the accounting profession's going concern assumption. Under such a doctrine of legal responsibility, the professional auditor would no longer be allowed to make unilateral decisions about the future prospects of a given firm, but instead, he would be required to supply financial statement users with all information that might be inherent to the making of their own investment decisions. Such a shift in legal responsibility would definitely have a material impact on the performance of the audit function. In this connection, the proposed statement on auditing standards by AudSec "Required Communication of Material Weaknesses in Internal Accounting Control" indicates the profession's growing concern with reporting on internal control weaknesses.

SUMMARY

As the computer became an integral part of the auditing environment, public accountants attempted to adapt their standards and techniques to deal with this new factor. Yet, while the accounting profession took action to implement the necessary adaptations, the courts failed to provide an adequate definition of the auditor's legal responsibilities in EDP engagements.

In *Adams* v. *Standard Knitting Mills, Inc.,* the federal court took the first steps toward defining these legal responsibilities. If later applied, this decision should affect the auditing profession in two ways. First, the *Standard Knitting Mills* decision could place severe limitation on the use of "auditing around the computer" as a replacement for adequate evaluation and testing of EDP controls. Second, the *Standard Knitting Mills* decision should broaden the concept of "full financial disclosure" employed by the public accountant in the preparation of audited financial statements. Although this first statement of the courts may have a significant effect on the EDP-auditing environment, the public accountant can be relatively sure that this is only a precursor to future legal decisions.

NOTES

[1] *Adams* v. *Standard Knitting Mills, Inc.,* 95,683 CCH Fed. Sec. Law Rept. (E. D. Tenn., 1976).

[2] Rule 10b-5, C. F. R. Section 240.10b-5. The rule specifically reads:
"It shall be unlawful for any person, directly or indirectly, by the use of any means or instrumentality of interstate commerce, or of the mails or of any facility of any national securities exchange,

a) To employ any device, scheme, or artifice to defraud.

b) To make any untrue statement of a material fact or to omit to state a material fact necessary in order to make the statements made, in light of the circumstances under which they were made, not misleading, or

c) To engage in any act, practice, or course of business which operates or would operate as a fraud or deceit upon any person, in connection with the purchase or sale of any security."

[3] Rule 14a-9, 17 C. F. R. Section 249-14a-9. The rule specifically states:

(a) No solicitation subject to this regulation shall be made by means of any proxy statement, form of proxy, notice of meeting or other communication, written or oral, containing any statement which, at the time and in the light of the circumstances under which it is made, is false or misleading with regard to any material fact necessary in order to make the statement therein not false or misleading or necessary to correct any statement in any earlier communication with respect to the solicitation of a proxy for the same meeting or subject matter which has become false or misleading.

(b) The fact that a proxy statement, form of proxy or other soliciting material has been filed with or examined by the Commission shall not be deemed a finding by the Commission that such material is accurate or complete or not false or misleading, or that the Commission has passed upon the merits of or approved any statement contained therein or any matter to be acted upon by security holders. No representation contrary to the foregoing shall be made."

[4] See generally: *SEC* v. *Texas Gulf Sulphur Company*, 401 F.2d 833 (2nd Cir. 1968).

[5] Standard Knitting Mills.

[6] Throughout the early part of this century, courts ruled that a contractual relationship between plaintiff and defendant is prerequisite to recovery of pecuniary losses. While the courts have sometimes relaxed this rule to allow recovery by those who were "the primary beneficiary" of a specific contract, the privity requirement remains entrenched in the common law. See generally: Prosser, William L., "Misrepresentations and Third Parties," *Vanderbilt Law Review*, 19 (March, 1966), 231–255; and *Glanzer* v. *Shepard*, 135 N.E. 275 (N.Y. 1922); and *Ultramares Corporation* v. *Touche, Niven and Company*, 174 N.E. 441 (N.Y. 1931); and *Rhode Island, Hospital Trust National Bank* v. *Swartz, Bresenoff, Yavner and Jacobs*, 455 F 2d 847 (4th Cir. 1972).

[7] Standard Knitting Mills.

[8] *Ibid.*

[9] *Ernst & Ernst* v. *Hochfelder*, 96 S. Ct. 1375 (1976).

[10] Standard Knitting Mills.

[11] See generally: *U.S.* v. *Simon*, 425 F2d 796 (2nd Cir. 1969).

[12] "Statement on Auditing Standards No. 1," (New York: American Institute of Certified Public Accountants, 1973).

[13] Standard Knitting Mills.

[14] *Ibid.*

[15] *Ibid.*

CHAPTER 6

AUDITING OF
INFORMATION SYSTEMS

It is difficult to study accounting information systems without giving some consideration to the audit phase. From initial planning to final testing, auditing aspects must be included to provide for a sound operating system. While there are many different aspects to the auditing of computer based systems, the role of auditing in the development and implementation stages of a system is primarily concerned with control. It is only after proper controls have been implemented into the system that the auditor (either internal or external) can successfully evaluate the effectiveness and reliability of the system.

The problems of control for computer systems are different from those of other systems and this requires not only new audit techniques but also new approaches to systems evaluations. Beyond evaluating controls surrounding a computer system, the auditor needs to employ methods for testing transactions to ensure that the programs produce accurate and complete results.

In addition to being the object of the systems audit, the computer is a valuable tool often used in the audit process, a benefit that was heretofore unavailable in manual systems. The articles included in this chapter include discussions of these computer audit problems and possible solutions, and alternative audit techniques.

In the first article, Cash, Bailey and Whinston provide a discussion of the more frequently used audit techniques. They provide a review of actual EDP audit practices and an overview of the literature. The basic purpose of this article is to provide a historical perspective as to the development of EDP systems. While it is not filled with historic detail, it does include the salient points in the development of EDP auditing, which are necessary for one to know to have a lucid understanding of the status of this predominant auditing area.

Another important feature of this article is the development of a new approach to large-scale systems auditing. The new method describes how the utilization of computer-related software can assist in the actual audit engagement. The authors also emphasize that an equal amount of importance should be given to both the manual and automated components of the total system. In a thorough review of the system's internal control, the manual aspects may in some situations overshadow the controls related to the computer system.

Throughout the article there is an emphasis on common terminology. The authors believe there has been much duplication of effort by those researching and developing this area because no one has codified the existing terminology. This, in part, is blamed on the rapidly advancing technology and the voluminous amount of literature that is being published to report the changing status of computer auditing. The terminology given greatest emphasis is that used in labeling the different approaches and methods of computer auditing. Figure 2 in the article provides an excellent summary of terms and synonyms as well as basic advantages and disadvantages. This article should be required reading for all students studying computer related topics.

In meeting the changing needs of EDP auditing, the second article, "Auditing in a Data Base Environment," by Reneau, explains the problems of auditing the fastest growing area of computer systems: data base applications. Reneau begins by contrasting file systems and data base systems in very understandable terms. As in most computer auditing articles, "control" is the theme. He discusses the types of controls generally found in a data base system and evaluates their desirability from the auditor's viewpoint. The four areas of concentration are: organizational independence, accessibility, operations, and applications. While many of the controls necessary for a data base system are currently in existence in file systems, the importance of particular controls varies. This article provides the reader with basic information on the control requirements in a data base system and should serve as a basis for drawing together the work of computer personnel and the auditor.

Another new and challenging area of computer related auditing is electronic funds transfer systems, EFTS. According to Richardson in "Auditing EFTS," such systems provide the auditing profession an opportunity to interact with both the financial and systems communities in developing an approach to audit procedures and systems analysis. Because EFTS will have an impact on many aspects of accounting, information systems, and business practices, it is very important to expose students to the concept and its present and future developments. The three areas of emphases in the article are: the extent a system will be influenced by EFTS, the necessary general controls for effective EFTS, and the application controls needed in EFTS.

After examining the basic approaches to computer auditing the reader is directed to the fourth article by Perry and Warner, "Systems Auditability: Friend or Foe?" In this article the authors discuss the CPA's role in computer auditing. They draw attention to the fact that auditing and its related control procedures have not kept pace with computer technology, especially in software. This pressing problem of the accounting profession prompted the authors to conduct a comprehensive study of the area of computer auditing. This article also presents current trends in EDP auditing and techniques which have proved to be successful.

The authors also consider the roles of both external and internal auditors in the area of control implementation. Table 1 presents a list of computer operation activities and identifies the person who has primary responsibility for conducting each activity. The responsibility for each activity is assigned to either management, the auditor, or data processing management. As in the previous articles, the concept of utilizing the computer as an audit tool is discussed. With such utilization, through the creation of computer programs, the audit of otherwise unauditable areas is possible. This computer-assisted audit technique is one of the areas that auditors must develop if they are going to maintain an equal status with ever-changing computer developments.

In evaluating the status of auditing and the computer, the authors examine different types of EDP audit practices, describe their uses, and report the frequency of such uses from their survey results. These results are presented in Table 2. It is interesting to compare the material in Table 2 with the general discussion of audit methodology presented by Cash, Bailey, and Whinston.

From their study, Perry and Warner evaluate the needs of the future, especially with the continued growth of computer technology in mind. New EDP controls are needed and better audit techniques are mandatory if continued auditor integrity is to be maintained. What is needed, according to these authors, is for accountants to become more aggressively involved in EDP development.

As an example of the problems and needs of an information systems audit, we have included "Auditing the Corporate Information System," by Lowe. This article presents flowcharts and checklists illustrating the problems of a typical systems audit. The author discusses common weaknesses and explains how the auditor should deal with them. The problem of measurement in the evaluation of systems is discussed as it relates to how the systems audit should be performed and what management expects from such a review. He emphasizes the need for a comprehensive plan and a follow-up procedure for correcting any weaknesses found during the evaluation process.

Without doubt, the student studying systems needs to become familiar with what will be expected by auditors of information systems. The readings in this chapter provide a basic understanding of the concepts of EDP auditing, the related problems faced by auditors, and how systems personnel and auditors can work together to improve the total information system.

A Survey of Techniques for Auditing EDP-Based Accounting Information Systems

JAMES I. CASH, JR., ANDREW D. BAILEY, JR.,
AND ANDREW B. WHINSTON

In recent years large numbers of papers have appeared in accounting and accounting-related journals that can be classified under the general heading of "Auditing in the EDP Environment." The research and implementation effort expended has been immense: however, as in many new areas, many of the efforts have been of a repetitive nature. The primary objective of this paper is to present a review of the extant literature concerning auditing and EDP systems. We hope that by providing a means of tracing the flow of EDP-auditing development, by noting salient points of similarity in "different" techniques and by relating these issues to the auditor's professional responsibilities, we will contribute to an efficient expansion of effort in EDP-auditing research. It may also contribute to the adoption of common terminology, enabling future efforts to avoid repetition of effort founded on misconception.

As might be expected when this sort of effort is expended in studying existing techniques, we believe we have identified a line of future effort with great potential. We propose a new approach to the auditing of large-scale systems. The proposal goes beyond EDP-auditing and strikes at the fundamental problems of large-scale systems auditing. As its genesis lies in the area of EDP-audits, this seems to be an appropriate vehicle for its introduction.

THE AUDITOR'S RESPONSIBILITY IN THE EDP–AUDIT ENVIRONMENT

The statement of auditing standards No. 1 (SAS 1) embodies the auditor's responsibility with respect to the accounting information system in general [AICPA, 1973].

In an EDP environment the second standard of field work relating to the "... proper study and evaluation of the existing internal control...." can be characterized as the study and evaluation of the "phases of processing." [Touche, Ross and Co., 1973]. This is essentially a question of the organization and control of the computer activities and follows along much the same line as a traditional evaluation of internal control. The unique aspects of this phase, with respect to computers, was addressed in SAS 3 in discussing the general and applications classifications of EDP accounting controls.

> *General Controls* comprise (a) the plan of organization and operation of the EDP activity, (b) the procedures for documenting, reviewing, testing and approving systems or programs and changes thereto, (c) controls built into the equipment by the manufacturer (commonly referred to as "hardware controls"), (d) controls over access to equipment and data files, and (e) other data and procedural controls affecting overall EDP operations. . . .

> *Application Controls* relate to specific tasks performed by EDP; their function is to provide reasonable assurance that the recording, processing, and reporting of data are properly performed . . . Application controls often are categorized as "input controls," "processing controls," and "output controls."

> *AICPA, 1974*

The auditor's responsibility goes beyond the evaluation of internal controls as indicated by the third standard of field work concerning ". . . sufficient competent evidential matter . . ." [AICPA, 1973].

In a computer environment this might be characterized as verification of the "results of processing" [Touche, Ross and Co., 1973]. Thus the auditor's responsibilities in evaluating the internal controls and the results of the processing of accounting data may be classified as follows:

1. Understanding the system
2. Verifying phases of processing
   A. General controls
   B. Application controls
3. Verifying results of processing

The existence of the computer has created a set of unique problems in each of these classifications. Numerous functions previously amenable to traditional means of control, for example, separation of duties, have been collapsed into the machine and its related support staff. The unique and sophisticated technical aspects of computers and the rapidity of development and adoption of new computer technology helps explain the mushrooming of literature in the area, and thus the need for an organized study of that literature. Figure 1 depicts the organization of this survey. The figure does not include a separate discussion concerning the development of an understanding of the system because the process of developing such an understanding is hopelessly entangled with the testing aspects of the classification. It involves psychological issues associated with processing data, that is, learning. As these are not primary issues in this paper we limit our observations in this area to those associated with the testing phases.

We also would like to note at this point that the structure of the survey is not the only possible one. However, we feel that it accommodates the issues under consideration in a fairly clear manner. As is noted in a number of comments throughout the paper, there are problems of uniqueness in classification that arise due to the multiple purposes and outputs of the techniques under discussion. We have attempted to note these points of conflict when they seemed critical. Further, the satisfactory application of these techniques, individual or in unison, is admittedly a function of the particular audit. Thus, our discussions with respect to strengths and weakness of the various techniques must be interpreted accordingly. We have attempted to confine our comments to advantages and disadvantages without the detailed development of specific settings; therefore, they should be viewed as considerations in performing a cost/benefit selection of techniques for particular audit conditions and not as absolutes.

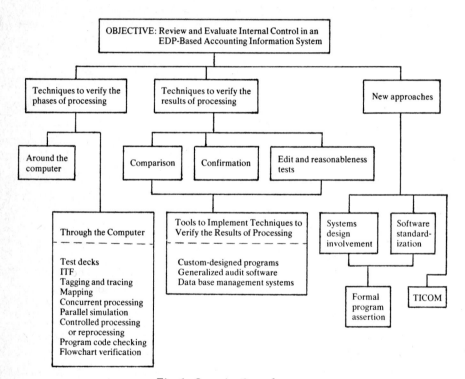

Fig. 1 *Organization of survey*

TECHNIQUES FOR VERIFYING THE PHASES OF PROCESSING

As previously discussed, the need to examine the processing system is based on compliance with the third standard of field work. The reliability or competency of accounting data output is directly related to the process that generates it. Therefore, to satisfy the standard that output data examined must be competent, it is logical and necessary to verify that the generating process is reliable.

The next section discusses "auditing around the computer" which was the original technique used when auditing an EDP-based system. That section pertains to techniques which were introduced as alternatives to the "around" technique. All the verification methods listed following this section can be generally classified as "auditing through the computer" techniques. Therefore, one can think of these two terms, "around" and "through," as classificatory.

"Auditing around the computer" has taken on the connotation of an undesirable auditing technique. This is only true when the technique is chosen because the auditor lacks understanding of the processing system and controls therein. In that case, the auditor is in violation of paragraphs 24–26 of SAS No. 3 concerning review of the processing system. If the term is being used to describe exclusion of the computer as an audit tool, the negative connotation is undeserved. The computer as an audit tool must stand the test of audit effectiveness. In some cases, an audit may be performed most effectively without the aid of a computer. This has caused some writers [Horwitz, 1976; Li, 1968] to use the terms "auditing without the computer" and "auditing with the computer" to describe the exclusion or inclusion of the computer as an audit tool. This distinction is made in order not to confuse our discussion concerning "around" and "through" techniques for verifying phases of processing with the issue of auditing "with" or "without" the computer.

AUDITING AROUND THE COMPUTER

This technique often is referred to as the "traditional manual approach" [Touche, Ross and Co., 1973]. Typically, the auditor selects source documents; traces associated entries through intermediate computer printouts; and finally examines resultant entries in summary accounts. Because this technique examines only the input-output relationship of data, it is often said to view the computer and its data-generating processes as a "black box." The basic advantages of this technique are: its low cost; low level of requisite technical expertise; and ease of comprehension by all persons involved—auditors, management and EDP personnel. The major disadvantages of this technique are: the intermediate printouts (audit-trail components) may not provide enough detail or simply will not be available; contemporary systems often produce data too voluminous for manual examination in a reasonable time frame; and no formal inference can be made concerning how the process handles data that are not examined.

The last disadvantage forms the basis for most arguments against auditing around the computer, that is verification of a given set of data's input-output relationship does not allow one to make assertions about the underlying process. An example cited by Mair [1971] was in an interest-computation program for a large savings institution. Interest calculated for depositor accounts were rounded to the lower penny (floor). Resulting fractions then were deposited to the account of the adroit programmer. If only a limited number of accounts are so treated, when the total number of accounts is large, the probability of discovering this type of error approaches zero. Alternatively, if all accounts are so treated, the auditor still may overlook the problem. Since auditors are concerned with statement fairness, it would not be unreasonable to expect that they would not be sensitive to fractions of pennies. And because "around the computer" techniques do not investigate computer programs, there is no chance that the auditor would discover the unique coding that provides our adroit programmer with extra funds. Thus, it is safe to say that such an error has a high probability of not being detected when auditing around the computer. In general, the around the computer technique will fail to detect exception conditions in voluminous and/or complex systems without high sampling and time costs. This is true despite the efficient handling of volume data by sampling techniques as the problem here is one of error definition and auditor perception. As it is impractical to make fractional penny payments, the auditor will recognize the need for rounding. Thus, a consistent rounding policy will not be viewed as an error observation, as it is not an error. Thus, sampling will disclose the rounding, but it is unlikely to disclose the fraudulent disposition of the nominal amounts to all but the most perceptive auditor. This most likely will be disclosed only by an examination of program code or highly detailed program flowcharts.

Because the examination of output, generated by the computer-based process, is an integral part of the around the computer technique, some writers misclassify this technique as a method of verifying the results of processing. This is unfortunate because while the tests may provide data relevant to substantive balances, it is fundamentally an aid in evaluating the reliability of internal controls. The basic techniques of confirmation, comparison and reasonableness and edit tests, which are used extensively in noncomputer audits for verifying results, are well-established and more appropriately identified as methods of verifying the results of processing. The techniques presented in the following section are clearly distinguishable upon close examination from the around the computer technique discussed. The techniques described there contribute directly to the verification of the results of processing and can be viewed as aids in applying the traditional techniques noted above.

AUDITING THROUGH THE COMPUTER

This technique is really a family of techniques that were introduced as alternatives to auditing around the computer. As a technique, it was the first used to describe the de-emphasis of the testing of records and the increased examination of the processing system [Milko, 1970]. As such, this technique has been displaced by many contemporary approaches and seldom is found in the literature. The logic underlying the introduction of this technique hinged on the hypothesis that if the processing system is reliable, then the records have an increased probability of being accurate. This assertion is most likely valid in computer processing environments. When the programs that constitute an accounting information system are written properly, they will comprise the most reliable and efficient accounting system in existence.

Typically, this technique as originally conceived, involved processing by the client's computer system, although no direct examination of program code was necessarily implied. In that sense, the first versions of this technique "used" the processing system but did not necessarily "examine" it.

A real difficulty encountered by many of the "through the computer" techniques involves gaining adequate assurance that client programs tested are, in fact, the programs used to process client data. Certain of the techniques discussed attempt to overcome this problem by accessing client programs during normal processing, for example, ITF. However, this can create timing and access difficulties. No absolute resolution of this problem currently exists short of the impractical suggestion that auditors retain control of all client programs and applications.

We have purposely not given a precise definition of this technique as most of the techniques that were introduced subsequent to "auditing around the computer" can be classified as "auditing through the computer." Therefore, we now proceed to comment on these techniques beginning with "Test Decks."

We would like to reemphasize that the audit effectiveness criteria applies in selecting techniques under the classification, "Auditing Through the Computer." That is, while we note potential advantages and disadvantages inherent in the techniques discussed, we do not suggest that these techniques lack usefulness in particular audit situations or that they might be applied in unison in an attempt to overcome particular disadvantages in one technique with advantages in another. We have not pursued the issue of optimal combinations in this paper as there are no unique solutions to this issue. Our purpose is to review this literature and provide insights into the techniques. Each auditor may then use these results in developing the audit program suited to the situation.

Test Decks

This term denotes the first technique associated with auditing through the computer. At its inception, the most common method of entering data into a computer system was via punched cards, thus, the term "decks." Currently, there are numerous other alternatives for data input. Therefore, the term "test data" is often used, but it still refers to the same basic technique. Another related term, "test data generator," is found in the literature and refers to an automated method of generating comprehensive test data.

The test data technique requires preparation of input data that are processed under the auditor's control by the client's processing system. The *perfect* set of test data contains every possible combination of input data, including erroneous data, that causes execution of all logic contained in the process under examination. The output generated by the test data usually is compared to the auditor's predicted output. Differences in the two sets of output are examined.

The major advantage of this technique is its improvement on the "around" approach with little increase in technical training by the field auditor and the potential for increased process examination by the test data designer. It can be a particularly effective technique if the variety of possible conditions is limited.

The auditor is forced to become familiar with the logic of the process being examined to design effectively test data. However, use of this technique does not necessarily imply that the auditor has adequately examined the process. First, the program tested may not be the one that processed client data; and second, identical sets of test data may give rise to identical outputs from different processes. Without complete control over client programs and directly examining the process itself, these problems cannot be resolved. Subsequently discussed techniques contribute to better resolutions of these problems than do test decks. However, a test deck addressing all possible inputs would contribute to an increasing probability that the process, however structured, would produce reliable output. Thus, the major problem associated with test decks is the design of comprehensive test data.

The design problem has two parts: the complex logic that may reside in a single process and the common existence of numerous integrated process modules that constitute the total processing system. Comprehensive test data that would address every possible system condition would approach infinity in length and development time. Special purpose software, termed "test-data-generators," attempt to improve the applicability of test data in complex systems by reducing the time required to construct the data and increasing the number of cases examined. Numerous generators have appeared on the market and have been reviewed and compared [Adams, 1973]. Given the auditor decision to use the "test data" technique, the only disadvantage of generators might be cost.

A good overview of verifying with test data, as it was initially proposed, is provided by Davis [1968]. This technique is usually thought to be incomplete or inconclusive in large, complex systems. The major contributing factor to that connotation is the procedure of examining only preconceived conditions in the process. However, it is used in conjunction with other techniques to form more effective audit methods, which are presented later.

Integrated Test Facility (ITF)

This technique is an extension of the "test data" approach and often is referred to as: the "minicompany" approach; "dummy-company" approach; "extended test data"; and "Auditor's Central Office" [Weiss, 1973]. Typically, the auditor initializes a dummy file and processes data through the regular processing system against the new file. The unique feature of this technique which distinguishes it from "test data" is that the test data are "integrated" into the regular system of processing. The term integrated also is used to imply that this technique may be used on a continuous basis during the business year.

Since this technique is related closely to the "test data" approach, its advantages and disadvantages are similar. As a result of entering the regular system of processing, an additional advantage of testing the actual system during operation is incurred. Likewise, random but continuous ITF runs during the business year increase the probability that the process audited at the end of the year was the one in effect during the year. The major disadvantages are predicated on methods of removing the "test data" from the system. The first method generally is referred to as "program modification." This method causes constituent processes to separate the test data before they are incorporated into important output or reports. An obvious drawback of this method is that the process logic associated with test data may be different from the logic associated with actual data. Also, the cost associated with execution time overhead and process modification may be high. The second method causes the auditor to enter "reverse journal entries" which negate the effects of the test data. The major disadvantage associated with this method is the inadvertant destruction of client files. Unintentional errors may go unnoticed and, when discovered, may require substantial effort for their correction as a result of entries that affect numerous activities within the system.

Tagging and Tracing (TT)

This technique is an extension of ITF that might or might not use "test data." Synonymous terms are: "tagging and picture taking"; "tracing marked data"; and "Audit Indicator" [Weiss, 1973]. This technique also has been called snap-shotting; however, this term refers to a particular proposed implementation of the TT technique [Perry, March 1974]. It typically involves marking or tagging client input data such that relevant information is displayed at key points in the processing system. The major advantage of this routine is the use of actual data and the elimination of special journal entries. The special logic required to display information may be subject to the same criticisms mentioned under ITF. However, one would imagine that the process code used to display information is not as complex as that used to partition data.

The combination of ITF and "tagging and tracing" have been shown to be effective in at least one installation [Weiss, 1973]. This combination is intuitively appealing since TT can be used to follow data through a complex system while ITF extends test capability by entering unusual or abnormal test data to examine exception conditions. This permits greater flexibility and somewhat reduces the impact of criticism leveled at "test data" related techniques. Still, there is no guarantee that all logic paths are transversed or that an indication of their existence will be provided. This shortcoming leads us to discuss the next group of techniques we choose to call "mapping" techniques. They often are referred to as TT techniques, but their emphasis on untraversed logic paths is a distinguishing factor.

Mapping

Mapping describes a number of techniques that attempt to identify logical paths in a process and determine whether all paths are traversed in a given run. "Missed branch indicators," "control monitors" and "logic supervisors" often are used to describe this technique. Implementation of this technique varies from resident supervisors (monitors) that provide statistics of logic paths traversed, to four-step integrated processes that list references to untraversed paths. Typically, process code is flagged at branches and other control points within the program to facilitate the analysis. COMBI (*COBOL Missed Branch Indicator*) and COTUNE are examples of popular implementations of this technique [Adams, April 1975].

Relative to the previously mentioned techniques, this is the first that "examines" process logic as opposed to "using" process code. Major advantages center on the ability to recognize and refer the auditor to specific types of code: redundant, inaccessible, exception and error. Disadvantages associated with this technique include: interpretability of output of some implemented versions (that is, to use the references output may require an unreasonably high degree of programming expertise); process overhead associated with supervisor-type programs; and preprocessing, performed by some mapping techniques may alter source code so as to camouflage malicious code.

This technique has been combined with other techniques, such as test data, to form more effective verification methods than the use of individual techniques afforded the auditor. The basic concept of a monitor or supervisor can be and has been expanded to represent a resident software auditor. Those efforts, termed "concurrent processing" are sometimes confused with mapping techniques. The distinguishing feature between the two techniques is the continuous residency of monitors in concurrent processing.

Concurrent Processing

Concurrent processing grew out of improved software technology for supervisory programs and the need to monitor unusual transactions and generate reports containing relevant data. Because the supervisor is omnipresent, this technique is alternatively referred to as "continuous processing," "concurrent auditing" and "continuous auditing by exception." It is designed specifically to detect exception or unusual conditions and to record information about the initiating transaction. Another term used to describe the actions of concurrent auditing is "threat monitoring," which highlights the association of this technique with computer data integrity and security [Martin, 1973; Cash, 1976; Perry, 1976; Parker, 1976].

Obviously, this technique does not examine process code. *This is the first technique in which the auditor might participate in the systems design function, inserting controls that hopefully detect "exceptions," which translates into "possibly malicious" conditions.* A tradeoff is made between examining a process for malicious code and designing a system that potentially detects malicious code. SCARF [Perry, February 1974] is an example of concurrent processing that appeared in the literature recently. Stone [1976] outlined an IBM industry application program (IAP) that possessed many desirable concurrent processor capabilities. The IAP, manufacturing management accounting system (MMAS), uses a monitor and interactive (IDE) facility to guide the operator through a processing cycle in a specified sequence and under specific conditions. "Systems Management Facilities" (SMF) has appeared as an audit tool in recent papers [Adams, September 1974; Schaller, 1976] that should be classified under this technique. It is a feature of

IBM's 360–370 operating system (OS and VS only) that may be used by the auditor to accumulate processing information. Kunkel [1974] provides a general overview and justification of this technique that, for the sake of brevity, will not be repeated here.

Examples of unusual conditions that concurrent auditors were designed to control typically are policies that simplify clerical procedures but may condone fraudulent activity. The accounts receivable system practice of accepting payments if they are within a given number of dollars of the invoiced amount is an example. Likewise, the ability to override prices, within certain tolerances, in a billing system is equally exploitable. This technique has been presented as a tool more applicable to the internal auditor. However, in light of the mammoth task of the external auditor in auditing large, complex EDP-based systems, it seems appropriate that the external auditor encourage the use of this type of technique and that he or she acquire and use the information generated.

Parallel Simulation

In parallel simulation, the auditor creates a set of application programs that "simulate" processing functions in "parallel" with the operational processing system. Mair [1971] outlined this technique as consisting of the following general procedures:

a) Define application functions that are to be verified

b) Understand processing logic

c) Define machine readable inputs and outputs of data to be used

d) Use audit software to prepare a process consistent with logic determined in (b)

e) Execute operational and simulated systems with data from (c)

f) Identify and examine discrepancies

Parallel simulation has been proclaimed as the best method for detection of fraudulent code and as one of the most powerful tools for verification of phases of processing. *Closer examination of this technique reveals that it is an automated version of auditing around the computer.* The authors describe this method as "auditing around the computer with the computer." All the disadvantages listed in the discussion concerning "auditing around the computer" are applicable, with one significant exception, that is, the number of data records that can be simulated is increased substantially. The example of the adroit programmer that rounds pennies and adds fractions to his or her account still illustrates a fraudulent activity that has a low probability of being detected, given a large number of accounts and a materiality measure of a reasonable magnitude. Since most financial programs round to cents, the .01¢ difference in several accounts easily could go unnoticed.

Parallel simulation is a substantial improvement over its manual analogue, particularly in the volume of transactions considered. Parallel simulation is a good example of a technique that on a cost/benefit basis may be found to be quite satisfactory in a wide variety of audit settings. When coupled with a GAS package, discussed subsequently, it is a formidable tool.

Controlled Processing or Reprocessing

A technique unrelated to those just mentioned in which the auditor "controls" the processing run using a client-processing system that has been tested by the auditor is controlled processing or reprocessing. This technique emphasizes authenticity of the processes generating financial reports once they have been certified (for example, see mapping) as conforming to given standards. The first term, controlled processing, refers to the use of a process, for example, at year end, that had been tested and maintained under the control of the auditor. The second term, reprocessing, refers to use of a process that the auditor has reviewed, tested and controlled to "reprocess" sample data from the period under audit. Note that these methods make no assertions about the process code except that it was certified before the use of these methods. Therefore, some other method for verifying correctness of the relevant process must be employed in combination with these techniques. These techniques should not be categorized as process verification methods because of shortcomings cited earlier for techniques that focus on comparative output as a means of asserting process correctness. Rather, these methods should be viewed as a means by which the auditor can check the consistency of processes used during and at the end of the audit period. They do address, in a limited way, the problem of detecting process code changes. Extensions to the basic methods defined by Davis [1968] have appeared in EDPACS [Shell, 1975].

Program Code Checking

Often referred to as "program listing verification," "desk checking" or "code checking," this method refers to detailed analysis of process code. It requires the highest level of expertise (on the part of the auditor) of any technique mentioned. Undoubtedly, it is the most time-consuming and cumbersome technique listed. Given a large complex system, it would be impossible to examine every line of process code. However, as with the other techniques listed, it can be used in conjunction with other methods to form an effective audit method in particular environments. For example, code checking and controlled processing would validate consistency between processes under examination.

Flow Chart Verification

An improvement on program code checking would be examination of schematics that represent the logic of a given process. Instead of line-by-line code checking, the process under examination can be used as input to a software routine that generates a logic flowchart which corresponds to the process code. (The June 1975 issue of the *Journal of Accountancy* contained a list of "automatic flowcharting" routines and an article by Moore [1975] that illustrated the use of this technique.) The "state-of-the-art" of automatic flowcharting can provide adequate detail for an auditor's preliminary review. However, where controls are to be relied upon, automatic flowcharting generally is not capable of providing the detail sufficient to assure the identification of program code failures. In some languages, the amount of detail can be so voluminous that it far exceeds the auditor's needs in preliminary review and, due to the difficulties of analysis, it may still be insufficient to assure the identification of malicious code. Obviously, the auditor could manually flow-chart the code to any desired level of detail but that would involve a line-by-line examination which reverts back to code checking.

In addition to the problems outlined above, the auditor has to be thoroughly familiar with flowcharting, which could be interpreted as another language. The problem of consistency between program examined and program used is also in evidence.

TECHNIQUES FOR VERIFYING THE RESULTS OF PROCESSING

As mentioned earlier in this paper, "confirmation," "comparison" and "reasonable-ness and edit tests" are the basic techniques for verifying the results of processing. They have been used for many years prior to the introduction of computer audit applications. These techniques may be implemented manually or with the aid of an EDP system. If an EDP system were used, the auditor would have the option of using custom-designed audit programs or generalized audit software. The following sections actually list EDP-based systems that aid the auditor in implementing the techniques listed above.

As previously noted, we recognize that there are classification problems as to whether a given technique is associated solely with "processing" or the "results of processing." This is largely due to the potential of multipurpose outputs of a given test. However, the technique classification used distinguishes the issues in a fashion consistent with their primary objectives. The reader is cautioned not to become rigid in considering the appropriate mix of techniques in a given audit situation.

Custom-Designed Computer Programs

EDP-based accounting information systems have forced the auditor to retrieve and analyze data stored in machine readable form. One alternative solution for the auditor is to have client programmers, or other EDP personnel, write code to access and analyze data files. These programs usually are designed for specific audit tasks, as opposed to generalized audit software (GAS) which addresses itself to a variety of tasks.

"Special purpose" programs, as they are sometimes called, decreased in popularity when GAS's were introduced. The major contributors were: high cost, long lead times needed for program development, low degree of flexibility to change with applications and additional verification required if the program was written by client personnel. However, custom-designed programs have increased in popularity with the recent introduction of complex data structure such as data base management systems (DBMS).

Generalized Audit Software (GAS)

Haskins & Sells introduced a software package called AUDITAPE in 1965 which was designed to assist auditors examining EDP-based accounting systems. Since that time, many software packages have been introduced with the same objective. Adams and Mullarkey [1972] surveyed these packages as they approached the crest of their effectiveness in 1972. GAS's, also termed "generalized audit packages" (GAP) and "generalized audit software packages (GASP), were developed especially for auditors and became known as "high level auditor computer languages" [Touche, Ross and Co., 1973]. In general these routines convert instructions written in terminology functionally related to audit activities into computer programs. Adams [1973] outlined requirements for GAS in an edition of EDPACS.

Porter [1969] distinguished between GAS's for a given industry and those claiming complete generality. Whatever the contextual setting, GAS's generally were thought to have the following advantages:

1. Allowed the auditor a high degree of independence from client's personnel
2. Reduced requisite level of EDP expertise and special training
3. Accessed a wide variety of records interchangeably without preparing a special program for each access
4. Allowed auditor to totally control programs

GAS's such as Touche, Ross's STRATA, have been used as the key element of parallel simulation discussed earlier.

Unfortunately, GAS's were designed for use with sequential file structures. Improved software technology for file processing was introduced in the early 1970's and has since grown rapidly. These improvements allowed for more complex data structure. The term often associated with generalized software for file processing is "data base management system" (DBMS). Weber and Litecky [1974] noted the effect of these systems on GAS's and proposed solutions that are discussed in the next section.

Data Base Management Systems

Management's need for integrated data files, reduction of data redundancies and buffer routines between user and data that separate logical and physical data structures led to the introduction of data base management systems. File structures to support such systems are too complex for use of generalized audit software as it existed in the early 1970's. Weber and Litecky [1974] and Weber [1974] noted this problem and suggested several solutions. One approach is to upgrade GAS technology to handle the more complex structure: however, this implies that every time a change occurs in the structure, a corresponding change would be incorporated into the GAS. Another approach was standardization of software interfaces which has all the associated disadvantages of standardizing a programming language. The last solution proposed was modification of data base management systems to include audit functions available to the auditor. This implied that GAS software should be incorporated into the DBMS. Of the three suggested solutions, the last seems the most viable in the long run.

The incorporation of GAS software in the DBMS increases auditor reliance on client systems. In our view, this may be an unavoidable condition given the increasing size and complexity of the audit problem. Thus, while GAS packages undoubtedly will continue to be a substantial aspect of future audits, techniques need to be developed that will satisfy the audit requirements and permit greater reliance on client systems.

SUMMARY OF TECHNIQUES

We have attempted to classify the techniques listed in the earlier discussion within the framework mentioned at the beginning of the paper. Our objective is to provide the auditor with a taxonomy of available techniques and references. Figure 2 contains this summary of the techniques and tools discussed.

FIGURE 2

SUMMARY OF TECHNIQUES AND TOOLS

Verification Objective	Technique	Synonyms	Advantages	Disadvantages	References
Phases of Processing	Auditing Around the Computer	"Traditional manual" and "black box" technique	Low cost; little required technical expertise; comprehension	Impractical in voluminous systems; no inference about unexamined data or process	Boutell, 1970; Cerullo, 1974; Davis, 1968; Horwitz, 1976; Jancura, 1974; Li, 1968; Mair, 1971; McRae, 1966; Milko, 1970; Poplawski, 1974; Touche, Ross & Co., 1973.
	Auditing Through the Computer	(General caption for following routines)			Boutell, 1970, 1965, 1965; Cloyd, 1967; Davis, 1968; Horwitz, 1976; Jancura, 1974; Li, 1968; Milko, 1970; Poplawski, 1974; Stuhldreher, 1969; Woellner, 1966; Wright, 1966.
	Test Deck	"Test data"; a related term is "test data generator"	Little technical expertise; increased process logic examination by data designer; effective if the variety of conditions is limited	Only preconceived conditions are tested; almost impossible to design comprehensive test data for complex systems; time-consuming; lacks objectivity	Adams, 1973; Chambers, 1975; Davis, 1968; Jancura, 1974; Li, 1968; Mair, 1971; Stone, 1975; Taylor, 1969; Touche, Ross & Co., 1973; White, 1972; Wohl, 1966.
	Integrated Test Facility (ITF)	"Minicompany"; "dummy-company"; "Auditor's Central Office" and "extended test data method"	Tests system in a regular processing mode; only moderate degree of technical expertise required; other advantages parallel "Test Deck"	Removing test data from system may cause destruction of client files; use of different or special process logic; other disadvantages parallel "Test Deck"	AICPA, 1975; Perry, 1973; Stone, 1975; Touche, Ross & Co., 1973; Weiss, 1973.
	Tagging and Tracing (TT)	"Tagging and picture taking"; "tracing marked data"; ("Audit Indicator and Snapshot" are specific implementations of this technique)	Use of actual data; can be more effective when used in combination with ITF	May also require special process logic not normally used; no guarantee that all logic paths are traversed; risk of code violation when entry points are known	AICPA, 1975; Perry, 1973; Stone, 1975; Weiss, 1973.

FIGURE 2 (*Continued*)

Verification Objective	Technique	Synonyms	Advantages	Disadvantages	References
	Mapping	"Missed branch indicator"; "control monitors"; "logic supervisors"	Refers auditor to undesirable code; examines process logic; once developed, easy to implement; can be used in conjunction with other techniques	Interpretability of output; high process overhead pre-processing may camouflage malicious code	Adams, 1975; Gould, 1973; Stone, 1975.
	Concurrent Processing	"Continuous processing"; "concurrent auditing"; "continuous auditing by exception"	Designed to detect "exception" conditions when they occur; can be used in conjunction with "threat monitoring" routines of a security system	Does not examine process code; most systems detect only anticipated "exceptions"	Cloyd, 1967; Kunkel, 1974; Perry, 1975, 1974; Schaller, 1976; Stone, 1976.
	Parallel Simulation		Allows independence of auditor from client personnel; facilitates examination of a larger number of transactions; only moderate level of technical expertise required	This technique is an automated version of "around the computer" technique and has the same disadvantages as that technique, except that it handles substantially larger samples (for a given time or process it may handle the population of transactions)	Mair, 1975; 1971.
	Controlled Processing or Reprocessing		Allows auditor to check for consistency of processes used during and at the end of the audit period; low technical expertise required	Does not verify process code directly; it is assumed another technique is used	Adams, 1974; Davis, 1968; Shell, 1975.
	Program Code Checking	"Program listing verification"; "desk checking"; "code checking"	Process logic examined in detail; auditor is intimately aware of process code content	Very high level of expertise required; very time consuming; practical only in relatively simple systems	Mair, 1971; McRae, 1966; Touche, Ross & Co., 1973; Weber, 1974; Adams, 1975.
	Flowchart Verification	Related term is "automatic flowcharting routine"	Improved readability over code checking; logic interpretability is improved	State-of-art of automatic flowcharters not sufficiently developed; cumbersome and time consuming if manual; another language	Moore, 1975; Stickler, 1972; Stone, 1975; Touche, Ross & Co., 1973.
Results of Processing	Custom-Designed Computer Programs	"Special purpose programs"	Aids in accessing data stored in machine readable form; forces familiarity with system	High cost; long lead times for program development; low degree of flexibility	Adams, 1974, 1973, 1972; Bryden, 1976; Christopher, 1968; Doherty, 1970; Johnson, 1974; Leishman, 1971; Merich, 1973; Merrill, 1972; Moore, 1970; Christopher, 1967; Niestrath, 1972; Raffensperger, 1973; Schick, 1969; Smith, 1973, 1972, 1971, 1969; Spinelli, 1970; Touche, Ross & Co., 1973; Welke, 1972; Wlodarek, 1970.
	Generalized Audit Software	"Generalized audit packages"; (GAP) "generalized audit software packages" (GASP)	Low cost when compared to special purpose programs; uses business oriented language; flexibility	Designed for use with sequential file structures; typically written for ease of implementation disregarding efficiency	Adams, 1974, 1973, 1972; Haskins & Sells & Co., 1966; Crabtree, 1969; Doherty, 1970; Johnson, 1974; Leishman, 1971; Li, 1970; Meikle, 1969; Merich, 1973; Merrill, 1972; Moore, 1970; Christopher, 1967; Piket, 1974; Porter, 1969; Raffensperger, 1973; Reid, 1971; Sady, 1970; Schick, 1969; Smith, 1973, 1972, 1971, 1969; Thibeau, 1970; Touche, Ross & Co., 1973; Wasserman, 1974.
	Data Base Management Systems		Can access more complex data structures; auditor not responsible for maintenance of access mechanism	Auditor relies on client's system to generate data for audit; increased level of technical expertise needed	Bjork, 1975; EDPACS, 1975; Rittersbach, 1974; Schroeder, 1974; Weber, 1976, 1975, 1974; Wlodarek, 1970.

Note: The value, advantages and disadvantages of any verification technique ultimately must be examined in the context of specific audit circumstances including non-EDP controls. Thus the existence of disadvantages relative to a technique does not preclude it from being the "best" alternative under the circumstances at hand. Relevant issues include auditor expertise, timing, cost and available alternatives yielding acceptable results.

NEW APPROACHES

Even though the current "state-of-the-art" in auditing the EDP environment is much advanced over that of the late 1960's and continues to improve rapidly, substantial room for improvement still exists. None of the techniques mentioned can serve as a stand-alone method for completely evaluating the EDP, even though combinations of techniques, for example, parallel simulation and GAS, may provide strong evidence in a given audit situation. In some sense, the "new techniques" supersede the prior classifications in that the implementation of the "new approaches" would provide a much stronger basis within which the previously discussed techniques still might be applied, even if it is on a more limited basis. Thus, the "new techniques" are potentially important in their own right and can increase the effectiveness of existing methods. Given the differences in audit environments, one omnibus technique may not be a viable alternative.

A general methodology or philosophy that outlines an approach to reviewing, evaluating and testing the system where the approach includes the seeds of its own improvement, seems imperative to performing the audit functions within the limits prescribed by generally accepted auditing standards.

Several new approaches to the problem have been proposed. They are included in this section because either they have not been implemented or do not conform to the classification given earlier. The reader will note that with the exception of software standardization the "new approaches" place heavier burdens on the auditor in terms of basic system development. As little actual practice exists in these areas, the following may be viewed as simply a report on new, and perhaps experimental, approaches. However, it is our opinion that these approaches ultimately may prove essential to the effective audits of large-scale complex DBMS.

Software Standardization

Standardization of process-related software is a frequently mentioned approach. Among the specific proposals we chose to classify under this heading are: standardized compilers, standarized object code (target languages), standarized programming languages (source code), and automatic code generators. The justification usually presented with these approaches is that with standardized software, uniform examination and evaluation procedures could be adopted. The difficulties writers associate with these techniques are consistent with problems incurred in any standardization effort. They are increased in the context of programming languages because clients develop accounting systems based on economic utility of interfaced hardware-software alternatives. That is, one client's criteria might be minimum hardware costs which implies a particular programming language, while another client might want a turnkey system which minimizes software cost but dictates a particular hardware configuration.

Systems Design Involvement

An approach proposed by AICPA's Computer Auditing Subcommittee's—Auditing Advanced EDP Systems Task Force [AICPA, 1975], is increased auditor participation in the system design. The success internal auditors have had with concurrent auditing probably led to this proposal; it is logical in that it includes proper controls at the inception of the system which enhance the reliability of the system in operation. For example, the system could include automatic sampling of transactions written on special auditor files for subsequent physical examination. More advanced possibilities include "computer to computer confirmation" [AICPA, 1975], a software technique that the auditor might specify as a part of the system design. Also, the inherent familiarity of the auditor with the resultant system more than meets the requirements listed in SAS No. 3.

Major issues of concern in applying this suggestion include: timing difficulties, remoteness from primary audit objective and auditor independence. Clients develop systems at their convenience; requiring auditor participation will increase the auditor's burden not only in the absolute amount of time demanded but also in the scheduling of time. The auditor's concern is primarily with statement fairness. Systems development is relatively far-removed from the statements. Is systems involvement necessary in a cost/benefit framework when statement fairness is the criterion? The issue of auditor independence is much discussed and needs no elaboration here. In our opinion, the expanding responsibilities being placed on auditors warrant serious consideration of a deeper involvement by auditors in basic systems design.

FORMAL SYSTEMS ASSERTIONS

Another approach currently being researched by the authors is a combination of the two mentioned above. It includes involvement of the auditor in the system design function and the introduction of a standard system development technique that allows formal assertions about the resultant system. The key phases of this methodology are shown below:

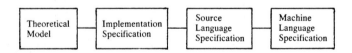

A left to right scan of this diagram follows one's intuitive view of the system development cycle. The contribution of this approach is a formal proof that the behavior of each component corresponds to the component that precedes it. This technique was used by the MITRE Corporation to develop and implement a security kernel for the Air Force [Burke, 1974]. The justification for promoting such a technique is exactly the same as examining processing control or internal control systems. If the generating system can be proven to be reliable, one has a higher degree of confidence that the resultant output is accurate. The association between auditing EDP systems for controls and security controls is very pronounced as indicated by the interest in security issues displayed by auditing organizations (for example, IIA's conference on auditing and security and EDPACS newsletter). Therefore, the interest of the auditor in having the client implement a "secure" processing system would reduce the auditor's concern in an EDP-based environment. This logic parallels that associated with the reduction in subsequent tests once the internal control system is proven highly reliable.

TICOM

Several new approaches center around software advances in the maintenance of stored data files. The term most frequently used is "data base management system" (DBMS). As mentioned earlier in this paper, they allow for very complex data structures which further complicated the auditor's problems. However, some writers have suggested how these advances might be helpful to the auditor. The auditor can use DBMS's as a tool in the audit function. First, it can be used as a retrieval mechanism to aid in the analysis of "processing results." Second, it can be used for simulating and evaluating the client's internal control system (manual and/or computerized). Several authors, for example, Weber [April 1975], have suggested how DBMS's can be used in the retrieval of data. Eventually, generalized audit software packages may be comparable to DBMS's and will perform this function similar to their current abilities. Automating the general internal control system evaluation will cause the auditor to do a much better job in a given time period allocated for that activity (as dictated by the audit program).

There does not exist a system so totally automated that no manual controls appear. Therefore, a thorough review and evaluation of a firm's internal control system encompasses much more than the scrutinizing of computer processing routines. More specifically, a method of examining and evaluating internal control should view manual and automated components of the total system in an equal fashion. In addition, it should be able to encode information flow through the organization so as to lend the auditor maximum support in the search for system weaknesses. Last, since it generally is accepted that the computer provides faster access of more detailed data than manual systems, it seems desirable to use advanced EDP technology in this analysis.

The authors currently are refining a model, TICOM (The Internal Control Model), that stores a description of a client's internal control system, *both manual and automated,* in a network data base structure, that exhibits characteristics such as those noted above. Another paper by the authors pursues TICOM issues further.

SUMMARY OF NEW APPROACHES

The "new approaches" discussed tend to place new burdens on the auditor in suggesting involvement in systems design and the use of automatic internal control description methods. These proposals are at the current frontiers of the audit function and may prove impractical. However, the increasing complexities in data management and their potential impacts on financial reporting and its related audit function suggest maintaining an open mind.

REFERENCES

Adams, D. L., "COMBI (*CO*bol *M*issed *B*ranch *I*ndicator) As An Audit Tool," EDPACS, (April 1975).

——, "Audit Review of Program Code-1," EDPACS (August 1975).

——, "SMF–An Untapped Audit Resource," EDPACS (September 1974).

——, "Audit Software–DYL-250 and DYL-260," EDPACS (July 1974).

——, "Audit Software Requirements," EDPACS (November 1973).

——, "A Survey of Test Data Generators," EDPACS (April 1973).

—— and J. F. Mullarkey, "A Survey of Audit Software," *Journal of Accountancy* (September 1972).

AICPA, Computer Auditing Subcommittee's Auditing Advanced EDP Systems Task Force, "Advanced EDP Systems and the Auditor's Concern," *Journal of Accountancy* (January 1975).

——, Auditing Standards Executive Committee, "The Effects of EDP on the Auditor's Study and Evaluation of Internal Control, *Statement on Auditing Standards No. 3* (December 1974).

——, Committee on Auditing Procedure, "Codification of Auditing Standards and Procedures," *Statement on Auditing Standards No. 1* (November 1973).

Bjork, L. A., "Generalized Audit Trail Requirements and Concepts for Data Base Application," *IBM Systems Journal No. 3* (1975).

Boutell, W. S., ed., *Contemporary Auditing* (Dickenson, 1970).

——, "Auditing Through the Computer," *Journal of Accountancy* (November 1965), pp. 41–47.

——, *Auditing With the Computer* (University of California Press, 1965).

Bryden, W. A., "A Case Study in Computer Auditing of a Small Company," *Journal of Accountancy* (March 1976).

Burke, E. L., "Synthesis of a Software Security System" (MITRE Corporation, September 1974).

Cash, J. I., W. D. Haseman and A. B. Whinston, "Security for the GPLAN System," *Information Systems* (October 1976).

Cerullo, M. J., "Procedures for Auditing Around EDP Service Bureaus," *Florida Certified Public Accountant* (July 1974), pp. 11–14.

Chambers, A. D., "Audit Test Packs and Computer Audit Programs," *The Computer Journal,* No. 2 (1975).

Christopher, D. W. and J. R. Keith, "Case Study of a Computer Audit Program: An Application of a Computer to the Audit of the Recording Function for Fixed Assets in a Heavy Industry Company," *Price Waterhouse Review* (Spring 1968).

—— and J. A. Richards, "Case Study of a Computer Audit Program," *Journal of Accountancy,* v. 123 (April 1967), pp. 69–73.

Cloyd, H. M., "Continuous Auditing–What is its Future?" *National Public Accountant* (January 1971).

——, "Auditing Through the Computer," *National Public Accountant* (January 1967), pp. 20–22.

Crabtree, M. G. and A. Oakley, "Interrogation Kit–a Description of Generalized Audit Program, ASK 360," *Accountancy* (Eng.) (November 1969), pp. 820–827.

Davis, G., *Auditing and EDP* (AICPA, 1968).

Davis, K. W. and D. R. Wood, "Computer Control and Audit," *Touche, Ross Tempo,* v. 18, (Autumn 1972), pp. 9–20.

Doherty, H. S. and J. L. Sorenson, "Use of Computers in Auditing," *Arthur Young Journal* (Special Issue, 1970).

EDPACS, "Auditing a Data Base System," (March 1975).

Gould, K. "Computer Performance Measurement Techniques," First Annual EDP Auditors Conference (1973).

Haskins & Sells & Co., "Auditape," *H&S Reports* (Autumn 1966), pp. 4–7.

Horwitz, G. B., "Needed: A Computer Audit Philosophy," *Journal of Accountancy* (April 1976).

Jancura, E. G., "Technical Proficiency for Auditing Computer Processed Accounting Records," *Journal of Accountancy* (October 1975).

—— and A. H. Bergen, *Computers: Auditing and Control,* (Auerbach, 1973).

——, *Audit & Control of Computer Systems* (Petrocelli, 1974).

Johnson, E. C. "Computer as an Audit Tool," *California CPA Quarterly* (June 1974).

Kiefer, G. H., "Systems Auditing with Test Decks," *Management Accounting* (June 1972), pp. 14–18.

Kunkel, J. G., "Continuous Auditing by Exception," *Management Accounting* (July 1974).

Leishman, R. O., "Computer as an Auditing Tool," *Internal Auditor* (January-February 1971), pp. 22–27.

Li, D. H., "Audit-Aid: Generalized Computer Audit Program as an Instructional Device," THE ACCOUNTING REVIEW (October 1970), pp. 774–778.

——, *Accounting-Computers-Management Information Systems* (McGraw-Hill, 1968).

Loebbecke, J. K., "Internal Control Evaluation: How the Computer Can Help," *Journal of Accountancy* (August 1975).

Mair, W. C., K. W. Davis and D. R. Wood, *Computer Control and Audit,* (Institute of Internal Auditors, 1976).

——, "PARALLEL SIMULATION–A Technique for Effective Verification of Computer Programs," EDPACS (April 1975).

——, *New Techniques in Computer Program Verification* (Touche, Ross & Co., Inc., 1971).

Martin, J., *Security, Accuracy and Privacy in Computer Systems* (Prentice-Hall, 1973).

McRae, T. W., "Need We Audit The Program?" *Accountant* (Eng.) (June 1966), pp. 806–807.

Meikle, G. R. and J. B. Gambles, "Auditape for Management and the Auditor," *Accountancy* (Eng.) (July 1969), pp. 493–500; (August 1969), pp. 583–591.

Merich, L. C., "Data Processing Auditing: Using a Computer-Assisted Approach," *California CPA Quarterly* (December 1973), pp. 36–37.

Merrill, W. W., "Auditing with the Computer–Basic Principles," *Massachusetts CPA Review* (January-February 1972), pp. 28, 31.

Milko, E. M., "Auditing: Through the Computer or Around?" *Management Accounting* (August 1970).

Moore, M. R. and R. H. Yocom, "The AY Audit/Management Systems: An Information Tool for Auditors and Managers," *Arthur Young Journal* (Special Issue, 1970).

Moore, R., "Computer Generated Documentation," *Journal of Accountancy* (June 1975).

Parker, D. B., *Crime by Computer* (Scribner's Sons, 1976).

Perry, W. E., "Using SMF as an Audit Tool–Accounting Information," EDPACS (January 1975).

——, "Using SMF as an Audit Tool–Performance," EDPACS (December 1975).

——, "Using SMF as an Audit Tool–Security," EDPACS (January 1976).

—— and D. L. Adams, "SMF–An Untapped Audit Resource," EDPACS (September 1974).

——, "Concurrent EDP Auditing: An Implementation Approach," EDPACS (February 1974).

——, "Concurrent EDP Auditing: An Early Warning Scheme," EDPACS (January 1974).

——, "Try ITF, You'll Like ITF," EDPACS (December 1973).

——, "SNAPSHOT–A Technique for Tagging and Tracing Transactions," EDPACS (March 1974).

Piket, T. P., "AUDIT Retrieval–the New Frontier for Auditors," *U.S. Army Audit Agency Pamphlet, no.350-2* (June 1974), pp. 16–22.

Poplawski, E. J., "Auditing Around or Through the Computer," *Magazine of Bank Administration* (November 1974), pp. 22–24.

Porter, W. T., *EDP Control and Auditing* (Wadsworth, 1974).

——, "Generalized Computer Audit Programs," *Journal of Accountancy* (January 1969).

Raffensperger, O. E., "Computer as an Audit Tool," *Internal Auditor* (November-December 1973), pp. 72–74.

Reid, G. F. and J. Demeak, "EDP Audit Implementation with General Purpose Software," *Journal of Accountancy* (July 1971), pp. 35–46.

Rittersbach and Harlan, "Auditing Advanced Systems," *Journal of Accountancy* (June 1974).

Sady, M. and R. J. Joyce, "Generalized Computer Programs–Are They Worth the Effort?" *GAO Review* (Fall 1970), pp. 48–54.

Schaller, C. A., "Auditing and Job Accounting Data," *Journal of Accountancy* (May 1976).

Schick, C. W. and V. J. Perrill, "Using the Computer as an Auditing Tool," *New York Certified Public Accountant* (January 1969), pp. 57–60.

Schroeder, W. J., "Memo on Installing a Data Base System," *Journal of Accountancy* (February 1974), pp. 81–82.

Shell, R. C., "Audit Control Over Computer Programs," EDPACS (March 1975).

Smith, C. O. and G. F. Jasper, "Using the Computer in Audit Work," *International Accounting* (Eng.) (April-June 1973), pp. 8–12.

—— and G. F. Jasper, "Using the Computer in Audit Work," *Management Accounting* (October 1972), pp. 34–38, 42.

—— and G. F. Jasper, "Using Computer-Aided Techniques in Financial Audit Work," *GAO Review* (Fall 1971), pp. 28–37.

——, "Useful Techniques for Examining Automated Data Processing Systems," *GAO Review* (Fall, 1969), pp. 27–35.

Spinelli, C. C. "Auditing Accounts Receivable by Computer–A Case History," *Journal of Accountancy* (April 1970), pp. 73–78.

Stettler, H. F., *Systems Based Independent Audits* (Prentice-Hall, 1974).

Stickler, V. D., "An Appraisal of Flow Charting as an Audit Technique," *Internal Auditor* (July/August 1972).

Stone, R. L., "Security and Integrity Controls in Small Computer Systems," *Journal of Accountancy* (February 1976).

——, "Who is Responsible for Computer Fraud?" *Journal of Accountancy* (February 1975).

Stuhldreher, W. F. "Can Auditors Actually Audit 'through' the Computer?" *U.S. Army Audit Agency Bulletin* (Summer 1969), pp. 33–36.

Taylor, A. R., "Audit of A. D. P. Systems Using Test Decks and Test Files," *Australian Accountant* (May 1969), pp. 206–210.

Thibeau, P. B., "Auditape: A Versatile Audit Tool," *GAO Review* (Fall 1970), pp. 55–59.

Touche, Ross & Co., National Accounting and Auditing Staff *Computer Controls and Audit,* (September 1973).

Wasserman, J., "Selecting a Computer Audit Package," *Journal of Accountancy* (April 1974), pp. 30, 32, 34.

Weber R. and A. M. Jenkins, "Using DBMS Software as an Audit Tool: The Issue of Independence," *Journal of Accountancy* (April 1976).

——, "Audit Capabilities of Some Data-Base Management Systems," Fifth IIA Conference on Computer, Audit, Control and Security (April 1975).

——, "An Audit Perspective of Operating System Security," *Journal of Accountancy* (September 1975).

—— and C. R. Litecky, "The Demise of Generalized Audit Software Packages," *Journal of Accountancy* (November 1974).

——, "This Business of Database Management and What it Means to the Accountant and Auditor," (University of Minnesota, Graduate School of Business Administration, October 1974).

Weiss, H. L., "The Use of Audit Indication and Integrated Test Facility Techniques," EDPACS (July 1973).

Welke, W. R. and K. G. King, "Using the Computer as an Audit Tool," *CPA Journal* (November 1972), pp. 930–932.

White, D. C., A. R. Whitesell and J. W. Bynum, "Using Test Decks in Financial Audit Work," *GAO Review* (Spring 1972), pp. 33–39.

Wlodarek, R. A., "Using an ADP Information Retrieval System in Auditing an Educational Assistance Program," *GAO Review* (Fall 1970), pp. 60–67.

Woellner, D. A. "Auditing Through Computers," *Federal Accountant* (Spring 1966) pp. 20–29.

Wohl, G. and M. D'Angelico, *Computer in Auditing—The Use of Test Data*, (Richard D. Irwin, Inc., 1966).

Wright, R. G., "Auditing Through the Computer," *Oklahoma CPA* (July 1966), pp. 7–14.

Auditing in a Data Base Environment

J. HAL RENEAU

With the increasing number of data base system applications in business entities, auditors are more frequently asked to assess the integrity of data processing systems that have some or possibly all applications operating in a data base environment. The purpose of this article is to provide an overview of differences between file systems and data base systems from a point of view most relevant to auditors, that is, a nontechnical view of the alternative structures with emphasis on control.

FILE SYSTEMS VS. DATA BASE SYSTEMS

File systems are designed for specific applications such as payroll, accounts receivable or inventory. All data associated with a specific application is stored in the application's files. Each file is completely associated with the specific program or programs for that application. For example, a payroll system is designed to perform functions such as computing net pay, accumulating year-to-date totals, writing checks, etc. The programs performing these functions operate with a file or files of data, such as the payroll master file. The payroll master file is associated with the payroll programs, but is completely disassociated from other applications such as accounts receivable or inventory.

The composition of the files, their internal organization and storage media are designed to achieve optimal performance of the application programs that process the files. When several programs process one file, reformatting, preprocessing or a decrease in efficiency usually results. A general overview of an accounting system under file processing is shown in Figure 1. Each application has its own program(s) and file(s). There is no direct logical relationship across the several applications or files.

Data base systems are designed so that many applications may efficiently operate on the same physical data base. Data previously contained in separate files is now contained in one or more common data bases. However, the logical data base, that is, the way the data base is viewed by an application program, is likely to be unique for every program.

A data base system can greatly reduce the amount of redundant data stored, yet efficiently support numerous application programs by letting each program have a unique logical view of the data base. In a file system, the field inventory part number might be included in the inventory master file, open purchase order file, vendor master file, back order file, and job costing detail file. This redundant data storage is eliminated in a data base system by storing inventory part number in only one physical location, but logically associating inventory part number with other fields such as quantity on hand, quantity on order, vendor name, unit cost, etc. Various application programs are allowed to use only those logical associations that are necessary to accomplish their processing function. For example, the logical association between inventory part number and vendor name is necessary for the purchase order preparation program but not required for the job costing program. Thus, a data base system can greatly reduce the amount of redundant data stored, yet efficiently support numerous application programs by letting each program have a unique logical view of the data base.

A data base is designed for generality and flexibility. It serves a community of users rather than a single logical function. Figure 2 shows a general overview of a data base system.

The application programs supported by a data base system may be the same as those used in the file system. However, the programs do not contain file descriptions. Instead, they contain a reference to a data description known to the system. The data description provides the interface between the data base and the application program which must access only specified data items. The data base contains all the company's data stored in some physical format. The data description block in Figure 2 defines a logical view of the data base to an application program. Each application program is likely to have a unique logical view of the data base.

Figure 3 shows a more detailed view of the functions performed in associating an application program with the proper data in the data base. The application program contains program specification information identifying the data it needs. In IBM terminology, this is the program specification block (PSB). The data base management system (DBMS) will then search its library to determine if the named program specification information exists and whether the particular application program is authorized to access this data. If the application program is allowed access to the requested data, the data base management system will again search its library to locate information that tells where the requested data resides in the data base. This is called a data base description (DBD) in IBM terminology. The data base management system then calls the data management language processor (DL/I for IBM), which retrieves the desired data from the data base and provides the data to the application program.

The DBMS library is a critical control area in the data base system. This library contains all the program specification information and data base descriptions for all

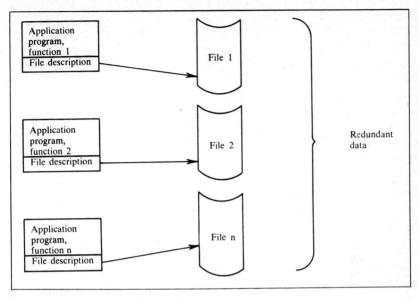

Fig. 1 *File processing system*

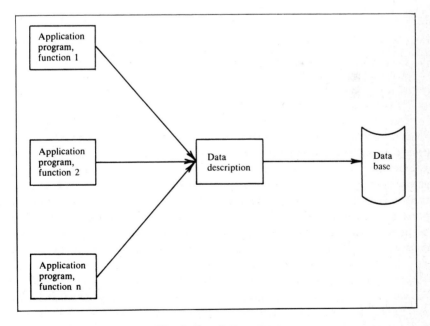

Fig. 2 *Data base system*

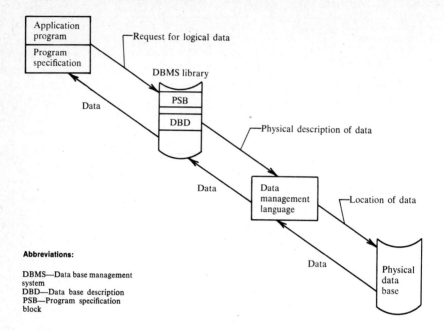

Fig. 3 *Functions in a data base system*

application programs. Once a program's data request is approved, the data base system automatically retrieves the data when requested by the program. The privacy and security information controlling what program may access what data is contained in the DBMS library.

FROM THE AUDITOR'S VIEWPOINT

When reviewing a data processing system, the auditor must gain assurance that proper controls exist in several areas of data processing. SAS no. 3 categorizes these as general controls and application controls.[1] A recent AICPA audit guide further describes these control areas, identifying 19 general controls and 12 application controls.[2] The differences in some of the control procedures and potential audit problem areas for file systems and data base systems are considered in the following paragraphs. The discussion highlights certain control differences between file systems and data base systems, but does not attempt to describe a complete set of

---

[1] Statement on Auditing Standards (SAS), no. 3, *The Effects of EDP on the Auditor's Study and Evaluation of Internal Control* (New York: AICPA, 1974), pars. 7–8.

[2] *The Auditor's Study and Evaluation of Internal Controls in EDP Systems* (New York: AICPA, 1977).

control procedures for a data base system because many controls are identical for the two systems.

Certain general controls over program development and program maintenance are different for file systems and data base systems. Basic controls such as approval of change request, revision of documentation, program testing and revision of backup and recovery procedures apply to both file and data base systems. However, a data base system requires additional controls. In file systems, program changes are generally directed at revising the logical operations performed on the file, for example, restructuring the program for increased efficiency or correcting a previously unknown logic error. The data accessed by the program typically does not change because the file is logically and physically dedicated to the program. A revision in the payroll program will not change the data contained in the payroll file accessed by the program, unless the file, too, is restructured and changed. In a data base system, the program operates on a data base rather than a file. The application program contains program specification information (see figure 27.3) which is processed through the data base management system to access the desired data. A change in the application program could involve a change in the logical operations performed on the data, a change in the data items accessed or both. Thus, general controls over program maintenance in a data base environment must ensure that any changes in the application program's specification information are necessary and properly authorized.

The possibility of accessing different data items in a given application program can have a cascading effect because a data item in the data base is likely to be accessed by several different application programs. For example, a program that updates personnel data for employees hired and terminated might be modified to delete the employee numbers for persons no longer employed by the company. This procedure might be used to help control against issuing checks to terminated employees or simply to conserve data storage. However, this modification might also destroy the logical association in the data base between employee number and year-to-date earnings for that employee, thus affecting other application programs. For this reason, general controls over program maintenance and development are more critical in data base systems. Program modifications must be reviewed by a responsible person familiar with all the application programs—the data base administrator (DBA).

Controls over access to the data represent another major difference between file systems and data base systems. In a file system, files dedicated to a particular application program need be on-line only when the program is processing those files. Thus, data access controls in a file system are mostly organizational. Typically the files are stored in a library and checked out to an operator only when the application program is scheduled to be run. Even if controls over access to program documentation which contain a description of the file(s) processed by the program are circumvented, physical access to the file is organizationally controlled by the librarian. In a data base system, control over access to data is more difficult to achieve by physical means. The data base contains data to support many application programs and must be available in the computer during the processing of all such application programs. Control over access to data in a data base system is centralized in the DBMS library while the DBMS is operational. The DBMS library contains security information to determine which data items may be accessed by each application program.

Another control problem related to data access is present in data base systems. While the DBMS software is running, any access to the data base is controlled by the DBMS software. However, like all software, the DBMS software requires maintenance which may be scheduled or unscheduled. When the DBMS software is not operational (down), the data base still exists in the system. It could be accessed, copied or deleted in the same manner as any other data while the DBMS software is not operational. Therefore, controls must be established to prevent any unauthorized access to the data base when the data base is not under the control of the DBMS.

General controls over organization and operations in data base systems, that is, ensuring that programs are processed in accordance with approved operating procedures, have many features common to file systems. Controls such as an operations procedure manual, operator instructions for each program, maintenance and regular review of a system log and controlling access to the system are necessary in both system configurations. In a data base system, additional controls are necessary. Any changes in the DBMS library must be controlled by a responsible official such as the data base administrator. A related control should govern the use of vendor-supplied utility programs to access the DBMS library. Such a program could be used to gain knowledge of the physical structure and all logical views of the data base by analyzing the program specification blocks and data base descriptions contained in the DBMS library (see Figure 3). In addition, a log of the DBMS library should be maintained and periodically reviewed by the DBA. The log should contain all additions or changes in the DBMS library and should log which programs used which program specification information in accessing the data base. These control procedures ensure that application programs accessed only those data items they are authorized to access and that any DBMS library changes were properly authorized.

DESIRABLE CONTROLS IN A DATA BASE ENVIRONMENT

Control features are discussed in four general areas:

1. Division of responsibility.
2. Access to data.
3. Operations.
4. Application programs.

Division of Responsibility

In division of responsibility, the need for segregation of functions between application programmers, systems analysts and operators remains the same as in file systems. In addition to those controls, additional organizational controls are required. A DBA should be responsible for the definition, organization, protection, efficiency and control of the data base. The DBA performs such functions as advising management in the selection of hardware and software, planning the structure of the data base, documenting the data base contents, consulting with users on data organization and retrieval methods, establishing security procedures and procedures for recovery in the event of data base destruction, and monitoring usage of the data base.

Organizational controls when a DBA function is present include the following:

1. The DBA should not be allowed unsupervised access to the computer room and should not be allowed to operate the equipment. Because the DBA is the only person with complete knowledge of the DBMS library contents and all application programs, he could easily gain access and manipulate any data items in the data base.
2. Only the DBA should have the authority to make changes in the DBMS library. Any changes to the DBMS library should be performed by a person independent of application program development.
3. The DBA should not be able to initiate transactions without user department approval. Because the DBA knows the functions performed by all application programs, he should have external authorization before entering transactions data.
4. The application programmer should know only the program specification information for his program. An application programmer has no need to know any data in the data base not directly associated with his application. This control is necessary in both file systems and data base systems, but is more critical in data base systems because physical control over the data is more difficult to achieve.

Access to Data

Because physical and organizational control over access to data is less feasible in a data base environment, additional controls are necessary. Suggested controls and justification for the controls are listed below.

1. Access to the DBMS library by utility programs should be adequately controlled, probably through the DBA.[3] Utility programs for functions such as listing the data base descriptions, or testing the data manipulation language could be used to gain unauthorized access to the data base.
2. There should be adequate procedures to prevent access to the data base when the data base is not under the control of the DBMS software. When the DBMS software is not operational, the physical data base still exists in the system and must be protected.

---

[3] Utility programs perform basic EDP functions independent of application programs.

3. The operating system log and the DBMS log should be reviewed by the DBA. This review should determine whether the data base has been accessed only when under the control of the DBMS, by authorized programs and in accordance with a processing schedule. This review is feasible only if supported by software to assist in summarization of these logs.

4. The DBA should control the use of maintenance-related utility programs. Utilities for initial loading of the data base and compression of items deleted from the data base should be controlled by the DBA because he is the one individual with complete knowledge of the data base structure. This control ensures that necessary maintenance of the data base is proper and authorized.

5. The live data base should be separate from the data base used for program testing. This control ensures that live data is not contaminated during program testing.

Operations

Many controls over operations in file systems are also necessary in data base systems. These controls include procedure manuals, operating instructions for all application programs, a processing schedule and provision for backup and recovery procedures. In addition to these controls, the additional controls listed below are necessary to ensure that control over operations is maintained.

1. The DBA should approve and log all changes to the DBMS library. This control is needed to ensure that only required data items are accessed by an application program.

2. The DBA should periodically review the DBMS library. The purpose of this review is to ensure that no unauthorized changes have been made.

3. A log of programs run and the program specification information used by the program should be maintained and periodically reviewed by the DBA. This control provides additional assurance that only authorized program specification information was used to access the data. In addition, this control will reveal any temporary changes made to the DBMS library, for example, establishing an unapproved program specification information entry in the DBMS library for one run of a program and then removing the library entry.

4. The DBA should approve all major modifications (both in-house and manufacturer) to the DBMS software. The DBA is the only person with complete knowledge of the DBMS system. He is thus the only person who can assess the control and data integrity impact of any modifications to the DBMS software. Many manufacturer modifications are minor technical corrections to solve software errors. Such modifications are exceptions to the above control and should not require DBA approval.

Application Programs

Control over application programs in a data base system, as with the previous control areas, has many attributes common to file systems. Controls such as documentation standards, programming standards, testing standards and backup and recovery procedures are necessary in both file and data base systems. However, the importance of such controls increases in a data base environment. Suggested controls over application programs in a data base environment are listed below.

1. There should be written programming standards that specify what type of data manipulation language (DML) calls can be used to access the data base that indicate what program actions are to be taken for each DBMS return code. The use of certain DML call verbs (insert, replace, delete) may be unnecessary for certain applications and should be restricted.[4] The presence of an error condition in the data base is typically indicated by a DBMS return code. Programs should provide for appropriate disposition of all possible DBMS return codes to ensure that processing errors are detected. The existence and enforcement of these and other programming standards are more critical in a data base environment because of the more integrated structure of the data base processing system.

2. There should be written documentation standards for all application programs, with the documentation reviewed by the DBA before the program is put into production. Documentation is a more critical area in data base systems because a common data base is accessed by multiple programs. The DBA must be able to determine the impact of new programs and program alterations on all other application programs.

3. There should be program testing standards that specify criteria for generating test data, review of the test results and retention of the test data and results. These controls are more important in a data base environment because of the cascading effect of errors, discussed in the previous section.

4. Backup and recovery procedures should be tested prior to implementation. As in file systems, such procedures should be tested simply to ensure that they adequately perform their functions. The testing is more critical in a data base environment because failure of any application program could alter the effectiveness of any other application program which accesses that data item.

CONCLUSION

One rapidly changing area in data processing technology concerns the manner in which data is stored and retrieved in the system. Under the traditional file system approach, a direct correspondence exists between the physical and logical structure

---

[4] DML call verbs are used in the application program to retrieve and/or modify data in the data base.

of data. Files are created to support a given application with minimal integration of data across applications. In a data base system, a physical data base is viewed as multiple logical data bases by the various application programs.

From an auditing viewpoint, necessary controls in a data base environment have certain features found in file systems, but certain controls are more critical. This article has presented a nontechnical distinction between file systems and data base systems, emphasizing control differences. This article should provide the auditor who is not expert in data base systems with basic information to both foster an awareness of control requirements in data base systems and serve as a basis for communication between the auditor and data processing personnel.

Auditing EFTS

DANA R. RICHARDSON

As financial information systems have grown in sophistication, the audit community has had to react to change—developing new methods and adapting existing techniques to a rapidly changing systems environment. As more advanced design concepts have been implemented, the auditor has been forced not only to augment and modify audit approaches but also to begin an introspective process of anticipating sweeping new dimensions in technology and systems design.

For the first time, a major change in technology—the advent of electronic funds transfer systems (EFTS)—provides the auditing profession with an opportunity to interact with both the financial and systems communities in developing an approach to audit procedures and systems analysis before the implementation of the technology is widespread.

This article will deal with the portion of EFTS that is related to payment-system transactions. The discussion will include

- The extent of the client's system.
- General controls in EFT systems.
- Application controls in EFT systems.

THE EXTENT OF THE CLIENT'S SYSTEM

Before an adequate study and evaluation of internal controls can be made, the auditor needs to define the extent of the financial system under review. In most conventional systems, the boundaries of the client's system are quite obvious. EFT systems, on the other hand, provide a potential for connecting many different organizations into one vast system. Though current standards do not specifically address this issue for EFT systems, their general guidelines do provide a conceptual framework for defining client-system boundaries in an EFTS environment.

AICPA Statement on Auditing Standards no. 3 defines the extent of the client's system of internal control as follows:

> An auditor's review of a client's system of accounting control should encompass all significant and relevant manual, mechanical, and EDP activities and the interrelationship between EDP and user departments. The review should comprehend both the control procedures related to transactions from origination or source to recording in the accounting records and the control procedures related to recorded accountability for assets.[1]

SAS no. 3 also requires the auditor to understand the flow of transactions through the client's system. It follows that if the points at which these transactions start and stop can be identified, then the boundaries of the client's system have been defined. SAS no. 1 states that

> Transactions include exchanges of assets or services with parties outside the business entity and transfers or use of assets or services within it. The primary functions involved in the flow of transactions and related assets include the authorization, execution, and recording of transactions and the accountability for resulting assets.[2]

Thus, in EFT systems, the point at which authorization for the transaction occurs and at which assets or services are exchanged will be the outer boundary of the system's flow of transactions. The system would then encompass all functions or procedures from the origination of these transactions through their ultimate recording in the books of account.

To illustrate the extent of client EFT systems, the following sections trace typical transactions through the three major categories of EFT services:

- Remote-banking services.
- Retail point-of-sale (POS) services.
- Direct deposit/preauthorized payment services.

Remote-banking Services

The most prevalent transactions in these EFT systems are deposits and withdrawals. With both types of transactions, an exchange of assets is consummated at the remote terminal. As such, the terminal should be considered part of a financial institution's system. Similarly, bill payments and account transfers affect an exchange of assets from the terminal, making the terminal the outermost node of the financial institution's system.

---

[1] Statement on Auditing Standards no. 3, *The Effects of EDP on the Auditor's Study and Evaluation of Internal Control* (New York: AICPA, 1974), par. 24.

[2] SAS no. 1, *Codification of Auditing Standards and Procedures* (New York: AICPA, 1973), sec. 320.20.

Retail POS Services

Through the use of POS terminals, these EFTS can provide three types of financial transactions at retail outlets: check verification transactions, check guarantee transactions and funds transfer transactions. The check verification process, though critical to the retailer's financial operations, should not be considered as generating an accounting transaction, because the process does not affect an exchange of assets or services per se. Check guarantee transactions, however, may or may not be considered accounting transactions, depending on the financial institution's procedures for processing and recording such transactions. In those situations in which the financial institution merely returns an authorization message to the retailer without changing the customer's records, the guarantee transaction is, in effect, no different from a check verification. If the financial institution does encumber customer funds as a guarantee transaction, one could argue that assets had been exchanged as a result of the transaction—though, in this case, exchanged between the financial institution and its customer rather than between the customer and the retailer. The actual funds transfer transaction in a retail POS environment permits the customer to purchase goods and services with an electronic payment instrument. Clearly, these transactions parallel remote-banking deposits and withdrawals. For the financial institution, the transaction originates at the POS terminal, and all parts of the system from the terminal to the financial institution should be considered. At the other end of the spectrum, the retail establishment has had no change in the extent of its system. It has, rather, accepted another form of payment.

In many retail POS systems, the participating financial institution may charge a fee for some or all transactions, with this fee being paid by either the retailer or the customer. When confronted with such situations, the auditor for the financial institution should consider all portions of the system related to the generation of both the receivable and revenue portions of such fee transactions.

The auditor for the independent switch should not find any extensive changes in audit procedures as a result of the introduction of EFTS technology. Neither the terminal nor financial institution portions of the EFT system should be considered part of the independent switch's system, because transactions are merely passed through the switch and are not recorded in the books of record for the switch. The auditor will be far more concerned with the portions of the message-switching software that count and balance transactions to determine the revenue charged by the switch for its function in the EFT system.

Direct Deposit/Preauthorized Payment Services

The functions of direct deposit and preauthorized payment systems closely parallel those of conventional payment systems. As such, these EFTS services pose no major change in the extent of the system but merely provide another mode of payment and/or receipt.

The above discussion has described the most common activities and transactions involved in EFT systems today. Certainly, as EFTS technologies evolve, the auditor will need to consider the functions performed within the EFT system and how these functions affect the client's systems boundaries and, therefore, the nature and extent of the auditor's review.

GENERAL CONTROLS EFTS

Professional literature dealing with controls in a data processing environment usually categorizes these controls as either general controls or application controls. General controls are those that affect the environment in which a particular accounting application is processed. These controls comprise

(a) The plan of organization and operation of the EDP activity, (b) the procedures for documenting, reviewing, testing, and approving systems or programs and changes thereto, (c) controls built into the equipment by the manufacturer (commonly referred to as 'hardware controls'), (d) controls over access to equipment and data files, and (e) other data and procedural controls affecting overall EDP operations.[3]

With the advent of EFT systems, many of the general controls applicable to batch systems will change in significance or may have new aspects of control that differ from traditional batch-oriented systems. In addition, new control elements themselves will surface for EFT systems in particular. The following discussion addresses these modifications in control techniques for each of the general control categories listed above.

Organization and Operations Controls

These controls are designed to ensure that incompatible functions are segregated among multiple individuals. In addition, they ensure that the actual production process in the EDP facility is structured to provide accurate, timely and reliable results.

Two critical elements in EFT systems are the plastic card and the personal identification number (PIN). It is therefore important that the stock of plastic cards, as well as the issuance of PINs, not be controlled by programming or operations personnel. Similarly, the programming and operations personnel should not provide a customer-service function for the data processing department that would interface with merchants or customers to authorize system transactions when remote terminals are inoperative.

Though systems development is typically considered a separate control area, organization controls can also have an impact on this process. Since most EFT systems rely heavily on programmed control features within the actual system software, it is important to segment the system development team sufficiently so that no one individual has a complete and detailed knowledge of the entire EFT system.

---

[3] SAS no. 3, par. 7.

Segregation of functions in EFT systems is discussed in more detail in Norman Lyon's article.[4]

System Development and Documentation Controls

These controls are designed to ensure that systems are developed, modified and tested only as specified and authorized. In addition, documentation of systems and their subsequent modifications should be sufficient to assure system continuity and maintainability as well as to evidence appropriate review and authorization.

Two system development and documentation control elements are particularly important in EFT systems: program modification control and system testing. Because EFT applications use various data communication technologies, program change control is crucial in an EFT environment to assure both system integrity and the proper functioning of the many segments in the system.

Adequate testing procedures are important to any data processing system. An EFT application requires particular attention to the testing of all of the various system interfaces. These "system links" provide the necessary hardware and software for each separate segment of the EFT system to accurately pass information to other parts of the system in such a manner that the information will be interpreted and processed correctly. These system interfaces should be tested when new financial institutions, new switches and/or new retailers are added to the EFT network. Similarly, the addition of new terminals to the system or even a new transaction type should also trigger system-interface testing.

Hardware and Systems Software Controls

Vendor-supplied hardware and software should have sufficient built-in controls to assure consistent and reliable processing as well as timely and accurate detection of hardware malfunctions. Since EFT systems require extensive data communications capabilities, both the hardware and software control facilities should be used to detect errors in data transmission and prevent the potential erroneous processing of transactions.

EFT software, at a system level, must provide additional features not required in traditional batch-oriented systems. These features should be designed to identify both the source and nature of the transaction and to appropriately append machine-sensible identifiers to the transaction. In essence, such system-level software provides much of the electronic audit trail, which, within the EFT environment, resides only within the individual transaction itself. Identifying data that should be appended to EFT transactions should include

- Time and date coding, to identify not only when the transaction was originated but also when subsequent processing was performed against the transaction in other segments of EFT systems.

---

[4] Norman Lyons, "Segregation of Functions in EFTS," *Journal of Accountancy,* (October, 1978), pp. 89–92.

- Transaction sequence numbers, which assist the system in controlling the totality of data processed.
- Terminal identification numbers, which permit subsequent determination of the remote terminal at which the transaction was entered.
- Merchant authorization and/or employee identification codes, which are particularly important in POS systems where the customer does not directly interface with the EFT system.

Access Controls

The American Institute of CPAs audit guide on internal controls in EDP systems states that

> Proper access controls will assist in the prevention or detection of deliberate or accidental errors caused by improper use or manipulation of data files, unauthorized or incorrect use of a computer program, and/or improper use of computer resources.[5]

These controls are important for EFT systems not only to provide accounting transaction controls but also to meet data privacy requirements. Access should be controlled in such a manner that one customer's data is not available to other customers and that one financial institution's data may not be accessed by other financial institutions, either deliberately or unintentionally.

As mentioned earlier, strict controls should be established over the stock of blank plastic cards, and, once embossed, these cards should be mailed only to existing customers. In "shared" EFT systems (where terminals are used by more than one financial institution), all participants in the system should exercise the same level of security and control over the plastic card stock. This is particularly important because all cards must be manufactured with the same physical characteristics to operate the shared terminals—with only minor cosmetic differences identifying the financial institution issuing the card.

For a transaction to be processed by an EFT system, the customer must input a separate PIN after insertion of the plastic card. This number assures that the card is used only by its authorized owner. Complex mathematical formulas are developed to assure accuracy of the PIN and its corresponding association with the account number embossed on the plastic card. Access to these encoding formulas should be strictly enforced, and, wherever possible, the formulas should be changed frequently.

Data and Procedural Controls

These controls are designed to provide for proper operation of the system on a day-to-day basis and to ensure the reliability of the data processed.

Because of the extremely short time frame from the initiation of transactions to their electronic authorization and the users' receipt of assets or services, the

---

[5] *The Auditor's Study and Evaluation of Internal Controls in EDP Systems* (New York: AICPA, 1977), p. 39.

responsibilities of an independent control group take on added importance as a detective control in EFT systems. The control group should have responsibility for monitoring both the integrity and totality of the transactions processed. In addition, this group should have responsibility for monitoring unsuccessful attempts at accessing the system. When a customer or user inserts the plastic card into the remote terminal, most EFT systems allow at least two attempts to enter correct PIN. Once the maximum number of attempts has been exhausted without success, the system, either through EFT software or through the terminal itself, ceases communication with the customer and may trigger mechanical action within the terminal to retain the plastic card. Careful monitoring of unsuccessful attempts at system access should alert management to the potential exposure of unauthorized use or malfeasance.

Many EFT systems will be implemented on a "shared" basis. In these shared systems, the agreements among all parties participating should be in writing and executed before the system is operational. These agreements have audit impact because they should provide a clear understanding of each party's responsibility for security and maintenance. In addition, these agreements should set forth fees to be charged for system transactions and should identify the parties who are liable for the consequences of errors or irregularities.

Contingency considerations, such as system backup and recovery, are important general controls in any EDP system. These backup, recovery and restore procedures are particularly important in EFT systems because of the real-time nature of such applications. Even with the best system design and hardware, systems will fail and adequate provisions must be established and tested to provide for both recovery from short-term failures and the ability to operate in an off-line mode in the event of prolonged outage.

General controls are designed to provide assurance that the environment in which the EDP application is processed is adequate to ensure timely and accurate processing. Weaknesses in these controls can have pervasive effects on the application controls affecting the EFT system itself.

The above discussion has attempted to illustrate some of the additional general control considerations required with the advent of EFT technology.

APPLICATION CONTROLS

Application controls apply to each specific EDP application rather than to the entire EDP environment. Their function, as defined in SAS no. 3, is "to provide reasonable assurance that the recording, processing, and reporting of data are properly performed."[6] These controls are typically categorized as

- Input controls.
- Processing controls.
- Output controls.

---

[6] SAS no. 3, par. 8.

Input Controls

The objective of input controls is to assure that all data is recorded correctly and not lost, added to or otherwise improperly changed.

The plastic card and PIN, when used together, currently provide the best means for assuring authorized input. To avoid the potential of theft or misappropriation through the mails, the plastic card and its associated PIN should be mailed separately to each customer.

The system should have access, at the time the transaction is entered, to a current file of lost and stolen cards. When the transaction is entered at the remote terminal, the system should first verify that the card presented at the terminal is not either lost or stolen. In addition, the system should permit only a limited number of attempts by the customer to enter the correct PIN before it discontinues any communications and advises the customer to contact a customer-service representative for assistance.

The system should also maintain a log of the number of valid accesses to a given account within a specific time period. This log could then be used to alert management of possible "overuse." This technique is similar to the approach adopted by many credit card systems in operation today. The system should also not permit large-dollar withdrawals from remote, unattended banking terminals.

To ensure that data is not lost, the system should have facilities to control both the totality of messages processed through the network (possibly by assigning unique transaction sequence numbers) and the totality of each message itself (possibly by counting and reconciling the number of characters transmitted in each message).

Processing Controls

These controls are designed to provide assurance that processing is performed only as intended. Some techniques used include

- Control totals.
- Limit and reasonableness checks.
- Run-to-run controls.

Each major component within the EFT system should maintain sufficient control totals so that a reconciliation is possible at the end of the day's operations. This balancing could include both transaction counts and dollar amounts maintained at the central computer facility, the independent switch and possibly even totals maintained by remote terminals themselves.

In addition to maintaining control as to the number of valid accesses to a given account, the system should have sufficient monitoring capability to scan transactions for unusual conditions or an unusual mix of transactions by terminal or merchant.

Output Controls

These controls are designed "to assure the accuracy of the processing result . . . and to assure that only authorized personnel receive the output."[7]

One output control technique in EFT systems might be the use of a transaction log file. At the end of the day's processing, this file, when processed with both the start-of-day master file and the end-of-day master file, could validate the accuracy of account posting and processing results.

Certainly, customers are still an important control element in any system. In EFT systems, they should receive a printed receipt for the completed transaction at the terminal. In addition, they should receive periodic and timely statements of account activity and should have the opportunity to challenge charges recorded against their accounts.

When an inquiry transaction is received regarding account status, the EFT system should limit the amount of information provided to that required to complete the proposed transaction. For example, in a check verification service, the retailer should receive an indication that the account is valid and has a balance sufficient to cover the check but should not receive the balance amount information. It may also be appropriate to restrict this type of inquiry transaction to only certain terminals. Thus, it would not be possible for a fraudulent user to query the system about the status of a particular account and then to process a withdrawal for the remaining balance (indicated by the inquiry)—all on the same terminal within a short time period.

SUMMARY

EFT systems blend many complex technological developments and many represent significant changes in payment systems within our economy. These changes may have a profound effect on both today's and tomorrow's auditor.

The profession is just embarking on in-depth research into audit procedures to deal with these EFT systems. The AICPA guidelines publication, *Audit Considerations in EFT Systems,* is a first step in this process.

Though the technology for EFT systems is available today, implementation has been slow because of proposed legislation, controversial litigation and considerable capital requirements. This situation provides one of the first opportunities for interaction by the accounting profession. Practitioners have the opportunity to learn how to deal with evolving systems as innovative audit procedures and advanced design and control techniques for assuring system auditability are developed.

---

[7] SAS no. 3, par. 8-c.

BIBLIOGRAPHY

American Institute of Certified Public Accountants. Statement on Auditing Standards no. 3, *The Effects of EDP on the Auditor's Study and Evaluation of Internal Control.* New York: AICPA, 1974.

American Institute of Certified Public Accountants. Audit and accounting guide, *The Auditor's Study and Evaluation of Internal Controls in EDP Systems.* New York: AICPA, 1977.

American Institute of Certified Public Accountants. Audit guide, *Audits of Service-Center Produced Records.* New York: AICPA, 1974.

American Institute of Certified Public Accountants. Computer services guidelines. *Audit Considerations in Electronic Funds Transfer Systems.* New York: AICPA, 1978.

Bank Administration Institute. *Security, Audit, and Control Considerations in the Design of Electronic Funds Transfer Systems.* Park Ridge, Illinois: BAI, 1977.

Systems Auditability: Friend or Foe?

WILLIAM E. PERRY
AND HENRY C. WARNER

Executive management, as well as regulatory agencies and the general public, have tended to rely increasingly on the audit community to help protect organizations against the hazards of inadequate control in electronic data processing systems. However, preliminary investigations into the problem revealed a dangerous gap: auditing and control procedures for EDP systems have failed to keep pace with the introduction of new technology and new concepts in EDP systems design.

It was these conditions that provided the impetus for conducting a comprehensive survey of the present status of EDP system auditability[1] and control. In addition to presenting the survey's principal findings and conclusions, this article will identify current trends in the audit of EDP and document what specific audit and control techniques now in use have proved to be of practical value.

Statements on Auditing Standards no. 3 and no. 9[2] have charged CPAs with addressing the problem of the effects of EDP on their evaluations of internal control and using the work of internal auditors. This article addresses those topics. It will explain how internal auditors audit computer-based applications. It will provide auditors with information on

---

[1] Auditability reflects the interrelationship between audit and control. The auditability of computer-based information systems refers to the features and characteristics needed to verify the adequacy of controls as well as to verify the accuracy and completeness of data processing results. Systems control pertains to the mechanisms within the total systems environment that ensure the accuracy and completeness of the computer-based information system and its output.

[2] Statement on Auditing Standards no. 3, *The Effects of EDP on the Auditor's Study and Evaluation of Internal Control* (New York: AICPA, December 1974), and Statement on Auditing Standards no. 9, *The Effects of an Internal Audit Function on the Scope of the Independent Auditor's Examination* (New York: AICPA, December 1975).

- The current state of the art of EDP auditing.
- The extent to which auditors should concern themselves with computing systems and operations.
- Internal control in organizations using data processing.
- The evolving role of the internal auditor in data processing.
- Computer audit techniques, both manual and computer assisted.
- An outlook for the future.

EDP AUDITING DILEMMA

The auditing profession has discussed the extent to which auditors should concern themselves with computing systems and computing operations. Auditors agree that the increasing use of computer technology in the processing of business data is having a significant evolutionary impact upon auditing.

Recent survey statistics[3] show that in 1966 more than 25,000 general-purpose computer systems were installed in the United States. In 1975, over 70,000 general-purpose computer systems were installed. One example of the growth of new technology in the computer field is data communications. Only 25 percent of the general-purpose computers installed in 1970 were equipped with data communications terminals. By 1975, 54 percent had terminals.

As new technology is successively introduced and applied, computer application systems and controls have become more complex. Consequently, as organizations become increasingly dependent on data processing, they also become more concerned about the continuing accuracy and completeness of data processing results. It is generally agreed that "the objectives and the essential characteristics of accounting control do not change with the method of data processing."[4] The implementation of such technology has, however, resulted in fundamental changes in the structure of computer application systems and controls. As a result, audit and control techniques appropriate to earlier business operations have, to some extent, become outmoded.

Beyond outlining the distinction between general and application controls presented here, it is not our purpose to discuss the relationship of the independent auditor and SAS no. 3. However, for those interested in a discussion of this type, a recent audit and accounting guide, *The Auditor's Study and Evaluation of Internal Control in EDP Systems,* prepared by the computer services executive committee of the AICPA, has been issued to provide the independent auditor with information on this subject.

---

[3] *Systems Auditability and Control: Executive Report, Audit Practices, Control Practices* (Altamonte Springs, Fla.: The Institute of Internal Auditors, April 1977).
[4] SAS no. 3, par. 10.

SAS no. 3 does distinguish between general controls and application controls to the extent that general controls relate to all EDP activities and application controls to specific tasks (see Figure 1).

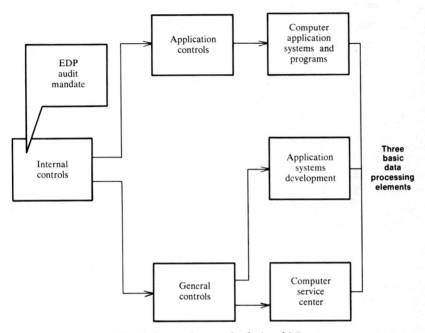

Fig. 1 *Internal control relationship*

The data processing function typically includes three basic elements of internal control:

• Computer application systems, which encompass manual procedures to originate and transmit input transactions to the data processing department; computer application programs that control the processing of transaction data, record maintenance and output report preparation; and procedures that guide computer service center personnel in the use of specific computer application programs and the handling of the associated input data and output reports.

• Computer service center operations, which encompass the facilities, equipment, personnel and general procedures that govern computer center operations, as opposed to procedures specific to individual application systems.

• Application systems development, which encompasses the personnel and general procedures governing the design, development, testing and implementation of the manual procedures and the computer application programs that make up computer application systems. This element also includes the modification and improvement of existing computer application programs. Some of the organizations interviewed during The Institute of Internal Auditors' SAC (*Systems Auditability and Control*) study reported that as much as two-thirds of their systems development work involved modifications and improvements to existing computer applications.

The responsibility for internal control tends to be fragmented. Internal controls governing the manual phases of transaction processing and recordkeeping tend to be the responsibility of line management in charge of specific organizational units. Users can be viewed as being responsible for establishing the requirements for controls within the computer processing phase of an application system. Data processing management typically is responsible for designing and implementing the controls governing automated phases of computer application systems and the controls governing other phases of data processing activities. In many situations, controls in these two areas reflect accounting and financial reporting control objectives. Unfortunately, controls are often established to meet the needs of various stages of manual and computer processing without being evaluated within the context of the total computer application system and its associated control objectives.

In the independent auditor's relationship with EDP systems, he must be concerned not only about his individual competency but also about the competency of others. This article discusses the addition of three powerful new allies to the independent auditor to assist in the performance of compliance and substantive tests in a highly structured computer-based information system:

- The internal auditor.
- Computer-assisted audit techniques.
- Control point identification.

THE STATE OF THE ART

In 1975 the Institute of Internal Auditors launched the SAC research project in an effort to improve internal auditing in a computerized environment. The field work was conducted by Stanford Research Institute (SRI) under a $500,000 grant by the International Business Machines Corporation.

The results of this study show that although data processing systems and internal audit techniques have been evolving, there has been little coordination between the two disciplines. From the standpoint of those managing the EDP facility, the internal auditors' mandate and their scope of activities are not clear. At the same time, internal auditors are faced with the task of investigating an environment in which most of them have only limited experience, knowledge and tools. Compounding these conditions is the fact that top management in many organizations has not been sufficiently informed to give adequate attention to the potential repercussions of inadequate EDP audit and control procedures.

One outcome of this study was the identification of a series of management actions designed to assure that computer-based information systems are developed with adequate controls, are auditable and do operate in a reliable manner. While it was not within the scope of this study to fix specific responsibility for these various management activities, Table 1 is indicative of the management concerns and the probable location of primary (P) and supporting (S) responsibility for each.

TABLE 1
INDICATED MANAGEMENT ACTIONS

| | Responsibility | | |
| | Executive management | Audit management | Data processing management |
Action			
Ensure that all management realize the importance of internal audit in data processing.	P	S	S
Issue a clearly defined internal audit mandate that specifies the responsibility of internal audit as it relates to all phases of data processing.	P	S	S
Clearly define the working relationship among users, internal auditors and the data processing department for the development and maintenance of computer-based information systems.	P	S	S
Encourage the development of new data processing control techniques and internal audit approaches to ensure the reliability of computer-based information systems.	P	S	S
Require the development of control guidelines.	P	S	S
Ensure that internal audit participates in the system development process.	P	S	S
Ensure the adequate preinstallation testing of computer-based information systems.	S	S	P
Ensure that periodic postinstallation verification takes place.	S	P	S
When auditing computer-based information systems, computer service center operations and system development, ensure that there are reviews of controls, tests to verify the controls and tests to verify the data.	S	P	S
Encourage data processing and internal audit to work together to achieve improved system audit and control capabilities.	P	S	S
Ensure that training programs are developed to provide the needed skills to audit data processing and also to reflect the internal audit discipline.	S	P	S
Upgrade the quality and quantity of EDP auditors. As a starting point, use individuals from the internal audit staff with a specific interest in data processing.	S	P	S
Add data processing personnel to the EDP audit staff for specialized data processing assistance.	S	P	S
Ensure that data processing, internal audit and external audit work together to develop required EDP audit tools and techniques.	P	S	S
Ensure that assessments of the internal audit function are performed jointly by internal audit and data processing.	P	S	S

P=primary.
S=supporting.

EVOLVING ROLE OF THE
INTERNAL AUDITOR IN DATA PROCESSING

SAS no. 9 describes the effects of an internal audit function on the scope of the independent auditor's examination. Paragraph 1 states that while the work of internal auditors cannot be substituted for the work of the independent auditor, the independent auditor should consider the procedures performed by internal auditors in determining the nature, timing and extent of his own audit procedures.

One area the independent auditor should consider to be the work of the internal auditor is in the evolving EDP audit specialty. The SAC study indicates that over 60 percent of the larger U.S. corporations now have internal EDP audit functions. Figure 2 shows the percentage of organizations that now have an EDP audit function and when that function was established.

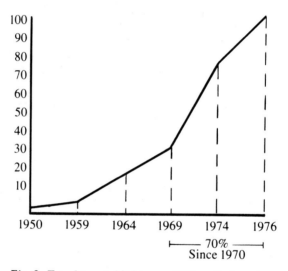

Fig. 2 *Trend in establishing an EDP audit function*

Note that 70 percent of the organizations that now have EDP audit functions instituted that function since 1970. Its development in larger organizations reflects greater reliance on data processing, increasingly complex management information systems and increasing reliance upon internal audit to verify the accuracy and completeness of data processing results.

INTERNAL AUDIT INDEPENDENCE

Internal auditors are becoming increasingly involved in evaluating internal controls relating to computer application systems. This is a result of their relatively independent perspective in reviewing internal controls in user areas as well as within data processing. It is important to note, however, that although the internal auditor may be used effectively in the review of internal controls and in making control recommendations, the responsibility for internal controls properly resides with data processing and the user groups responsible for the preparation and processing of transactions, recordkeeping and resulting management reports. The role of the internal auditors is to judge the adequacy of controls and to recommend control improvements. Responsibility to implement and maintain appropriate controls resides with data processing function and user organizations.

Audit committees, themselves relatively new, are increasingly interested in their organizations' data processing activities. Again, survey statistics indicate that in 70 percent of the large corporations with audit committees that committee has communicated with the organization's internal auditors regarding data processing activities.

In reviewing the competence and objectivity of internal auditors to perform such functions, paragraphs 6 and 7 of SAS no. 9 state that the independent auditor "should inquire about the qualifications of the internal audit staff" and that he "should consider the organizational level to which internal auditors report the results of their work."

Other factors that relate to internal audit independence and, therefore, the extent to which the independent auditor's scope may be affected include the following:

- Independence to plan and pursue audit work within the scope of the written mandate.
- Access to and support from top management for internal audit plans and programs.
- Support of the organization's external auditors.
- Access to consultants from outside the organization.
- Access to all phases of the organization including data processing.

COMPUTER-ASSISTED AUDIT TECHNIQUE

A number of challenges confront the auditor of computerized operations. Among them are

- A comparative invisibility of data, records and transactions.
- The centralization or aggregation of activities or transactions.
- The resequencing of the steps of traditional procedures.
- Integration of processing functions, which frequently has the side effect of eliminating formerly available audit trails.

- Creation of new applications in company operations.
- Supporting systems of far greater complexity than traditional manual operations.

Finally, it is worth noting that the modern company is frequently dependent on the operation of its computer systems for its ability to conduct business. This places a high priority on the auditing and control functions.

The recognition that computer technology is a source of problems and challenges to the auditor should not obscure the fact that the same computer technology can serve as a considerable aid to auditability and control.

The computer is not only a powerful device for accomplishing its intended tasks of computing, data communications, process control and so on; it is also an ideal instrument for keeping records and producing information about its own activities and the nature of its work. Such records, statistics and analyses about its own activities can often be compiled concurrently with the main tasks it performs. If this characteristic and these capabilities of the computer are deliberately exploited by the auditor, they can be very powerful and useful tools for this work.

The auditor should not overlook the "analysis power" of the computer when applied to the auditor's work. The existence and the availability of a computer may make it possible for the auditor to create computer programs designed to do major audit analyses that otherwise would have been performed manually (if at all).

Related to these features, but nevertheless significantly different, is the computer's potential capacity to support automated checks and controls. If internal auditors participate in the design of a major computing system, they can aid in creating provisions for automatic real-time monitoring and checking facilities which will be operative during routine operations on the system. Such automated facilities are important in on-line real-time systems.

The SAC study identified 28 practices used by internal auditors in performing their internal audit function. These practices included techniques for compliance and substantive testing plus practices for managing the function and participating in the development phase of data processing applications. Thirteen of these audit practices were found to be used in both the auditing of developments and modifications as well as the auditing of production systems. These 13 practices are listed in Table 2, together with a brief description of the practice and percentage of use information.

CONTROL POINT IDENTIFICATIONS

Transactions are the basic elements of business operations and consequently the primary subject matter of internal control. SAS no. 3, par. 25, states that the auditor's review "should be designed to provide an understanding of the flow of transactions through the accounting system. . . ." Because of the complexity of today's computer-based information systems, such an understanding of transaction flow is not easily attainable. One method of obtaining such an understanding is to examine data as it passes specific system control points.

TABLE 2
EDP AUDIT PRACTICES AND THEIR USE

EDP audit practice	Description of practice	Developments and modifications*	Production systems*
		Percentage of survey respondents that used each practice in the audit of	
Generalized audit software	A set of computer programs that have the capability to process computer data files under the control of input parameters supplied by the internal auditor.	12.5%	32.6%
Manual tracing and mapping routines	Manual analysis of program language and logic to determine patterns of usage.	22.9%	31.2%
Test data method (e.g., test-decking)	Verifies processing accuracy of computer application systems by executing these systems using specially prepared sets of input data designed to produce preestablished results.	27.1%	26.6%
Parallel operation	Use of one or more special computer programs to process "live" data through test programs.	32.2%	23.1%
Tagged transactions	Flagging transactions in "live" operations for later review.	12.0%	20.9%
Snapshot	Picture-taking of selected transactions through the flow of transactions.	10.0%	18.4%
Systems performance monitoring and analysis (e.g., SMF, SCERT)	A feature of the computer operating system software or a separate program that provides the means for gathering and recording information to be used for evaluating systems usage.	8.2%	15.8%
Program source code comparison	Comparison of two copies of a program made at different times to verify that program change and maintenance procedures are being followed correctly.	9.6%	14.5%
Control flowcharting	Technique provides the documentation necessary to explain the system of control.	8.3%	9.0%
Program object code comparison	Same as program source code comparison except the comparison is performed after program compilation.	4.7%	8.9%
Integrated test facility (mini or dummy company)	Uses auditor-developed fictitious or dummy entity within the framework of the regular application processing cycle.	4.2%	5.0%
Modeling (simulation)	A procedure to compare estimates of expected values to actual values to identify potentially important differences.	9.5%	7.6%
Automatic tracing and mapping routines	Computer analysis of source language and logic to determine if any program segments are not being utilized.	3.6%	3.9%
Other		6.5%	10.5%

* Percentages are based on actual responses to the SAC project mail survey, weighted to reflect the probable response distribution of all organizations in the sampling frame. The organizations in this sample represent the approximately 3,000 largest (nongovernment) U.S. organizations with computer systems.

The third standard of field work requires that "sufficient competent evidential matter . . . be obtained through inspection, observation, inquiries, and confirmations to afford a reasonable basis for an opinion regarding the financial statements under examination." Some important methods of determining where and how to gather evidence will include the use of client documentation—control documentation, system flowcharts, program flowcharts, program listings, etc.

A unique combination of such documentation is shown in Figure 3. As an example, control point 4 (access control) would include a definition such as a security application, which controls access to all applications within the total system and verifies that the operator is an authorized user of the system and that his personal profile of clearances includes the transaction he has requested. The important point being made here is not the method of control used, but the fact that the system has been analyzed and documented from a control perspective.

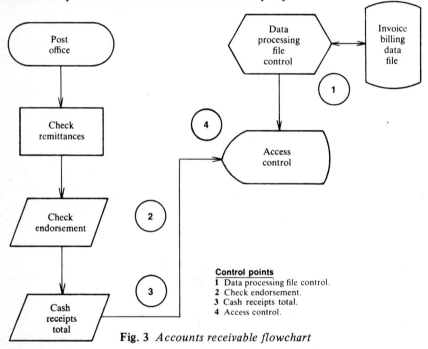

Control points
1 Data processing file control.
2 Check endorsement.
3 Cash receipts total.
4 Access control.

Fig. 3 *Accounts receivable flowchart*

While still not widely used, control documentation and the identification of specific system control points is now becoming recognized by auditors as well as many system designers as an essential element to computer system understanding.

SAC IMPACT

To date over 55,000 copies of individual SAC project reports have been distributed. This distribution included sending complete sets of the three reports (on executive, data processing and audit practices) to over 4,000 chief executive officers around the world. Initial report distribution began in May 1977. A number of chief executive officers, after having read the executive report, have asked their audit and data processing managers to initiate an assessment of their organizations' audit and control practices.

The General Accounting Office, already considered to be a leader in the computer audit field, reports that the SAC study has helped it in its continued development of computer audit capability by aiding it in structuring courses in computer reliability assessment. The GAO is also reviewing some of the computer audit techniques (i.e., those not currently used by the GAO) reported by SAC to determine where they can be used most effectively.

While it is much too early to determine the true impact of this EDP auditing research effort, it appears the SAC project has presented something useful to those primarily concerned with systems auditability and control. An important dialogue has started among executives, data processing managers and the auditors. It is anticipated that this dialogue should result in closer cooperation between auditors and data processing personnel. Such considerations were sadly lacking in the early years of computer systems development.

CONCLUSION

A major conclusion of this two-year study calls for top management to initiate periodic assessments of their organizations' audit and control programs pertaining to the data processing environment. CPAs will be asked to provide input to these periodic evaluations. It appears that the CPAs' answers may well be based on

- An evaluation of current audit and control practices and an assessment of data processing capabilities within the internal audit staff.

- An identification of likely future trends in the development of computer-based information systems and data processing technology.

- Formulation of programs to improve both the audit and the control capabilities in the data processing environment.

To accomplish these objectives CPAs will need to consider new factors such as the adequacy of control guidelines, the scope of internal audit activities, internal audit involvement in data processing and their competence to perform in this area.

AN OUTLOOK FOR THE FUTURE

The outlook is for a continuation of the trends that have characterized the growth of data processing in recent years: the automation of more business functions, an increasingly complex data processing environment and greater management reliance on computer-based information systems. Because audit and control capabilities have not kept pace with the expansion of data processing and the introduction of new technology, new data processing control techniques and audit approaches are needed to ensure the integrity of business information.

The IIA's study pointed to several conclusions that tend to lessen organizations' capability to control and audit computerized applications. Without additional efforts in this area, CPAs will need to undertake additional audit steps to ascertain the adequacy of internal controls. These study conclusions are as follows:

- As a result of the growth in complexity and use of computer-based information systems, needs exist for greater internal audit involvement relative to auditing in the data processing environment.

- There is an important need for EDP audit staff development because few internal audit staffs have enough data processing knowledge and experience to audit effectively in the data processing environment.

- Few current EDP audit tools and techniques meet the needs of the EDP auditors as they approach the task of verifying the accuracy and completeness of data processing activities and results. New tools and techniques are needed.

- Internal auditors must participate in the system development process to ensure that appropriate audit and control features are designed into new computer-based information systems.

CPAs can foster the role and capability of the internal audit function in the computerized business environment. This can be accomplished by including specific recommendations in their management letters that are supportive of an aggressive and organizationally independent internal audit function which is both skilled and involved in data processing.

CHAPTER 7

ACCOUNTING
APPLICATIONS

The readings included in this chapter bring together many of the relationships among accounting, computers, information systems, and other business functions that have been referred to in earlier chapters. Without the proper interactions between accounting and all of the other functions of the organization the effectiveness of the entire system will be reduced. While six readings cannot attempt to expose one to all accounting-related applications, these selected articles provide samples of the diversification in the systems area that are found in many modern organizations.

The first article, by Doppelt, "Down-to-Earth Marketing Information Systems," examines the primary system of most organizations—the system for selling their goods and services. Major trends in recent years have indicated the importance of developing specific marketing plans and measurements. As a member of the management services division of a large CPA firm, the author shares his experiences of working with many different types of marketing systems. He discusses the vital role that the accountant has in relation to the marketing information system and how he or she can work to improve the system. In his work the author has found that many marketing systems have been neglected over the years, and a major part of the article analyzes the reasons for such neglect. In putting the marketing information system back on a sound foundation several improvements are recommended. Because of the many necessary interfaces between marketing and the other organizational functions a list of basic data sources is given and discussed. The success of any concentrated effort to improve planning and control in the marketing system will depend on the support of top management and their involvement with other related areas such as accounting.

An area which has not received a large amount of attention but which is very important to many types of organizations is materials requirements planning (MRP). MRP is a formal type of inventory management system and Keegan, in "Some Second Reflections on MRP," discusses how it works and warns that it sometimes does not work. An MRP system can greatly help management reduce inventory levels and improve the cost accounting system as it relates to inventories. The author discusses how the concept was developed and the inputs necessary for proper operations. MRP is an application which should be familiar to all accountants because of its flexible utilization, and any organization which has inventory might be a candidate for MRP. However, as Keegan is quick to point out, MRP can be ineffective if it is not properly implemented and monitored.

In connection with the Keegan article, "Aiding Decision Makers with a Generalized Data Base Management System: An Application to Inventory Management," by Bonczek et al, provides follow-up on MRP within the context of data base management systems. This reading examines the attributes of data base management systems as related to decision making and inventory management. The authors elaborate on the fundamental features of the data base structure and discuss the two primary aspects of data bases. Following this discussion they examine the different varieties of data base systems. Examples drawn from actual experience in MRP are used to illustrate the concepts and potential benefits of generalized data base systems.

Although the authors discuss inventory management, the major contribution made by the article is the well-organized presentation of data base management systems concepts, using inventory as the basic example throughout. The authors view data base systems as a tool of managerial decision making with inventory management simply being one use of the tool.

A topic that all accountants should be familiar with is that of computerized general ledger systems. In "Developing a Computerized General Ledger System," Lubas provides the reader with the basics of how such a system works. He elaborates on the input requirements, output reports, data collection, and controls. By use of a flowchart he illustrates the relationships of the ledgers and journals to the information system. The two primary advantages to such a system are standardization and availability of accounting information. As a result of these advantages the related decision-making activities should be improved through timeliness and easy data access.

Closely related to the general ledger system is the financial reporting system. Hill and Rutherford, in "Computerized Financial Data Reporting System," explain the financial reporting system of a large corporation. The system is defined as one that can capture and manipulate data into a data base and then perform data analysis for the various organizational areas. The key to the success of the system is its flexibility, which is discussed by the authors. For the accountant the main advantage to such a system is that it enables him or her to concentrate on report analysis rather than report generation.

The last article included in this chapter was selected to illustrate a specific industry application. Hancock, in "An Approach to Hospital Data Processing Development," describes the needs for computers in the nonmedical activities of hospitals. While the health care field is one of the largest of the nation's industries, it has been very slow in developing computerized systems. The author discusses the need for a comprehensive information system and the requirements for implementing such a system in a hospital. The described system is well developed and most of the system needs of a hospital could be met with such a system.

Although it is necessary to learn the basic techniques of system design and the applications of computer systems, one cannot fully grasp the problems nor appreciate the advantages until actual systems work is undertaken. The next two chapters provide these opportunities with cases based on actual situations.

Down-to-Earth Marketing Information Systems

NEIL DOPPELT

As the cost-price squeeze continues to handicap many companies, increasing attention is being paid, not only to every effort to cut costs but also to every possible way to increase sales and profits. This has focused attention on marketing efforts—and marketing management—as it has never been directed before.

The accountant, whether he is internal or external, has a vital role to play in this increasing attention to marketing activities.

This concentration, while it is rather belated in some companies, is only an acceleration of trends that have been visible for some time.

Actions to improve the management of marketing activities and to increase senior management's understanding of marketing functions have been prompted by three key factors:

1. More companies are adopting a definition of marketing operations that goes beyond the simple mechanics of selling products to consumers. This "marketing concept" begins when the company interprets the consumer's needs and desires, both quantitatively and qualitatively; follows through with all the business activities involved in the flow of goods and services from producer to consumer; and ends with those services necessary to aid the consumer in getting the expected utility from the products he has purchased. In order to adopt the marketing concept in deed as well as word, companies must approach the market place with respect and flexibility, rather than trying to succeed with brute force.

2. Investments in advertising, sales promotion, market research, salesmen, and new product development are increasing. Possible profit improvements by making more effective use of marketing resources are often much larger than the prospects of achieving significant product cost reductions.

3. The outputs of the marketing department are critical to orderly and efficient operations throughout the organization. Marketing forecasts and budgets become the basis for production schedules, cash flow projections, and profit plans. Conversely, lack of detail, accuracy, or timeliness in marketing planning can impair the profit potential for products or services that are otherwise strong and competitive.

PAST NEGLECT–WHY?

If marketing is so important, why do many companies find themselves with fragmented or nonexistent planning and control systems in this area? Several reasons can be pinpointed:

• Partially by design and partially by accident, marketing often becomes isolated from other operating departments. Senior executives accustomed to dealing with straightforward information about machine hours, inventory turns, and sales volume are reluctant to dig into the supposedly less precise areas of marketing decisions. In some cases marketing managers themselves have contributed to this situation by overemphasizing subjective judgment as the basis for their strategies—even though most marketing executives are at least as fact-oriented as their counterparts in other functions.

• Marketing information needs have usually been satisfied on a piecemeal basis by using data sources and reports really designed for other management purposes, such as financial reporting, production control, and accounting. This "hand-me-down" method sometimes looks like an economical way to solve continuing marketing information problems. Basic information needs go unfulfilled, however, since important aspects of customer identification, cost allocations, and external market conditions cannot be captured unless special provisions are made for doing so.

• EDP techniques have been successfully applied first where dollar savings or operating advantages have been easily recognized; accounting, inventory control, order entry, and production scheduling usually get top priority. The benefits of better information for the marketing function are difficult to quantify in dollars and cents.

• The concepts behind a marketing information system may be misinterpreted by senior executives. At one extreme, they may expect such systems to deliver the answers to the most difficult kinds of questions—the effectiveness of advertising and promotion, for example. At the other extreme, the systems approach may be dismissed as just another sales reporting scheme. Neither concept is correct. As is detailed in this article, many problems can be solved or their current solutions improved upon with better marketing information. Imperfect answers to tough questions are usually better than no answers at all, and sales reporting is only one element of a basic system.

When the pressures to develop effective systems for marketing become great enough, these historical problems succumb to good management judgment and a "marketing information system" begins to sound like the right answer.

The primary objective of a marketing information system is to improve marketing management's ability to identify profitable sales opportunities, to make the most effective use of sales force personnel, to allocate advertising and sales promotion expenditures efficiently, and to react quickly and correctly to changes in market conditions. The "system" itself can be broadly defined as an organized set of procedures, information-handling systems, and reporting techniques designed to provide the information needed to plan and control marketing activities.

These definitions of objectives and system content are necessarily long because a substantial amount of information is required to manage the marketing function and there are many different kinds of tasks carried out within that function. Regardless of the eventual complexity of a marketing information system, the guiding philosophy is simple: Better information helps capable men do a better job.

A good problem solver usually has the answer sketched out in his mind before he sets to work. The same logic applies to the design of a system to meet the information needs of marketing management—the most important information needs should be anticipated before the first interview is scheduled. The following list is offered as a guide to the kinds of information marketing managers want, whether the products involved are building materials, breadsticks, or bonds:

CUSTOMER INFORMATION

- Where is volume concentrated?
- Who are specific major customers, both present and potential?
- What are their needs for products?
- What are their needs for sales coverage and service?
- What order activity and volume are expected?
- What are the differences in profitability between types and classes of customers?
- Where is performance significantly short of expectations?

PRODUCT INFORMATION

- What are the relative profitabilities of products at the gross margin level? After direct marketing expenses?
- Which elements of variable product cost are influenced by marketing decisions? What is the current cost structure?
- Which products tend to respond most favorably to sales promotion at the wholesale, retail, and consumer levels?
- What are the major advantages and disadvantages of current products in the eyes of consumers, relative to competitive products?
- What factors have the greatest influence on sales volume?
- What is the status of volume and profitability relative to objectives?

SALES FORCE INFORMATION

- What area and which customers are assigned?

- What call activity is required, both for protection of present volume and development of new business?

- Do current compensation systems motivate the desired mix of salesmen's activity?

- What is current performance relative to objectives?

This list can be expanded, of course, into the detailed questions concerning the "right" strategies for pricing, advertising, sales promotion, and new product development. However, information systems do not make strategic decisions—managers do, by the best use of their experience and the information and analytical tools available to them.

A basic marketing information system should be designed to provide most or all of the customer/product/sales force information listed above. Focusing on the *decisions* each manager must make as part of his normal job responsibility helps to define what his information requirements are and how his outputs of plans and forecasts can best be integrated into the information system.

Like any other systems development project, the design and installation of a marketing information system must be undertaken with care and organized effort. A good first step is to charter a temporary Task Force, including knowledgeable men from marketing, accounting, and data processing. These individuals, assigned full time for the duration of the project, can provide the broad and intensive effort required to produce a conceptual systems design for all aspects of the system and to participate in the implementation of the design. The Task Force approach helps to avoid the disappointment of sporadic, stop-and-start marketing systems projects.

VARIED SKILLS REQUIRED

Each member of the Task Force can make important contributions to the project. The marketing representatives (there could be more than one) should have overall responsibility for the successful completion of the project. The system will be designed, after all, to meet the needs that they identify and interpret. The accounting representative's skills will be needed because accounting systems in particular are likely to require revision in order to accommodate marketing information needs. The data processing man should participate in the planning of changes in data collection and reporting systems, as well as in their implementation. Given the flexibility and capacity of current electronic data processing techniques (if they are required) and the skills available to design manual systems, the output of the Task Force should be in agreement with user needs.

The users are, of course, marketing managers with a wide variety of responsibilities and outputs, as is illustrated in Exhibit 1. These managers are charged with preparing plans covering sales volume, advertising and promotion programs, customer service, and sales force operations. Each of these plans and associated budgets becomes integrated into a marketing plan (product emphasis) and a sales plan (customer or territory emphasis). Other functional areas, shown on the right of the exhibit, rely on the marketing department's outputs as the basis for their own schedules, projections, and objectives.

Exhibit 1

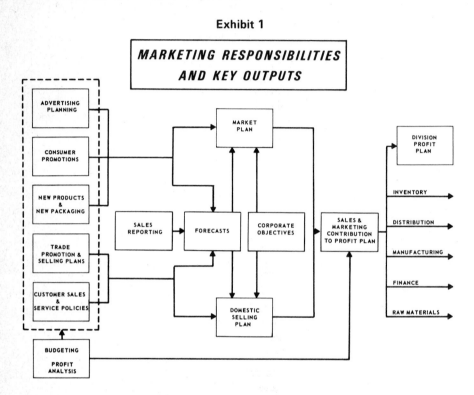

The varying tasks of marketing executives might suggest separate data files and reporting systems for each kind of planning and monitoring activity. Such a system would be inefficient, however, and a more economical approach would utilize basic data sources for a variety of purposes.

The interfaces between marketing and other functional areas can present problems if users on either side are forced to work with data formats and definitions that are cumbersome or unfamiliar, simply to avoid a data processing step. For example, marketing managers may be comfortable with "cases" while production scheduling personnel prefer to work in terms of "pounds." A common unit is not necessarily required for both marketing and production as long as the two different units can be defined in terms of one another and procedures installed to maintain compatibility.

As discussed previously, it is not necessary that each marketing manager have a separate information system. The problems (and opportunities) in marketing information systems design arise from the need to utilize available sources for a wide variety of information requirements. Basic data sources usually consist of the following:

- Invoices or other documents recording shipments of specific quantities to specific customers,
- Accounting ledgers recording the disposition of funds for specific purposes,
- Salesmen's call reports showing the frequency and nature of their activity,
- Reports of inventory status, product costs, and project status,
- Planning documents showing expected levels of activity for product volume, price levels, sales force activity, marketing expenditures, and projects, including statistical forecasts based on historical data,
- External data, collected and analyzed for the purpose of establishing priorities among products, customers, and areas.

The list of basic sources has several implications for marketing systems design work. First, most of the documents and records are designed for users in other functional areas such as accounting, production, and distribution. If they are to be utilized as part of a marketing information system, it will be necessary to modify the ways in which other users handle and distribute the basic sources. Second, plans are included as a source of information; they are also important outputs of the marketing management effort. Both aspects of the planning process are critical since information flows *within* as well as *between* functions. Finally, models and simulations are not included in the list; they represent "second generation" information systems projects for most companies. Managers can make better use of these sophisticated tools after they have fully explored the benefits of new procedures and reports.

The following example illustrates how basic data can be rearranged to provide marketing management with valuable information.

Case 1. A manufacturer of cosmetics utilized department stores, chain drug stores, and variety and specialty outlets for his channels of distribution. Each of his many products required substantial support in the form of special promotions, cooperative advertising arrangements with retailers, and partially or completely subsidized in-store sales personnel. As part of a larger effort to exercise more control of these expenditures, procedures were installed to identify expenses directly attributable to the different classes of retail outlets, in addition to product-by-product budget control. These procedures required subsidiary ledgers to accumulate marketing and selling expenses by class of trade. Exhibit 2 shows one of the resulting trade-class profitability reports.

Customer class profitability data had not been available before, and the new reports enabled management to pinpoint profit improvement opportunities. Exhibit 2 illustrates another key point about marketing information systems: They provide the tools for decision making, but not the decisions themselves. Based on the new cost and profit data, management could conclude that department store business was just not worth having, or it could conclude that the prestige and exposure afforded by department stores was worth the costs and low profit levels involved. Other alternatives involving changes in promotional programs could also be considered. The key to the decision remains the factual information provided by one element of the marketing information system.

Exhibit 2

TRADE CHANNEL PERFORMANCE

COSMETIC COMPANY

	% OF NET SALES	
	DRUG STORES	DEPARTMENT STORES
COST OF GOODS, FREIGHT, COMMISSION, INSURANCE	56%	53%
CO-OP ADVERTISING	3	10
SALESGIRL SALARY SUPPORT	0	21
COMMISSIONS IN OUTLETS	12	11
	71%	95%
CONTRIBUTION TO PROFIT & OVERHEAD	29%	5%

In contrast to other functional areas, marketing operations depend heavily on data originating *outside* the organization. External data from government publications, trade associations, business periodicals, and syndicated services provide marketing managers with indicators of market and product potential. In turn, these measures of potential establish the basis for assigning salesmen to particular geographic areas, industries, or customers; for allocating advertising and promotional dollars to specific buying groups or areas; and for forecasting volume performance.

Case 2. A small manufacturer of copper wire relied on his customers' buying expectations, as reported by his salesmen, to establish volume forecasts. Actual performance, however, was usually far short of forecast. By utilizing trade and government publications that reported on activity of his customers' customers, he was able to adjust his projections downward to compensate for the tendency of end-users of copper wire to place multiple orders as protection against stock-outs. It was found that these multiple orders were inflating the purchasing expectations of the manufacturer's direct customers.

The Task Force must identify the most appropriate sources for external data and pinpoint why, how, and by whom such information will be used. The availability of external data can have major effects on the organization and reporting of internal data. For example, geographic definitions used internally (such as districts and regions) may require realignment in order to provide direct comparability with external statistics dealing with countries or accepted industry trade area designations. Product groups also may have to be reorganized in order to match the categories found in trade literature or government publications. The tasks of rearranging and reclassifying internal data usually require extensive recoding and wholesale changes in key master files.

Planning is one of the most important elements of sound management—it provides the basis for evaluating performance and exercising control. Unfortunately, planning procedures that should be part of the most basic marketing information systems tend to get pushed aside in the rush to design and install new reporting systems. Planning systems are usually an afterthought even though the simplest report serves little purpose without some predetermined benchmark against which results can be measured.

Case 3. The sales manager in a textile company supervised the activities of some 80 salesmen and district managers. He found that continued hiring of salesmen did not seem to improve overall performance, even though his field managers insisted that more men were required to cover the market. A more formal and effective way to plan sales force activity was adopted, as shown in Exhibit 3. The new sales planning procedures called for:

- identifying key customers;
- defining minimum call frequencies by customer class;
- assigning salesmen to territories of approximately equal potential; and
- developing sales objectives for key customers and territories based on potential and past performance.

The sales plan in this example covers a six-month selling season and specifies call frequencies for each major and prospective account, as well as cumulative volume objectives. The summation of such territory plans becomes the basis for assigning salesmen and for checking total volume objectives against corporate goals. The sales manager must adjust the total of the individual account objectives downward to reflect probable account losses from season to season.

Exhibit 3

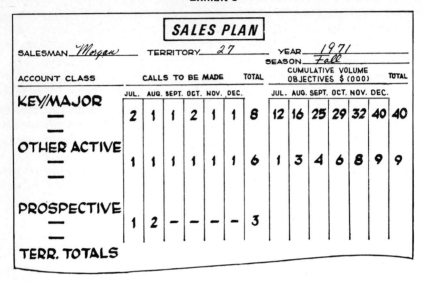

Controls over sales force activity were facilitated by regular reports like the one shown in Exhibit 4. The primary measures of performance—volume, call activity, price maintenance, and new account acquisition—are all monitored versus objectives using data from two basic sources, call reports and orders. A profit index is used to give the salesman an indicator of profit contribution without requiring the sales manager to distribute detailed profit margin data throughout his organization.

Exhibit 4

CALL REPORTS   ORDERS

PERFORMANCE REPORT

SALESMAN _Jones_   TERRITORY _14_   PERIOD THROUGH _March 31, 1971_

	SALES VOLUME			PROFIT INDEX		CALLS	
	PLAN	ACTUAL	LAST YR.	PLAN	ACTUAL	PLAN	ACTUAL
KEY/MAJOR							
—	7,200	8,100	6,500	100	104	4	4
ALL OTHER							
—							
NEW							
—							
• TOTAL	90,000	100,000	75,000	100	102	210	196
• COMMISSION	XXX			XXX		XXX	XXX

• ACCOUNTS	PLAN	ACTUAL
RETAINED	40	43
NEW	8	10

The Task Force responsible for marketing systems design needs to define the responsibilities, formats, and timing necessary to produce plans for product sales, sales force manpower levels and call frequency, promotion and advertising expenditures, and summary budgets and profit contribution plans for the entire marketing and sales function. Exhibit 5 illustrates the timing of plan preparation and the relationship between planning and reporting. In this example planning begins early in the year with the review and updating of long-range and new product plans. Other basic plans and forecasts are developed throughout the year, some sequentially and others concurrently. A "pause" in the fourth quarter provides for updating statistical forecasts with the most recent data available, prior to the final coordination and approval sessions necessary to establish objectives for the coming year. On the reporting side, progress is monitored against each plan on a monthly or quarterly basis.

Exhibit 5

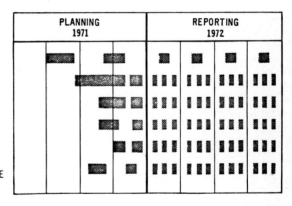

PLANNING TIME FRAME

Once a Task Force begins to ask marketing managers what their reporting needs are, requests are likely to come thick and fast. Some managers have useful personal systems that they would like incorporated into any new system. Others will see the project as an opportunity to satisfy their curiosity, but they have no specific uses in mind for the information they request. These requests must be evaluated in light of the overall marketing approach either in use or contemplated by management. Even with experienced assistance on board to help sort out priorities, the eventual list of needs can be very long. The volume of reports can be staggering when levels of detail and reporting frequencies are considered.

Part of this problem comes about from confusion between data and information. Detailed reports of every individual sales transaction and marketing expenditure provide raw data only and are often unusable due to their bulk. Summaries, groupings, and limited report distribution procedures are required to make reports readable and manageable. Exception reporting techniques would also simplify reporting, but few systems utilize exception reports to more than a minor extent. Managers are reluctant to work with less than complete information at the levels of detail most convenient for them.

Exhibit 6 illustrates a technique that parallels the exception report concept. The graph is based on the volume contribution of each account, arranged largest first. Thus in this example, the top 10 per cent of accounts contribute 74 per cent of total volume. The importance of these accounts warrants frequent, detailed reporting on their activity, although the reports themselves will be relatively "thin"; key accounts are usually less than 20 per cent of the total number of accounts. The small accounts contribute relatively little volume and thus detailed reports of their activity do not add much to a manager's understanding of current market conditions. Some systems are designed to summarize the smallest accounts (perhaps several thousand of them) into a single line for reporting purposes.

Exhibit 6

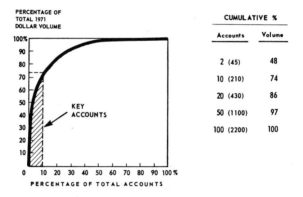

The "key account" approach works equally well with product line reporting, especially for those companies that manufacture a large number of product variations that are distinguished by minor differences in size, color, packaging material, or shipping quantity. As the costs of electronic data storage decrease and the time pressures on marketing managers increase, information systems tend to emphasize more storage and less reporting.

Various parts of this article have focused on the reasons for directing effort toward a marketing information system; the basic user needs, data sources, and design techniques for such a system; and some of the potential problems involved. The focus has been on developing a basic system that will reflect the marketing approach and key information needs of marketing management.

The success of any concentrated effort to improve planning and control in the marketing function will depend most heavily, however, on the active support of senior management. "Active support" means defining the scope of the project, assigning qualified personnel on a full-time basis, participating in regular progress report sessions, and recognizing that a broad and detailed examination of needs and alternatives must precede implementation.

Most companies, large and small, have yet to scratch the surface in this critical area. Although designing and installing even a "down-to-earth" marketing information system can involve some hard work, a quick look at the resources allocated to the marketing function should be sufficient incentive to get started.

Some Second Reflections on MRP

DANIEL P. KEEGAN

In the last several years, many organizations have attempted to install materials requirements planning (MRP) systems. Although some companies have been successful, many others have been disappointed by the results.

A careful analysis indicates that this has occurred for many reasons. Perhaps the single largest flaw, however, is not in the technique but in the zeal of its advocates. A historical perspective is worthwhile to understand this phenomenon.

For many years, professional literature was so crowded with new mathematical techniques supporting MRP's rival system, statistical inventory management, that the advocates of MRP had trouble being heard. Naturally they began to shout louder about the benefits of MRP—but they did not acknowledge any shortcomings.

Finally, through the efforts of organizations such as the American Production and Inventory Control Society and certain computer manufacturers, the advocates of the two systems were synthesized just short of open warfare. However, during the conceptually embryonic days of MRP, a great deal of useful dialog concerning its pitfalls was not evaluated in an objective manner. Consequently, many organizations embarked upon MRP installations without adequate forewarning that birthpangs could be expected.

DATA INTEGRITY

To understand what can go wrong with MRP, it is necessary only to recognize that this technique is completely dependent upon accurate, up-to-date information. MRP, in both a theoretical and practical sense, absolutely breaks down in the face of incorrect data.

Why is MRP so dependent upon correct data? MRP minimizes inventory investment by determining precise timings for replenishment, thus resulting in little, if any, safety stock. Since the objective of MRP is to "squeeze" out the excess inventory associated with less precise methods, such as re-order point techniques, there is no tolerance for error. Otherwise, manufacturing relives the familiar lost battle for "want of a nail." (In reality, lot sizing protects somewhat against error and even MRP systems have safety stock—although it may be called something else.) If the chain of accuracy is broken, an MRP system leaves the plant in a very vulnerable situation because there is no "excess" inventory to compensate for the planning error. The chain of accuracy also extends further than may be obvious on the surface. It includes:

The bill of material: MRP will suggest that the wrong items be manufactured or fail to indicate that some items are needed if the bills are incorrect.

The perpetual inventory records: MRP will incorrectly net manufacturing requirements if the perpetual inventory records do not correspond with actual stockroom balances. (If the system automatically prepares shop paperwork and picking lists, incorrect perpetual records are even more of a problem.)

Manufacturing (or purchasing) lead times: MRP will schedule production during the wrong time period if lead time information is incorrect. Furthermore, incorrect data concerning one part may have a domino effect on the schedules of other parts.

Scheduled receipts: MRP offsets requirements against expected receipts of detailed parts and purchased items. If these receipt timings are not current, the entire plan may be in jeopardy.

The main reason that MRP is so vulnerable to incorrect data, then, stems from the very nature of the technique. An MRP system is an *integrated* system relying upon bits of data from various information sources, analyzed and processed algorithmetically (i.e., in a well-defined manner) based upon the assumption that the data is correct.

One could reasonably ask, "Doesn't every computer system rely on correct data? Isn't the case for correct data in MRP overstated?" Of course, the answer to the first question is yes, but MRP requires even higher standards of data integrity. Contrast MRP to payroll, general ledger accounting, sales analysis, or other types of financial systems. Although the answer really depends upon the actual scope of these systems and what they have been designed to accomplish, generally these are transaction processing systems which indirectly affect the planning functions of management. MRP, on the other hand, is an analytical system which is executed primarily to enhance planning. In the former case, while there may be some consternation if an error is found, corrections can be made and future operations are not especially affected. In the case of MRP, however, errors have an immediate and direct bearing on the future.

PLANNING FEEDBACK

A second area in which materials requirements planning systems seem to have broken down centers around the tracking of work in process inventory. Most MRP implementation plans call for building of the item master file (perpetual records) and the product structure file (bill of materials) as first installation steps. Such an approach is very logical, particularly if the plan anticipates the need for keeping the perpetual records accurate after they are first established. Unfortunately, however, the amount of time required to build these data bases is often underestimated and there is the tendency to push forward into other MRP elements too soon. The next usual step is to record scheduled receipts; and then to proceed in generating materials plans.

Scheduled receipts, though, are rarely ever received on schedule. A necessary ingredient for planning is feedback and control. Without some mechanism for adjustments, the materials plan will continue to be based upon previous periods' scheduled receipts, while the factory is undoing this plan operation by operation. For most companies, additional attention to the feedback mechanism is warranted; it is necessary to track items in production and adjust the timings of scheduled receipts accordingly.

To establish the timings of manufactured-parts scheduled receipts and monitor actual results, two additional data bases must be established. The first is the so-called standard routings file, which contains each operational step that the item must complete as well as the time required to begin processing and complete the operation. The second contains the same data but is created when a specific manufacturing order is placed for the item. This file also serves as a repository for actual information concerning the current status of the order and is used for control and feedback. Equivalent information is needed for purchased items. Once these files of data have been created and feedback mechanisms established, the materials plan can be adjusted based upon the actual arrival of scheduled receipts or management action can be forthcoming to keep work in process on schedule.

Until very recently the importance of work in process tracking was not emphasized by MRP literature. Therefore, in many cases, an organization's MRP system was vulnerable to plans based upon inadequate feedback. This deficiency is particularly apparent in companies with long manufacturing processes.

MANUFACTURING ACCOUNTING

In the evaluation of MRP thinking, there has been a tendency to exclude the financial aspects of inventory management from professional literature. In fact, there seems to be a commonly held view that if an organization sets out to enhance manufacturing control and cost accounting at the same time, neither effort will be very successful. This attitude is unfortunate for two reasons:

- MRP systems most often fail for lack of data integrity—the very perspective that accounting invariably brings to any system development project.
- MRP systems unlock the information which not only enhances manufacturing planning and control but also makes practical some very advanced concepts of cost accounting.

Nonetheless, there is some truth to the prevalent attitude regarding manufacturing control and cost accounting. It is not that the objectives are irreconcilable—these two subjects are different sides of the same coin—it is that an organization can absorb change only in the right dosage and at the right time. In other words, an organization should not set out to do too much.

On balance, however, MRP system development projects can be enhanced if cost accounting requirements are identified as part of conceptual design. In such a case, it will be seen that the materials control systems provide information needed for product cost buildups, stockroom inventory valuation, purchase price variance and analysis, work in process valuation and analysis, engineering change cost analysis, labor efficiency monitoring, and overhead rate development and monitoring.

Since several years may be required to develop and install a materials requirements planning system, it is important to identify the cost accounting implications of additional information sources in the early stages of the system life cycle. In this way, system adjustments to accommodate accounting needs can be made before programming commences. All too often, the MRP system development effort is disrupted because cost accounting opportunities present themselves as afterthoughts.

What is often diagnosed as a deficiency in the MRP system may actually be a deficiency in accounting for inventory, caused by accounting concepts which are obsolete in the face of revised techniques of materials management. Such a situation often occurs in a job shop environment where, previous to MRP, purchased material was charged directly to a job. With MRP, more precise purchasing and ordering becomes possible, but material will most likely be issued from stock. If an actual cost system were possible prior to MRP, a standard cost system would be called for after MRP.

These are the types of cost accounting considerations which should be addressed along with the new MRP system.

MRP: WHAT SHOULD BE DONE?

Today, almost every corporation has either installed an MRP system or is in the process of such an installation. MRP can enhance management planning and control, resulting in reduced inventory levels. Before committing itself to a plan of action oriented toward implementing such a system, however, management should be aware that MRP is dependent upon very accurate underlying data and a work-in-process tracking and feedback mechanism. MRP also unlocks new opportunities to improve cost accounting and some thinking about this subject should take place concurrently with MRP conceptual design.

There is a much higher chance that an organization will not be disappointed with its materials control system if it recognizes that:

- *MRP will not cure acne:* Be skeptical of those who will oversell the concept.

- *MRP, absolutely, breaks down in the face of incorrect data:* Data integrity shortcuts will result in situations which are worse than no MRP system.
- *MRP becomes ineffective without feedback:* Work in process tracking (and purchased item tracking) brings reality to the planning process.
- *MRP unlocks the door to effective manufacturing accounting.*

THE EVOLUTION OF MRP AND
OTHER MANAGEMENT INVENTORY SYSTEMS

Work completed two or three decades ago in operations research resulted in some well developed techniques for controlling inventory levels. These techniques dealt with such important aspects of inventory management as when to replenish inventory and how much to order.

The re-order point has been reached when the stock is at a level equal to that which will be needed during the time to replenish it. The amount to be ordered equals a quantity that best balances the cost of holding inventory with the cost of its replenishment. Other techniques were put forward as to the amount of stock required to compensate for variation in usage and variations in replenishment timing. The theoretical purpose was to maintain an acceptable level of customer service without having an infinite amount of inventory in stock.

Often the body of knowledge that served as a basis for such techniques was referred to as statistical (or scientific) inventory management because much of the underlying theory was based upon mathematics, especially statistics.

In application, statistical inventory management (let's call it SIM for brevity's sake) met with mixed results. The economics of "the cost of holding" versus "the cost of replenishment" was very difficult to measure and the notions of service levels or stockout costs became almost impossible to define. Nevertheless, even today these concepts result in fairly well balanced, low cost inventory programs when applied to certain classes of inventory (such as wholesalers').

But when SIM was applied to manufacturing inventories, results often were much less satisfactory. In such cases, other techniques such as MRP will work better.

Enter MRP

Unfortunately for the proponents of SIM, manufacturing inventories simply do not fit within its concepts of demand/replenishment. Although cases of tomato juice stocked by a wholesaler may be shipped to retail stores in a fairly stable manner (say, an average of 50 cases per week), the demand for subcomponents of a complex manufactured product is anything but stable—even if the end product is shipped at a fairly uniform rate. Because raw materials become machined into detailed parts, and detailed parts are combined into sub-assemblies, and sub-assemblies are configured into higher level sub-assemblies, and all these activities take place within lot size constraints, the demand for raw materials, parts, and sub-assemblies appears to be very erratic—not uniform at all. In such a case, which is typical of manufacturing inventories, SIM theory (and practice) falls apart.

A very important breakthrough in thinking came about when the nature of "independent" versus "dependent" demand was explicitly defined. The demand for tomato juice may be independent of factors other than the market; however, the demand for detailed parts is *wholly dependent* upon decisions to complete a number of sub-assemblies. Therefore, in theory (and only in theory), the reorder time for detailed parts can be determined exactly by knowing the number of sub-assemblies which will be required, and there is no need to maintain a safety stock of these items. In such a case, the investment in manufacturing inventories can be minimized.

Stripped to its essentials, MRP is simple counting. First, count the number of items to be shipped, determining the number of sub-assemblies; explode these sub-assemblies into the number of parts, and translate this amount into demand for raw materials. MRP has the added benefit that this technique is much less dependent upon stability of demand. Within some fairly wide latitude, MRP well accommodates rapidly increasing or decreasing demand for final products. (SIM techniques react poorly to such conditions unless helped by large doses of management judgment.)

The Computer

Counting of manufacturing requirements has existed for many years. In fact, when applied to manufacturing companies, SIM often replaced large numbers of production schedulers who were manually developing materials plans. Nevertheless, MRP is a by-product of the computer era. Developing an effective material plan is actually very difficult, requiring frequent references to large files of data, a facility for synthesizing many pieces of information, and extreme accuracy. In other words, MRP takes a computer that is programmed as follows:

- Start with known requirements for end products, spare parts, and management's plans for increasing or reducing the number of end products in inventory.

- Determine the amount of stock which is on hand and in production and reduce these requirements accordingly.

- Determine the sub-assemblies which will be required by referencing the bill of material. Net these requirements by what is on hand and what is in production.

- Determine the time required to complete these assemblies, offset sub-assembly requirements by this time factor.

- Determine lot sizes in accordance with the rules specified for the item.

- Go to the next level of the bill. . . . repeat,

- and the next,

- and the next.

- Finish with raw materials, still netting requirements against on-hand and on-order. Determine raw material lead times and denote requirements in the correct time frame.

- Prepare a report for management review indicating material shortages by time frame: suggest appropriate lot sizes (. . . or . . . prepare shop orders and purchase orders).

While simple in concept, MRP, because of the various types of data which must be analyzed and processed, may actually strain the capability of a very powerful computer. Recently, revised techniques have been developed for modifying the plan once established. These techniques offer promise in reducing computer processing time but they do not directly address some of the more fundamental problems of MRP.

Aiding Decision Makers with a Generalized Data Base Management System: An Application to Inventory Management

ROBERT H. BONCZEK, CLYDE W. HOLSAPPLE
AND ANDREW B. WHINSTON

INTRODUCTION

Management is the art and science of deciding how to coordinate human and material resources subject to some set of objectives and constraints. Some of these decision problems are structured and capable of being resolved almost automatically; other problems are of the semistructured or unstructured variety. This lack of structure typifies complex, non-routine problems that are subject to conflicting interests and require judgment (i.e., qualitative inputs), and for which there is a paucity or disorganization of information. Efforts to resolve such problems are usually exploratory in nature, such that each discovery often suggests unforeseen factors that also deserve exploration. Hence the problem may be viewed as undergoing a series of redefinitions or refinements.

The exploratory activity is essentially the process of interrogating a data base. The way in which the data are organized and the available data manipulation methods have definite implications for managerial performance. Not only are data values themselves important, but the relationships among data values of various types are also indispensable information. The data base must be organized such that all pertinent relationships are captured, no matter how intricate they may be. This by itself is insufficient, for there must also exist a facile mechanism for extracting both standard and non-standard configurations of data values for purposes of display or input to application programs. In the exploratory activity, many of the types of reports desired are not standard, and they change rapidly; delays (e.g., writing programs to produce each newly desired report) certainly detract from the exploratory process. Thus it is imperative that we address two related issues. The first involves a facility for data organization that can accommodate complex relationships in an integrated data structure; that is, a single structure capable of supporting the data needs of different decision makers. The second issue concerns the way in which the user of a data base interfaces with that data base and with relevant application programs, so that both structured and unstructured decision processes are supported.

In this presentation, we discuss a generalized data base management system in terms of the aforementioned considerations. This generalized system, GPLAN (Generalized Planning System), has been implemented with a high-level query capability which allows it to be utilized by those who are unfamiliar with computer programming languages. GPLAN is generalized in the sense that it supports the information and analysis needs of decision makers regardless of their application areas. In order to illustrate the data base concepts and techniques involved (as well as their practical utility), we draw an example from the application area of inventory management. Since inventory management is an activity that pervades the entire production planning and control process, it impacts on other functional areas of management. Data related to inventory management is therefore subject to integration with data required for activities such as sales forecasting, job shop scheduling, accounting, etc. Specifically, we examine the information processing requirements for material requirements planning because of its broad applicability and its significance in the inventory management field. A requirements planning algorithm is itself a highly structured aspect of inventory management. The information needed to support this algorithm may be used to support other formal analyses and various unstructured lines of inquiry. The latter is useful in handling non-routine or exceptional situations not covered by the formal analyses. Exploratory interrogation of an integrated data base allows us to discern the relationships between data pertaining to various functional areas.

Our prime purpose is that of portraying the method and utility of a general tool of managerial decision making. We trust that the inventory management example is suggestive of the way in which this tool can be utilized in other applications, be they limited in scope or integrated, specialized or general, structured or unstructured in nature. The presentation commences with a cursory review of requirements planning concepts in order to establish the terminology used in ensuing examples of data structure and manipulation. It must be emphasized that although we use the example of requirements planning, the data base techniques presented are applicable to a host of operations problems such as job shop scheduling, PERT, queuing problems, transportation problems, etc. Given this background, there follows a description of the fundamental features of data base structure and a classification of the varieties of data base structures. Finally, there is an examination of the power of generalized network structures and of a query system interface based thereon, with respect to supporting structured and unstructured decision processes. That is, the query system is a single mechanism with which the non-programming user can both request the execution of formal analyses and engage in exploratory information retrieval.

MATERIAL REQUIREMENTS PLANNING

A brief outline of some of the basic concepts involved in material requirements planning (MRP) is presented in order to establish the terminology of this paper. Material requirements planning is a method of inventory management that is especially applicable in situations where inventory items are demand dependent. That is, the inventory consist largely of components that are used in the construction of other inventory items that themselves may be components needed for the assembly of still other items carried in inventory. Given a particular item and projections of the units of that item that are needed in each time period within some planning horizon, a bill of materials allows us to deduce the number of each of its components needed in each time period. Depending upon the order-size policy (e.g., lot-for-lot, EOQ, etc.), the scheduled receipts for each component at the beginning of each period follow directly, as do the corresponding expected units on hand at the end of each period. Furthermore, the lead time required for procurement of a component (along with the above information) implies the order size of the component for each time period. Since each component may itself be composed of other components, we can follow the same procedure to ascertain the gross requirements, expected inventory on hand, scheduled receipts and planned order releases for each of its constituents in each time period.

The procedure is used iteratively, commencing with final products or component modules and their associated demand forecasts (called master schedules) and culminating with raw materials requirements. Thus the master schedules are "exploded" through increasingly detailed levels of resolution, generating time-phased material requirements plans at each level. These material requirements in turn have important implications for capacity and manpower requirements. Another significant point is that the same component may be used in the construction of many other components. In some applications, it may occur that final products are primarily custom-made, very numerous and not amenable to demand forecasts; in this case, it is impractical to deal with bills of material of final products for purposes of material requirements planning. Instead, MRP analysis is predicated upon master schedules and bills of material for modules that, in their various combinations, can be used to assemble a relatively large number of final products [8]. In response to a specific customer request (which may perhaps never be repeated), pertinent modules are combined in order to generate the bill of material for this product.

FUNDAMENTAL FEATURES OF DATA BASE STRUCTURE

Within the present scope, a data base is considered to have two aspects: a logical structure (or schema) and a collection of data values organized on the basis of this structure. The schema serves as a blueprint that specifies not only the pattern of data base architecture, but also the types of data values that may be used to build the data base. All data base structures can be described in terms of three fundamental features: data item types, record types, and sets. The structure is composed of various data item types that are related to each other through the mediums of record types and sets. Each data item type is identified by name and refers to a distinct kind of data. For example, COMPONENT-NAME is a data item type that refers to a particular collection of data values (e.g., "BOLT," "SCREW," "ROTOR," "HOUSING," etc.) that are names of components. Each data value associated with a given data item type is said to be a data item occurrence of that type; "BOLT" is a data item occurrence of COMPONENT-NAME.

There are two ways in which data item types may be related to each other: aggregation and association. A record type is an aggregation of data item types. For example, the record type COMPONENT may be composed of data item types COMPONENT-NAME, COMPONENT-ID, QUANTITY-ON-HAND, QUANTITY-ON-ORDER; and a record occurrence of COMPONENT consists of the item occurrences "BOLT," "B1385," "239," "600." In Figure 1a, a record type is indicated by a rectangle enclosing the names of its data item types. Association is accomplished by means of defining sets. In order to avoid confusion, we note that the concept of a set [4] [11], as used here, is unrelated to the mathematical notion of a "set." A set is defined in terms of an owner record type and a member record type such that there is a one-to-many relationship between owner and member occurrences. In other words, there are many occurrences of the member record type associated with each occurrence of the owner record type; for a given set, however, a particular member occurrence may be associated with no more than one occurrence of the owner record type. In Figure 1b for instance, SET1 indicates that there may be several STATUS occurrences associated with each COMPONENT occurrence; the occurrence of COMPONENT denoted by the COMPONENT-ID "B1385" may own these three STATUS occurrences: "WEEK1," "239," "600"; "WEEK2," "153," "500"; "WEEK3," "37," "550." This occurrence structure is portrayed in Figure 1c. Rectangles with rounded corners are used to indicate record occurrences of the type shown in the right margin. In this example there is one occurrence of COMPONENT and three occurrences of STATUS. These occurrences are associated by SET1 in the manner shown; an arrow between two record occurrences means that they are associated with one another through the set name appearing in the right margin opposite from the arrow. The arrow points from the owner occurrence to the member occurrence.

Not only does a set furnish information about the relation among owner and member record types, but it also allows the member occurrences associated with an owner occurrence to be logically ordered according to some criterion (e.g., LIFO, FIFO, sorted according to the values of some data item type contained in the member record type, etc.). For example, member occurrences of SET1 may be ordered in an ascending manner based on the values of their data item type WEEK.

Figures 1a and 1b depict alternative methods of organizing the same four data item types. The method of aggregation requires that an occurrence of one data item type has a strictly one-to-one relation with an occurrence of another item type. Hence, the data base having the structure of Figure 1a must contain redundant data values for COMPONENT-NAME and COMPONENT-ID in order to accommodate the expected status for more than a single time period. Using the previous example, we would have the following three occurrences of the record-type COMPONENT (as shown in Figure 1a):

"BOLT," "B1385," "239," "600"

"BOLT," "B1385," "153," "500"

"BOLT," "B1385," "37," "550"

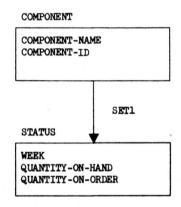

COMPONENT

| COMPONENT-NAME |
| COMPONENT-ID |
| QUANTITY-ON-HAND |
| QUANTITY-ON-ORDER |

a. The record type COMPONENT

COMPONENT

| COMPONENT-NAME |
| COMPONENT-ID |

SET1

STATUS

| WEEK |
| QUANTITY-ON-HAND |
| QUANTITY-ON-ORDER |

b. Association of item types via a set relation

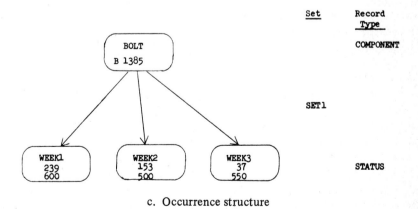

c. Occurrence structure

Fig. 1 *Structural features of a data base*

The ordering of these record occurrences with respect to a set may be used to indicate time periods. In contrast, utilization of the data structure illustrated in Figure 1b requires only one occurrence of the data value "BOLT" and one occurrence of the data value "B1385." For large data bases, the issue of redundancy is important, not only with regard to storage considerations, but also from the standpoint of maintaining data base consistency when changes in data values are made. When a data value is to be modified, one must be certain that all occurrences of it within the data base undergo the modification; this becomes a non-trivial problem as the data base becomes voluminous, and it is compounded when the data base is scattered over several storage mediums and under the auspices of dissimilar data management systems. The update problem is considerably simplified where data structures are designed that eliminate redundancy and where the data base is integrated within the confines of a single (and necessarily generalized) data management system. Regardless of the degree of redundancy (which is an aspect of what is termed data integrity), there remains the issue of data security concerning who can have access to what data for what purposes (e.g., update) [6].

VARIETIES OF DATA BASE STRUCTURE

Using the terminology and pictorial notation developed in the previous section, we can abstractly illustrate the sorts of data base structures that can exist. The simplest data base structure consists of a single record type (e.g., Figure 1a). A more complex situation occurs when the data base is organized according to a number of disjoint record types. Figure 2a presents a linear structure; that is, each record type is the owner of no more than one set, nor is it the member of more than one set. A data base may consist of data values organized on the basis of several disjoint linear structures. The more flexible tree structure is shown in Figure 2b. In this kind of structure a record type may be the owner of more than one set, but it can be the member of no more than one. Hence, there is a unique path between any two record types. The most general of all data structures is the network (Figure 2c), since the record type, the linear structure and the tree are special cases of it. In a network structure a record type may be the owner of more than one set and also the member of more than one set.

Figure 3a presents a very simple network structure; it is a network because there is a record type that is the member of more than one set. This type of network structure denotes a many-to-many relationship between occurrences of COMPONENT and PERIOD. That is, a COMPONENT is USED in many time PERIODS; and during a time PERIOD, use is made of numerous COMPONENTS. This relationship is mediated by occurrences of the record type STATUS, each of which indicates projections and plans with respect to a particular component for a particular time period. Figure 3b shows an example of this at the occurrence level. Both USES and USED satisfy the definition of a set (e.g., each occurrence of PERIOD may have many occurrences of STATUS associated with it, but no occurrence of STATUS is associated with more than one occurrence of PERIOD).

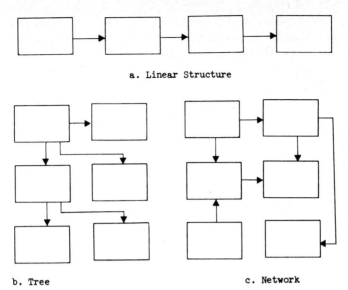

a. Linear Structure

b. Tree   c. Network

Fig. 2 *Varieties of data base structure*

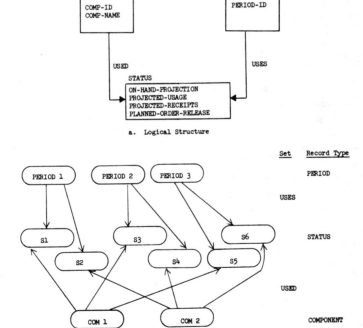

a. Logical Structure

b. Occurrence Structure

Fig. 3 *Many-to-many relation between occurrences of COM-PONENT and occurrences of PERIOD*

With this logical configuration, it can be seen that each occurrence of STATUS identifies a relationship between a single period and a single component. As will be seen in a subsequent section, many-to-many relationships may be combined to form more complex networks.

LIMITATIONS OF TREE STRUCTURES

The limitations described here apply not only to tree structures but to linear structures as well, since the latter constitute a special case of the former. Indeed the linear structures suffer from considerably less flexibility than the tree. The limitations are examined primarily in terms of amenability to the formation and maintenance of an integrated data base, and facility of the user/data base/application interface. Therefore, the methods for manipulating the data of a given type of data base are very important. A language for performing such manipulation is termed a Data Manipulation Language (DML). And a language for defining data structures is called a Data Description Language (DDL). These concepts are illustrated in the following two examples of primitive data management.

The FORTRAN language has the capacity for manipulation of data in the form of linear structures. As such, FORTRAN commands can be viewed as a DML that allows the manipulation of data organized into the structure defined in FORTRAN declaratives. In effect, these declaratives form a DDL that allows linear structures. A simplistic data management system can be built by writing a collection of FORTRAN programs that manipulate data residing in a group of sequential files. Typically, these programs perform sorts, merges, and extractions of data from various files, and with subsequent computation, display it in some reports. Every time a new kind of report is needed, new programs are written. Such a system may well suffice in situations where the number of data item types is small, the inherent relationships among data items are simple, the kinds of reports needed are static, and the users have the skill and time to write programs. As a second example, the Data Division of a COBOL program can serve as a DDL and the commands of the Procedure Division serve as a DML. This DDL admits the use of tree structure and the DML provides enhanced data manipulation facilities relative to FORTRAN commands. The standard COBOL language, then, can provide the basis for a rudimentary data management system similar to that described for FORTRAN, but more flexible. See [12] for the proposal of a more sophisticated tree-base data management system.

We first of all observe that in systems organized in this fashion, the user serves as the interface between the data base and application programs that use the data; the tasks of fitting data to programs and of writing programs compatible with existing data structure are human ones. And these tasks become very cumbersome as the data base tends towards increasing integration. The term integration is used to designate a condition wherein the data base is capable of being accessed by users with different data needs, such that a given user has some data needs in common with some of the other users; but the total information needs of one user are not identical to those of another. One might say that there is a "many-to-many" relationship between users and data item types.

Thus it can be seen why the task of being an interface between an integrated data base and the programs that access it is cumbersome: the tendency toward integration implies more data item types, more data values, more complex relationships among data items, and more complex data manipulations in order to obtain the necessary information for report production. In environments where trees are the only data structures available, this circumstance of more volume and more complexity must necessarily result in either a proliferation of the number of disjoint trees or an inordinate increase in the complexity of record types in a smaller number of trees. Both approaches entail significant degrees of redundancy with the attendant difficulties of inefficiencies and the maintenance of internal consistency. This volume and complexity has a decidedly negative effect upon performance of the human interface. The magnitude of disjoint trees and/or the inner complexity of record types is a direct consequence of the lack of a mechanism to handle all data item relationships within the confines of a single data structure. The network data structure provides such a mechanism.

Prior to examining the capacities of a network data structure, mention must be made of a common method for ameliorating the user/data base/application interface problem that is to some extent independent of the type of data base structure employed. This involves the replacement of the human interface between applications and data base with software. Software accepts user requests (which may be more or less procedural) and responds by interfacing the appropriate data with an application routine from a library of applications; results of the execution are returned to the user. While such "self-contained" systems alleviate many onerous details from the user's concerns, a major drawback is a very limited degree of flexibility with regard to the integration of additional data item types into the existing data base, and the consequent introduction of additional application routines for processing that data. The basic difficulty is that such systems are designed to support a special, limited managerial function. The result is the existence of several self-contained systems (e.g., one for MRP, one for PERT/CPM, one for accounting, etc.), each of which has a data base that contains some of the same data item types as the other systems' data bases; once again, there is the problem of data consistency within an organization. Following a depiction of network capacities, we describe a generalized data management system that supports a network data base, allows user interaction through a non-procedural, English-like language, readily allows the addition of programs to its application library, and provides a novel set of DML commands that effect basic data structure manipulations.

NETWORK REPRESENTATION OF A DATA
BASE FOR MATERIAL REQUIREMENTS PLANNING

The basic structure (Figure 4) for representing bills of material is quite compact. We use the term "component" to denote an item in inventory, regardless of whether it is a raw material, subassembly, module or final product. There is an occurrence of the record type COMPONENT for every item in the inventory. The COMPOSES set indicates that each component may appear on many bills of material; the COM-POSED OF set shows that each component may be composed of many materials. Therefore, each occurrence of MATERIAL is owned by a component having a bill of material (via the COMPOSED OF relationship) and by a component that appears on that bill of material (via the COMPOSED relationship). An occurrence of the data item AMOUNT indicates how much of the latter component is needed to construct the former. Each of the record types contains user-desired data item types describing it; these include items for tracking a project's progress.

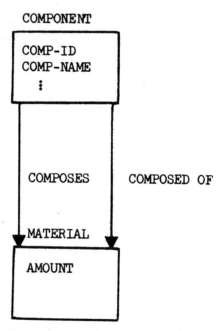

Fig. 4 *A general data structure for organizing information concerning bills of materials*

In order to account for time-phase aspects of MRP, we simply introduce the additional sets USES and USED as depicted in Figure 5. These sets have already been described in references to Figure 3. Observe the features of this logical structure with respect to the information required for MRP analysis. Multiple final products (or modules) are accommodated by the component record type. These may be distinguished from other occurrences of COMPONENT, which represent lower-level components and raw materials, by the values of the corresponding occurrences of COMPONENT-NAME and COMPONENT-ID. A master schedule is essentially the projected usage of a final product (or module) in each of the time periods.

Notice that any desired bills of material may be represented by, or built from this logical structure; a given component may appear in many bills of material. Thus, the structure contains the information necessary for execution of the MRP procedure. Results of this execution are stored in the appropriate occurrences of the record type STATUS in order to provide a basis for maintenance of the requirements plan. Maintenance is necessitated by changes in master schedules stemming either from revised forecasts of demand, or from changes in the availability of some raw material or component. Finally, the depicted record types may be defined to include item types for data about the history of component usage.

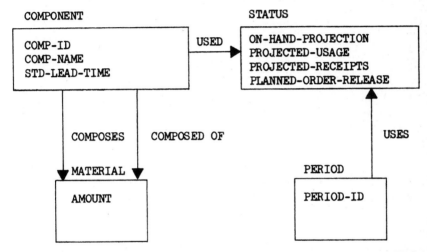

Fig. 5 *Basic logical structure of data requirements for time-phased MRP*

Figure 6 portrays further elaborations suggestive of the ways in which information concerning inventory management may be integrated with information needed for other functional areas of management relating to production planning. The record type SUPPLIER denotes either in-house or external suppliers of components. Since a supplier may supply more than one component and a component may be supplied by more than one supplier, we have constructed two many-to-many relationships between COMPONENT and SUPPLIER. The first indicates options available in ordering components by associating a particular component with its alternative suppliers via record occurrences of OPTIONS. Each occurrence of OPTION provides such information as the lead time, minimum and maximum order quantities, and various cost data with respect to a particular component and a particular supplier. This information furnishes the basis for trade-off analyses (e.g., costs vs. lead times) in production planning. The second many-to-many relationship that associates COMPONENT with SUPPLIER is used to track the progress of a job or shipment. That is, a given component may be scheduled to have more than one supplier, and conversely a particular supplier may be scheduled to complete several jobs of a single or many components. Such information is useful in tracking the progress of various jobs and shipments.

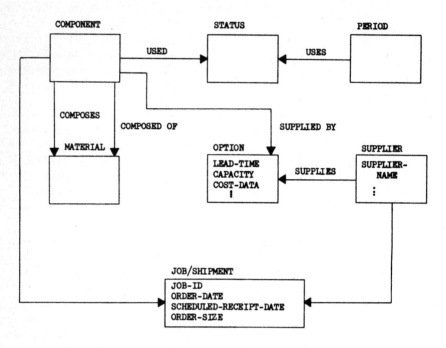

Fig. 6 *Elaborations of the basic information structure for MRP*

These data structures have been included to help illustrate the efficacy of the network data structure in terms of compactly representing complex data relationships and providing an organized method for integrating various types of data into a unified logical structure. Further extensions to the logical structure in Figure 6, to handle other types of data (e.g., accounting information, job shop scheduling data), may be made with respect to particular organizational protocols and settings. This basic structure, subject to modifications for the idiosyncrasies of a specific context, is capable of providing data needed to support the typical MRP analyses. The reader attempting to represent the relationships portrayed in Figure 6 in linear or tree structures, or in tabular form, will appreciate the power of the network concept in terms of giving an organized, compact means for conceptualizing data and its relationships, as well as its treatment of the aforementioned issues of redundancy, consistency and specialization. The ensuing sections address the topic of interfaces with a network data base, which preclude the need for a manager to be an expert in the technicalities of data base management.

INTERFACES WITH A NETWORK DATA BASE

Given a DDL that permits the definition of logical network data structures, a DML is required that allows the storage, modification and extraction of data values for a particular structure. Specifications for such a language have been proposed by the CODASYL Data Base Task Group [7]. One implementation partially based upon these specifications is the GPLAN (Generalized Planning System) Data Management System [1] [4] [10]. This DML is utilized within the framework of a host language, e.g., FORTRAN, COBOL. Each command in the DML consists of a FORTRAN subroutine call. Thus, these DML subroutines essentially extend the FORTRAN language to give it complete data manipulation capability with respect to data organized into network structure. An important feature of this method of implementation is its high degree of machine independence; i.e., subject to a few minor modifications, this DML can be used on any machine that has a FORTRAN compiler and some sort of random access mass storage facility. One special group of these DML commands allows a user to perform structural manipulations on an already existing data base (e.g., the addition or deletion of item types, record types or sets) [4].

For large, integrated data bases a DML that supports network data structures is superior to one that does not; for the user is no longer required to keep track of a collection of trees (with its previously mentioned limitations), but has a compact and organized method for utilizing data from a single repository. Moreover, in such a situation the user does not need to know the entire structure if only a small portion of the network is of personal concern. Each user may be allowed to have a simplified view (called a subschema) of the entire logical structure [4] [5]. In order to access the data or interface it with pre-existing applications routines, the user is still required to write programs using DML (even though the number or size of programs may be less, due to the power of DML commands that operate on a network). So with respect to the ease of interface, the network-based DML is inferior to specialized, self-contained data management systems. The objective, therefore, is a data-manipulating system that provides a facile interface for the user, i.e., it minimizes the amount of effort and computer expertise required of the user. The system must also furnish a generality that allows it to be used in a wide variety of managerial contexts, including the situation where decisions are to be based upon 1) an integrated (rather than compartmentalized) data base, and/or 2) rapidly changing information needs. This has been the motivation behind the development of an English-like, non-procedural, general query system capable of interrogating network data structures.

QUERY LANGUAGE FOR A NETWORK DATA BASE

The query language (GPLAN/QS [2] [3]) discussed here extricates users from the position of interfacing programs with a data base; the user is not required to be a programmer. The query system provides the appropriate interface in response to non-procedural requests by the user. That is, the user's query needs merely to specify what is to be done; there is no statement of the procedures to be followed in order to accomplish the task. An example of a very simple command is

LIST ALL SUPPLIERS OF COMPONENT.ID = 'B1385'

(To avoid confusion with the minus sign, data item names are not hyphenated in the query language.) Upon receipt of this command the query system analyzes the request, sets up the necessary DML commands, executes those commands and provides the user with the requested information. The system is designed such that it permits the selective (or unconditional) retrieval of any configuration of data; and furthermore it allows the execution of application programs using any desired (and mundane) data from the data base. The basic query syntax is

<COMMAND><RETRIEVAL CLAUSE><CONDITIONAL CLAUSE>

The command identifies the application program to be executed; in the above query, LIST indicates that a report generator is to be executed. The retrieval clause allows the user to specify the data to be retrieved for execution; this retrieval is contingent upon the conditions specified in the conditional clause.

Figure 7 provides an overview of the system. The library of application routines has two categories: standard and special. The standard library of applications consists of such commands as LIST, PLOT, REGRESSION, STATISTICS, and data modification routines. Special application libraries contain routines used in the functional areas of management supported by the data base (e.g., canned programs for various MRP analyses, job shop scheduling, resource assignment, etc.). Methods for incorporating a routine into a special library are examined in [9]. The user is allowed to submit retrieval clauses of arbitrary complexity. This clause may contain not only names of data items to be retrieved, but also allows arithmetic operations using data items or literals and the introduction of both single variable functions and multivariate functions. The conditional clause is composed of a Boolean expression that may contain literals, data item names, relational operators, arithmetic operators, logical operators, single-variable functions, and multivariate functions. The query language also allows the use of noise words, synonyms and various other cosmetic features for the convenience of the user. Given the basic information structure of Figure 6, some sample queries are:

LIST SUPPLIER.NAME FOR COMPONENT.ID = 'B1385' AND·
   LEAD.TIME<'3'
LIST COMPONENT.ID, COMPONENT.NAME AND PERIOD.ID IF
   PLANNED.ORDER.RELEASE>'500' AND SUPPLIER.NAME =
   'ACME'
LIST ON.HAND.PROJECTION, PROJECTED.USAGE,
   PROJECTED.RECEIPTS, PLANNED.ORDER.RELEASE AND
   PERIOD.ID FOR COMPONENT.ID = 'B1385'
LIST AVERAGE PROJECTED.USAGE FOR
   COMPONENT.ID = 'B1385'

LIST MAXIMUM PLANNED.ORDER.RELEASE FOR
    COMPONENT.ID = 'B1385'
PERFORM MRP.ANALYSIS FOR COMPONENT.ID = 'M3'

The last query utilized an application from the special library. The query: LIST COMPONENT.IDS AND AMOUNT FOR COMPONENT.ID = 'M2' will result in a bill of material for the module "M2." Observe that some queries are more prone to be asked by certain types of users than others. So through this query system, different types of users can access the same data base to meet their divergent information needs. Each manager can extract and enter (subject to security constraints) data that are germane to his own individual perspective. Since a single data base is used, the data changes made by one user are automatically reflected in other users' outputs which are based on the data that is altered. The flexibility allowed by the facility for selective retrieval of any data configuration is extremely useful for the generation of non-standard reports. Such reports are essential to resolution of non-routine, unstructured problems, to trouble-shooting activities and to the identification of heuristic methods. The query system provides such reports on a timely basis in response to non-procedural, English-like queries.

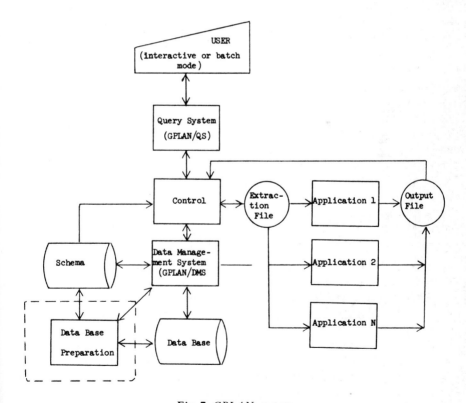

Fig. 7 *GPLAN system*

CONCLUSION

In the face of decreasing costs for computer hardware and the increasing complexity of situations with which managers must contend, the increasing use of computerized data management systems is imminent. The manner in which data is managed, with respect to its organization and manipulation, has important consequences for managerial decision making. The two principle issues, then, are the capacity to organize data such that their intricate interrelationships are taken into account, and the existence of a facility that enables users (who are not programmers or computer experts) to query the data base for assistance in solving both structured and unstructured decision problems. Of particular interest is the ease and flexibility with which data base interrogation can be conducted; for the manager's time is presumably too valuable to be consumed in the pursuit of writing programs or frequently explaining to programmers the kinds of reports that are needed.

We describe a system that directly addresses both issues. The system's outstanding features may be summarized as follows: utilization of the network variety of data base; selective retrieval of any configuration of data from a particular network structure; automatic execution of any desired application program from a standard or special library of applications; user interface with a data base and applications by submitting English-like, non-procedural queries; and generality that allows tailoring to specific applications and provides a basis for integration of planning (and control) activities. Although MRP examples were used to illustrate this system, it must be emphasized that the system is general insofar as it aids the resolution of a wide variety of other decisions that involve complex data relationships (not to mention simple relationships) and that are subject to varying degrees of integration with each other; e.g., material requirements planning, queuing problems, scheduling problems, transportation problems. Moreover, the system provides a convenient means for producing both standard reports and one-time reports to aid both structured and unstructured decision making.

REFERENCES

[1] Bonczek, R. H.; J. I. Cash; W. D. Haseman; C. W. Holsapple; and A. B. Whinston. *Generalized Planning System/Data Management System Reference Manual: Version 3.0.* West Lafayette, Ind.: Krannert Graduate School of Management, Purdue University, August 1975.

[2] Bonczek, R. H.; W. D. Haseman; and A. B. Whinston. "Automatic Path Determination of a Network Data Base." West Lafayette, Ind.: Krannert Graduate School of Management, Purdue University, April 1976. (Technical report.)

[3] Bonczek, R. H.; W. D. Haseman; and A. B. Whinston. "Structure of a Query Language for a Network Data Base." West Lafayette, Ind.: Krannert Graduate School of Management, Purdue University, April 1976. (Technical report.)

[4] Bonczek, R. H.; C. W. Holsapple; and A. B. Whinston. "Extensions and Corrections for the CODASYL Approach to Data Base Management." *International Journal of Information Systems,* Vol. 2 (1976), pp. 71–77.

[5] Bonczek, R. H., and A. B. Whinston. "A Generalized Mapping Language for Network Data Structures." *International Journal of Information Systems,* Vol. 2 (1977), pp. 171–185.

[6] Cash, J. I.; W. D. Haseman; and A. B. Whinston. "Security for the GPLAN System." *International Journal of Information Systems,* Vol. 2 (1976), pp. 41–48.

[7] CODASYL: Data Base Task Group Report. *ACM,* April 1971.

[8] Garwood, D. "Stop: Before You Use the Bill Processor. . . ." *Production and Inventory Management,* Vol. 11, second quarter (1970), p. 43.

[9] Haseman, W. D., and A. B. Whinston. "Automatic Program Interface." *The Computer Journal,* Vol. 20 (1977), pp. 222–225.

[10] Haseman, W. D., and A. B. Whinston. *Introduction to Data Management.* Homewood, Ill.: Irwin, 1977.

[11] Nijssen, G. M. "Set and CODASYL Set or Coset." *Data Base Description.* Edited by B. C. M. Douque and G. M. Nijssen. Amsterdam: North-Holland Publishing Co., 1975.

[12] Shu, N. C.; B. C. Housel; and V. Y. Lum, "CONVERT: A High Level Translation Definition for Data Conversion." IBM Research Report RF 1515.

Developing a Computerized General Ledger System

DANIEL P. LUBAS

The primary objective in developing a computerized general ledger system is to satisfy the wants and needs of the user. To meet this objective, a system was developed that would increase the accuracy and control of the company's accounting data. It reduced the manual (clerical) requirements of producing, controlling, and maintaining ledgers for those users who were on a completely manual system. Finally, the system established a base for an accounting information system that could provide results and information to satisfy other internal and external systems.

INPUT REQUIREMENTS

The first step in meeting these objectives was to identify the data elements required to support the general ledger system. In order to obtain this identification the users were asked to prepare a list of all the elements they would like to see as output from this system. We found that a number of the items were actually outputs to subsystems (i.e., accounts payable, accounts receivable and payroll) and therefore did not need to be included in this system. We also found that other items listed were available from other systems and would not be included in order to reduce duplication. After continued contact with the users, a list of general ledger system data elements was compiled.

OUTPUT REPORTS

The second step was to define the output reports required by the system. After numerous proposals and counterproposals, we determined that the system should contain a total of six output report formats. Four of these report formats would be produced on a monthly basis. The remaining two reports would be provided after each system load and edit to monitor the system and maintain the necessary system controls. A brief description of each report and its content follows.

General Ledger

The general ledger would be produced primarily on a monthly basis but could be produced during the month or in a subsequent month if the conditions warranted. In keeping with traditional general ledger layouts, each unique general ledger account and its detail would start on a new page. If the general ledger account was supported by a subledger, only totals would appear in the general ledger with all details appearing in the subledger. The last page of the general ledger would contain total debits and credits for the month-to-date, and trial balance figures that could be reconciled against the month-to-date and trial balance figures as they appear in the most current summary control run printed prior to the running of the general ledger. A pile-up general ledger would be produced at year end to replace the individual monthly general ledger. See Exhibit 1.

Subledgers

The subledgers would be produced primarily on a monthly basis but could be produced during the month or in a subsequent month if the conditions warranted. As in the case of the general ledger, each unique subledger account and its detail would start on a new page. In addition, it would contain a functional departmental breakdown by month and year listed for each department that incurs a charge relative to the appropriate subledger account. These totals would also be divided by charge classification code that provides a grouping of charges by type for information and reporting purposes (i.e., payroll, depreciation, taxes).

Subledger Summary

The subledger summary would be produced at the end of each subledger. It would contain the total debits and credits for the account range contained in the subledger. These figures would reconcile with the appropriate general ledger account. The subledger summary would also contain a functional departmental summary that would list, by department, charge classification code totals by month and year.

Operation and Maintenance Work Order Summary

An operation and maintenance work order identifies individual construction projects, type of project, or class of expense. The operation and maintenance work order summary would be produced on a monthly basis after completion of the printing of the subledgers. The summary would contain detail totals by account for each operation and maintenance work order. It would also contain a charge classification code summary that lists monthly, year-to-date, and to-date totals by charge classification code.

Exhibit 1 GENERAL LEDGER

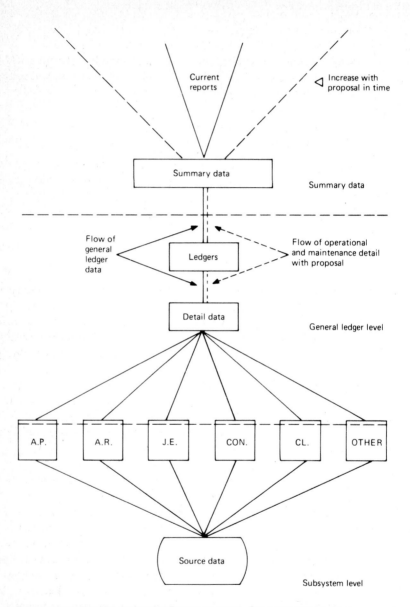

This schematic reflects the general ledger system developed. The system captures data from numerous manual and mechanized systems and feeds a summary data that produces reports for top management.

Summary Control Run

The summary control run would be produced at the end of each entry and edit run. The report consists of a list of month-to-date net totals for all the accounts containing subledgers and other accounts selected by the user. It would also list month-to-date net totals for selected charge classification codes. Total debits and credits for month-to-date and trial balance figures would be reflected, along with the total accounts payable and accounts receivable contras produced.

Journal Register and Error List

The journal register and error list would be produced after each submission of transactions to the system and would identify correction entries by a description of the error after the line in error. The journal register and error list would provide both physical batch and hash control totals. The physical batch totals would be provided when the batch is accepted as correct and loaded on to the accepted records file.

COLLECT AND PROCESSING DATA

The third step in the development was in determining how to collect and process the information needed in the system. The first area considered is the collection of data. The source data are collected from each user in the form of transactions representing actual data. The information submitted falls into three categories: manual input transactions, computerized interface input, and system control input.

Manual input transactions would consist of all general journal entries. The accounts payable and accounts receivable entries would be manual for the users who do not have mechanized systems and those whose mechanized systems could not be interfaced. Data from some mechanized systems in which the interface is planned for the future would also be submitted manually.

Computerized interface transactions would consist of data that would be passed automatically from the existing mechanized subsystem to the general ledger system for processing.

System control input would be accomplished by both the user and the mechanized system. Each user would be responsible for correct submission of transactions with a central coordinator combining all efforts for final consolidation. In addition, each user would maintain a control log of transaction batch produced for each batch to be verified with the journal register and error list. Each user would be directly responsible also for submission of correction entries into the system. Batch control for mechanized submissions would be accomplished automatically; therefore a control log would not be required for those types of entries.

After defining how the data would be gathered, the processing flow is developed. Source documents (i.e., journal entries, accounts payable and accounts receivable vouchers) would be grouped by batch. Each batch would contain documents of one source type and would be control numbered. Batches would be forwarded to data processing for keypunching and verification, after which they would be submitted to the edit run. Any number of batches could be submitted into one edit run and all types of batches could be submitted simultaneously. In addition to the three sources described above, mechanized entries from other subsystems would be extracted. These entries would maintain their original mechanized identity to simplify error correction procedures.

Batches entered into the edit program would pass in sequential fashion through validity and compatibility checks. Records found to be in error would be flagged with a descriptive error message and all the records of the batch would be written on the error file. Error records would be assigned an identification key so that only the record in error need be corrected. If an error exists on a batch record, that batch number would be uniquely referenced for later correction. Records and batches that are clean would be processed through a control program which would accumulate data and print specific account and charge classification totals on the summary control run.

Errors would be corrected via a separate error correction program. To correct the errors, the identification key would be used to match up with and overlay the error record on the error file. The facility to add and delete records on the error file would also be available. The entire error file would then reprocess through the edit program as though the errors were normal batch entries. An important item to note is that whenever an error is detected, a correction entry is required via the general ledger system, regardless of whether or not a correction entry was made to a mechanized subsystem.

The edit run could be invoked as often as each user desired. On the last edit run of a particular period, however, the error tape would have to be cleared of all error transactions. No general ledger/subledger programs would be initiated if any error records remained. The primary reason for this is to hold the entire batch in suspense whenever an error occurs for any record on the batch. Ignoring that batch for the general ledger print would seriously affect financial statistics.

CONTROLS

During development of the processing area the users requested numerous controls. After detailed research a comprehensive network of controls that could be divided into three basic areas was developed. They are manual, automatic computerized, and manually initiated computerized controls.

Manual Controls

In order to ensure accurate submission of data and proper and complete acceptance of the data into the system, the following manual controls would be instituted:

- *Single source document.* All manual input, including corrections to the system, would be in one standard format on a standard form. This provides ease in submission of information, a standard base for audit, and eliminates errors that arise from multiple types of forms and transactions.

- *Hash totals per batch.* The hash total would be derived by disregarding the sign for the amounts and accumulating the amounts. The hash total would ensure that all entries in the batch are entered to the system.

- *Month-to-date controls.* Each user location would maintain month-to-date totals that the location feels are essential to determine the accuracy of the summary control report produced by the system.

- *Review of output reports both daily and monthly.* With proper review of key reports produced by the system, the location could discover and eliminate errors that could be considered valid by the system. An example of this is the charging of an expense to the wrong valid account.

Automatic Computerized Controls

These controls are initiated and maintained by the system during edit-update and in numerous control jobs throughout the general ledger system.

- *Accounting validation file.* The major elements of all input transactions would be validated by the accounting validation file. Selected proper compatibility checks would also be made where possible.

- *Detail element validation.* Elements including but not limited to the following would be checked for accuracy: voucher number, accounting month, improper blanks, alpha or numeric characters.

- *Amount verification.* Amounts would be verified in the following manner: debits must equal credits on input transactions; batches must equal hash totals submitted.

- *Control file.* A control file would be maintained that would include current month values by account code, work order qualifier, and charge classification code. This file would be used to produce a summary control run in order that manual checks of data could be made. The control file would also be utilized to determine the accuracy of mechanized procedures.

- *Journal register and error list.* These reports would be produced whenever input to the system is made. They would indicate errors submitted to the system and suspense account entries created to eliminate those errors. A complete listing of data submitted during the edit update would also be provided. The journal register would also provide the capability to determine missing journal entries.

Manually Initiated Computerized Controls

In order to provide audit capabilities and ensure complete accuracy of the system, the following could be initiated upon request.

- *Control procedures.* These procedures check the various data files of the system to assure that they are in balance. Total detail value of the holding file is checked against the control file. Details are checked to summary and summary is checked to the control file. These procedures are also initiated to verify the accurate back-up of current day's transaction input.

RESPONSIBILITIES

The final step in the development of the system was establishing responsibilities. The decision was made that each user would be responsible for the timely submission of transactions relating to his own company. In order to monitor, control and coordinate system processing properly, each user is required to appoint an individual to act as his site controller. The site controller would accumulate and verify transactions, develop batch totals and enter them on the batch source document, submit transactions in batch form for keypunching and entry into the edit program, review the journal register and error list and reconcile all errors, or initiate the proper activity to resolve the errors and finally initiate and review the general/subledger reports.

Although the system is based upon data submitted by various locations, a single, common accounting system is desired with standardized procedures. Therefore, a system coordinator was appointed to review and approve much of the policies and procedures and further coordinate the system processing. While each user is responsible for collecting and preparing input for processing, the system coordinator reconciles system outputs with each user's site controller and also serves as the centralized communication point for resolution of inquiries and questions regarding the system and its functions.

CONCLUSION

With this design of a computerized general ledger system, standardization and availability of accounting information can be obtained. This will provide for easier analysis on a system-wide basis and eliminate the manual preparation of many schedules, reports, and ledgers. System control can be maintained at all times and any future expansion or additions will be along common lines requiring a single approach rather than satisfying numerous individual requirements.

Computerized Financial Data Reporting System

DAN J. HILL
AND GAROLD L. RUTHERFORD

Our Financial Data Reporting System (FDRS) described in this article is a computer system through which basic accounting data can be maintained, updated and printed according to user requirements. It is one of the computer systems being used by our company to capture and manipulate data into a universal data base and to provide a means of analyzing these data for various business segments.[1] In addition, it provides financial data reports to both division and location levels.

SYSTEM PHILOSOPHY

The Financial Data Reporting System incorporates a philosophy centered around financial data storage and retrieval in a most flexible manner. To accomplish this, three major developments were necessary to enable us to:

1. Establish a maintainable data base containing the level of financial data required to generate divisional, as well as locational, reports,

2. Provide accounting personnel with tools necessary to define report specifications and to generate reports containing data under their cognizance (without restricting any user to the specifications of another user), and

3. Develop a report generation system that is complex, yet flexible enough to support the above-mentioned items.

DATA BASE CONTENT

Data base files are established for each major reporting location, all of which contain multiple profit centers. The data base consists of two types of files: financial

---

[1] In this article, the authors describe the Financial Data Reporting System implemented by Collins Radio Group of Rockwell International. The FDRS System provides interface with the Rockwell Corporate Financial Data System.

data and report specifications. Financial data files contain prior fiscal year actuals and current fiscal year actuals, as each period is processed. Report specification files contain report column specifications and report line specifications. Identifiers for all records consist of location code, profit center identification, overhead class code, account number, and service function code.

SYSTEM DESCRIPTION

The Financial Data Reporting System applies to any department or division company-wide, where all reports are profit-center and account oriented. In order to assure a reporting package flexible enough to satisfy the requirements of month-to-month financial data preparation, the report specifications consist of two controlling factors.

Column Matrix Identifiers (CMI)

The first of these is report column definition, referred to as "column matrix identifiers" (Exhibit 1). Basic correlation between this portion of the report description and data records is provided by profit-center identifiers. These CMI records will control the column content of all reports. Many combinations of specifications are available, i.e., multiple profit centers may be included in a single column; groups of columns can be totaled; and, in general any arithmetic computation may be performed between columns. A maximum of 24 columns is allowed within any given report. Also included in these CMI records are parameters that control the printout each column will portray: month or period specification that allows an on-going situation (specifying the number of months prior to the current month, corresponding month of prior year, and so forth); type of data (actuals, current period or year-to-date); type of financial printout (dollars and cents, rounded dollars, rounded thousands, rounded millions to two decimal places, percent); number of print spaces to be allocated for each report column; report column headings.

Exhibit 1
COLUMN MATRIX IDENTIFIERS

	Record identity field	Record continuation field	Column no. of report field	Data type field	Period field	Format field	Equation field	Column width field	Column title 1 field	Column title 2 field
PCI	A	B	C	D	E					
COL	A	B	Ø	Ø	E					

There are two kinds of column matrix identifiers. One specifies basic data such as profit center identifiers (PCI) to be included in particular report columns. The second specifies how information is to be summed with respect to other columns (COL). The column matrix identifiers themselves are:

- *Record continuation field.* This field indicates whether or not there are multiple records that define this particular report column. If blank, it indicates only one record for this column. "0-9" or "A-Z" specifies a sequence of multiple records.
- *Column number of report field.* This field must be "0-24." When zero, it indicates an explicit definition of the length of line description. A specification of "1-24" indicates the exact column being defined.
- *Data type field.* This field specifies the type of financial data, whether it is year-to-date or current-period actuals.
- *Period field.* This field specifies the relationship to the current fiscal period as shown on the report request entered at batch process time.
- *Format field.* This field specifies whether the value is in dollars and cents, rounded dollars, rounded thousands, millions to two decimals, or percent.

Line Matrix Identifiers

The second portion of report specifications consists of groups of parameters describing each line content of a report. These are referred to as "Line Matrix Identifiers" (Exhibit 2). Basic correlation between this portion of the report description and data records is provided by company account numbers. In addition to account identifiers within LMI tables, there are records that provide line titles, summations,

Exhibit 2
LINE MATRIX IDENTIFIERS

Line identity field	Record identity field	Record continuation field	Line control field	Column designation field	Equation field	Line title field
A	ACCNT	B	C	Ø	123250, 127453, 123456, 123500-01-02-04	E
A	EXTRN	B	C	D	(CMI, LINE, COL) + (CMI, LINE, COL)	E
A	SPECL	B	C	D	(CMI, COL) + (LINE, COL) * 100	E
A	SPECL	B	C	Ø	(LINE) + (LINE) + (LINE) + (LINE)	E
A	TITLE	Ø	C		Ø	E
A	TRANS	Ø	Ø	COL, COL, COL, COL		Ø

transfer of data from one report to another, and entries that retrieve data from some external report previously processed. In general, any mathematical computation desired can be accomplished with these line parameters. In addition to these specifications, there are parameters defining line spacing on reports, and column-to-column interaction. (Particular columns from this report or previous reports may be individually specified so that any data combinations can be accomplished.)

There are five kinds of line matrix identifiers: account record specifications, external record specifications, special record specification, title record specification and transfer record specification. The line matrix identifiers themselves are:

- *Record identity field.* This field consists of a four-digit line number. These are arbitrary numbers that are assigned for use by other fields/records within LMI table. They do not appear on output reports of financial data.

- *Record continuation field.* This field indicates whether or not there are multiple records that define data for this record type and line number. If blank, it indicates only one record for this line. A "0-9" or "A-Z" specifies the sequence of multiple records.

- *Line control field.* This field specifies the printer carriage control to be performed before this line is executed. This may indicate a page eject or a space of a specified number of lines before next print line. If blank, it assumes data is to be placed on the next print line.

- *Column designation field.* This field specifies the particular columns to receive this data. If blank, it assumes all columns are to receive data according to the calculation specified in the equation field.

- *Line title field.* This field contains a line title to be displayed on the report. The title may be indented to improve the legibility of the report. Maximum length of the title is 41 characters. If the equation field extends over into this field area, then multiple records should be used and the line title supplied on subsequent records.

FLEXIBILITY

By using the above two factors to control reports, an unlimited amount of flexibility is available. CMI and LMI tables are established for standard reports. Users need only refer to the report number to generate that report. If a non-standard report is desired, users have the ability to develop CMI and LMI tables to generate these reports.

In conjunction with the column and line specification philosophy, a report generator was developed to compile these parameters. Updating capabilities are available so that users may change the contents of a report with no programming intervention. A data base of financial records is established and maintained so that any data item is accessible through report specification.

INTERFACE

Monthly input data for actuals are provided by interfacing with the company's Accounting Data System, using the general ledger summary from this system. These data are retained on files separate from the financial data base until after a closing period is completed. When this summary general ledger is available, each reporting group reviews its trial balance and prepares any necessary post-closing entries. A review of the monthly reporting requirements will indicate whether or not report specification changes should be made. If so, these will be prepared at this time. Creation and update of report specification tables are accomplished in processings separate from report generation. Procedures are established to validate these specifications so that the user can be confident the tables will produce the desired reports. Each reporting location is completely independent of other locations, and all reporting is on a request basis.

Control cards accompanying job requests will contain parameters specifying the exact processing required, for example, location code to be processed, calendar date to be displayed on report, fiscal period of current month, kind of data and explicit report selection. Exhibit 3 illustrates report request records.

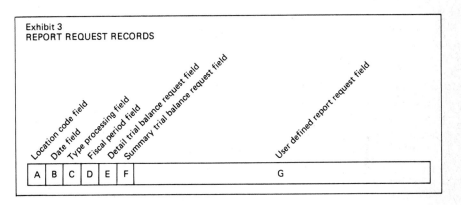

Exhibit 3
REPORT REQUEST RECORDS

These report request records are not stored on any file. These records are submitted with each processing. There are seven fields in the report request:

- *Location code field.* This field specifies the company location code for which processing is desired.
- *Date field.* This field specifies the calendar date (six characters) to be displayed on the report—month, day, and year.
- *Type processing field.* This field specifies that this is a processing of actual data.
- *Fiscal period field.* This field specifies the fiscal month that this processing represents.

- *Detail trial balance request field.* If blank, this field indicates that no detail trial balance is requested. If "1", it specifies that a report is requested.
- *Summary trial balance request field.* If blank, this field indicates that no summary trial balance is requested. If "1", it specifies that a report is requested.
- *User defined report request field.* This field specifies the reports to be generated. Users have previously established report specifications for these reports. Order of request represents order processed.

All monthly input data (post-closing entries) is first read in and then checked for valid codes. If invalid conditions are detected, they are printed on an exception report. Records found to be valid will be added to the appropriate location storage files for monthly data, and a post-closing entry report will display the entries for this batch processing. If no post-closing entries are available, the control advances to an interrogation of reports requested. There are two fixed reports; namely, a detail trial balance and summary trial balance. Either, both, or neither of these may be selected. If either of the two is selected, the report(s) will be generated. If no trial balance reports are selected, processing proceeds to an analysis of the user-designed reports requested. These user-designed reports are ones that have previously been defined and stored in files containing CMI and LMI report specifications. If no user-designed reports are requested, processing for this cycle is terminated.

MERGING MONTHLY AND HISTORICAL FILES

The next step in the processing merges monthly data files with historical data base files for the location requesting reports. Request records are examined to determine which specification tables are to be used for the processing. The tables selected are scanned, and all account and profit-center identifiers are extracted. Since all data are account and profit-center oriented, a separate record is generated for each account number/profit center found in the specifications. These expanded records are matched by account number and profit center with data base records, and a dollar amount is then added to the expanded records for the particular type of data requested. The system is now ready to compile the reports in the order specified by users.

COMPILING THE REPORTS

All data from expanded records for a given report are brought into a matrix and the appropriate specification tables are again interrogated to determine which lines are to be composed of data from an external file (having been generated by a report processed previously), which lines are to be totaled, and which lines are to be transferred to an external file for use in other reports, line description, line spacing, and other defined computations. After this portion of the matrix is completed, column specifications are again analyzed to determine what action is to be taken on each column within the report matrix: which columns are totals, which columns are differences, which columns are to be divided into other columns, and which columns are to be suppressed in printing. The matrix now contains all information and the report is printed. After processing each report, location transfer files are updated with data generated in that report. This procedure of report generation continues until all reports are processed.

CLOSING CYCLE

The FDRS month-end closing period is usually four working days. During this period, each reporting location will continue to analyze its reports, submit post-closing entries, update the report specification tables and generate updated reports until responsible personnel sign off on the data file content. These data are then used as input to the FDS Interface System.

After the closing cycle is complete, all monthly files are merged with existing historical data base files. At the end of the fiscal year, all historical data base files are updated so that prior year data (two years prior at this point) are removed and data from the year just past are placed in these positions.

CONCLUSION

The Financial Data Reporting System develops a computer system for data storage and report generation. This system gives all company accounting personnel the ability to maintain financial data and to define report descriptions without dependence on programming personnel.

In accomplishing the above purpose, the system enables each division or location to concentrate on report analysis, and furthermore provides:

1. An interface with the company's Accounting Data System. (This system provides basic monthly input to FDRS),

2. Post-closing entries to the trial balance,

3. A system under user-design and control (i.e., each reporting location/division has the ability to design and maintain report specifications),

4. A reasonable throughput time so that several turnarounds are possible during the working day,

5. A system for storage and retrieval of historical data, and

6. A means by which our group can interface with the corporate Financial Data System.

An Approach to Hospital Data Processing Development

SIDNEY HANCOCK

Even though the health care field constitutes the nation's biggest non-defense industry, it is one that has exploited the computer only to a very limited extent. The need certainly exists for progressing beyond the usual batch accounting applications, but clearcut guides as to how an individual hospital should proceed are few. Fragmented computer industry development, rapid growth in hardware technology, professional staff resistance to change, hospital budget pressures, costly user and vendor mistakes, and other factors have combined to make significant progress a difficult and challenging proposition.

REQUIREMENTS-PRESSURES FOR DATA PROCESSING DEVELOPMENT

The Hospital as an Information Processor

It is estimated that hospitals in this country spend one-quarter to one-third of their budgets on acquiring and communicating information. Perhaps half of this is for functions that can be automated, including patient care, medical audit, and financial management. A comprehensive information system (yet to be installed in any hospital) would include the following:

1. Online collection of data at its source, including patient identification and location, service requests, and medical data;

2. Online inquiry to a computerized "medical record" including clinical and requisition data for the duration of the patient's stay;

3. Automatic routing of entered or preprogrammed requests for services and supplies to supporting departments;

4. Operational tools within ancillary service departments such as clinical lab (specimen labels, worklists, cumulative patient reports, unfinished test lists, etc.); and

5. Reports for use in administering the patient's stay and financial management of the facility.

Cost Control in a Labor-Intensive Industry

It is common knowledge that the medical care industry is under pressure to reduce inflationary pressures. Computerization is an attractive possibility for cost containment in clerical payroll, reduction of lost patient charges, and increased productivity of professional staff. On the other hand, assigning a cash value to many of the productivity benefits is very difficult. For example, it is hard to price the value of an immediate, accurate, legible drug request in the pharmacist's office.

Demands for Improving Patient and Physician Service

This has not yet become a major factor because of the limited number of installed information systems. The importance will vary with facility size, also. Within a few years, however, competition for physicians and patients will be affected by the extent of automated support provided for administrative and patient care functions.

Reporting to Government Agencies

The most compelling reason for using computers in hospitals may turn out to be the need for compliance with government regulations. These include utilization review requirements, professional standards review organizations, and national health insurance legislation. The extent of reporting and controls necessary to comply may necessitate computer support in all but the smaller facilities.

In summary, recent and anticipated future pressures in the health care industry are bringing about the situation where the need to extend computer use in the hospital cannot be ignored.

OPPORTUNITIES: POTENTIAL FOR APPLICATION DEVELOPMENT

Basic Accounting Systems—Level A

These are the primary accounting-financial applications that are typically implemented first, usually in sequential batch mode.[1] Selected functional characteristics to be expected are listed for each application. Each must provide adequate internal controls and audit trail information, and proper integration with related systems, in addition to the items listed.

General Ledger
1. Accrual method of accounting
2. Separate identity of fund entities
3. Compatibility with American Hospital Association chart of accounts

Patient Billing

1. Coordinated "family" of controlled source documents
2. Posting of patient and revenue ledgers upon discharge and at least subsequent monthly intervals
3. Revenue accumulation by type of service, organizational and functional origin
4. Integration of data from admissions and medical records
5. Data to satisfy reporting requirements of third party insurors

Accounts Receivable

1. Cycle billing
2. Ability to charge interest on delinquent accounts
3. Flexible access to volume and aging statistics by groups or types

Accounts Payable

1. Central control of all materials and services required other than payroll
2. Vendor, product, or service reference file
3. Processing at volume-efficient intervals compatible with other costing and financial reporting
4. Cost distribution by organizational department, service function or type of cost incurred

Personnel and Payroll

1. A file of each employee's personal data and employment history
2. Periodic reports on composition of staff
3. Reference payroll dollars and hours and report by individual, job class, shift, and department or service function
4. Account for, and report on, absence and vacation statistics

Purchasing and Procurement

1. Documented controls of authorized and approved commitments to acquire material and services
2. Integration with a receiving procedure
3. Detailed and summary listing of items delivered and items outstanding
4. Identity code for commodity or service classes

Cash Disbursements and Receipts

1. Based on pre-numbered, controlled documents
2. Ability to provide reporting access for effective cash management and budgeting

Property and Plant System

1. Identification of major equipment items by individual nomenclature and number for equipment group or class type, and organizational or functional location
2. A perpetual inventory and custodial responsibility for major and movable items
3. Flexibility to change depreciation method

Inventory

1. Item control and perpetual control on high value and narcotic items
2. Overall control by predetermined markup on low value items
3. Standardized nomenclature and item identity numbers
4. Predetermined pricing and rate schedules
5. Ability to provide detail and summary listings of usage and on-hand quantities by item or class

Budgeting and Reporting

1. For annual formal budget planning revised and updated at least semiannually
2. Financial reporting in a structure comparative to the budget
3. Reporting to satisfy requirements of the governing body and third parties
4. Revenue and direct cost reporting by organization and service function
5. Overhead and indirect cost distribution on recognized bases
6. Flexible and timely management-reporting capability
7. Integration with census and other statistical data.

Online Administration Systems—Level B

Level B represents an online extension to the batch accounting applications, and may require a second computer. Such an approach has the advantage of providing a duplexed backup in case the online processor fails.[2] Level B systems offer data collection, message switching and inquiry capabilities. They transmit orders, capture charges for one day, prepare a census, may or may not report lab results, and may be queried regarding current charges. Level B systems are generally limited to interdepartmental communications and data entry support for Level A applications. They stop short of the automated medical record and the intra-departmental clinical systems which comprise the "Medical Information System" of Level C. The Level B functions include the following:

Admission-discharge-transfer. The foundation for Level B system is a current, online patient file which correctly identifies the patient and his bed location during the hospital stay. The admitting department is responsible for entering the correct data promptly, and their reward for the effort includes computer-prepared census reports.

Some users have extended the A.D.T. system to include a utilization review function. A diagnosis for each patient is entered upon admission and the system produces an average length of stay and expected discharge date. On the day prior to projected discharge, a listing is printed including the patient's name. The review coordinator consults the attending physician and requires an explanation if the patient's stay is to be extended. The purpose is to comply with the requirements of professional standards review organizations. Use of the computer spares the coordinator the task of reviewing scores of medical charts every day.

Data collection and message switching. This system is designed around the patient-ordering process, particularly for ancillary services. The terminal first presents the nurse with a display of patients and room numbers. The nurse selects one, and then chooses from a menu of displayed functions: "order drugs, lab tests, x-ray, dietary, etc." Then the system leads the nurse through a selection process to isolate the particular drugs, lab tests, etc. desired.

As the data collection function is concluded, a printer in the ancillary service department prints out labels and the patient's bill is charged. At any time, the orders submitted for a patient may be reviewed and errors corrected. In some cases, these systems also allow for lab test result entry and transmission to the floors.

The advantages of this application area include greater accuracy and promptness of service and supply orders, the capture of lost charges, and reduced clerical activity.

Patient billing extensions. As an adjunct to the online capture of billing data at its source, the system automatically computes what insurance benefits are available to the patient. Records of all major insurance policies and their benefits are maintained in the system. On a daily basis, the online patient's transactions are posted to the batch billing system.

Inquiry. The inquiry functions allow access to what amounts to a subset of the patient's chart for the current stay. Identification, location, service order, and charge data are accessible to authorized users. Additional inquiry files may be kept such as lists of physicians, their specialties, biographical data, etc.

Clinical Systems—Level C

The clinical systems are distinguished by the presence of medical data as well as administrative data in the automated chart, further automation in the patient care administration process, the inclusion of systems which serve as intra-departmental operational tools as well as sources of chart data, such as the lab system, and a very comprehensive and accessible medical information reporting system based on added types of data, integrated data bases and data management techniques.[3] Level C systems affect individual departments and functions as follows:

Nursing. A Level C system would support patient care management, and therefore nursing, in the preparation for a routine surgery. The patient's name or number, surgeon's number or name, and the operation are the only inputs required. The system generates a list of secondary orders normally associated with the surgery and displays them for verification by the nurse.

As a result, the nursing floor receives orders for pre-op care such as bathing and feeding. The supply department receives an order to send a pre-op preparation kit to the patient's floor and to provide transportation for the patient. Dietary is given instructions for feeding the patient. X-ray and pathology departments receive pre-established orders and enter results online to the patient's "chart." Reports for nursing may include "medications due" lists by hour, "daily orders summary," and "reminder notices" for overdue work.

Pharmacy. The pharmacist is aided by orders printed in the pharmacy, online access to review patient orders, and patient profiles on allergies. He also has information on drug incompatibility and has medications priced.

Radiology. The basic application here is text entry and retrieval for the report. A primary purpose is to speed the availability of the report to the requesting physician. The most effective approach in this respect is to have the radiologist key the text online. This eliminates the dictaphone, typist, and the time lost in review, correction and distribution.

Clinical laboratory. This can be a very complex application which provides labels, specimen collection lists, worklists, analog-digital converters and specialized keyboard terminals for results entry, various lab management reports, billings, and cumulative patient reports for the chart. These systems normally use a dedicated minicomputer, and may be installed as stand-alone systems.

Patient screening. These systems are used for health testing. The purpose is to reduce the professional time required in taking the history and ordering appropriate tests. The patient supplies answers to questions produced by the machine. This involves the logic to generate question sequences based on patient responses. Marksense cards and CRT terminals are typically used.

CONSTRAINTS ON DEVELOPMENT: STATE OF THE INDUSTRY

Vendor Environment

The relative complexity of the applications at the B and C levels, combined with the limited size and financial resources of the users, have produced a situation where most application software development is performed by vendors rather than by users. The result of this is that user hospitals must conform somewhat to the operating procedures, coding structures, and data formats designed by the vendor, although table driven design and user-generated CRT screen formats provide some tailoring capability.

Industry development has, furthermore, been very fragmented; there have been many vendor entries to, and departures from, the industry. IBM has chosen not to enter the software battle for Level B and C systems, although they possess most of the dedicated small system market with the Systems 3 and 32.[4] Most installed systems are limited to Level A applications, but less than half of all users have in-house systems. Other arrangements include service bureaus, multiple hospital shared systems, timesharing, and facilities management contracts. There are wide variations in application offerings, terminal types, and processor types. In short, there are many options, some definite risks and no specific approach which is clearly superior to all others.

The continued improvement in price/performance of data processing systems is very applicable to medical care. This is particularly applicable to processors and direct access storage; for example, the minicomputer is playing a rapidly expanding role. This means that economically feasible applications and the means of implementing them are subject to constant change, which is a big reason for the projected doubling of annual industry revenue over the next four to five years.

User Environment

Level A and B systems have been fairly well accepted. Of nearly 6,000 hospitals participating in a recent A.H.A. study, 60 percent have some form of computerization. Dr. Stanley Jacobs, former director of computer systems for A.H.A., has predicted that by 1980 at least 50 percent of all short-term general hospitals with over 200 beds will have Level B systems.

The commitment to Level C systems is less widespread here, but the growth is significant. A study by Creative Strategies, Inc., in San Jose, California, has forecast a tripling of industry revenue from $20 million in 1976 to $60 million in 1979, compared to a total industry market estimate of $380 million in 1979. Some of the reasons for the limited adoption of Level C systems include:

1. Objections by nurses and doctors to cumbersome data entry, bulky chart reports, etc.;

2. Concerns over security and privacy of medical data;

3. Reluctance to adopt the problem-oriented medical record necessary for computerization;

4. Cost and performance problems with installed systems; and

5. The prospective of more comprehensive software, and smaller, less expensive, more reliable machines to operate and back up online patient care systems.

RECOMMENDATIONS

Anticipate Legal Requirements

This is not possible in a literal sense. Reports cannot be developed until the requirements are known. However, by keeping abreast of legislative developments there is some hope of being able to plan for new system developments which may be indicated. This area is important because compliance is not likely to be a matter of choice, the impact may be very significant (as was for example the effect of Medicare on Level A systems), and purely manual compliance may be very expensive except for small hospitals.

Consider Alternative Implementation Approaches

While complete medical information systems are too complex and costly to be designed and developed by individual hospitals, medical and hospital staff people have demonstrated a reluctance to conform to the requirements of package systems. Fortunately, the industry offers a growing variety of application designs, hardware configurations, operations and financial arrangements, and implementation tools. In such an environment it is incumbent on hospital management to explore the alternatives in a comprehensive and thorough study, before making significant commitments to a course of development.

Maintain Flexibility

Considering the pace of technological change in data processing generally, and in health care systems in particular, plus the fragmented character of the industry, we must be prepared for system conversion on relatively short notice. There are some things which can be done to make this as painless as possible:

1. *Establish good D.P. documentation practices*—The average data processing shop has a patchwork of documentation because of the fact that programmers don't like to do it. This makes maintenance or conversion extremely difficult. The answer to this is to set up standard forms and procedures, and make them an integral part of the design and implementation process rather than a chore to be completed after installation.

2. *Use standard implementation tools and techniques*—Such things as common languages and coding techniques, industry-standard file management systems, and standard hardware configurations can help to minimize the impact of conversion to new systems and/or vendors.

3. *Avoid binding long-term vendor commitments*—This is another hard-to-achieve objective, because the vendors try to counteract by making short-term contracts very expensive. However, contracts with small companies in data processing are negotiable. One object of such negotiation should be to insure escape clauses in case the vendor does not meet his commitments.

4. *Maintain top management awareness*—In effect this says that system benefits, ease of implementation, conversion costs, etc. should not be oversold. Conservative projections and good communications are always desirable in project development of this sort.

Establish Long-Range Plans

The process of going from a Level A to a Level C system, or even to Level B represents a sizeable growth in system design complexity. The jump from sequential batch to online to data base/data communications systems is a long one. It is highly preferable to have top management decide where it wants to go at an early stage. How far do we want to go with the automated medical record? What size of operation will we be supporting five years from now? What changes in medical center operation, patient care management, staffing patterns, reporting formats, etc. will result from the systems we plan to install? Can we prepare for them in advance? What assurance do we have that near-term system developments will integrate easily with longer-term plans? These and other questions should be addressed on a five- and ten-year basis to insure a unified, integrated growth-path for hospital systems development.

CONCLUSION

The medium-sized hospital finds itself no longer able to ignore the propect of computerization. Current and impending government reporting requirements, the rising cost of clerical and professional services, and the demands of competition will continue to exert pressures toward administrative and clinical computer systems. On the other hand, the relative size of investment required, an immature vendor environment, and the potential impact on traditional methods of health care management may create a great deal of uncertainty as to how and when to proceed. In my opinion, the objective should be to steer a course which keeps up with the industry without being a pioneer, manages change as smoothly as possible, and operates on a cost-effective basis.

NOTES

[1] Much of this section is drawn from an article written by Dr. James V. Hansen, "Progress in Health Care Systems," *Journal of Systems Management,* April, 1975.

[2] The use of cathode ray tube terminals in the hospital makes this a significant step in terms of operational impact and the sophistication of data processing.

[3] A full-blown Level C system has yet to be installed anywhere.

[4] The main vendors include McDonnell-Douglas, Honeywell, Technicon, Spectra Medical, N. C. R., Shared Medical Systems, Meditech, and IBM.

CHAPTER 8

CASE:
GARDEN CHEMICALS,
INCORPORATED

INTRODUCTION

This case study is concerned with the document and information flows in a medium-size, growing organization. Especially in the areas of order processing, shipping, and billing, the case provides an opportunity for students to discern possible improvements in a manual system of document generation and handling. Emphasis may be on the improvement of the manual system and/or the conversion of it to a computerized system. The case allows for flowcharting, internal control evaluation, document design, data base improvement, and system redesign. This case should be assigned after the student has been exposed to systems flowcharting and document flows. For most courses the assignment of either part I or II is sufficient to expose the student to overgrown manual systems, and to provide the opportunity to convert a manual system to a computer system. The assignment of only part II is generally recommended. Depending upon the level of the students the assignment of parts III and IV may provide a capstone for the accounting and systems areas.

Possible Assignments

For assignments I and II each requirement may be assigned separately as the students progress through the course. For example, after students cover the topic of "feasibility studies," requirement II D may be assigned. Each lettered assignment requires approximately equal time and may be used for one period.

I. Purchasing/Accounts Payable/Inventory

   A. Flowchart present system.

   B. Identify strengths and weaknesses.

   C. Redesign system with computer application.

      1. Purchasing system.
      2. Accounts payable system.
      3. Inventory system.

    D. Develop data base schemas for each area.

    E. Redesign documentation of system, i.e. sales invoices, etc.

II. Order/Shipping/Billing

    A. Flowchart present system.

    B. Identify strengths and weaknesses.

    C. Develop improved manual system using flowcharting as basis.

    D. Calculate cost savings of new system.

    E. Design a computer system for the:

        1. order entry system.
        2. shipping system.
        3. billing system.

    F. Design the necessary documents for the improved system, i.e. the purchase order form, etc.

III. Other Subsystems

    A. Flowchart each of the other areas described in the case.

    B. Identify the strengths and weaknesses of each subsystem.

    C. Redesign and flowchart the subsystems

        1. assuming manual redesign, or
        2. assuming computer implementation.

IV. Develop an integrated computer system for the company including all areas described:

    A. Determine size and type of computer system needed.

    B. Perform a feasibility study.

    C. Flowchart the integrated system.

    D. Require programming of selected areas.

    E. Design selected source documents for the system; include both input and output type documents.

THE COMPANY

Garden Chemicals, Incorporated, is a wholesale distributor of liquid chemical products for lawn and garden use.

Since the firm's founding in 1970, it has grown rapidly in sales volume due largely to the success of its principal product, Weedoom, a selective herbicide prepared from alcohols and other chemicals. In addition to Weedoom, the other 45% of the company's sales consists of:

a) Other specialty chemical products blended and bottled by the company, and

b) Jobber items purchased in tank car lots and canned or bottled for resale.

Garden Chemical currently sells its products to retail dealers in 39 states and to one exporter. The company's 47 salesmen operate out of 20 district sales offices. No inventory (except samples) is carried in the district offices: all shipments are made from a single central warehouse.

The company maintains the general ledger on a cash basis. Worksheets are prepared at the end of each period recapping unpaid invoices and other accruals in order to create operating statements on an accrual basis. There is a substantial volume of such invoices handled each period. As a result, the financial statements are not completed until the 20th of each month.

No journal entries are prepared; in lieu thereof, two general accounting clerks enter standard worksheet entries in an adjustment column of the worksheet to arrive at interim report figures.

PURCHASES/ACCOUNTS PAYABLE/INVENTORY

1. Inventory Control

Kardex inventory records are posted at the warehouse. Each inventory item is on a separate card which contains a record of all changes and permanent information.

Receipts are posted to the perpetual inventory records from copies of the purchase invoices and issues are posted from copies of the sales invoices.

Production reports are maintained for each blending or manufacturing process. These reports show the quantity of the products used and the quantity produced. These reports are then posted to the perpetual records.

Since there are no raw materials nor work-in-process accounts, the material costs from the production reports do not enter into the general books. There is only one general ledger account for all stock called "inventory." Labor and overhead are applied to inventory in total each month based on a percentage of sales. At the year end, the time the physical inventory is taken, the manufactured and blended products are priced at standard costs. All variances from standard existing during the year are picked up at that time.

2. Purchasing Procedures

All purchasing is done by the purchasing agent. Except for routine items, purchases are made only on the basis of signed requisitions from authorized persons. Purchase orders are prepared for all purchases but quotations are not first obtained nor is the purchase price entered on the purchase order.

Eight copies of each purchase order are prepared and distributed as follows:

#1 and #2—Supplier.

#3 and #4—Purchasing department files in numerical order.

#5 and #6—Freight and invoice checking section. The fifth copy is used to match up with freight bills. The sixth copy is used as a numerical control for a check-off of invoices as they are received. It is destroyed when the order is complete.

#7 and #8—Warehouse. The seventh copy is filed numerically for warehouse record and the eighth copy is given to the receiving dock to put them on notice of a shipment. It is destroyed when the shipment is complete.

3. Receiving of Merchandise

The central receiving point is the dock. A three copy receiving report is prepared for each receipt. The receiving reports are not prenumbered. The copies are distributed as follows:

#1—Filed at warehouse for any future reference.

#2 and #3—Forwarded to invoice checking clerks in the office where they are held until the invoice is received from the branch.

4. Processing of Suppliers' Invoices

Two copies of all invoices are received from the suppliers at the sales branches. The unit cost is computed and entered on a perpetual inventory record. This record is kept at the branches in case the salesmen wish to refer to it. The original copy of the invoice is then forwarded to the main office for processing. The duplicate is filed pending receipt of a cost sheet from the main office confirming the correctness of the branch's unit cost computation. This unit cost is used by the salesmen at the branches for reference purposes as to how much sales discount can be allowed on specific items.

The original invoice next goes to the controller who logs it in on a control worksheet by date due. This worksheet is then furnished to the payable clerk for his or her control. The invoice then goes to the invoice checking section where it is matched with the receiving report copies 2 and 3. It is also matched with the sixth copy of the purchase order and the items received are checked off the purchase order. When the shipment is complete, the purchase order is destroyed. The cost of each item on the invoice is computed and entered on the third copy of the receiving report. This third copy is then filed by date received, by branch.

The invoice and the second copy of the receiving report next go to the purchasing department where they are matched with the fourth copy of the purchase order pulled from the file. If it is a completed shipment, the fourth copy of the purchase order is attached to the invoice. If it is a partial shipment, the fourth copy is placed back into the file and held until final shipment. The quantity received is posted at this time to both the third and fourth copies of the purchase order. The third copy then becomes a permanent numerical file record.

The invoice, together with the second copy of the receiving report and the fourth copy of the purchase order is forwarded to the comptometer section where the clerical accuracy is checked. The documents then go to the payable section for payment.

5. Accounts Payable

When the invoice and receiving report are forwarded from the purchasing section, the payable clerk enters the distribution. Each supplier has a code number which is entered on the invoice. The invoices are next batched and taped in total and by account distribution. This distribution is then posted, in summary form, to a payable register.

The invoices are then sorted by supplier and posted to accounts payable ledgers. The total postings are balanced to the batch totals.

The invoices are next filed by supplier. From the payment control worksheet, the clerk pulls invoices as they are due for payment. If any invoices are missing, the clerk finds where they are being delayed and expedites them.

6. Payments of Suppliers' Invoices

After pulling the invoices from the file, the payable clerk types a two-part check and sends the original to the supplier. The top portion of the check is the remittance advice and each invoice being paid is entered in that section.

The second copy of the check is posted to a check register and then filed in numerical order. The check register is then used as the media for the posting to the individual accounts payable ledgers. The copy of the check is filed numerically and the paid invoices are filed alphabetically.

ORDER/SHIPPING/BILLING

1. Sales Department

   a. Order Editing Clerk

      1) On receipt of a customer order, it is entered in an order register. The following details are recorded:

> Date of receipt
> Customer's order number
> Customer's name
> Sales order number (assigned serially from previous entry)

      2) Sales order number is entered on the customer's order.

      3) Customer's order is checked against credit exception file. If exception applies, the order is sent to the Credit Department for clearance. When returned, the order is processed through regular routing beyond this point. If not approved, it is so indicated on the order and the order is returned to sales and filed by customer name.

4) Each line item is checked against catalog data to assure proper catalog number, description, and price.

b. Order Typist

1) The customer order is passed to a typist who types a sales order in triplicate. The following data are recorded:

Date of customer's order
Name and address of customer
Name and address of consignor
Sales territory
Customer's order number
Sales order number
Shipping instructions (if provided by customer)
For each line item:
Catalog number
Quantity
Description

2) The first copy of the sales order is mailed to the customer as an acknowledgement. The second copy is sent to the warehouse. The third copy is filed alphabetically in an open order file with the customer's order.

2. Warehouse

a. Inventory Clerk

On receipt of the sales order, each item is checked for availability:

1) If an item is available, the quantity called for is posted as a deduction on the inventory record.

2) If an item is not available, the date, sales order number, and quantity are posted to the back-order section of the inventory record and the quantity figure is circled on the sales order.

3) If an item is partially available, the quantity available is posted as a deduction, the back-order quantity figure is circled on the sales order, and the quantity available is written to the right of the circle.

4) If all items on the order are back-ordered, a back-order entry is made for each item as in (2) above. The sales order is held by the Inventory Clerk until any one of the items is available and then released for further processing. (Back-orders are handled in the same manner. See back-order preparation procedure explanation in a following section.)

b. Warehouse Clerk

1) The sales order is passed to the Warehouse Clerk who places it in a "waiting for shipment" file in sales order number sequence.

2) Sales orders are assigned to Packers for assembly of items and packing in sales order number sequence.

c. Packer

When the items have been packed, the Packer writes in the quantity shipped beside the quantity ordered and also enters the number of cartons and total weight on the sales order. The cartons are marked with the sales order number and set aside.

d. Warehouse Clerk

1) The sales order is returned to the Warehouse Clerk who enters the following data from the sales order in a shipping register:

> Date packed
> Sales order number
> Number of cartons
> Total weight

2) Shipping and routing instructions are determined from reference data and entered on the sales order if these instructions have not been provided by the customer.

Note: All shipments are made on a "freight collect" basis and freight charges are therefore collected by the carrier directly from the customer.

e. Shipping Typist

1) The sales order is then passed to the typist for preparation of a shipping order (serially numbered) in five copies, one shipping label for each carton, and bills of lading. The following data are entered on the shipping order:

> Date
> Customer's name and address
> Consignee's name and address (if different from above)
> Sales territory
> Customer's order number
> Sales order number
> Number of cartons
> How shipped
> Total weight

For each item:

> Quantity ordered
> Quantity shipped
> Catalog number
> Description

2) Copies are distributed as follows:

#1 to the Warehouse Clerk with the shipping labels and bills of lading

#2 to Billing as notice of shipment

#3 the shipping order number is recorded on the second copy of the sales order which is then sent with the third copy of the shipping order to the Order Edit Clerk.

#4 is filed in shipping order number sequence

#5 to sales branch.

f. Warehouse Clerk

1) Labels are applied to the cartons. The first copy of the shipping order
• is placed in one carton as a packing list and the cartons are sealed.

2) Two copies of the bill of lading are given to the carrier; the third is filed by bill-of-lading number.

3. Sales Department

a. Order Edit Clerk

1) The shipping order is checked against the sales order for accuracy.

2) The sales order is checked for back-ordered items. If any item has been back-ordered, the sales order is stamped to indicate that a back-order is to be prepared.

3) The sales order copy is then passed to the Order Typist and the shipping order is given to the Pricing Clerk.

b. Order Typist

1) The original customer order and the sales file copy of the sales order are pulled from the open file and the inventory copy of the sales order is attached.

2) If the order is complete, the order documents are placed in the closed order file alphabetically by customer.

3) If any item has been back-ordered, a back-order is typed in duplicate and one copy is sent to the warehouse; the other is attached to the original order documents which are then returned to the open order file.

Note: The processing of back-orders through shipping, sales review, pricing, and invoicing is identical to the treatment of original sales orders.

c. Pricing Clerk

1) Refers to the customer file, obtains and enters the customer class code on the shipping order copy.

2) Refers to price lists for customer class, obtains and enters unit prices based on volume discounts.

  d. Comptometer Operator

  1) The shipping order is passed to the Comptometer Operator, who extends unit price and quantity for each item, enters the extension on the shipping order, and calculates and enters the total amount.

  2) The shipping order is then sent to billing.

4. Billing Department

  a. Invoice Typist

  1) The second copy of the shipping order, when received from the warehouse, is filed in a "waiting for billing" file in shipping order number sequence.

  2) On receipt of the priced copy of the shipping order, the second copy is pulled and attached.

  3) An invoice (serially numbered) is typed (in nine copies) with the following data entered:

> Invoice date
> Customer name and address
> Consignee's name and address
> Customer's order number
> Sales order number
> Sales territory
> How shipped
> Number of cartons
> Total weight

> For each item:

> Quantity ordered
> Quantity shipped
> Catalog number
> Description
> Unit price
> Total price

> And: Total amount invoiced

  4) The invoice set is passed with the copies of the shipping order to the Invoice Checking Clerk.

  b. Invoice Checking Clerk

  1) The invoice is checked against the shipping order for typing accuracy.

2) Extensions and total amount are checked.

3) Invoice copies and shipping order copies are distributed as follows:

    #1 and #2—Mailed to the customer

        #3—to Accounting (Accounts Receivable)

        #4—attached to and filed with the shipping order copies (invoice number sequence)

        #5—to Accounting (sales distribution)

        #6—to Accounting (salesman commission)

        #7—filed by sales order number

    #8 and #9—to salesman

OTHER SUBSYSTEMS

1. Sales and Cost of Sales Analysis

The accounting section receives the sales analysis copy of each sales invoice. The items are coded by product grouping and any trade discounts or freight allowances shown on the invoice are allocated to all product groups shown on the invoice.

The invoice copy is then sent to the inventory clerk who enters on the invoice the average cost of each item. This is taken from the perpetual inventory record.

The invoice copy is then returned to the sales analysis clerk who summarizes the cost on each invoice by product group totals.

The invoices are next listed into a 54-column sales register. The gross sales amount and cost by product grouping are distributed by columns and totaled at the end of the month.

2. Accounts Receivable

All receivables are machine posted on a Burroughs F100 Sensimatic bookkeeping machine. Charges are posted from copies of the sales invoice and cost is posted from cash receipt advices.

At the end of each period, open item statements are typed from the ledger cards. This is done in the first 10 days of the month and the receivable checking clerks spend full time during that period in this task. The statements are prepared in three copies—original to customer, second to credit manager who prepares an aging from the copies, and third to the branches.

The Company has established credit limits for their customers and the sales branches are not to allow credit greater than the limit. In order to keep current as to a customer's status, the sales branches file the statement copy and all cash receipts are entered thereon during the month. An open invoice file by customer is also maintained for the current month's invoices.

3. Cash Receipts

Cash is received by the sales branches and at the main office.

As cash is received at the branches, a clerk types a two-part cash receipt advice for each check or cash item. Customer remittance advices, which accompany almost all checks, are attached to the original copy of the cash receipt advice. The clerk then prepares a three-part deposit slip. The original of the deposit slip is forwarded to the bank, the second copy is forwarded to the main office with the cash receipt advice, and the third copy is filed.

The second copy of the cash receipt advice is used for checking off the payments against a copy of the prior month's customer statement received from the main office. All payments are checked off this statement copy until the next month's statement copies are received.

The home office processing is the same except that the second copy of the cash receipt advice is sent to the sales branches.

The original copies of the cash receipt advices are used for posting to the ledgers. The copies are first forwarded to the four receivable checking clerks who match payments with open items on ledger cards. At this point, they enter the date paid by each item on the ledger card. The purpose of this is to simplify open item statements at month-end.

The receipt advices are next forwarded to the bookkeeping machine operator who posts the cash receipts to the individual accounts. The total is balanced to a tape of the advices and this total is then posted to the general ledger from the receivable proofsheet.

4. Reporting

Each month the company prepares a balance sheet and a profit-and-loss statement. In addition, a profit-and-loss statement is prepared for each branch. In order to obtain this information a general ledger is maintained for each branch. A separate one is kept for the home office but all these profit-and-loss accounts are allocated to the branches. The president receives a consolidated balance sheet and profit-and loss statement listing the accounts by account title.

In addition to these statements a statement of sales by product line is prepared, showing gross sales and gross profit.

5. Payroll

Employment is authorized by the sales branch managers, the office manager or the treasurer. Rates of pay and subsequent changes are authorized by the joint agreement of the president, executive vice president, treasurer and office manager. The office manager then verbally informs the payroll clerk of the change.

Clock cards are used by the warehouse employees. In addition to the clock card, each employee fills out a daily distribution card turned in daily to the payroll department. For office personnel, a time sheet is turned in biweekly by each employee.

The gross pay and deductions are computed and entered on the front side of each clock card or time sheet. Standard deductions are entered from the individual earnings records filed alphabetically by employee.

Distribution is taken each day from the distribution cards and entered on a worksheet. Each card has an average of four account distributions. The payroll clerk sends the worksheet to the general ledger section after balancing to the gross pay entered on the payroll register.

After gross pay has been computed on the clock card and time sheets, a payroll register is prepared. The total of this register is balanced to total distribution. Checks are then typed from the register and distributed to the employees. The payroll register is used also for posting to the individual earnings records and then filed by the payroll clerk for his or her subsequent reconciliation of the payroll account.

APPENDIX I BALANCE SHEET

Assets	December 31, 1978		December 31, 1977	
Current Assets				
Cash		$ 277,990		$ 572,660
Accounts receivable	$1,607,480		$1,310,510	
Less—Reserve for				
bad debts	52,030	1,555,450	42,420	1,268,090
Merchandise		4,679,070		4,040,650
Prepaid expenses		45,720		41,720
Total current				
assets		$6,558,230		$5,923,120
Notes receivable		26,840		19,660
Investments		20,450		20,450
Fixed assets	1,175,670		984,600	
Less—Reserve for				
depreciation	598,310	577,360	434,210	550,390
Total assets		$7,182,880		$6,513,620

Liabilities				
Current liabilities				
Notes payable		748,490		658,560
Accounts payable		788,980		603,510
Accrued expenses				
and taxes		431,110		525,290
Accrued income taxes		75,830		97,500
Container deposits		184,010		158,910
Total current				
liabilities		$2,228,420		$2,043,770
Notes payable		329,280		168,110
Capital stock		1,531,790		1,531,790
Earned surplus		2,845,660		2,522,220
Capital surplus		247,730		247,730
Total Liabilities				
and Owners Equity		$7,182,880		$6,513,620

APPENDIX II STATEMENT OF INCOME

12 Months Ending December 31

	1978		1977	
Sales	$12,648,950	100%	$10,920,880	100%
Cost of Sales	10,342,620	82%	8,734,120	80%
Gross Profit	$ 2,306,330	18%	$ 2,186,760	20%
Selling, General and Administrative Expense	1,690,270	13%	1,339,450	12%
Operating Income	$ 616,060	5%	$ 847,310	8%
Other Income (net)	57,380	–	42,720	–
	$ 673,440	5%	$ 890,030	8%
Provision for Taxes	350,000	2.5%	450,000	4%
Net Income	$ 323,440	2.5%	$ 440,030	4%

APPENDIX III MISCELLANEOUS SALES DATA

1. Customers

   1,550 active customers as of January 1, 1979.
   4,000 total accounts.
   New customers–20 per month; 14 net increase.
   10% of customers require a credit check.
   20% of customers account for 80% of the sales order volume.

2. Customer Orders–Volume Averages

   1st Quarter–170 daily–average 4 line items.
   2nd Quarter–250 daily–average 4 line items.
   3rd Quarter–250 daily–average 4 line items.
   4th Quarter–420 daily–average 6 line items.

3. Order Processing Cycles

   1st through 3rd Quarters–5 days.
   4th Quarter–7 days.

4. Back-Order Volume

   75% of all orders shipped complete.
   25% of orders–1 item back-ordered.

5. Sales Items

   Total inventory items–2,850.
   Active items–2,175.

APPENDIX IV NUMBER OF EMPLOYEES

Present clerical personnel are engaged full-time related to their main assigned functions.

		First 3 Quarters	Fourth Quarter
a.	Sales Order Processing		
	1. Order editing clerks, Senior	6	6
	2. Order typists	11	14
	3. Pricing clerks, Junior	6	7
	4. Comptometer operators	4	4
b.	Warehouse		
	1. Inventory record clerks, Senior	3	3
	2. Warehouse clerks, Junior	2	2
	3. Shipping typists	6	8
c.	Billing		
	1. Invoice typists	8	10
	2. Invoice checking clerks, Junior	4	4
d.	Receivables		
	1. Supervisor	1	1
	2. Checking clerks, Senior	4	4
	3. Posting clerks, Junior	4	4
e.	Cash receipts		
	1. Cashier	1	1
	2. Clerks, Junior	2	2
f.	General Accounting		
	1. Supervisor	1	1
	2. Assistant supervisor	1	1
	3. General clerks, Senior	6	6
	4. Sales and cost of sales clerks, Senior	4	4
	5. Purchase invoice checking clerks, Junior	4	4
	6. Payroll supervisor	1	1
	7. Payroll clerks, Junior	4	4
g.	Purchasing		
	1. Supervisor	1	1
	2. Assistant supervisor	1	1
	3. Clerks, Junior	3	3

APPENDIX IV (Cont.)

		First 3 Quarters	Fourth Quarter
h.	Purchase Invoice Checking		
	1. Clerks, Junior	4	4
i.	Accounts Payable		
	1. Supervisor	1	1
	2. Clerks, Senior	5	5
j.	Credit		
	1. Clerks, Junior	4	5
k.	Sales Branch Clerical		
	1. Clerks, Senior (in each of 20 branches)	5	5

APPENDIX V PAYROLL COSTS

Payroll Costs—Clerical
Per Hour

	Per Hour
a. Clerks, Senior	$ 5.00
b. Clerks, Junior	4.50
c. Typists	3.50
d. Supervisors	10.00
e. Machine operators	5.50
f. Assistant supervisors	7.00
g. Keypunch operators	4.00
h. Payroll fringe benefits	15%

Example of Calculations

	Hours	Rate	Emp.	Weeks	Total
First Quarter					
Senior Clerks	39 hrs. × 5.00 × 11 × 13 =				$ 27,885
Junior Clerks	39 hrs. × 4.50 × 14 × 13 =				31,941
Typists	39 hrs. × 3.50 × 25 × 13 =				44,362
					$104,188
Fringe benefits of 15%					× 115%
Total Costs					$119,816

Average straight time hours worked per week by each of the accounting and order processing clerks

a. 1st quarter—39
b. 2nd quarter—42
c. 3rd quarter—41
d. 4th quarter—49

APPENDIX VI FORMS AND COSTS

		Set Usage				Total Dollars
	Copies	First Quarter	Second Quarter	Third Quarter	Fourth Quarter	5¢–Set 1¢–Copy
Sales order	3	11,050	16,250	16,250	27,300	$ 5,700
Shipping order	5	3,800	20,300	20,300	34,100	7,950
Bill of lading	3	13,800	20,300	20,300	34,100	7,100
Labels	2/order	27,600	40,600	40,600	68,200	1,800
Invoices	9	13,800	20,300	20,300	34,100	12,400
Back-order set	2	2,750	4,050	4,050	6,800	1,250
						$36,200

Example of Calculations

Days: 365 − 104 weekends − 7 holidays = 254
Assume 63 days per quarter
Order volume

	Orders	Total Including Spoilage	Back Orders
		(2 days volume)	(25%)
1st quarter	170 × 63 = 10,710	11,050	2,750
2nd and 3rd quarters	250 × 63 = 15,750	16,250	4,060
4th quarter	420 × 63 = 26,460	27,300	6,800

Other Volumes–Per Month Average

a. Purchase order–2,200
b. Checks issued–2,050
c. Cash receipts–4,000

CHAPTER 9

CASE:
CENTURY PLASTICS
COMPANY

INTRODUCTION

This case concentrates on the control aspects of a computerized information system. Three areas are presented for analysis—payroll, order entry, and procurement. Each or all of the functional areas may be assigned and either the individual or team approach may be used. This case should be assigned after the student has been exposed to both computer controls and accounting controls. The requirements are generally more effective if given progressively during term.

Possible assignments include:

I. For any or all three systems the possible requirements are:
   a) Evaluate existing or design systems flowchart
   b) Evaluate the controls surrounding the system
   c) Make suggestions as to how to improve system
      1. Specify weaknesses
      2. Correspond improvements to a given weakness(es)

II. Make a general evaluation of the company's control system.
   a) Accounting controls
   b) Computer and system controls

III. Prepare a listing of the procedures that could be used to "test" the system and the types of transactions that you would test.

BACKGROUND

The Century Plastics Company is a wholly owned subsidiary of the Baker Corporation, a nationwide manufacturer and distributor of toys and cookware. The Century Plastics Company manufactures and distributes Baker Corporation products exclusively in the southern states. Century Plastics Company has nine manufacturing plants at various locations throughout the South and a central office located in Atlanta, Georgia. At each plant, there also is a warehouse from which products are distributed. The company has annual sales of about $330,000,000 and employs about 20,000 people.

The data processing requirements of the company are extensive. Payroll preparation, customer billings and collections, and disbursements to suppliers are the major large-volume EDP tasks. Century Plastics has ten data processing units; nine of these units (one at each plant location) are responsible for the routine, repetitive, high-volume tasks described above. Their work is carried out with a small staff and machine operators who have little or no previous training or experience. No programming is done at these units.

In June, 1979, as Mr. Al Sanders was reviewing the negative comments received from his CPA about the condition of his management information system, he realized that as controller of Century Plastics he had neglected the role of accounting in the development of the information system since the company acquired its computer 11 years ago. Having just replaced the retired head of the internal auditing department with an aggressive young accountant, he decided to give the specific task of improving internal control to her. Ms. Edwards was to select two or three other members from either the accounting or systems analysis staffs and make the necessary recommendations to improve the accounting controls related to the information system and the computer. Mr. Sanders asked that they initially concentrate their work in the areas of payroll, order entry, and procurement.

THE ELECTRONIC DATA PROCESSING CENTER

The tenth unit, the Electronic Data Processing Center (EDPC), is located in the central office at Atlanta, and its work is quite different from that of the other nine units. This work consists principally of many small, difficult, one-time jobs rather than high-volume, repetitive jobs. The unit is primarily concerned with providing management information reports requested by various departments of Century Plastics. Some of this work, however, is routine because some jobs are required by the customer departments on either a monthly or quarterly basis. At any give time during the year the center is responsible for nearly 300 projects.

Organizationally, the EDPC is evaluated as a separate cost center and reported as a line group to the Accounting Department. Although job costs are compiled, the EDPC does not charge customer departments for its services. To make sure, however, that only those jobs in the company's best interests are undertaken, a staff group called the Procedures Staff monitors all activity. Its function is to examine all proposals, to evaluate their usefulness from the company's viewpoint, and to correlate them with the present schedule of the EDPC. If this group feels that a job is to the overall advantage of the company, it is discussed with the EDPC, and a joint agreement is reached as to whether or not to run the job in the center.

The staff also helps to arbitrate situations where the EDPC, because of timing or scheduling problems, is unable to handle all the work expected of it. The staff negotiates with the center so that a mutually satisfactory agreement can be reached between the EDPC and the customer department.

PAYROLL

The following description is of a typical payroll operation that may be found in any of the nine plants. This is one of the routine, repetitive, high-volume tasks referred to above. Each plant and the home office is responsible for their own payroll.

Processing

Transaction cards (Exhibit 1) are keypunched from the following source documents:

1. Weekly time cards,
2. Employees' exemption certificates,
3. Authorized rate change forms approved by the personnel department,
4. Authorized new employee forms approved by the personnel department,
5. Authorized employee termination forms approved by the personnel department.

Transaction cards, after keypunching, are not subject to key verification. Master file cards for terminated employees are removed during a presort operation and are processed on a separate run. Master file cards contain the information shown in Exhibit 2.

Three types of changes in input media are recognized by the program:

1. *Changes in number of dependents.* A change in the number of dependents for an employee will appear in field #5 of the payroll transaction card; for all other employees this field will be blank. The new number of dependents is used during the processing run for the current period and is punched in the updated master card for future processing runs.

2. *Pay rate changes.* A change in the regular rate of pay for an employee appears in field #6 of the payroll transaction card; for all other employees this field will be blank. This new rate is used during the processing run for the current period and is punched in the updated master card for future processing runs.

3. *New employee.* The code digit "1" is punched in field #7 on the transaction card for all new employees; for all other employees this field will be blank. The program interprets this to mean that there is no master record for this transaction card; an updated master card will be punched for future processing runs.

The computation phase of the program is designed to take account of the following aspects of payroll processing:

1. All hours worked in excess of 40 are paid at the rate of 1½ times the regular rate of pay;
2. The first $20,000 of each employee's gross earnings is subject to an FICA rate of 6.05%;

Exhibit 1 PAYROLL TRANSACTION CARDS

Field 1—Name _____
    01-20

Field 2—Department Code and Employee # _ _ _ _ _ _ _ _
    21-25

Field 3—Rate _ _ _
    26-28
	Field 4—Dependents _
	    29

Field 5—Change in Dependents _
    30

Field 6—Pay Rate Change _ _ _ _
    31-34

Field 7—New Employee _
    35
	Field 8—Employee # _ _ _ _ _
	    36-40

Field 9—Vacation accomulation rate _ _ _
    41-43

Field 10—Hours worked _ _
    44-45
	Field 11—Last Payroll _
	    46

Exhibit 2 PUNCHED CARD INPUT-OUTPUT

Master Card

    Field 1:   Employee number;
    Field 2:   Number of dependents
    Field 3:   Regular rate of pay
    Field 4:   Gross earnings to date
    Field 5:   FICA deductions to date
    Field 6:   Federal withholding tax to date
    Field 7:   Other deductions to date

3. Federal income tax withholdings are computed as follows:

    a)   exempt weekly earnings = number of dependents X $20.00,
    b)   taxable earnings = gross earnings − exempt earnings
    c)   taxes withheld = taxable earnings X 22%.

The program provides for the possibility that exempt earnings may exceed gross earnings and no tax will be withheld in such situations.

4. "Other deductions" represent union dues, credit union deposits, savings bonds deductions, and so forth. For any one employee, these deductions are fixed in amount, except that union dues are deducted only once a month. Since these deductions are not a function of gross earnings, the possibility exists that the total of all deductions (including FICA and income tax withholdings) will exceed gross pay. In that event, the program provides for "other deductions" to be reduced to the extent of any "negative" net pay, resulting in a net pay of zero for the current period.

Exhibit 3 illustrates a "typical" weekly payroll processing run within the company. While not every plant uses this exact system they all have the same input-output documents. This flowchart does not illustrate terminated employee processing.

Processing Controls

Several processing controls are used in each payroll system. The first three are checks of the validity or reasonableness of the input data. Deviations, based upon the first three process controls, will result in "error messages," which are discussed below.

Both the master file and the transaction file are presorted in ascending employee number sequence prior to the processing run. No duplication of employee numbers should appear in either file. The sequence check is to assure that both files are in proper sequence prior to processing the transaction.

The self-checking digits are designed to detect errors in keypunching of the employee number. In this particular application, the self-checking digits are recorded in field #2 of each transaction card. They are a function of the employee number and are computed as follows:

1. The units position of the employee number is multiplied by one,

2. The tens position of the employee number is multiplied by two,

3. The hundreds position of the employee number is multiplied by three,

4. The thousands position of the employee number is multiplied by four,

5. The sum of the four products is computed and subtracted from 1,000 to produce the self-checking digits.

Exhibit 3 TYPICAL PAYROLL FLOWCHART

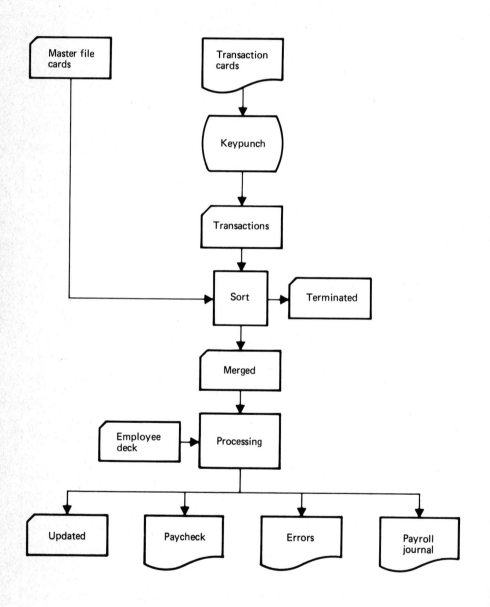

The reasonableness or limit check of gross pay calculations is designed to pick up inadvertent computational errors or keypunching errors in the number of hours worked (or provide special approval for what may be excessive overtime). The reasonableness check on gross weekly pay is $1,000.

The record count is a control total which is verified against pre-established numbers relating to the total number of employees included in the master file and the total transaction cards that have been processed.

Output

Exhibit 4 provides a description of the printed output of the processing run. The updated master file, of course, becomes the input for the next processing run and provides the data necessary for various periodic reports to users outside the company—the federal government relative to FICA and withholding taxes, the union relative to union dues withheld, and so forth. The master cards and the payroll cards are produced by an "on-line" card punch.

The payroll cards provide the input data for two separate processing steps. Both steps are carried out on an "off-line" printer and are controlled by wired board programs. Step one is the production of the payroll journal as described in Exhibit 4. The other processing step results in the production of payroll checks. In check preparation, the payroll card deck is merged with an "employee identification deck" which contains the following information:

a) Field 1: Employee name
b) Field 2: Employee number
c) Field 3: Employee social security number

The merged deck provides the input data for the payroll checks.

The error messages are printed out on an electric typewriter attached to the console. When an error message is printed out, no further processing of that transaction card takes place. The system is programmed to proceed to the next transaction card without halting. Errors are investigated, new cards punched as necessary and a second run is used to process the exceptions. The error message normally contains only the employee's number and the class of error. Details of error messages are as follows:

Error Message #1: A sequence error exists; either a duplicate employee number or an incorrect ascending sequence has been used.

Error Message #2: Incorrect self-checking digits; either the employee number or the self-checking digits have been recorded incorrectly.

Error Message #3: Sum of deductions exceeds gross earnings; all the details of gross pay and deductions are printed out in addition to "EM #3" so that "other deductions" which may have been reduced by the amount of any negative balance may be adjusted in subsequent pay periods.

Exhibit 4 PRINTED PAYROLL OUTPUT

Payroll Journal

Column 1:   Employee number
Column 2:   Hours worked
Column 3:   Gross earnings–this period
Column 4:   FICA deductions–this period
Column 5:   Income tax withheld–this period
Column 6:   Other deductions–this period
Column 7:   Net pay–this period
Columns 8–15: Gross pay broken down by cost centers based upon cost center code included as part of employee number.

Printed Error Messages

Printed error messages list the employee number and the class of error (except as noted in case) as follows:

1476–error message 3

Error Message #4: The limit check of $1,000 in gross pay has been exceeded.

Error Message #5: A transaction card without the code digit "1" for which there is no master record (new employees must have code digit "1" to indicate no master record exists).

After each payroll run the plant telephones the home office to place a funds transfer into the plant payroll bank account. No formal documentation of this transaction is forwarded to the home office. The internal auditing staff makes infrequent audits of each plant's payroll processing.

ORDER ENTRY SYSTEM

Sales orders are transmitted by salesmen from the 43 sales branches to the home office. Each order is processed on a disc-oriented computer system consisting of four disk storage drives, four magnetic tape units, a card-reader-punch, a line printer, and a console typewriter. For branch transmission of orders, a teletypewriter system is used with orders recorded on punched paper tape. Data on paper tape are converted to magnetic tape in batches with use of a punched-paper-tape reader. Off-line equipment includes keypunch and verifying machines and a card sorter.

The branch office is responsible for pricing the orders, based upon catalog prices for standard items. For special items of a nonstandard nature, prices are based upon estimates prepared by the home office.

Processing

The standard order form is used to prepare a punched paper tape for transmission of the order to the home office. While the punched paper tape is being prepared, a two-part copy of the sales order is produced on an automatic typewriter. One copy of the sales order is kept in a manual open order file pending proof from the home office that the order was received properly. The second copy is distributed to the salesman.

The branch office maintains master paper tapes for all its customers. The master tape contains uniform customer information such as name, address, number, geographic code, credit class, branch office and salesman. In transmitting an order, the customer information from the master tape is transmitted first, followed by the order tape containing variable information, such as shipping point, items ordered, quantities and cash discounts. The order tape also indicates whether the order will be filled from branch stock or whether it must be shipped from a plant. The receiving station at the home office receives orders in random sequence from the entire network and produces a punched paper tape of the information sent by the branches. It also initiates the Today's Order File along with the paper tape.

As the data are received at the home office and as the punched paper tape is prepared for orders received, sales orders are simultaneously created by the computer at the home office. Six copies of the sales order are created with distribution to sales; customer; shipping and stores (three copies, one of which is the packing list copy and another is a delivery receipt); and branch, to be compared with copy created at time-of-order transmission.

The punched paper tape is next converted to magnetic tape, at which time a record count is established on orders received from each branch. After this run, the orders are also checked by the computer for completeness and for illogical conditions such as incorrect salesmen code for a particular branch. Once the data are edited, the valid orders (now on magnetic tape) are processed as input to update the Open Order File, maintained on a disk pack. During the order-entry run, a Daily Orders Entered Register is printed. This register provides a listing of all orders processed with the Open Order File for the day and provides a dollar total of all orders processed. Today's Order File is used subsequently to update the inventory file and to update the accounts receivable files (credit analysis).

During the conversion process a few input validity checks are made on the input data. A test is made to determine whether the customer number is numerical. Order numbers and salesmen's codes are tested to see whether they are for the correct branch. If the order is to be split between two locations or two salesmen, the program determines that the percent relationship adds to 100.

Invalid orders are matched manually with the six part standard order and both are returned to the branch office for correction and retransmission. Only valid orders are placed in the Open Order File.

The Today's Order File contains all valid orders in random order number sequence. The tape is sorted by the computer before processing with the Open Order File and a new tape is written with daily orders in order number sequence. A record count is maintained throughout the program and is recorded on the trailer label of the sequenced tape.

Order changes are received from the branch offices on the same teletypewriter network except that a punched paper tape is not prepared. Order change cards are keypunched, keyverified, and processed with Today's Order File, in order number sequence, and the Open File, also in order number sequence. Order change cards are also used in the Accounts Receivable Updating system.

In the Order Entry system, the computer operations produce both machine-readable output and visible output for subsequent use and distribution. This output includes:

1. Updated Open Order File, on magnetic tape and printed listing.
2. Stock Items Listed on Order File, on magnetic tape.
3. Today's Orders Entered, on punched cards and printed listing.

The updated Open Order File is used in the Invoicing system while the Stock Items Listed on Order File is used for inventory updating and control and for production scheduling.

The Daily Orders Entered Register lists the order number, shipping point, items, and quantities. This register also shows a complete print-out of every order that is rejected because of a duplicate order number. One of the two copies of this register is mailed to the branch office entering the orders and is used by the branch to determine that all orders entered by the branch have been processed. The other copy is sent to the Accounting Control Group, where the total of all orders entered by all branches is compared to the total orders entered that appears on the Daily Orders Entered Register.

The order change cards are also used to produce a Daily Order Change Register, which is a listing, by branch, of all changes made to orders on the Open Order File. The register shows order number, the change made, the kind of change, and the sales value of the change. This report is mailed to the branch offices daily.

Today's Orders Entered cards are used in subsequent processing as part of the Invoicing system and Accounts Receivable Updating system.

Invoicing

The home office does the invoicing for all shipments made. The invoices are prepared by the computer by processing the Open Order File, which contains data on the order shipped—including the unit price and transaction data on shipments. The source document creating shipment transactions is the shipping and stores copy of the order. On this document, shipping personnel indicate the quantity shipped, shipping method, freight information, and special charges (Exhibit 5). This information is in addition to the standard information already printed on this copy of the standard order form (quantity ordered, customer, and branch information).

The shipping documents arrive for keypunching in the input-output section of data processing from the various shipping points of the company.

After review, the shipping documents are sent to be keypunched and keyverified; no batch or control totals are developed at this point. After punching and verification, the cards are transferred to the computer center for processing. The data on the cards are converted to data on magnetic tape. The updated Open Order

File is then used for the next day's processing of orders to be entered while the Stock Items Shipped tape is used to prepare sales analyses and for inventory updating. The punched cards are used in the Daily Status Report processing program and the Accounts Receivable program.

Three copies of the invoice are sent to the customer and one copy each is sent to the Accounting Control Group, the salesman, and the branch office which originated the sale. The original copy of the invoice includes a stub which the customer is requested to return with his or her payment.

In a second processing run, the card deck is read into the computer with the Daily-Monthly Status Report File on magnetic tape and Today's Order Entered card deck, produced by the Order Entry system. The Daily-Monthly Status Report File is in product code sequence and both card decks are sorted into the same sequence before processing with the Status Report program. The updated Daily-Monthly Status Report File is used in processing the next day's Daily Status Report while the Invoice Control Report is distributed to the Accounting Control Group for review and follow-up as required. The Invoice Control Report includes the following information:

1. The total number of invoices prepared by the computer.

2. The total number of shipment cards read but not invoiced because there was no order number in the Open Order File.

3. The total number of invoices prepared for partial shipments.

4. The total dollar amount of invoices written.

The Daily Status Report indicates, by product, orders entered for the day, month to date, and last month to date; backlog today and a month ago. The report also shows total orders, total billings, and total backlog. The total orders can be compared to the total orders on the Daily Orders Entered Register resulting from the initial processing of orders. The total billings for the day are sometimes compared with total billings shown on the Daily Cash Receipts-Sales Register, the output of subsequent processing in this system.

Accounts Receivable Updating

The Accounts Receivable Records are maintained on portions of two disk files. One file contains the basic Accounts Receivable Records containing data such as account balance, amount on order, credit limit, credit history, delinquency history, and sales history. The other file contains data on the details supporting the account balance—such as unpaid invoices—and "suspense" items—such as customer payments for which a specific invoice is not initially identifiable and credit memorandums unassigned to a specific unpaid invoice.

The Accounts Receivable Files are updated with normal transactions such as cash receipts, billings, credit memos, and new orders. Other types of transactions include new accounts and changes to permanent data in customer accounts, such as credit limit, customer names and addresses, etc.

Exhibit 5 SHIPPING COPY

ORDER FORM

TO						DATE	

SHIP TO			BILL TO			

STREET & NO.			STREET & NO.			

CITY	STATE	ZIP	CITY	STATE	ZIP

CONFIRMATION TO FOLLOW?	CUSTOMER ORDER NO.	DEPT. NO.	TERMS		

SHIPPING DATE	VIA	☐ PREPAID ☐ COLLECT ☐ PREPAID & CHARGE

QUANTITY	ITEM NUMBER	COLOR & DESCRIPTION	PER DOZ.	AMOUNT
			TOTAL	

SIGNATURE

The cash receipts are initially received in the mail room where all company mail is opened. Checks are forwarded to the cashier who prepares an adding-machine tape of the checks. The payment identity stubs returned with the customer checks are forwarded to the keypunching section and cash receipts punched cards are prepared. For customer payments for which no stubs are returned, the input-output group prepares appropriate source documents for keypunching. The other primary input transactions are the billings and the day's orders prepared as a result of previous processing described earlier.

All credit memorandums for returned merchandise are initiated by the accounting control group or the branches upon receipt of a returned material receiving report. Branches forward their memorandums, approved by the branch manager, to the home office for approval. All credit memorandums in excess of $2,000 must be approved by the controller before they can be posted to accounts receivable. All other credit memorandums must be approved by the assistant controller. Miscellaneous credits also originate in the input-output control group to correct invoicing errors. These are processed the same as material-returned credits. There is no formal method for handling damaged merchandise.

Accounts Receivable processing produces the following output:

1. Updated Accounts Receivable Basic Record File, on magnetic tape.
2. Updated Open Order File, on magnetic tape and printed listing.
3. Exception Report Cards, on punched cards.
4. Daily Cash Receipts and Sales Register.
5. Cash Deposit Slip.

The aged trial balance is prepared weekly and at the end of each month by computer processing of the accounts receivable master tape files. The aged trial balance lists, in customer number sequence, all invoices, credits, and debits by date, number, and amount. All open invoices are aged according to 30-day, 90-day and over-90-day categories.

The Daily Cash Receipts and Sales Register is prepared in customer number sequence and shows, for each customer having transactions that day, the cash receipts and/or billings information applicable to that account. If there is no activity in the account, it does not appear on the statement. Cash receipts information includes gross amount of the billings, discount earned, and net amount paid. The billings information includes invoice number and gross amount of billings with the amount applicable to material, transportation, and sales tax shown separately. The balance in the customer's account after the transactions have been posted is shown, along with grand totals for cash receipts and billings. Total sundry cash receipts are shown separately as well as the total balance of all accounts receivable and the number of invoices processed during the day.

The Cash Deposit Slip itemizes each receipt and is prepared in duplicate. Both copies are sent to the cashier for agreement with the remittance adding machine tape he prepared and for use in depositing the daily collections.

The Accounting Control Group compares the total billings printed on the Daily Cash Receipts and Sales Register with the total billings shown on the Daily Status Report and the Invoice Control Report prepared as part of the Invoicing system.

Daily Exception Report

An exception report is prepared daily by processing the exception transaction resulting from the accounts receivable update run. These transactions are produced as the result of programmed controls in the computer program that cause the accounts receivable transactions to be posted to the accounts receivable magnetic tape files.

Exception Report Card entries may be classified as exceptions to operational policies, errors in input data, and/or information disclosure.

The exception codes and an explanation of the codes are:

1. Order received today, from new customer.
2. Account opened today.
3. Order received today, no credit limit on record.
4. Order received today, from delinquent account.
5. Order received today over credit limit. A credit limit check is not made until the order is received, processed for shipment, and posted to the accounts receivable files. The computer program then compares the total of the customer balance and orders entered with the amount of the credit limit on the customer record.
6. Inactive account (no sales last two years).
7. Account closed today.
8. Account with credit balance.
9. Item delinquent today.
10. Delinquent item, paid today.
11. Cash discount not taken, allowable, within six-day grace period.
12. Cash discount taken, not allowable.
13. Cash discount not taken, allowable, less than $5.00.
14. Unassigned payment in item record. Customer remits payment without identity stub and the payment cannot be identified.
15. Unassigned credit in item record. All credits, except those for the same amount as in invoice or group of invoices, are processed unassigned until payment is received for the remaining amount due in the invoice for which the credit applies.
16. Difference in amount between accounts receivable balance and total of open items in item record file.
17. Confirmation of change. Change is printed out.

18. Answer to query. Exception report shows what is in a customer's record.

19. Error Card—this card shows the type of error in input and information which is not processed because of the error.

PROCUREMENT DEPARTMENT

The last area of concern to Mr. Sanders was the inefficiency of the purchasing related functions. An organization chart of the Procurement Department is shown in Exhibit 6. As a purchase requisition is received (two copies) from the manufacturing plants it is logged in by the administration clerk. The date and time it was received are stamped on the back of the requisition. Each job number specified on current purchase requisitions is checked against those recorded in the open work authorization report of each plant. This step insures that the job is still open and that the original material cost estimates and allocations have not been exceeded. If the job is closed or if costs as estimated have been exceeded, the requisition is returned to the requisitioner for authorization. All approved requisitions are forwarded to the Quality Control Section. Quality and reliability terms are checked by Quality Control, and the requisitions are returned to the administrative clerk, who then delivers them to the chief purchasing agent or the subcontracting officer, as applicable.

The chief purchasing agent reviews the requisitions and forwards them to one of the specialist buying groups: Plastics, Office Supplies, Plant Supplies, or Hardware. The buyer or subcontracting office then searches for sources of supply. If a request for a quote has been previously handled, he begins with this information. If the item has been procured previously, the item price history card is analyzed to determine previous sources used, prices paid, dates purchased, and quantities purchased. Vendor rating cards are reviewed to determine delivery and quality performance of the vendors being considered. For purchase orders of $300 or more, formal requests for bids are required, unless the item is a sole-source item or a customer-specified-brand item or is acquired for emergency reasons. Emergency reasons occur when a production foreman requests stock items on a special requisition form after a bill of materials has been filed.

Purchases of the company are characterized by many small-volume, low dollar-value purchase orders, with a small percentage of items kept in stock (many of these are office and plant supplies). About 35 percent of the purchase orders are for less than $50.00, 50 percent are for less than $100.00, and 85 percent are for less than $500. For example, total value of items procured during 1979 was about $160 million. This value covered about 85,000 line items on 30,000 purchase orders. Of the 12,000 different line items used over a period of time, about 3,000 items are in stock.

About 400 of the high-volume items are purchased through long-term agreements with quantity discounts based on the volume purchased. There are eight major sources of supply which account for about 60 percent of the total dollar volume of purchases and the total number of purchase orders. Twenty sources of

Exhibit 6 PROCUREMENT DEPARTMENT ORGANIZATION

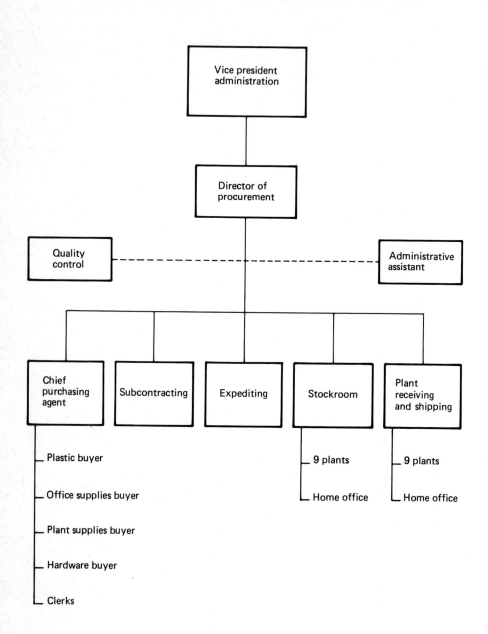

supply account for 80 percent of the total dollar volume of purchases and total number of purchase orders.

Orders are usually placed by phone, but a confirmation copy of the purchase order is sent if required. For items purchased locally by plants under $50.00 per order, a special local purchase form is prepared by the buyer, and the Receiving Section dispatches a vehicle to the vendor to pick up the items. The vendor records cost information on the local purchase order form, but bills the company only once a month. The driver delivers the items to the Receiving Section where quantities are verified and recorded on the local purchase order form. The items are forwarded to the inspection area, then delivered to the stockroom or to the user as specified on the original requisition.

Copies of the local purchase order form are distributed as follows:

2—Procurement
  1—filed by job number
  1—filed by purchase order number
2—Controller
  1—Accounts Payable Section (after items are processed through Receiving and Inspection)
  1—Cost Accounting Section
1—Receiving Section file (by purchase order number)
1—Inspection Section file (by purchase order number)
2—Requisitioner (after receipt and inspection)
  1—Material specialist
  1—Production control officer
1—Stockroom (with items)

At the time a vendor is selected, the buyer or subcontracting officer completes the sections of the regular purchase requisition dealing with vendor name, vendor number, location of vendor, purchase order number, quantity ordered, delivery date, unit price, tax, terms, FOB, shipment instructions, and related data. If the vendor is new, the buyer contacts the Accounts Payable Section of the controller's office to obtain a new vendor number. The duplicate copy of the purchase requisition is then returned to the material specialist in the Production Division and the original is given to the Procurement Administration Section for typing of the purchase order.

The typed purchase order is checked by Quality Control to ensure correct quality and reliability terms. These terms are spelled out on the reverse side of the forms and are coded numerically. The applicable numerical codes are typed on the front of the purchase order. The purchase orders are then signed: by the buyer for orders less than $7,500; by the chief purchasing agent for orders less than $12,000; and by the director of procurement for orders over $12,000. The subcontracting officer also signs orders for less than $12,000. Distribution of copies of the purchase order is as follows:

2–Vendor (if required)
2–Controller
   1–Accounts Payable Section
   1–Cost Accounting Section
2–Requisitioner
   1–Material specialist
   1–Production control officer
3–Procurement
   1–Numerical file (purchase order number)
   1–Buyer file (by vendor, alphabetically)
   1–Expediting Section follow-up copy (by date due)
1–(Master)–Receiving Section (filed by purchase order number in open file)

As shipments are received, the receiving clerk pulls the master purchase order copy (which has space provided to record quantities, dates delivered, and inspection data). A record is made of the quantity received of each line item and the date it is received. Xerox copies of the purchase order (which now serves as a receiving and inspection report) are made and distributed as follows:

2–Controller
   1–Accounts Payable Section
   1–Cost Accounting Section
2–Requisitioner
   1–Material specialist
   1–Production control officer
1–Procurement (Expediting Section)
8–Inspection (with materials)
1–(Master)–Receiving Section (filed by purchase order number in pending or
   completed file, depending on whether shipment is a partial or total order)

The Expediting Section pulls the follow-up copy and the receiving data are entered. If the order is complete, the follow-up copy is placed in a completed purchase order file (numerically by purchase order number). If the shipment is a partial one, the updated follow-up copy is returned to the pending file (by date due).

When materials are inspected, the results of the inspection are recorded on the copies of the purchase order (receiving and inspection formats). If there are no defects in quality, distribution of the eight copies is as follows:

1–Stockroom (with materials)
1–Inspection file (by purchase order number)
2–Requisitioner
   1–Material specialist
   1–Production control officer
4–Destroyed by Inspection area

If a partial or total reject occurs, distribution is as the foregoing except the four copies which were destroyed in the case of acceptable materials are distributed as follows:

    2—Controller
        1—Accounts Payable Section
        1—Cost Accounting Section
        1—Procurement Expediting Section (to correct follow-up copy and determine disposition of defects)
        1—Receiving Section with defective items to await disposition instructions (accepted items are forwarded to Stockroom)

The procurement expediter coordinates disposition of defects with the material specialist and the vendor. He notifies the Receiving Section and the disposition is effected.

Mr. Sanders believes that the lack of computer usage in this area has been unfortunate and that more applications are possible along with improvements in control and efficiency. He believes that procurement should be closely tied to the cost accounting system, which is almost completely computerized.

The Cost Accounting Section of the controller's office compiles the estimates of materials required (copy of bill of materials), labor hours and costs (copy of job control sheet), and fixed overhead costs (allocated by the Cost Accounting Section). These estimates are made up by job number and contract number and are used as standards of performance. The Cost Accounting Section forwards the estimates to the Data Processing Department for keypunching and preparation of the open work authorization master file. The open work authorization report is made up from the outstanding or open work orders. As daily timecards are received by Cost Accounting, they are forwarded to Data Processing and the open work authorization master file is updated. Similarly, material usage reports are received by Cost Accounting and forwarded to Data Processing for updating of the work authorization report. Actual fixed-cost allocation data are forwarded to Data Processing for updating the open work authorization report.

Receiving report data, as received by Cost Accounting, are forwarded to Data Processing for updating the raw materials master file. As materials are requisitioned from the stockroom by the work stations (by means of stockroom requisitions), Cost Accounting furnishes the stockroom requisition data to the Data Processing Department to transfer material data from the raw materials master file to the work-in-process master file. Finally, as a job is completed, a copy of the shipping report is furnished the Cost Accounting Section, material data are transferred from the work-in-process to the finished goods inventory master file, and the accounts receivable master file is increased accordingly.

The Accounts Payable Section receives copies of purchase orders, receiving reports, and rejection reports. Data Processing is furnished data pertaining to purchase commitments (in terms of purchase orders issued for stock items only) and increases in raw materials inventories (receiving reports for all items). A weekly purchase order commitment report is prepared by Data Processing for stock items by purchase order numbers. A weekly stock catalog is prepared for stock items for each plant. Data Processing also prepares a monthly report on usage of stock items which is used by Procurement to determine maximum and minimum levels and to screen out slow-moving items.

A point of distaste for Mr. Sanders is that one plant may order something that another plant has in stock and is not currently using. Communication between plants is a major problem.